CW00558509

Empowering Squatter Citizen

Local Government, Civil Society and Urban Poverty Reduction

Edited by
Diana Mitlin and David Satterthwaite

London • Sterling, VA

First published by Earthscan in the UK and USA in 2004

ISBN: 1-84407-101-4 paperback
1-84407-100-6 hardback

Typesetting by MapSet Ltd, Gateshead, UK
Printed and bound in the UK by Creative Print and Design (Wales), Ebbw Vale
Cover design by Danny Gillespie
Cover photo © copyright Janet Jarman

For a full list of publications please contact:
Earthscan
8–12 Camden High Street
London, NW1 0JH, UK
Tel: +44 (0)20 7387 8558
Fax: +44 (0)20 7387 8998
Email: earthinfo@earthscan.co.uk
Web: **www.earthscan.co.uk**

22883 Quicksilver Drive, Sterling, VA 20166-2012, USA

Earthscan publishes in association with WWF-UK and the International Institute for
Environment and Development

A catalogue record for this book is available from the British Library

Library of Congress Cataloging-in-Publication Data

Empowering squatter citizen : local government, civil society, and urban poverrty
reduction / Diana Mitlin and David Satterthwaite (editors).
     p. cm.
  Includes bibliographical references (p.) and index.
  ISBN 1-84407-101-4 (pbk) – ISBN 1-84407-100-6 (hardback)
   1. Urban poor–Government policy–Developing countries–Case studies. 2. Urban
poor–Services for–Developing countries–Case studies. I. Mitlin, Diana. II.
Satterthwaite, David.

HV4173.E46 2004
362.5'561'091724–dc22

                                                                    2004002311

This book is printed on elemental chlorine-free paper

Contents

Part I: Introduction

Part II: Government Initiatives

Part III: Civil Society Initiatives

Part IV: Drawing Some Conclusions

List of Tables, Figures and Boxes

Tables

Figures

Boxes

About the Authors

Volume Editors

Diana Mitlin (Chapters 1, 8, 9, 10 and 11) is an economist with the Human Settlements Programme of the International Institute for Environment and Development (IIED) in London and teaches part time at the Institute for Development Policy and Management (IDPM) at the University of Manchester. She also works on urban poverty issues within the Centre for Chronic Poverty and the Centre on Regulation and Competition at IDPM. She is a member of the editorial board of *Environment and Urbanization* and is the editor of *HiFi News*, a newsletter on innovations in housing finance. Email: diana.mitlin@iied.org

David Satterthwaite (Chapters 1, 10 and 11) is a senior fellow at IIED and also on the teaching staff of the London School of Economics and the Development Planning Unit at University College London. He has been the editor of the international journal *Environment and Urbanization* from its inception in 1989. Much of his work is on seeking ways through which external agencies can be more effective in supporting poverty reduction in urban areas and more accountable to low-income groups. He also co-authored the book *Squatter Citizen* with Jorge E Hardoy (Earthscan, 1989) to which this volume is a follow-up. Email: david@iied.org

Chapter Authors

Somsook Boonyabancha (Chapter 2) is director of the Community Organizations Development Institute (CODI). She is also founder and secretary general of the Asian Coalition for Housing Rights. Trained as an architect at Chulalongkorn University, she joined the Thai government's National Housing Authority in 1977, initially working on slum upgrading. In 1988, Ms Boonyabancha set up the Asian Coalition for Housing Rights with a number of key professionals in the region and this coalition has been active in many nations in Asia, fighting forced evictions, promoting alternatives to evictions and supporting active regional exchange and learning among groups in the region. She is also a member of the Millennium Project Taskforce 8 on Improving the Lives of Slum Dwellers. Email: achr@loxinfo.co.th

Emma Porio (Chapter 3 – principal author) is professor and head of the department of sociology and anthropology at the Ateneo de Manila University in Quezon City, Metro Manila, Philippines. Email: eporio@ateneo.edu. She is very grateful to Christine S Crisol, Nota F Magno, David Cid and Evelyn N Paul for giving the best of their technical and social skills, and would not have completed this study without them. The study on which this chapter is based would not have been possible without the excellent collaboration provided by the following research partners: Anna Marie Karaos (Urban Research Consortium/Institute of Church and Social Issues), Ma Lourdes Rebullida (Urban Research Consortium/University of the Philippines), Ma Lina Mirasol (Urban Research Consortium/Fellowship for Organizing Endeavor), Napoleon Amoyen (Urban Research Consortium/Ateneo de Davao University), Francisco Fernandez, Ana Oliveros, Vikki Horfilla and Miriam Quizon (National Congress of CMP Originators of the Philippines).

Priscilla Connolly (Chapter 4) is a British-born architect with a doctorate in history who has lived and worked in Mexico since the early 1970s. She has undertaken extensive research and consultancy on housing and urban development both in non-governmental and academic contexts. Other research interests include urban employment, construction history, government investment and environmental policies. Priscilla currently teaches urban sociology and planning at the Universidad Autónoma Metropolitana at Azcapotzalco, Mexico City, where she also coordinates the Urban Observatory Project (OCIM:SIG). Email: pcd@correo.azc.uam.mx

Alfredo Stein (Chapter 5) is the programme officer for the Development Co-operation Section of the Swedish Embassy, in Tegucigalpa, Honduras. In this role, Mr Stein is responsible for the supervision of municipal and urban housing projects in Honduras. He has worked for the past 18 years with different international development agencies in low-income housing and local development programmes in Honduras, El Salvador, Nicaragua, Costa Rica, Guatemala, Argentina, Chile and South Africa, including working as Sida's consultant to PRODEL from 1994 to 1999. He is also a member of the Millennium Project Taskforce 8 on Improving the Lives of Slum Dwellers. Email: alfredo.stein@sida.se

Asiya Sadiq (Chapter 6) is an architect and planner educated at the Dawood College in Karachi and in Leuven (Belgium) and is currently assistant professor of architecture and planning at the NED University in Karachi.

Salim Alimuddin (Chapter 6) is an architect and planner educated at the Dawood College in Karachi and at the Asian Institute of Technology in Bangkok. He has been working with the Orangi Pilot Project-Research and Training Institute since 1989 and is currently joint director of its Housing and Sanitation Programme.

Arif Hasan (Chapter 6) is an architect and planner in private practice in Karachi. He is chairman of the Urban Resource Centre and the Orangi Pilot Project-Research and Training Institute and visiting professor at the Faculty of Architecture and Planning at the NED University in Karachi. He is also a member of the Millennium Project Taskforce 8 on Improving the Lives of Slum Dwellers. Email: arifhasan@cyber.net.pk

Debora Cavalcanti (Chapter 7) is a researcher associated with the Brazilian non-governmental organization Cearah Periferia. Trained as an architect and urban planner with a Masters in habitat and development at the Universite Catholique de Louvain, Belgium, she is currently undertaking a PhD at the London School of Economics. Email: debora_cavalcanti@hotmail.com.br

Olinda Marques (Chapter 7) is a sociologist and coordinator of the Department of Architecture, Urbanism and Technology of the CEARAH Periferia, coordinator of the Programs Casa Melhor and PAAC. Email: olindacearah@bol.com.br

Teresa Hilda Costa (Chapter 7) is a social worker and coordinator of the project 'Force of the Woman' in Cearah Periferia. Email: cearah@fortalnet.com.br

Ted Baumann (Chapter 8) was manager of the *uTshani* Fund from 1994 to 1997 and is now a freelance development consultant based in Cape Town. He continues to work with the South African Homeless People's Federation and Shack Dwellers International, supporting their networking initiatives with other non-governmental organizations, government and international agencies. Email: tedb@iafrica.com

Joel Bolnick (Chapter 8) was director of People's Dialogue on Land and Shelter from its inception until 2001 and is currently coordinator of the Community Organization Urban Resource Centre in Cape Town. He coordinates support to Shack/Slum Dwellers International groups in Africa through the Slum/Shack Dwellers International Secretariat. He is also a member of the Millennium Project Taskforce 8 on Improving the Lives of Slum Dwellers. Email: boluick@courc.co.za

Sheela Patel (Chapter 9) is the founder-director of SPARC (The Society for the Promotion of Area Resource Centres), the non-governmental organization in the Indian Alliance of SPARC, *Mahila Milan* and the National Slum Dwellers Federation where she has worked since 1984. She is also on the board of Shack/Slum Dwellers International and a member of the Millennium Project Taskforce 8 on Improving the Lives of Slum Dwellers. Email: sparc1@vsnl.com

Preface

This edited volume develops a theme that has been central to the work of the Human Settlements Programme at the International Institute for Environment and Development (IIED) since its foundation in 1977 – what possibilities exist within urban centres or particular urban neighbourhoods to address the deprivations faced by those with low incomes?[1] The preparation of this volume also reflects one of the core organizing principles of this programme's work – namely, the collaboration with individuals and organizations in Africa, Asia and Latin America.

A note on terminology may help the reader connect this volume to the Human Settlements Programme's previous work. Until 1995 the term 'poverty' was not used much in the programme's work because its main focus was on the need to find ways of improving housing and living conditions and infrastructure and service provision for those who were living in tenements, cheap boarding houses or informal settlements, and also to address the environmental health problems and the health burdens that they faced. During the 1970s, 1980s and early 1990s, these were not considered to be aspects of poverty. The programme's work was based on an understanding that civil and political rights – including the right to organize and make demands – were a central part of addressing these problems. So, too, was the need for strong, accountable and democratic local government and legal systems that were more supportive of the needs of low-income groups.

Today, these issues are usually discussed within a 'poverty' framework – with the recognition that poverty is caused not only by inadequate income but also by many other (usually interconnected) deprivations, as discussed in Chapter 1. But during the 1980s and early 1990s, because governments and international agencies defined and measured poverty using poverty lines based only on income levels or consumption levels, the deprivations relating to housing and living conditions, lack of basic services, lack of civil and political rights, inadequate local governments and anti-poor legal systems were generally not discussed as part of 'poverty', although the relationship between income levels and the extent and depth of these deprivations were explored. Within our programme, the book *Squatter Citizen* (Hardoy and Satterthwaite, 1989) documented the extreme deprivation of the housing conditions in which the urban poor lived and the

---

1 David Satterthwaite has been working at IIED since 1974 and in its Human Settlements Programme since 1978. Diana Mitlin began working at the Human Settlements Programme in 1989 and currently works part time with this programme and part time with the Institute for Development Policy and Management at the University of Manchester.

ways in which laws and government structures contributed to these, while *The Poor Die Young* (Hardoy et al, 1990) documented the health problems faced by the urban poor, and *Environmental Problems in Third World Cities* (Hardoy, Mitlin and Satterthwaite, 1992)[2] included documentation of the environmental health problems suffered by the urban poor. But these deprivations and risks were not discussed as aspects of poverty.

It was in 1994 that we first sought to bring the non-income aspects of deprivation into a 'poverty' framework – including those aspects that had strong links with income levels and those that had weak or no links with income levels. This was encouraged by an international seminar on urban poverty that we organized with the CROP programme (Comparative Research on Poverty) at the University of Bergen. From this, in 1995, came two special issues of the IIED journal *Environment and Urbanization* on urban poverty. The editorial in the April 1995 issue highlighted how the papers it included demonstrated the inadequacies of, and inaccuracies in, the official ways in which urban poverty was defined and measured, and how and why the scale of urban poverty was underestimated (*Environment and Urbanization*, 1995a). The editorial in the October 1995 issue discussed how to integrate the different ways of reducing poverty, including increasing incomes and addressing the other deprivations and the inter-linkages between them (*Environment and Urbanization*, 1995b).

Since 1995, both in our own work and in the work of others that we have published, we have sought to promote an understanding of urban poverty that includes consideration of housing conditions, tenure, service provision, the rule of law and civil and political rights (including 'voice' and the right to influence policy and practice on the ground). This work drew, in particular, on the work of Jorge Anzorena (especially the *Selavip Newsletter*), on the authors of papers that were published in the two issues of *Environment and Urbanization* in 1995 (including Wratten, 1995; Amis, 1995; Kanji, 1995; and Rakodi, 1995) and also on Moser (1993; 1996) and Moser, Herbert and Makonnen (1993), which focused on urban poverty. It also drew on the work of Robert Chambers, Tony Beck and Bob Baulch, which focused more on rural poverty but expanded the understanding of poverty (see Beck, 1994; Chambers, 1995; and Baulch, 1996) and on the many detailed case studies of urban poverty and multiple deprivations faced by the urban poor that we have published in *Environment and Urbanization*.[3]

Another set of writings that was particularly important for expanding the understanding of urban poverty stemmed from non-governmental organizations (NGOs) that were working with organizations and federations of the urban poor – including the work of authors who are featured in this book (for example, Boonyabancha, 1996; 1999; Patel, 1990; Patel and d'Cruz, 1993; Patel and Mitlin, 2001; and Bolnick, 1993; 1996).

Many other specialists have contributed to this broader, multidimensional

---

2 This was superseded by a much updated and expanded version in 2001 (Hardoy, Mitlin and Satterthwaite, 2001).

3 See, for instance, Pryer (1993), Kanji (1995), Latapí and de la Rocha (1995), Navarro (2001), Huq-Hussain (1995), Alder (1995), Yapi-Diahou (1995), Benjamin (2000), Rakodi, Gatabaki-Kamau and Devas (2000), Urban Resource Centre (2001) and Asian Coalition for Housing Rights (2001).

view of poverty – see, in particular, the work of Amartya Sen (especially Sen, 1999) and the United Nations Development Programme (UNDP) human development reports (and their Human Development Index). By 2001 even the World Bank was acknowledging that a broader view of poverty was needed in its 2001 *World Development Report* (World Bank, 2001). However, this report, like most other general works on poverty, still had difficulty in recognizing that urban contexts and certain urban characteristics produce, or can produce, particular forms and mixes of deprivation, or extremes of deprivation, that are not well captured by frameworks that had been developed for identifying rural poverty or 'poverty' in general. There are similarities between the list of multiple deprivations that came out of our work and our collaboration with the groups mentioned above and Sen's five sets of 'freedoms', although our work focused on urban contexts and concentrated more on the relationships of the urban poor with local institutions, including politicians, government agencies and NGOs, and on the extent to which they have opportunities to develop their own initiatives and negotiate support for them from local organizations.

Finally, a note on the title of this book: *Empowering Squatter Citizen* was chosen because the case studies in this book are initiatives that address the concerns raised in the book *Squatter Citizen* that IIED's Human Settlements Programme published 15 years ago. *Squatter Citizen* also included a discussion of emerging shifts in the attitudes and policies of local and national governments and international agencies towards those that better address the needs of low-income urban dwellers – and the case studies in this book demonstrate how much these have developed since then.

Diana Mitlin and David Satterthwaite
June 2003

References

Alder, G (1995) 'Tackling poverty in Nairobi's informal settlements: developing an institutional strategy', *Environment and Urbanization*, vol 7, no 2, October, pp85–107

Amis, P (1995) 'Making sense of urban poverty', *Environment and Urbanization*, vol 7, no 1, April, pp145–157

Asian Coalition for Housing Rights (2001) 'Building an urban poor people's movement in Phnom Penh, Cambodia', *Environment and Urbanization*, vol 13, no 2, pp61–72

Baulch, B (1996) 'The new poverty agenda: a disputed consensus', *IDS Bulletin*, vol 27, no 1, pp1–10

Beck, T (1994) *The Experience of Poverty: Fighting for Respect and Resources in Village India*, Intermediate Technology Publications, London

Benjamin, S (2000) 'Governance, economic settings and poverty in Bangalore', *Environment and Urbanization*, vol 12, no 1, pp35–56

Bolnick, J (1993) 'The People's Dialogue on land and shelter: community driven networking in South Africa's informal settlements', *Environment and Urbanization*, vol 5, no 1, pp91–110

Bolnick, J (1996) 'uTshani Buyakhuluma (The grass speaks): People's Dialogue and the South African Homeless People's Federation, 1993–1996', *Environment and Urbanization*, vol 8, no 2, pp153–170

Boonyabancha, S (1996) *The Urban Community Development Office, Thailand*, IIED Paper Series on Poverty Reduction in Urban Areas, IIED, London

Boonyabancha, S (1999) 'The Urban Community Environmental Activities Project, Thailand', *Environment and Urbanization*, vol 11, no 1, pp101–115

Chambers, R (1995) 'Poverty and livelihoods: whose reality counts?', *Environment and Urbanization*, vol 7, no 1, April, pp173–204

Environment and Urbanization (1995a) 'The underestimation and misrepresentation of urban poverty', Editorial, pp3–10

Environment and Urbanization (1995b) 'Urban poverty – from understanding to action', Editorial, pp3–10

Hardoy, J E and D Satterthwaite (1989) *Squatter Citizen: Life in the Urban Third World*, Earthscan, London

Hardoy, J E, D Mitlin and D Satterthwaite (1992) *Environmental Problems in Third World Cities*, Earthscan, London

Hardoy, J E, D Mitlin and D Satterthwaite (2001) *Environmental Problems in an Urbanizing World: Finding Solutions for Cities in Africa, Asia and Latin America*, Earthscan, London

Hardoy, J E, S Cairncross and D Satterthwaite (eds) (1990) *The Poor Die Young: Housing and Health in Third World Cities*, Earthscan, London

Huq-Hussain, S (1995) 'Fighting poverty: the economic adjustment of female migrants in Dhaka', *Environment and Urbanization*, vol 7, no 2, April, pp51–65

Kanji, N (1995) 'Gender, poverty and structural adjustment in Harare, Zimbabwe', *Environment and Urbanization*, vol 7, no 1, April, pp37–55

Latapí, A E and M González de la Rocha (1995) 'Crisis, restructuring and urban poverty in Mexico', *Environment and Urbanization*, vol 7, no 1, April, pp57–75

Moser, C O N (1993) *Urban Social Policy and Poverty Reduction*, Working Paper, Urban Development Division, TWURD WP No 10, October

Moser, C O N (1996) *Confronting Crisis: A Summary of Household Responses to Poverty and Vulnerability in Four Poor Urban Communities*, Environmentally Sustainable Development Studies and Monographs Series No 7, World Bank, Washington, DC

Moser, C O N, A J Herbert and R E Makonnen (1993) *Urban Poverty in the Context of Structural Adjustment: Recent Evidence and Policy Responses*, TWU Discussion Paper DP No 4, Urban Development Division, World Bank, Washington, DC

Navarro, L (2001) 'Exploring the environmental and political dimension of poverty: the cases of Mar del Plata and Necochea-Quequén cities', *Environment and Urbanization*, vol 13, no 1, pp185–199

Patel, S and C D'Cruz (1993) 'The Mahila Milan crisis credit scheme: from a seed to a tree', *Environment and Urbanization*, vol 5, no 1, pp9–17

Patel, S and D Mitlin (2001) *The Work of SPARC and Its Partners Mahila Milan and the National Slum Dwellers Federation in India*, IIED Working Paper 5 on Urban Poverty Reduction, IIED, London

Patel, S (1990) 'Street children, hotel boys and children of pavement dwellers and construction workers in Bombay: how they meet their daily needs', *Environment and Urbanization*, vol 2, no 2, October, pp9–26

Pryer, J (1993) 'The impact of adult ill-health on household income and nutrition in Khulna, Bangladesh', *Environment and Urbanization*, vol 5, no 2, October, pp35–49

Rakodi, C (1995) 'Poverty lines or household strategies? A review of conceptual issues in the study of urban poverty', *Habitat International*, vol 19, no 4, pp407–426

Rakodi, C, R Gatabaki-Kamau and N Devas (2000) 'Poverty and political conflict in Mombasa', *Environment and Urbanization*, vol 12, no 1, pp153–170

Sen, A (1999) *Development as Freedom*, Oxford University Press, Oxford

URC/Urban Resource Centre (2001) 'Urban poverty and transport: a case study from Karachi', *Environment and Urbanization*, vol 13, no 1, pp223–233

World Bank (2001) *World Development Report 2000/2001: Attacking Poverty*, Oxford University Press, Oxford and New York

Wratten, E (1995) 'Conceptualizing urban poverty', *Environment and Urbanization*, vol 7, no 1, April, pp11–36

Yapi-Diahou, A (1995) 'The informal housing sector of the metropolis of Abidjan, Ivory Coast', *Environment and Urbanization*, vol 7, no 2, October, pp11–29

Acknowledgements

It is unfortunate that only our names are listed on the cover of the book as it draws on the work of so many authors. The final chapters, which list us as authors, also draw heavily on the insights provided by the case study authors. These chapters were also much improved by comments from Priscilla Connolly (the author of Chapter 4) and from our colleague at IIED Gordon McGranahan.

This book has particular debts to three sets of people. The first (as with so much of our work) is to Jorge Hardoy and Ana Hardoy. Jorge Hardoy was insisting that civil and political rights and freedoms were not means to development but central to development during the early 1970s, and he was also stressing the critical importance of local governments.[1] Few would dispute these now; but not many people recognized this during the early 1970s. This book's title *Empowering Squatter Citizen* was chosen because its main themes address the issues raised in the 1989 book *Squatter Citizen* that Jorge Hardoy wrote with one of us. The debt to Ana Hardoy is for what we have learned from her practical approaches to realizing what Jorge Hardoy had identified – on-the-ground work with squatters and their community organizations. From 1987 onwards, Ana Hardoy and her team at IIED-America Latina have been working in informal and illegal settlements in Buenos Aires and in other urban centres of Argentina, seeking to support resident-directed initiatives to improve conditions and to encourage more productive relations between urban poor groups and local authorities.

The second debt is to a group of individuals that has sought to work with urban poor groups in new ways and whose work helped us to develop this book. They include all the other authors in this book – although special mention needs to be made of Sheela Patel, Somsook Boonyabancha, Ted Baumann, Alfredo Stein, Arif Hasan and Joel Bolnick because of how much we have learned from working with them – and also the federations of the urban poor with whom several of them work. Thanks are also due to people from many other NGOs whose work is not covered in this book or only peripherally mentioned – for instance, Beth Chitekwe, Anna Muller and Jorge Anzorena.

---

1 Comment from David Satterthwaite: When I first read Jorge Hardoy's written work in 1974, when he was advising Barbara Ward (the president of IIED) on a book she was writing on urban issues (and I was her research assistant), I remember being surprised by his insistence that civil and political rights and freedoms were not means to development but central to development. At that time, it was fashionable to discuss whether some curtailment of such rights could be justified by greater possibilities for social and economic advancement. I also remember being struck by his focus on the importance of local government and of what we now term local 'governance' to development – again, well before this became a key theme in development discussions.

The third set of people that deserve special thanks are those within international agencies that have supported our work. Some of the case studies were funded by the UK government's Department for International Development (DFID) and the Swiss Agency for Development and Cooperation (SDC) – and special thanks are due to Michael Mutter (DFID) and Francoise Lieberherr (SDC). The Swedish International Development Cooperation Agency (Sida) also helped to fund the work on which this book drew – and special thanks are due to Pelle Persson and Goran Tannerfeldt.

Diana Mitlin and David Satterthwaite
July 2003

List of Acronyms and Abbreviations

ACHR   Asian Coalition for Housing Rights
AFB   Anjuman Falah Behbood (Pakistan)
ANC   African National Congress
ASB   Anjuman Samaji Behbood (Pakistan)
AURIS   Instituto de Acción Urbana e Integración Social (the Institute
            for Urban Action and Social Integration, Mexico)
BANOBRAS   Banco Nacional de Obras y Servicios Públicos (National Bank
            of Public Works and Services, Mexico)
BASIS   Bacolod Shelter Development Project (the Philippines)
BNDES   Banco Nacional de Desenvolvimento Econômico e Social
            (National Bank for Economic and Social Development, Brazil)
BNH   Banco Nacional da Habitação (National Housing Bank)
C3   City Community Challenge
CBO   community-based organization
CEARAH   Centro de Estudos, Articulação e Referência sobre
  PERIFERIA Assentamentos Humanos (Centre for the Study, Organization
            and Research of Human Settlements)
CENVI   Centro de la Vivienda y Estudios Urbanos (Mexican NGO)
CHAI   Carmina Homeowners Association, Inc (the Philippines)
CIDA   Canadian International Development Agency
CLIFF   Community-led Infrastructure Financing Facility (India)
CMP   Community Mortgage Programme (the Philippines)
CODI   Community Organizations Development Institute (Thailand)
COPEVI   Centro Operacional de Vivienda y Poblamiento AC
            (Operational Centre for Housing and Human Settlement,
            Mexico)
CPAC   Community Project Administration Committee
CROP   Comparative Research on Poverty programme
DESAL   Centro para el Desarrollo Económico y Social de America
            Latina (Centre for Social Development, Santiago)
DFID   Department for International Development (UK)
DWUP   Division for the Welfare of the Urban Poor (the Philippines)
FBFF   Federação de Associações de Bairros e Favelas de Fortaleza
            (Federation of Neighbourhoods and Squatter Settlements of
            Fortaleza, Brazil)
FDUP   Foundation for the Development of the Urban Poor (the
            Philippines)
FONHAPO   Mexican National Popular Housing Fund

FOSOVI	Fondo Social de la Vivienda (Mexican NGO)
FOVI	Fondo de Operacion y Financiamiento Bancario a la Vivienda (Mexico)
FOVIMI	Military Housing Fund (Mexico)
FOVISSSTE	Housing Fund of the Health and Social Security Institute for State Employees (Mexico)
FUMHAB	Fundo Municipal de Apoio à Habitação Popular (Municipal Fund for the Support of Popular Housing, Brazil)
FUPROVI	La Fundación Promotora de Vivienda (Fund for Housing Promotion, Costa Rica)
GDP	gross domestic product
GLAD	Group Land Acquisition Programme (the Philippines)
GRET	Groupe de Recherche et d'Echanges Tecnologiques (Group for Research and Technology Exchange)
HUDCO	Housing and Urban Development Corporation (India)
IBRD	International Bank for Reconstruction and Development (World Bank)
IIED	International Institute for Environment and Development
IMF	International Monetary Fund
INDECO	National Institute for Community Development and Popular Housing (Mexico)
INFONAVIT	Institute of the National Workers' Housing Fund (Mexico)
INIFOM	Instituto Nicaragüense de Fomento Municipal (Nicaraguan Municipal Development Institute)
IPLAM	Instituto de Planejamento do Município de Fortaleza (Institute of Planning, Brazil)
IRA	Internal Revenue Allocation (from the national government of the Philippines)
ISSFAM	Social Security Institute of the Armed Forces (Mexico)
JICA	Japanese International Cooperation Agency
MDF	Municipal Development Fund (the Philippines)
MDGs	Millennium Development Goals
NGO	non-governmental organization
NHA	National Housing Authority (Thailand)
NHMFC	National Home Mortgage Finance Corporation (the Philippines)
NSDF	National Slum Dwellers Federation (India)
OCT	Orangi Charitable Trust (Pakistan)
OPP	Orangi Pilot Project (Pakistan)
PAAC	Programa de Apoio à Auto Construção (Better Home and Programme of Support for Self-building, Brazil)
PAG-IBIG	Home Development Mutual Fund (the Philippines)
PAN	National Action Party (Mexico)
PHNAI	Planas Homeowners Association, Inc (the Philippines)
PRD	Party of the Democratic Revolution (Mexico)
PRI	Revolutionary Institutional Party (Mexico)
PRODEL	Local Development Programme (Nicaragua)

PRONASOL	National Solidarity Programme (Mexico)
PROVICAC	National Federation of Industrial Housing Promoters (Mexico)
RMK	Rashtriya Mahila Kosh (India)
RTI	OPP Research and Training Institute (Pakistan)
SAHOP	Secretariat for Human Settlements and Public Works
SCHPs	Sociedades Comunitárias de Habitação Popular (Community Societies for Popular Housing, Brazil)
SDC	Swiss Agency for Development and Cooperation
SELAVIP	Latin American and Asian Service for Low-Income Housing
Sida	Swedish International Development Cooperation Agency
SILAIS	Sistemas Integrales de Salud (Nicaraguan Integrated Health Systems)
SMCC	Samahang Magkakapitbahay ng Cabezas Compound (the Philippines)
SNMB	Samahang Nagkakaisang Magkakapitbahay ng Ilaya (the Philippines)
SPARC	Society for the Promotion of Area Resource Centres (India)
UCDO	Urban Community Development Office (Thailand)
UK	United Kingdom
UN	United Nations
UNDP	United Nations Development Programme
UNESCAP	United Nations Economic and Social Commission for Asia and the Pacific
URC	Urban Research Consortium (comprising NGOs and academics, Ateneo de Manila)
US	United States
USAID	US Agency for International Development
VAHAI	Villa Arandia Homeowners Association, Inc (the Philippines)
WASA	Water and Sewerage Authority of the Faisalabad Development Authority (Pakistan)
WHO	World Health Organization

Part I

Introduction

Chapter 1

Introduction

Diana Mitlin and David Satterthwaite

What this book is about

This book presents case studies of eight initiatives designed to address the deprivations faced by the urban poor[1]: four that were government initiatives and four that were civil-society initiatives (although each of the civil-society initiatives sought to work with government). Despite their differences – including the different bases from which they developed, their different goals and the very different economic and political contexts within which they occurred – all were more 'bottom-up' and supportive of community-based organization and action than is the norm. Also, all of the initiatives sought to build or strengthen local processes (both governmental and community) with the capacity for sustained activity (that is, avoiding one-off initiatives) and, where possible, to reach increasing numbers of people. Equally, they all aimed to demonstrate that there were possibilities of reaching very large numbers of the urban poor – and most did so. This also meant that the success of the initiatives depended upon keeping down the costs of the interventions per person or household – in part so that external funding provided by governments or international agencies reached more people, and in part because this increased the proportion of the funding that low-income groups could afford to repay. Inevitably, the more that can be funded from what individuals or households can afford to pay, and the less the

---

1 One difficulty facing this book concerns what term should be used to describe the people who are its principal focus: individuals and households living in urban areas who suffer from deprivations that are commonly termed poverty. These people can be described as 'low income'; but as the book stresses, it is not their low income that is the primary cause of many of the deprivations that they suffer. They can be termed 'the poor'; but this means that external observers or organizations may forget the knowledge, skills and resources that they have and that they can bring to addressing these deprivations. In this book, those who are facing deprivations that are part of 'poverty' are generally referred to collectively as 'the poor' or as 'low-income groups'; but we hope the reader will note the limitations of these terms.

reliance on external funding, the greater the possibilities of reaching more people.

Although most of the initiatives included components to support lower-income groups in obtaining better incomes, this was not their primary focus and some had no explicit component to do so. All concentrated more on addressing other deprivations. Governments and international agencies generally define urban poverty only by income level, with poverty measured by the number of people or households with incomes that are below an official income-based 'poverty line'. But poverty can also be seen in terms of the multiple deprivations that those with low incomes suffer, many of which are a result of their social, economic and political relationships (or lack of them) with local organizations. For example, in most urban centres in Africa, Asia and Latin America we can witness the failure of local organizations to provide safe, sufficient water and good-quality sanitation and drainage to the homes and neighbourhoods of large sections of the population. There are comparable failures of local organizations to provide large sections of the urban populations with healthcare, schools and emergency services – and where these services are provided, the quality of provision is often poor. Large sections of the urban population in these regions also have little or no 'rule of law' provided by local judiciaries, legal services and police forces and therefore no protection from landlords, loan sharks, employers who pay below subsistence wages and contravene health and safety standards, and other potential perpetrators of crime. They often have no accountable government institutions, and frequently face only clientelist politicians and bribe-seeking public employees as they struggle to earn sufficient income, access entitlements, get better services and avoid eviction. As will be discussed in more detail below, many of these deprivations are the result not of people's low incomes but of the failure of local government or of other organizations.

A consideration of urban poverty from the perspective of the failure of local organizations with regard to shelter and services, the rule of law and democratic processes is particularly important for the nations that are the focus of this book – low- and middle-income nations in Africa, Asia, and Latin America and the Caribbean. This makes them distinct from most high-income nations. While urban poverty in high-income nations may also be considered from the perspective of institutional failure, most of the urban poor in these nations have access to safe, sanitary accommodation (with piped water, internal plumbing, sanitation and drainage), access to schools, healthcare, emergency services and, generally, protection by the rule of law and the police, and inclusion within local and national democratic processes.[2]

There are large variations between nations, and between different urban centres within nations, in the scale of the inadequacies in each of these spheres and in the proportion of the population that has to cope with these inadequacies.

---

2 This is not meant to imply that the services available to the lowest-income groups and the homeless are adequate in high-income nations; but there are differences in scale and degree – for instance, when it is common in low- and middle-income nations for 20–60 per cent of cities' populations to live in illegal dwellings with most having no regular, safe piped-water supply and no sanitation, and with most of the inhabitants having no access to healthcare, medicines or emergency services if they cannot pay market prices for them.

There are some urban centres in low- and middle-income nations that have managed to greatly reduce the proportion of people suffering these deprivations; there are many that have minimized the proportion suffering some of these (for instance, ensuring that nearly everyone has easy access to safe, sufficient water). In relation to the nations from which the case studies are drawn, a much higher proportion of the urban population of most major Mexican cities has water piped to their home and good sanitation than in Faisalabad in Pakistan and the cities described in the case study on India. While recognizing this diversity, it is still valid to consider why local governments and other local organizations fail to serve large numbers of urban dwellers, and – in many nations – such high proportions of all urban dwellers.

Why focus on urban areas?

There are three reasons for the focus on urban poverty reduction in Africa, Asia, and Latin America and the Caribbean: the scale of their urban populations (and the increasing proportion of urban populations in the total populations in each region); the scale of deprivation among urban populations; and the possibilities for urban poverty reduction provided by local organizations, including those from civil society. We suggest that the scale and depth of urban poverty in these regions has been underestimated, as has the potential to reduce it through local organizations and processes, and this book concentrates on the potential of local organizations to reduce urban poverty. The scale and depth of urban poverty in these regions has been documented elsewhere (see, for instance, Tabatabai with Fouad, 1993; UNCHS, 1996; Mitlin and Satterthwaite, 2001; and Montgomery et al, 2003), so this is only briefly summarized below.

During the 1990s, there was a growing recognition among many researchers and international agencies that urban areas had been neglected, as can be seen by the growth in the literature on urban areas.[3] When our own institute (the International Institute for Environment and Development – IIED) began a research programme in 1977 that focused on the deficiencies in housing conditions and basic services in urban areas, it was difficult to get funding and many funding agencies refused to support work on urban deprivation. Some even questioned whether there was any urban deprivation. The growing recognition that the scale of urban deprivation has been underestimated has, in part, been driven by a recognition of the scale of the urban population in low- and middle-income nations. Most of the world's urban population and most of its largest cities are now in Africa, Asia, and Latin America and the Caribbean and only a very small proportion are in nations that have graduated from being 'low- and middle-income nations'. As Figure 1.1 shows, nearly half of the world's urban population lives in Asia, and between them India and China have one-quarter of the world's urban population.

---

3 One indicator of this is the work on urban areas published by our own publisher, Earthscan. When *Squatter Citizen*, our first book with Earthscan, was published in 1989, Earthscan had very few books on urban issues, whereas now it has more than 30 books in print on this topic.

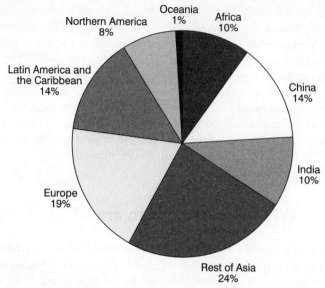

Source: United Nations, 2002

Figure 1.1 *Regional distribution of the world's urban population, 2000*

Latin America and the Caribbean are already predominantly urban, with three-quarters of their population living in urban areas in 2000. Although many may still think of Africa and Asia as predominantly rural continents, both have around two-fifths of their population in urban areas (United Nations, 2002). Africa now has around 350 million urban dwellers – far more urban dwellers than Northern America.

Figure 1.2 shows the contrasts between the growth in urban populations and rural populations by region between 1970 and 2005. The growth in Asia's urban population is much larger than that of its rural population – not surprisingly, as so many rural dwellers moved to urban areas. In Africa, the growth in the number of urban and rural dwellers is about the same, even though the urban population was so much smaller than the rural population in 1970. In Latin America, virtually all population growth from 1970 to the present has been in urban areas.[4] Most of the world's largest cities are also within low- and middle-income nations,

---

4 The data from many of the censuses held between 2000 and 2002 was not available for the data set on which this figure is based and some nations have had no census in the last 10 to 15 years. We suspect that this figure may overstate the growth in urban populations, especially in Africa where there is a lack of recent census data for many nations and where, in many nations, economic stagnation and decline has lessened or halted the growing concentration of economic opportunity in urban areas. In some, civil war or internal strife makes any consideration of urban change problematic (and with large streams of displaced people or refugees swelling many city populations). However, the fact that urban population growth has been on a much larger scale than rural population growth in Asia over the last 35 years, the fact that virtually all population growth in this period in Latin America and the Caribbean has been in urban areas, and the fact that Africa has had a very rapid growth in its urban population are not in doubt (see Satterthwaite, 2002).

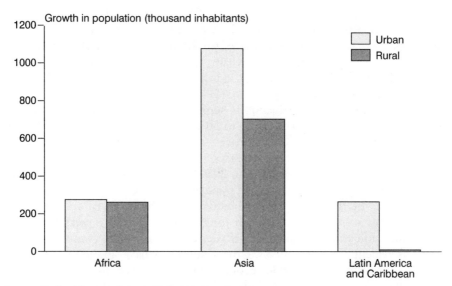

Source: Derived from statistics in United Nations (2002)

Figure 1.2 *Growth in urban and rural populations, 1970–2005*

especially in Asia where such nations have around half of the world's largest 100 cities and more than half of all cities that have more than a million inhabitants. Low- and middle-income nations in Latin America have more of the world's largest 100 cities and more 'million-plus' cities than North America.[5] However, it can be misleading to focus only on large cities as in virtually all regions of the world more than half the urban population live in urban centres with less than half a million inhabitants (United Nations, 2002)[6] – including a significant proportion in urban centres with less than 50,000 inhabitants.

The main reason for this rapid shift of population from rural to urban areas is that most of the growth in economic activities has been in industry and services that are located in urban areas. Most low-income countries and all middle-income nations now have more than half of the value added in gross domestic product (GDP) coming from industry and services – virtually all of which is located in urban areas (World Bank, 2002). Many have less than 20 per cent of their GDP coming from agriculture.[7] In general, the nations with the most rapid economic growth rates are also those with the largest increases in

---

5 These calculations come from the International Institute for Environment and Development's (IIED's) city database, which draws on United Nations (2002) and on data gathered from over 200 censuses.

6 Asia is the exception as it is said to have 49.8 per cent of its urban population in cities with 500,000 or more inhabitants.

7 These figures on the proportion of gross domestic product (GDP) in industry and services can be misleading. A considerable part of the growth in industry in most low-income nations is from forward and backward linkages with agriculture – for instance, the production and sale of agricultural machinery, fertilizers and other agricultural inputs, cold stores, and packaging and processing industries (Hardoy and Satterthwaite, 1986, Tacoli and Satterthwaite, 2003).

their level of urbanization (UNCHS, 1996; Satterthwaite, 2002). Political independence also brought a strong boost to urbanization levels in Asia and Africa; but this boost was concentrated around the dates when independence was achieved, especially when this was also the time that apartheid-like controls on the rights of the inhabitants to live in urban areas were lifted (UNCHS, 1996; Satterthwaite, 2002).

United Nations (UN) projections suggest that virtually all the growth in population anticipated in the next 25 to 30 years will be in urban areas (United Nations, 2002). Asia is expected to have less rural dwellers in 2030 than it has now, while its urban population increases 70 per cent between 2005 and 2030. Even in Africa the rural population in 2030 is expected to be only 31 per cent larger than it is today, while the urban population is expected to be 121 per cent larger. It may be that these projections overstate the speed of this shift to a predominantly urban world, especially for Africa where such increases in levels of urbanization will only take place if the region has more economic success than was evident during the 1990s. Urbanization may have slowed or stopped in many nations because of serious economic problems (see, for instance, Potts, 1995; 2001); but this has been hidden by the lack of censuses or delays in processing new census data. Projections made during the 1980s and 1990s on the size of urban populations and large city populations by 2000 proved to be too high for most nations and many large cities (Satterthwaite, 2002). It may be that current projections for levels of urbanization and large city populations up to 2025 will also prove to be too high, especially for nations which do not have considerable economic growth. But the long-term trend towards an increasingly urbanized world is not likely to change, even if it may be slower in many nations than the UN projections suggest and less concentrated in very large cities (Satterthwaite, 2002).

In relation to the numbers on urban poverty, it is now broadly accepted among researchers and development agencies that there are hundreds of millions of urban dwellers facing absolute poverty in low- and middle-income nations (Cairncross et al, 1990; WHO, 1992; UNCHS, 1996; World Bank, 1999), although there is disagreement about their actual numbers and the extent of their deprivations, and how they compare in numbers and the extent of their deprivations to rural populations.

According to official government statistics, between one-third and one-half of the urban population in many low- and middle-income nations have incomes below the poverty line; in some nations more than half are below the poverty line.[8] But in most nations, and in most global estimates, urban poverty is underestimated for three reasons:

1 *The depth of urban poverty is hidden by aggregate statistics 'for urban populations' since most middle- and upper-income groups live in urban areas and this pushes up urban averages – for income, consumption, access to basic services and health outcomes.* Statistics on income levels, service provision or health outcomes (for example, infant

---

8 See World Bank (2002, Table 2, pp236–237), Aegisson (2001), UNCHS (1996) and Satterthwaite (2004).

or under-five mortality rates) 'for urban populations' are usually significantly better than those 'for rural populations'. But aggregate statistics 'for urban areas' can hide the fact that the poorest half of the urban population may be as malnourished, ill and exploited as the poorest half of the rural population. In many low-income nations, under-five mortality rates in urban areas are between 100 and 200 per 1000 live births, which means that among poorer urban populations these mortality rates are often likely to be between 200 and 400 – that is, between one-fifth and two-fifths of all children born to urban poor families die before the age of five (see, for instance, Hardoy et al, 2001; APHRC, 2002; UN Habitat, 2003). According to a review of available data, childhood mortality, stunting and underweight are generally lower in urban compared to rural areas, whereas acute malnutrition or wasting (as measured by a low weight-for-height ratio) and morbidity from infectious diseases are often higher (Ruel et al, 1998). However, there is considerable heterogeneity in poverty, morbidity, mortality and nutritional status in urban areas, and generally the intra-urban differences in these are greater than the rural–urban differences (Ruel et al, 1998). So, the problems of service provision and poor health outcomes among lower-income groups in urban areas may be very serious, but they may be obscured in any urban average because of the concentration of well-fed, well-served middle- and upper-income groups in urban areas.

2   *The scale and depth of urban poverty is underestimated because official poverty lines make little or no allowance for the higher costs of most necessities in urban areas (or particular cities).*[9] In many nations, the same income-based poverty line is used for urban and rural areas, even though the costs of land for housing, shelter and basic services are generally higher in urban areas or particularly high in certain cities. For instance:

- Many low-income households in cities spend between 20 and 33 per cent of their income on renting a single room; payment of rent for housing is rare in rural areas and, if paid, is likely to take a much lower proportion of a household's income.
- Many low-income households in large cities live far from income sources, so transport costs to and from work and services take up 5–15 per cent of their income.
- Many low-income urban dwellers spend 10–20 per cent of their income on purchasing water from vendors or kiosks and on using public toilets.

Access to healthcare and to schools may be more expensive in urban areas, as governments or those that run healthcare centres and schools charge more than in rural areas. However, it is difficult to compare rural and urban areas because lack of access to infrastructure and services is often the result of distance for rural populations and exclusionary social and political structures for urban populations. Low-income urban dwellers may live 50 metres from a sewer and 100 metres from a hospital and secondary school, but have as little possibility of using these as a rural dweller who lives 20 kilometres from the nearest sewer, hospital or secondary school.

---

9 This is discussed in more detail in Satterthwaite (2004) and Mitlin and Satterthwaite (2001).

The number of urban dwellers with below poverty-line incomes would be significantly higher if allowances were made in setting income-based poverty lines for the higher prices of many necessities. This is not to claim that urban poverty is worse than rural poverty or that there are more poor people in urban areas than rural areas (although for much of Latin America and some North African and Asian nations, this is so).

3   *The scale and depth of poverty is underestimated because most measures of poverty do not take into consideration living conditions, as well as other key aspects such as asset bases, safety nets and civil and political rights.* Although the literature on poverty often refers to people 'living in poverty', in most nations, calculations or estimates of the number of people suffering from 'absolute poverty' are based only on income or consumption levels, not on living conditions. Our work with Sandy Cairncross in 1990, drawing on a large number and range of city and neighbourhood studies, suggested that there were at least 600 million urban dwellers in Africa, Asia and Latin America who had homes of such poor quality and so lacking in basic infrastructure and services that their lives and health were constantly at risk (Cairncross et al, 1990). This estimate was subsequently endorsed by the World Health Organization (WHO, 1992) and the UN (UNCHS, 1996). Given that the urban population in low- and middle-income nations has increased by over 600 million since 1990, the number of urban dwellers currently living in 'life- and health-threatening' conditions is likely to be much higher than 600 million. Our work with Gordon McGranahan that reviewed all available information on provision for water and sanitation in urban areas suggested that, by 2000, at least 680 million urban dwellers in low- and middle-income nations lacked adequate provision for water and at least 850 million lacked adequate provision for sanitation (UN Habitat, 2003). Chapter 7 points out that in Brazil, with its predominantly urban population, 84 per cent of all new housing units in the second half of the 1990s were built informally, mostly by low-income groups with no access to formal finance.

One point about rural areas needs to be noted. By emphasizing that the scale and depth of urban poverty has been underestimated, we are not advocating a redirection of funding from rural poverty reduction to urban poverty reduction. It may be that the scale and depth of rural poverty has also been obscured by crude or inappropriate poverty definitions and measures. In addition, as the work of our research programme has long emphasized, the multiple links between rural and urban areas limit the validity of considering 'urban' and 'rural' poverty separately as many low-income urban households rely on rural links or assets, while many low-income rural households rely on remittances from urban family members or urban employment opportunities, including seasonal work and commuting (Tacoli, 1998). It is also impossible to consider rural and urban areas separately when considering how to improve most forms of service provision, access to information, the rule of law and democratic processes since many services and organizations that serve rural populations will be in local urban centres and many have responsibilities to serve both rural and urban populations. What this book highlights in terms of urban poverty reduction is the importance of focusing attention on building strong, effective local processes that help to address the multiple deprivations faced by large sections of the urban population (most of whom have limited income levels) – processes that involve and are accountable to this population. Local organizations and local processes for poverty reduction may have considerable validity for rural populations, too.

The eight case studies

The eight case studies in this book are about local or national initiatives and organizations that seek to address the deprivations suffered by low-income urban populations.[10] This reflects our belief that too little attention is given to the current and potential role of local organizations and processes in reducing urban poverty. We also believe that too much attention is given to the role of international agencies, without considering the local processes that they need to support in order to be effective (see Chapter 11). The case studies consider both the strengths and the limitations of these local processes. The limitations are considered in terms of what the initiatives do not provide and whom they do not reach, as well as in terms of the larger economic, social and political processes that underpin poverty and that are beyond the abilities of any local or national organization to change. All of the government initiatives examined support programmes in many different urban centres; as in all government agencies, each initiative is located within complex government structures, where it has to struggle to obtain legitimacy and resources. Each initiative is also one among various government programmes that attempt to reduce urban poverty. Each continues to struggle to make changes in the way that they operate and interact with low-income groups and their organizations (often in the face of strong opposition from others within government). All of the government programmes also draw on external funding for part of their work, which adds another layer of complexity since all external funding comes with requirements and conditions. For the civil society programmes, two operate in many urban centres (and are formed by national federations); two focus their attention in particular cities. In each, the scale and nature of what can be achieved is inevitably linked to what government agencies can be persuaded to do (or to stop doing), and what external funders can be persuaded to support.

The smallest initiative within the eight case studies, the work of the Anjuman Samaji Behbood in Faisalabad (see Chapter 6), is unusual in that it sought to demonstrate what could be achieved with regard to improving provision for water and sanitation without international donor or government funding. Here, costs were recovered from those who received the improvement to allow the initiative to expand – although some external funding was drawn from an international non-governmental organization (NGO) – WaterAid – to provide loan capital for required infrastructure investments that people could not be expected to pre-finance. As Chapter 9 discusses, all of the case studies sought to

10 One of them, CODI, also addresses rural poverty.

keep down their dependence on external funding through mechanisms for recovering some of the costs from beneficiaries.

The case studies were chosen with the help of the network of individuals and organizations with whom we work in Africa, Asia and Latin America. They were not chosen because they had shared characteristics. Some had a comparatively narrow focus: FONHAPO's name as the Mexican National Popular Housing Fund emphasizes its particular focus, whereas the Thai government's Community Organizations Development Institute suggests a broader focus (which is borne out by its work programme as described in Chapter 2). Despite their diversity, what they share is an attempt to address aspects of urban poverty by particular government agencies and civil society organizations or alliances. They were also not chosen as 'best practices' or 'success stories', although all case studies have sought to develop more effective ways of working with low-income groups and their organizations in addressing some aspects of poverty and have had positive outcomes.

The eight case studies represent considerable diversity with regard to:

- the kinds of nations and cities in which they are located;
- their main focus;
- the basis on which they are funded (ranging from those that rely on demand from low-income households or draw on community or local resources, to those that draw on funding from national governments and international agencies);
- the organizations involved in their formulation and implementation (see Table 1.1);
- what the organizations involved identify as the underlying problems and the chosen strategies for poverty reduction.

The case studies were also selected to reflect a diversity in which aspects of poverty they sought to address.

These case studies are not intended as evaluations, although all reflect on achievements and limitations and consider what constrained the effectiveness of initiatives. For six of the case studies, the author or some of the authors are staff from organizations who were involved in the initiatives. The other case studies were prepared by external (local) researchers.

Understanding urban poverty

Although it is still common for governments and international agencies to define, measure and monitor poverty on the basis of individual or household income levels or consumption levels, the last 10 to 15 years has brought a recognition of the inadequacies in doing so. Furthermore, of the multiple deprivations that most of the urban poor face, many of these deprivations have little or no direct link to income levels, while many relate much more to political systems and bureaucratic structures that are unwilling or unable to act effectively to address these deprivations.

Table 1.1 *The eight case studies*

Case study	Nation	Funding	Lead organizations involved in the initiative
Government initiatives			
Urban Community Development Office and the Community Organizations Development Institute	Thailand	Primarily Thai government (and cost recovery from loans)	Community organizations and networks of community organizations, often working with local government
Community Mortgage Programme	The Philippines	National (some cost recovery)	State (with active civil society)
Mexican National Popular Housing Fund (FONHAPO)	Mexico	Primarily national (some cost recovery)	State (with active civil society)
Programme for Local Development (PRODEL) operating in eight cities	Nicaragua	International, municipal and community	National NGO, municipal governments, national bank, community organizations
Civil society initiatives			
Anjuman Samaji Behbood in Faisalabad	Pakistan	Local demand, international NGO, cost recovery	Community organizations and a local NGO
Work of *Cearah Periferia* and the Casa Melhor/ Better Home and Programme of Support for Self-building (PAAC) programmes	Brazil	International NGOs, municipal funds, cost recovery	NGO with support from grassroots organizations and the municipality
Work of the South African Homeless People's Federation in different cities	South Africa	Community savings, local resources, national funds, some international funds	Savings and credit groups and their federations and local NGO
Work of the Society for the Promotion of Area Resource Centres (SPARC)–Mahila Milan–National Slum Dwellers Federation (NSDF) in different cities	India	Community savings, local resources, some national and international funds	Savings and credit groups and their federations and local NGO

Box 1.1 outlines eight different aspects of poverty. There is widespread recognition among governments and international agencies that lack of infrastructure and services are aspects of poverty, even if most do not incorporate indicators relating to these deficiencies in their measurements of poverty. Box 1.1 also includes aspects that are rarely considered in official discourses on poverty (and are less easily measured), such as lack of voice and power within political systems and bureaucratic structures, inadequate protection of poorer groups' rights by the law and discrimination (for instance, discrimination that is based on gender, age, religion or caste).

Some of the aspects of poverty listed in Box 1.1 are not exclusive to groups with limited incomes. For instance:

- In many societies, many of those with incomes that could be considered adequate in terms of paying for necessities lack voice within political systems and receive inadequate protection from the law (for instance, in terms of health and safety at work or protection from violence and other crimes).
- Some of the aspects of poverty noted above can be the result of non-democratic political systems that restrict the civil and political rights and freedoms of most or all 'non-poor' individuals and households as well as 'the poor'.
- In many urban centres, it is not only those with inadequate incomes who suffer from inadequate provision of 'public' infrastructure and services, since large sections of the population with the capacity to pay for good-quality infrastructure and services do not receive it; the deprivations they suffer that arise from, for instance, inadequate provision of water, sanitation and drainage, are more closely related to inadequacies within the service-providing organizations.

The list in Box 1.1 also has the limitation that many of the deprivations are linked and that one may cause another (for example, lack of income preventing an individual or household affording to buy, build or rent better-quality housing or to afford healthcare), while addressing one may also mean that others are resolved (or lessened). The deprivations suffered by low-income groups are generally the result of the interrelations between these different aspects. As Navarro (2001) describes, a five-person low-income household with only one income earner (who is illiterate), living in a rented room in an illegal settlement on a floodplain, cannot be categorized as having five distinct problems – namely, low-income, high-dependency ratio, lack of education, insecure tenure and unhealthy housing – because they are all related. It is often those households who face such multiple deprivations who are also the most vulnerable; a small change in one factor can result in increasing hardship and acute poverty. The last two deprivations might be seen as failures of civil and political rights rather than as aspects of poverty. But we feel that this list represents a more realistic characterization of the deprivations that large sections of the urban population face. As several of the case studies will show, it was through organized groups of the urban poor getting more voice and greater possibilities of participation that many of their other (material) deprivations were lessened. The list is also useful as a reminder of the

---

BOX 1.1 DIFFERENT ASPECTS OF POVERTY

1   Inadequate and often unstable income (and, thus, inadequate consumption of necessities, including food and, often, safe and sufficient water; frequent problems of indebtedness, with debt repayments significantly reducing income available for necessities).

2   Inadequate, unstable or risky asset base (non-material and material, including educational attainment and housing) for individuals, households or communities.

3   Poor-quality and often insecure, hazardous and overcrowded housing.

4   Inadequate provision of 'public' infrastructure (for example, piped water, sanitation, drainage, roads and footpaths), which increases the health burden and often the work burden.

5   Inadequate provision of basic services, such as day care/schools/vocational training, healthcare, emergency services, public transport, communications and law enforcement.

6   Limited or no safety net to ensure that basic consumption can be maintained when income falls or to ensure access to housing, healthcare and other necessities when these can no longer be paid for.

7   Inadequate protection of poorer groups' rights through the operation of the law, including laws, regulations and procedures regarding civil and political rights; occupational health and safety; pollution control; environmental health; protection from violence and other crimes; and protection from discrimination and exploitation.

8   Poorer groups' voicelessness and powerlessness within political systems and bureaucratic structures, leading to little or no possibility of receiving entitlements to goods and services; of organizing, making demands and getting a fair response; and of receiving support for developing their own initiatives. In addition, there is no means of ensuring accountability from aid agencies, non-governmental organizations (NGOs), public agencies and private utilities and of being able to participate in defining and implementing their urban poverty programmes.

Low-income groups may also be particularly seriously affected by high and/or rising prices for necessities (such as food, water, rent, transport, access to toilets and school fees).

Source: This table has been developed and modified since first drafted in 1995, and earlier versions of it have been published in various papers or book chapters. It draws on many other people's work, especially Moser et al (1993), Amis (1995), Chambers (1995), Wratten (1995), Baulch (1996), Moser (1996) and Moser (1998).

---

many possible entry-points through which deprivations can be reduced (see Chapter 10).

In many cities, there are large sections of the population who, according to government-defined poverty lines, are not poor but who live in poor-quality, overcrowded housing that lacks basic infrastructure and services. However, as noted earlier, this is usually more closely related to the unrealistically low level at which the income-based poverty line is set in relation to the real costs of necessities in that city, rather than to the fact that non-poor groups live in poor-quality housing.

The shift from seeing poverty as primarily 'lack of income or under-consumption' to one that recognizes other aspects brings obvious difficulties for agencies who seek to define, measure and monitor poverty. There are two particular problems: how to define poverty and how to measure it (and, thus, monitor it). With regard to defining poverty, there are obvious valid generalizations about who is poor and the immediate causes of their poverty in urban centres in low- and middle-income nations in terms of their lack of income (and, perhaps, its irregularity); their lack of assets; the nature of their work (informal, insecure, often hazardous, always poorly paid); and the poor quality of their homes and the basic infrastructure and services to which they have access (and related health risks). Measures for some of these can be incorporated within assessments of poverty. For instance, some nations now have an index of unsatisfied basic needs that monitors progress in improving housing conditions and some forms of infrastructure and service provision. But there will be considerable diversity in the scale and relative importance of these deprivations and of the priority given by individuals and households as to which they want addressed first.

There is less possibility of valid generalizations with regard to, for instance, levels of violence and other crimes, insecurity, illegality, and lack of social/community organization to help address and/or cope with deprivation, the scale and nature of discrimination (and who suffers from it), and the lack of civil and political rights, including 'voice' and the capacity to access entitlements (for instance, access to schools, clinics, medicines and subsidized food staples). Their importance as immediate causes of poverty vary considerably between cities and between districts within cities; also often in each city and city district over time. In addition, even within a neighbourhood or a household, the scale of the influence of any of these factors and their relative importance will also vary between people – for instance, between men and women and boys and girls (relating to differences in their tasks and roles, as well as their biology); between different age groups; and between different occupational groups. This sets a challenge for any external agency wishing to address urban poverty – whether they are NGOs, government agencies (from local, regional or national governments) or international agencies. This highlights why action is needed on many fronts. It also highlights why support from external agencies for poverty reduction programmes has to occur in a form that allows priorities to be influenced by those suffering the deprivation and to be sufficiently flexible to address the causes of deprivation within each particular location or social group and at the household or individual level. As Chapters 10 and 11 elaborate, some of the most effective poverty-reduction initiatives were those that provided individuals, households or organized community groups with access to resources whose actual use was determined by these individuals, households or community groups.

The multidimensional nature of poverty also makes it difficult to measure 'who is poor', to monitor trends in the number or proportion of people who 'are poor' and to see who moves into or out of poverty. Apart from the fact that it is important to learn how to support poverty reduction (which implies a need to define what constitutes poverty reduction and how it can be measured), there are also many powerful interests who want to demonstrate that poverty is diminishing and to claim that they are contributing to this reduction – especially governments and international agencies. The shift throughout the 1990s among the international development assistance agencies to more explicit commitments to reduce poverty and to set core targets whose achievements could be measured and monitored (which culminated in the Millennium Development Goals) occurred, in part, from their need to demonstrate their effectiveness to an often increasingly sceptical tax-paying population in high-income nations. But what does this shift imply for the relationship between these agencies and the people whose deprivations they are meant to address?

This focus on achieving a limited set of measurable targets brings both advantages and disadvantages. The obvious advantage is that most of the outcomes are important for low-income groups – for example, reduced infant, child and maternal mortality; control of malaria, tuberculosis and HIV/AIDs; and better provision of water and sanitation. The disadvantage is the possibility that this will mean top-down interventions by external agencies, which may contribute to achieving targets, yet fail to address most of the deprivations noted in Box 1.1 – especially those related to 'voice', participation, the rule of law and accountability. We believe that strengthening and supporting local processes and local organizations that work with, and are accountable to, the urban poor (including their own organizations) is a critical part of achieving the Millennium Development Goals (MDGs). It is such institutional changes that will drive the local reforms that contribute to achieving targets. More significantly, it is only such local organizations that can redefine the goals and strategies that are appropriate to poverty reduction. This is an issue to which we will return in Chapters 10 and 11. But perhaps it should be noted here that most national governments and international agencies would not see the work of the eight organizations that are described in Chapters 2 to 9 as being central to the achievement of the MDGs. On this, we beg to differ and hope that this book helps to substantiate the case for more support for these kinds of organizations.

Local organizations' and external agencies' orientations to urban poverty reduction

Before presenting the case studies, it is worth outlining different orientations that local organizations or external agencies may take in working with the urban poor. Each of the programmes described in Chapters 2 to 9 has a professional design component that seeks to identify and address the causes of poverty and these can be classified within four orientations: market; welfare provision; claim-making on the state; and self-determined solutions. In many of the case studies, more than one of these orientations is evident as they can complement each other (see Chapters 10 and 11).

A *market orientation* seeks to increase low-income groups' incomes or assets, or to pay for improved housing, infrastructure and services through measures that obtain full-cost recovery or through local entrepreneurs implementing programmes that respond to real demand. With limited grants or subsidies available from governments or international agencies, many initiatives seek to integrate the poor within local market systems. Much emphasis is placed on reducing the discrimination that the poor face (either in general or specific groups) – for instance, through ensuring that they can get credit, infrastructure or services from institutions that previously would not accommodate them. Credit often plays an important role since it allows low-income households to make larger payments to cover the capital costs of equipment and/or materials necessary for enhancing their incomes, or to pay for the cost of improved infrastructure (or connection to it), or of improving their own homes, with the repayments being spread over time. The great advantage of a market orientation is that if significant improvements for low-income households are possible at a cost that they can afford and for which they are prepared to pay, there are much better prospects for sustaining the improvements and for greatly expanding the number of people reached. Better integration into labour markets or markets with self-employment opportunities can help low-income households to secure higher and more stable incomes.

Welfare provision within agencies offers services or particular forms of assistance or improvements (for instance, 'slum-and-squatter' upgrading programmes) to those in need. Here, no measures may be taken to recover costs, as is the case in many upgrading programmes. This form of provision may be provided by an NGO, often fulfilling a role that government agencies should provide – for instance, provision of water, waste removal, healthcare or the support of centres that assist particular groups (such as centres for street children) – with no measures to recover costs through user charges. This is the most conventional role for local NGOs. This form of provision has not been attractive for the organizations whose work is discussed in Chapters 2 to 9 because it offers no possibility of 'going to scale' and depends so much on external funding.

Claim-making on the state may occur with the support of local NGOs or international NGOs who are active in advocating citizen rights and in putting pressure on local authorities or other state agencies to provide infrastructure or services to the poor and, where needed, to provide squatters with legal tenure. This usually concentrates on reducing the 'voicelessness and powerlessness' of poorer groups and, to some extent, on the inadequate protection of poorer groups' rights through the operation of the law. Other campaigns may focus on issues such as land-use rights or landlord–tenant relationships (for example, anti-eviction struggles), workers' rights (such as unionization, safe working conditions and non-discrimination), women's rights or the rights of specific groups at risk.

Self-determined solutions may involve autonomous actions or actions that combine community and state support in non-traditional ways, and which offer an increased role for local urban-poor organizations. This approach is of particular interest to NGOs because it can combine direct action, working with low-income groups to improve conditions, with a strong interest in improving the performance of local governments and their relationships with low-income groups (such as improving local governance). This is also the approach that explicitly recognizes and seeks to act upon most or all aspects of urban poverty described earlier. NGOs working in this area recognize that they must strengthen the bargaining power and capacity for organization and action of low-income groups and their organizations. Some government programmes also recognize this – as can be seen in the discussion of the Urban Community Development Office/the Community Organizations Development Institute (UCDO/CODI) in Chapter 2 and, in part, within the other government programmes. Behind this approach is a recognition that the other approaches (and most official 'solutions') often do not work well for the poorest groups. Part of the discussion in Chapter 11 is structured around considering the orientation of the eight case studies with regard to the four above approaches.

Conclusions

The case studies presented in this book are offered for their significance to learning and understanding. The record, to date, of development professionals in reducing urban poverty is not very promising.[11] Too many initiatives have offered too little to too few people. Although few project evaluations have been so critical as one conducted of a multilateral programme that stated 'there is no evidence that this project has benefited anyone',[12] many have had little lasting impact on the ground.

These case studies show that it is possible to reduce many of the deprivations faced by the urban poor and to make significance improvement in their lives. Chapters 2 to 9 present the case studies; Chapters 10 and 11 try to draw conclusions about why they have achieved some success and what this implies for the roles and approaches of external agencies – from local governments and NGOs to national governments and international agencies.

References

Aegisson, G (2001) *Building Civil Society: Starting with the Basics*, One World Action, London

Amis, P (1995) 'Making sense of urban poverty', *Environment and Urbanization*, vol 7, no 1, April, pp145–157

APHRC (2002) *Population and Health Dynamics in Nairobi's Informal Settlements*, African Population and Health Research Centre, Nairobi

Baulch, B (1996) 'The new poverty agenda: a disputed consensus', *IDS Bulletin*, vol 27, no 1, pp1–10

Cairncross, S, J E Hardoy and D Satterthwaite (1990) 'The urban context', in J E Hardoy, S Cairncross and D Satterthwaite (eds) *The Poor Die Young: Housing and Health in Third World Cities*, Earthscan, London, pp1–24

Chambers, R (1995) 'Poverty and livelihoods; whose reality counts?', *Environment and Urbanization*, vol 7, no 1, April, pp173–204

Hardoy, J E and D Satterthwaite (1989) *Squatter Citizen: Life in the Urban Third World*, Earthscan, London

Hardoy, J E, D Mitlin and D Satterthwaite (2001) *Environmental Problems in an Urbanizing World: Finding Solutions for Cities in Africa, Asia and Latin America*, Earthscan, London

---

11 The criteria used by governments to define and measure poverty are reviewed in Jonsson and Satterthwaite (2000) and Satterthwaite (2004).

12 This comes from a confidential report that we were permitted to read but asked not to reference.

Jonsson, Å and D Satterthwaite (2000) 'Income-based poverty lines; how well do the levels set internationally and within each country reflect (a) the cost of living in the larger/more prosperous/more expensive cities; and (b) the cost that the urban poor have to pay for non-food items', Paper prepared for the Panel on Urban Population Dynamics, Committee on Population, National Research Council/National Academy of Sciences, Washington DC

Mitlin, D and D Satterthwaite (2001) 'Urban poverty: some thoughts about its scale and nature and about responses to it', in S Yusuf, S Evenett and W Wu (eds) *Facets of Globalization; International and Local Dimensions of Development*, World Bank, Washington DC, pp193–220

Montgomery, M R, R Stren, B Cohen and H E Reed (eds) (2003) *Cities Transformed; Demographic Change and its Implications in the Developing World*, The National Academy Press, Washington, DC

Moser, C O N (1996) *Confronting Crisis: A Summary of Household Responses to Poverty and Vulnerability in Four Poor Urban Communities*, Environmentally Sustainable Development Studies and Monographs Series No 7, The World Bank, Washington, DC

Moser, C O N (1998) 'The Asset Vulnerability Framework: Reassessing Urban Poverty Reduction strategies', *World Development*, vol 26, no 1, pp1–19

Moser, C O N, A J Herbert and R E Makonnen (1993) *Urban Poverty in the Context of Structural Adjustment; Recent Evidence and Policy Responses*, TWU Discussion Paper DP #4, Urban Development Division, World Bank, Washington, DC

Navarro, L (2001) 'Exploring the environmental and political dimension of poverty: The cases of Mar del Plata and Necochea-Quequén cities', *Environment and Urbanization*, vol 13, no 1 , pp185–199

Potts, D (1995) 'Shall we go home? Increasing urban poverty in African cities and migration processes', *The Geographic Journal*, vol 161, part 3, November, pp245–264

Potts, D (2001) 'Urban Growth and Urban Economies in Eastern and Southern Africa: an Overview', Paper presented at a workshop on African Urban Economies: Viability, Vitality of Vitiation of Major Cities in East and Southern Africa, The Netherlands, 9–11 November

Ruel, M T, J L Garrett, S S Morris, D Maxwell, A Oshaug, P Engle, P Menon, A Slack and L Haddad (1998) *Urban Challenges to Nutrition Security: A Review of Food Security, Health and Care in the Cities*, IFPRI, Washington, DC

Satterthwaite, D (1997) 'Urban Poverty: Reconsidering its Scale and Nature', *IDS Bulletin*, vol 28, no 2, April, pp9–23

Satterthwaite, D (2002) *Coping with Rapid Urban Growth*, RICS International Paper Series, Royal Institution of Chartered Surveyors, London

Satterthwaite, D (2004) *The Under-estimation of Urban Poverty in Low and Middle-income Nations*, IIED Working Paper 14 on Poverty Reduction in Urban Areas, IIED, London

Tabatabai, H with M Fouad (1993) *The Incidence of Poverty in Developing Countries; An ILO Compendium of Data*, A World Employment Programme Study, International Labour Office, Geneva

Tacoli, C (1998) *Bridging the Divide: Rural–Urban Interactions and Livelihood Strategies*, Gatekeeper Series no 77, IIED Sustainable Agriculture and Rural Livelihoods Programme, London

UN Habitat (2003) *Water and Sanitation in the World's Cities; Local Action for Global Goals*, Earthscan, London

UNCHS (1996) *An Urbanizing World: Global Report on Human Settlements, 1996*, Oxford University Press, Oxford and New York

United Nations (2002) *World Urbanization Prospects; The 2001 Revision; Data Tables and Highlights*, Population Division, Department of Economic and Social Affairs, United Nations Secretariat, ESA/P/WP/173, New York

WHO (1992) *Our Planet, Our Health*, Report of the WHO Commission on Health and Environment, World Health Organization, Geneva

World Bank (1999) *Entering the 21st Century: World Development Report 1999/2000*, Oxford University Press, Oxford and New York

World Bank (2002) *Sustainable Development in a Dynamic World; Transforming Institutions, Growth and Quality of Life; World Development Report 2003*, World Bank and Oxford University Press, New York

Wratten, E (1995) 'Conceptualizing urban poverty', *Environment and Urbanization*, vol 7, no 1, April, pp11–36

Part II

Government Initiatives

Chapter 2

A Decade of Change: From the Urban Community Development Office to the Community Organization Development Institute in Thailand[1]

Somsook Boonyabancha

Introduction

This chapter describes the experiences of the Urban Community Development Office (UCDO) in Thailand in addressing urban poverty and how these fed into a new institution into which its programmes were integrated in 2000: the Community Organizations Development Institute (CODI). UCDO had a clear pro-poor, anti-exclusion agenda since its formation in 1992. It provided loans for new housing, housing improvement and income generation to community-managed savings groups, drawing from a capital base equivalent to US$50 million provided by the Thai government. Other programmes developed, drawing support from other agencies, including support for neighbourhood improvement and community-managed revolving funds. UCDO also increasingly provided support to networks of community organizations that took over many of the management tasks. Over time, this meant that UCDO shifted from managing a fund to support housing and land projects to managing a fund to support community networks that change the ways in which cities are planned and governed and that also addresses housing and land issues. This support of networks was widened and further consolidated once UCDO became part of CODI.

1 This chapter is a condensed version of a longer, more detailed paper. See Boonyabancha, S (2003) 'A Decade of Change: From the Urban Community Development Office (UCDO) to the Community Organizations Development Institute (CODI) in Thailand', Poverty Reduction in Urban Areas Working Paper 12, IIED, London. This can be downloaded at no charge from www.iied.org/urban. CODI and its predecessor UCDO also publish regular newsletters about their work; for more details see www.achr.net/country_news.htm; http://codi.or.th/ (click on the English sign at the bottom for the English version).

The emergence of the Urban Community Development Office

Recent official estimates suggest that as much as 37 per cent of Thailand's urban population live in some 5500 urban poor communities characterized by poor services and, often, inadequate infrastructure and housing conditions. Of these communities, 3750 have problems of insecure tenure as they are squatting on public land or renting land. The National Housing Authority (NHA) estimates that over 100,000 urban poor households are under imminent threat of eviction.

In 1990, the National Economic and Social Development Board began to look for new ways of addressing the problems of the urban poor communities.[2] It was widely recognized that their living conditions had not been improved by economic growth, especially for those squatting on land or renting illegally. Nor had conventional approaches worked well. Public housing represented only around 7 per cent of the total housing stock, and many urban poor households who had been provided with alternative land for relocation by the National Housing Authority were having considerable problems with repayments due to insufficient income (which often fell because of the lack of employment prospects in the new sites). Some sold their plots and returned to the city as squatters. The board initially thought that the answer was to generate more income in low-income communities so that households could afford to buy land and housing. As the first step in a substantive poverty-reduction programme, a study team led by Phaiboon Watthanasiritham was set up under the National Housing Authority to consider how to address the problem of poverty. By December 1990, the concept of an Urban Poor Development Fund had been established and the first steps towards establishing it were undertaken. Mr Watthanasiritham was asked to be the first managing director of the office set up to manage the fund.[3]

The study was a critical part of the development of this new fund for the urban poor. The process brought together community groups, activists, community federations, non-governmental organizations (NGOs), civic groups, entrepreneurs and government staff who were active in urban poor development issues. Through discussions, many ideas were shared and refined. A body of interested organizations developed that later came to support the operation of UCDO. The study proposed that an Urban Poor Development Fund be established (as a new institutional form in Thailand) to support urban community development activities and provide low-interest loans to community organizations for income generation and housing.

Initially, the fund would operate within the National Housing Authority. This allowed its rapid establishment, although from the outset it was intended that it would eventually become autonomous. The organization would be governed by

---

2 The term 'communities' is used throughout Thailand to refer to those individuals living in low-income settlements.

3 Mr Watthanasiritham was a highly respected individual with experience in both the public and private sectors. He had been the first director of the Thai stock exchange and, at the time, was running Rural Reconstruction and Development, a large NGO.

a board, which would institutionalize partnership as it drew members from government staff, academics and community representatives. There was considerable advantage in setting up the fund as a special unit within the authority, as it was able to operate with considerable freedom and flexibility without having to struggle for special legal status in its early years.

Many factors contributed to the changed policy towards the urban poor and the development of the fund:

- Rapid economic growth during the second half of the 1980s was accompanied by growth in the middle classes and by many large infrastructure and construction projects; but income disparities between the rich and poor increased. The income share of the top 20 per cent of income earners grew from 51 per cent during the early 1980s to more than 60 per cent during the early 1990s, while the share of the bottom 20 per cent fell from 5 per cent to 3 per cent.

- The rapidly expanding real estate housing market was not able to reach the poorest 30 per cent of the population.

- Economic growth attracted more people to cities because of better economic prospects, while rapid business growth and state infrastructure investments increased land prices. Squatter communities who had been left alone for years were now threatened with eviction as landowners sought to sell land and take advantage of higher prices. By the end of 1980s, 24 per cent of Bangkok's population lived in 1500 low-income settlements and most were threatened with eviction. Squatter communities had no legal protection, no matter how long they had been established. And, as noted above, the programmes to relocate squatters were not proving successful.

- Unusually, government finance was available for new programmes. Land revaluation, combined with long-standing restrictions on government expenditure, had produced a surplus.

- There was broad support within government for such a fund. Rapid economic growth, especially in industrial, commercial and construction sectors, had resulted in greatly increased needs for labour. The government supported an urban poverty reduction programme to enable skills and expertise to be developed. They also thought that small entrepreneurs would be able to find a niche alongside major traders. The administration of Prime Minister Anand Punyarajun, appointed after the coup d'état in 1992, established new funding mechanisms that supported the idea of the fund. There was also a growing interest in participation and in the role of civil society, together with a willingness to explore how the state might support local governance. As elsewhere, there were moves to decentralize government responsibilities to a local level. This opened new possibilities for devolved and participatory working methods.

- There were precedents on which to draw, both within government and from NGOs. During the 1980s, the government had supported land-sharing schemes, where part of the land site on which urban poor communities squatted was returned to the landowner while the inhabitants received secure tenure in reblocked communities on the other part (see Angel and

Boonyabancha, 1988) and some community-driven housing developments During the 1970s and 1980s, NGOs such as Human Settlements Foundation, Plan International, People's Organization for Development, the Building Together Association, Duang Prateep Foundation and the Human Development Centre established initiatives in community organization, savings and credit groups and housing development. Community groups were actively looking for more resources.

- There were increasing numbers of successful experiences elsewhere in Asia with programmes such as Grameen Bank in Bangladesh and the Community Mortgage Programme in the Philippines (see Chapter 3), showing that community development through savings and credit was viable, potentially leading to large-scale development opportunities.

- Savings and credit groups had long been functioning in rural communities both informally and formally, and there was also some experience with urban community savings and credit groups.

These factors help to explain why it was possible for a significant government financial contribution to be made to a new fund to provide loan capital for housing improvements and income generation. As a result, the institutional structure would be inclusive of different interests, would be consultative with regard to the direction to be taken and would be supportive of community needs. While these different factors did not define the kind of institution that would be established, together they offered legitimacy to an open process of exploration based on a number of key areas. The major problem was recognized as the need to find a solution for housing problems in urban areas, especially the problem of eviction. The availability of finance and the recognized need for new systems of governance enabled the setting-up of a new institution to address housing issues. The experiences of NGOs, other Asian programmes and Thailand's urban and (particularly) rural communities all suggested that a major thrust of the new institution should be savings and credit.

The common perception was that urban communities needed two kinds of support. On the one hand, there was a need for a financial system that was more flexible and directed more to the needs of low-income groups as they developed enterprises or other income-earning opportunities. On the other, rising inequality, combined with a widespread recognition that the benefits of economic growth should be shared, allowed a strong social development orientation. In part, the fund was a response to the large gap that had been created between the formal and informal systems of urban development.

Setting up the UCDO

As a result of the study team's report, the Urban Community Development Fund was capitalized and UCDO was set up in 1992 to manage it. The government granted it a revolving fund of 1250 million baht (at that time equivalent to US$50

Box 2.1 The advantages of community-based savings and loan activities

- Community savings and loan activities draw people together on a regular and continuous basis. They offer opportunities for members of low-income communities to develop their strengths gradually through making collective decisions about concrete activities that affect the community.
- The financial mechanisms are grounded in daily activities; saving and lending are quick, simple and related to the real daily needs of the urban poor as defined by the poor themselves.
- Savings and loan activities provide the urban poor with their own resource base to address their basic needs.
- The process creates ongoing learning within the community about each other's lives, about how to manage together and how to relate to external systems with greater financial strength in order to satisfy more than day-to-day needs. It is a process that every community member can relate to and that everyone can be involved in controlling. It is a gradual process that provides the community with the capacity and confidence needed for a true and comprehensive self-development process. Consequently, the poor can enjoy the pride that comes from being the owners of a process, and not merely recipients waiting for benevolence from outsiders.

Thus, savings and loan activities are not simply an end in themselves – rather, they are a means to strengthen community processes so that people can work together to satisfy their multiple and diverse needs.

Source: Boonyabancha (2001)

---

million) through the National Housing Authority.[4] The programme developed by UCDO sought to improve living conditions and to increase the organizational capacity of urban poor communities through the promotion of community savings and loan groups, and the provision of loans for housing improvement, new housing and income generation at subsidized interest rates to community organizations. The community organizations then on-lent to their members. From the outset, the Urban Poor Development Fund has been accessible to all urban poor groups who organize themselves to apply for loans for their development projects.

For the urban poor, savings and loan groups offer a simple, direct and uncomplicated way of addressing some of their immediate day-to-day needs. Savings and credit groups become a significant entry-point for a community's own development process, enabling them to come together as a community and to strengthen their relationship with the formal system of urban development. The importance of savings is elaborated in Box 2.1. The new fund offered opportunities for communities to obtain additional resources for their own development projects.

---

4 The Thai baht's value in relation to the US dollar varied between 1992 and 2002 from around 25 baht to 47 baht per US$1. Where exchange rates between the baht and the dollar are given, the rate used is the one current at that time.

Table 2.1 *UCDO loans available from 1992*

Type of loan	Purpose of loan	Annual interest rate	Maximum term
Revolving funds	Used as a revolving fund for a savings group	10 per cent	1 year
Income generation	Individual or group business investment	8 per cent	5 years
Housing (project)	Housing project for a community with immediate problems purchasing land and constructing housing	3 per cent for a loan of less than 150,000 baht; 8 per cent for a loan of between 150,000 and 300,000 baht*	15 years
Housing (non-project)	For repair and extension of houses and utilities	10 per cent	5 years

Note: *The higher interest rate for larger loans was introduced in 1995 in response to increased requests for housing loans and to a fear that low interest rates were encouraging an overextension of housing-related debts.

The UCDO had five initial objectives:
1 Stimulate community savings and loan groups, co-operatives and savings networks.
2 Develop managerial and financial management systems of community savings and loan groups, with learning processes and capacity-strengthening of group leaders and members.
3 Establish community savings and loan groups in order to achieve various development activities such as income generation, housing and environment–development projects, as well as community welfare.
4 Provide different kinds of loans – including those for community revolving funds, income generation and housing improvement – to all urban poor groups who organize themselves to apply for loans for their development projects (see Table 2.1).
5 Promote community action planning for other related activities to be implemented by communities.

The principles adopted to manage these activities are to:

• Strengthen local associations, with the understanding that community organizations are key actors in the development of low-income communities.
• Provide integrated loans for development projects, with the understanding that the loan is an instrument of development.
• Stimulate collaboration with other local groups such as government organizations, NGOs, academics and the business sector, while ensuring that the community organization is at the centre, and with the understanding that people-led partnership is essential to pro-poor development.

Through integrated loans (which could be used for housing, income generation or revolving funds), UCDO sought to strengthen community management

Table 2.2 *UCDO loans available in 2000*

Type of loan	Annual interest rate (per cent)*	Maximum term (years)
Revolving funds	10	3
Income generation	8	5
Community enterprise	4	7
Housing improvement	8–10	5–15
Housing project	3–8	15
Network revolving funds	4	5
Revival	1	5
Miyazawa – to reduce community crises and debt	1	5
Guarantee	Fixed rate +2	Flexible

Note: *In most cases, the community will add a margin of about 5 per cent on this rate charged by UCDO.

capacity and responsibility for self-determined and self-managed community processes. Of the three main types of activities for which loans were provided, the revolving funds loans were more unusual and more flexible than those for housing and for income generation. When communities first start saving, they accumulate capital that they are encouraged to lend to their members. These are small loans that may be used for emergencies (such as a shortage of food, medical needs and school fees) or for small income-generation activities. Revolving fund loans boost the capital held in community savings funds, enabling groups to better address members' needs for small and immediate financial liquidity. While often the least well-understood type of fund by people outside the UCDO, revolving loan funds were perhaps the most flexible form of intervention that it offered. Communities had to expand their collective capacity in finance and in decision-making to successfully manage the funds. The economic crisis in 1997 encouraged UCDO to respond to new needs, and by 2000 it had developed a more diversified loan system in response to the increasingly complex forms of social organization and financial mechanisms that it was promoting. Various types of loans provided finance for numerous development options that were implemented, decided and controlled by community organizations themselves (see Table 2.2).

Any group is eligible to receive any of the loans available, provided that it has a demonstrated financial management capacity through the administration of its own savings and loan activities. The fund requires a simple loan proposal (and has clear rules), and once a group fulfils the criteria, it can obtain loans. Once staff learn of the group's needs, they will explore ways of assisting and facilitating community processes. Loans can be released within a month, if the correct procedures are followed.

Stronger savings groups enabled new options to develop. Increasingly, loans and development processes came to be implemented through community 'networks' rather than through the UCDO itself. Network is the closest English word to the Thai term *krua kai*. Networks are assemblages of groups that come together around common aims – and they can be tightly organized or loose assemblies. There are networks of communities in the same city or province that use collective strategies to negotiate with city and provincial authorities or to influence planning processes, or who simply work together on specific problems of housing, welfare, livelihoods or access to basic services. There are networks based around occupations (for instance, taxi and *tuk tuk* co-operatives), pooled savings and co-operative housing. There are also networks based on shared land tenure problems (for instance, networks of communities living under bridges in Bangkok and communities living on Crown property, along railway tracks and beside canals who have tenure or landlord problems) who work together to find joint solutions and negotiate together for land rights and entitlements.

Networks are formed as groups join together because of the benefits of joint learning and action. Networks apply for capital and they distribute the funds to their members, reducing the administrative burden and enabling more localized decision-making that responds to local needs. Networks represent a considerable increase in collective community capacity, as leaders adjudicate over competing claims and disputes and, more importantly, make choices about how resources can be used most effectively to address needs. The UCDO ensures that funding is available to address all the needs that the network puts forward, while the experience of networks in managing investment and debt means that requests are carefully considered and evaluated. UCDO can rapidly disburse large amounts of money through networks. Perhaps more importantly, when the key node of decision-making is a staff member in the UCDO, the process can slow down and become rigid. Networks represent active and ongoing social organizations, and are under continuous pressure from membership organizations so that there is less danger of stagnation and delay.

When the fund was established, the board calculated that it could be self-sustaining with an annual average interest rate of 7 per cent. This would cover all administrative expenses, including the community development process (an estimated 4 per cent), with a small allowance for inflation (which was relatively low). The setting of terms and conditions for the loan process was a political rather than a technical issue. The idea of a 'shared' interest rate, with a proportion remaining with the community organization, had developed during the initial study phase, drawing on the experience of earlier loan funds. These groups (and later the networks) were allowed to add a margin to cover their own costs and to give themselves additional funds either for development costs or for their community welfare fund. The margin or additional rate depends upon agreement within the community, and ranges between 2 and 10 per cent.

Achieving the aggregate figure of 7 per cent return was an objective used to design the interest rate structure for the various loans, considering the amount of capital, repayment period and use made of the loans. Some board members were worried that UCDO loans would undercut existing financial markets – but they did not do so because the community added to UCDO's interest rate. Eventually, the board agreed that the interest charges would be shared with the savings schemes.

The community can decide on the amount and period of repayment, provided that it does not exceed the maximum terms of payment outlined. Groups may decide to repay daily, weekly, fortnightly or monthly. Communities must make regular loan repayments according to the agreement or by the tenth of every month. Delay or default without reasonable notice will result in a fine. More recently, groups who maintain repayment schedules receive awards and certificates. Network loans have much greater flexibility as repayment schedules may only require repayments to be made every six months. This assists the network in addressing the needs of members and uses group experience to support the weaker members.

Community loan proposals of up to 1 million baht are agreed through a recommendation to the managing director, while loan approvals above this amount have to be approved by a loan committee that includes external specialists. Loans above 20 million baht have to be approved by the board. After approval has been given, the community and UCDO sign a mutually agreed community development plan, together with a loan contract. After 1998, community networks became stronger and many loans are now made to them for further on-lending. In general, network loans may be up to 5 million baht.

All committee members are required to sign their names as guarantors to the loan scheme. In housing projects, the land title or housing itself may also be used as collateral.

Institutionalized partnership at the highest level

Since its inception, the UCDO has been governed by a board, with members appointed from various development partners. Unusually, this includes community representatives elected by community members themselves. As such, the UCDO is a new kind of Thai institution, one that promotes institutionalized partnership. The board has always had complete power to make all policy decisions, even during the period when it was a special organization under the National Housing Authority. The board is made up of the following groups:

- four representatives of government organizations (the Bank of Thailand, the Finance Ministry, the National Housing Authority and the National Economic and Social Development Board);
- four elected community leaders; and
- three professionals from NGOs and the private sector.

The board is chaired by the governor of the National Housing Authority, and the UCDO managing director is secretary to the board.

Through this board, the process of partnership is embedded within the programme. All relevant and concerned groups are represented and community leaders have equal status with government officials and other development actors. Having community representatives sitting on the highest policy-making committees has made the programme more transparent and participatory.

The UDCO works with national government agencies, local authorities, NGOs, federations and professionals. All are regarded as potential development partners to be supported and strengthened through collaboration in implementing the programme. In several cities, there have been successful attempts to bring all urban groups together as an Urban Community

Development Committee. Activities are subcontracted to NGOs and municipalities, providing funding to draw them into the programme. All such contractual arrangements are for a specific period to avoid dependency on the UCDO and to prevent the community from being dominated by the professional agency.

The fact that the funds were in the form of a revolving fund allowed greater flexibility in managing a new development process that is being led by people within communities. Communities can access the funds directly, without negotiations with a government department and without a long bureaucratic procedure. This new way of managing the fund allowed financial resources to be delivered directly to, and managed directly by, communities. Funds were available quickly to support the pace of community-managed development. This offers an alternative to conventional, expensive, externally managed development for the urban poor, which so often means long delays before funding is available and then a need to spend the money more quickly than community processes require when it finally arrives.

From the outset, it was agreed that any profit earned through the fund should help to subsidize the administrative and development costs. With the average interest rate (return) set at 7 per cent, the planned division was:

- 4 per cent for administration and development activity costs;
- 1 per cent reserved for bad loans;
- 1 per cent for special community activities; and
- 1 per cent to go back to the fund.

However, the actual average interest achieved across lending to all savings schemes was only 5 per cent. This shortfall was caused by the high percentage of housing loans requested in the initial years, with an interest rate of 3 per cent. However, only one-third of the total fund was being loaned and the rest remained on deposit, earning interest that could compensate for the shortfall. Therefore, the average annual interest gained from all the monies in the fund has averaged 7 per cent. Total expenses for all development activities and management costs have averaged 3 per cent a year. When the UCDO merged to become CODI at the end of 2000, the UCDO fund had grown to about 1700 million baht (much expanded from the original grant of 1250 million baht, although less when measured in terms of US dollars).

Expansion through diversification

As activities developed around the community savings and loan process generated by UCDO, and when so many community activities and networks emerged and began working actively with other local development actors on a large scale, other agencies chose to support this work with contributions to specific programmes. Since 1996, there have been several joint development projects between the UCDO and other development programmes – see Box 2.2. These include the Urban Community Environment Development Fund aided by

---

Box 2.2 UCDO: NEW ACTIVITIES, EXISTING NEEDS

Urban community environment activities

These are small grant funds for local environmental improvements, such as walkways, water supplies, drainage systems, recycling activities, day-care centres, tree planting and community playgrounds. A joint committee of community and local authority representatives administers the grants. Funding came from the Danish government and passed through the Urban Community Development Office (UCDO).

Urban Community Development Foundation

This is an NGO and sister institution to UCDO that helped to develop links with other agencies, including the United Nations Economic and Social Commission for Asia and the Pacific (UNESCAP) and the Japanese government's Overseas Economic Cooperation Fund and Japanese International Cooperation Agency (JICA).

Miyazawa Community Revival Loan Fund

This fund assists those savings schemes that faced financial difficulties as a result of the economic crisis. The Japanese government's aid package to Thailand enables recovery loans charged at 1 per cent per annum, and allows groups to restructure debts and undertake income-generation projects. Networks typically on-lend at 5 to 6 per cent, thereby creating a welfare fund for those facing particularly acute difficulties.

Collaboration with the World Bank Social Investment Fund

After the failure of conventional approaches to ensure the speedy release of funds to those most in need, the UCDO suggested that the community networks might help. After the initial proposals from six networks were accepted, the process went ahead. Resources are allocated as one-off grants to communities for education, welfare (those with HIV, the sick and the elderly) and income generation, with community management of the funds. The funds are also made available as grants, loans or partial loans, and are designed as temporary measures in response to economic crises. Funding is provided by a World Bank grant.

Community enterprises

A number of agreements have emerged between savings groups and private and public agencies. For example, in Bangkok, the Housewives' Savings Group secured a contract to make school uniforms from the Bangkok Metropolitan Authority, and the Community Handicrafts Promotion Centre received a contract to make souvenirs for the Asian Games. Many networks are now buying rice from wholesalers and sell on to their members.

---

a US$1.3 million grant from the Danish government, which supported a wide range of community-managed projects for environmental improvement. Community welfare activities also got a boost, as some US$6 million was channelled through UCDO from the World Bank's Social Investment Programme. This emerged from a rescue package offered to the Thai government in 1998. Some 40,000 households have benefited. The US$6 million supported community-managed revolving funds that acted as safety nets and emergency funds – for instance, to help pay school fees or to support elderly people or those who are sick or unemployed. Funds could be made available as grants, loans or partial loans.

From the outset, there was an understanding that the UCDO's development approaches had to be holistic; but between 1992 and 2000, a number of factors led to diversification into new areas. Firstly, the emphasis on partnership and collaboration resulted in many new links. Over the years, some of these links grew into joint activities and then into more formal programmes. Secondly, the organization was open to suggestions from other groups to explore new initiatives. New programmes were allowed to develop with their own strategies and approaches, and these became individual 'windows' that communities could approach to address specific needs. This allowed new kinds of activities to begin and minimized the risk to existing activities if they did not work. Each new strategy had its own advantages and limitations. Communities could learn what worked for them and why. Thirdly, the multiple needs of urban poor communities meant that there was a constant pressure to expand existing opportunities and a constant interest in exploration. If a formal agency came to the UCDO with a new idea, it was possible to link them to communities (and later networks) who wished to work with them.

From crises to opportunities

The 1997 economic crisis

In spite of the UCDO's activities, the problems of poverty resulting from unbalanced economic growth in Thailand continued during the second half of the 1990s. The Eighth National Social Economic Plan (1997–2001) sought to address inequitable development and to re-orient the country's development towards people's needs, social equity and environmental sustainability. Then, during the first half of 1997, Thailand was badly hit by the Asian economic crisis. Many private sectors and financial institutions collapsed, causing serious unemployment and widespread reductions in incomes. The urban poor also faced grave problems. To better inform their response, the UCDO commissioned a study of the urban poor in 1998 (see Box 2.3). According to this survey, 64 per cent of the urban poor had less income than in 1997 and increasing debts. Savings activities in many communities also faced crisis and near collapse.

However, eviction pressures were reduced by the downturn in economic activities. Furthermore, the crisis resulted in new government programmes with new development opportunities in communities on a massive scale. Perhaps most importantly, the crisis provided an opportunity to bring people together to rethink and review Thailand's development direction and to recognize the need for structural change in political systems, economic development options and the use of the natural environment.

Box 2.3 Urban poverty in Thailand, 1997 and 1998

A survey undertaken in 1998 covered 5745 households (26,813 people) in 130 communities. Half were in Bangkok, while the rest were drawn from other cities. All were within the lowest 10 per cent income bracket in Thailand. The survey was structured to ensure that it drew from different areas, networks and kinds of community (for instance, covering rental housing and squatters). Among those in the survey, 26 per cent owned their house and land, 26 per cent owned their house and rented land, 19 per cent rented a house or room, and 21 per cent owned their house in a squatter settlement. In addition:

- 72 per cent were wage earners (including factory and construction workers and temporary labourers); 18 per cent were small traders (including more than twice as many women as men); 6 per cent had jobs in the private sector; and 7 per cent classified themselves as unemployed.
- 21 per cent of those working had less work than before the crisis.
- 64 per cent said that their income had fallen between 1997 and 1998, with the average reduction in income being 24 per cent (3900 baht per month).
- 56 per cent said that their income was now insufficient to meet their basic needs and the average shortfall was 3000 baht.
- 55 per cent of households had debts, with the average debt being 72,000 baht; average loan repayments per month were 3800 baht.
- 35 per cent of families had borrowed from private money lenders (at an annual interest rate that averaged 180 per cent); 28 per cent from savings groups; 10 per cent from family and friends; 10 per cent from co-operatives; and 14 per cent from formal financial institutions.

UCDO responses and the growing importance of networks

Since its inception in 1992, the UCDO has developed links with a wide range of established federations, community organizations, savings groups, NGOs and other government organizations. Campaigns were organized to stimulate savings and loan activities in as many urban poor communities as possible. From the beginning, the UCDO sought to establish a participatory process at the grassroots level to ensure that the urban poor would be involved from the start of all activities. The UCDO was anxious that the urban poor perceived the fund as a 'fund of the poor, for the people', to which they wanted to contribute their efforts, rather than as a government fund – in which case their efforts would be focused on maximizing financial benefits for themselves.

The 1997 crisis brought immense pressure on the UCDO's operating processes during a significant period of adjustment and structural change. The financial difficulties faced by the poor resulted in many loan defaults. Questions were raised about many parts of the process. How could the risks associated with debt be both reduced and better managed? How could local organizations be strengthened so that they could help their members who were facing repayment difficulties? When was lending simply not appropriate? What were the preferred development options of the poor, and how could they identify and realize these options? The questions raised by the crisis resulted in increased pressure for change and the lending systems were subject to review.

The growing importance of networks of community organizations to UCDO's work was noted already. Changes in operating procedures and development processes primarily came from the creation of community networks within individual cities or across constituencies. There are several reasons for this new emphasis on community networks that reflect both the economic crises and the nature of the development process supported during the first years of the fund:

- As savings schemes became stronger, there was increasing emphasis on city development processes linking community groups with local authorities. Groups from the same city who have similar experience and have been active for some years often met at local authority development forums. As local authorities were drawn into the programme, they began to have ideas about how their role might be extended. City-based networks began to develop a life of their own.
- The savings schemes initiated by UCDO activities were scattered throughout the country. UCDO staff recognized the need to link communities to share and work together in their constituencies, to be self-supporting and to use self-learning among similar community groups. Staff and communities wished to use the experience and capabilities of the stronger groups to set up and support the new and weaker groups.
- As noted in Box 2.3, between 1997 and 1999 the economic crisis significantly affected the urban poor, including their savings and loan groups. The non-repayment rate increased from 1 to 2 per cent in 1995 to about 7 to 8 per cent in 1998–1999, and several community savings and credit groups were on the verge of collapse. The fragility and vulnerability of isolated savings groups was recognized, as was the need for a mechanism that provided local support. For debt not to increase vulnerability, it was critical to find ways of transferring repayment responsibilities from individuals to the collective. This led the UCDO to explore new directions, to bring groups together through networking (or what could be termed horizontal support) and to support networks that could help groups to manage debt repayment problems and improve auditing.
- Several of the interventions and programmes introduced since 1996, such as the community-driven environment and development activities and the community welfare programme, started to implement the decisions and work of the networks rather than that of single groups. The new approach proved to be extremely efficient in enabling communities to implement large numbers of projects in infrastructure, housing–community planning, education, and health and welfare. These projects identified productive connections and extensions for themselves. As community experiences with networking increased, so has the demand for support.

Thus, a very significant aspect of the work of the UCDO (and, subsequently, of CODI) is the linking together of urban poor savings and loan groups in the same city and district, or with similar development issues and common interests, to form many different *community networks*. Networks are organized at various

---

BOX 2.4 NETWORKS: SOME EXAMPLES

Bangkok Co-operative Housing Network

This network was set up in October 1994 and now has a membership of 17 groups with over 14,000 households. The network helps housing co-operatives to become established, successfully solve their problems and better manage their debts.

Buri Ram Community Network

Buri Ram is a city in the poorest region in Thailand. This network has a membership of 11 groups and 1000 households. It was set up in 1999 to help groups better manage their debts. A network loan from Miyazawa (at 3 per cent interest a year) has enabled them to relieve the debt problems of their members, to lend to many groups and to enable development to start again.

Bangkok Taxi Co-operative Network

This network has 214 taxi drivers as its members (divided into four groups for each of the major Bangkok zones). The network enables members to buy taxis rather than rent them from agents (who end up with most of the profits). Recent activities include a new network-owned petrol station with a repair workshop.

Khon Kaen Community Network

This is mostly made up of groups who live in squatter settlements and who make their living recycling rubbish in this north-eastern city. The network has built a recycling centre to allow fair prices for recyclers and has put in place a community welfare programme. Its membership includes 21 groups and over 1200 households.

Chiang Mai Network

The Chiang Mai network has undertaken environmental and housing activities for its 26 groups and 3000-plus household membership. This includes dredging canals, protecting historic walls and preventing environmental degradation in and around the canals.

---

levels – from national, regional, within-city, zonal and district-wide. They are organized around similar interests and problems, such as networks among those sharing the same landlord or those facing eviction. No particular format for community networks has been prescribed; but these have developed according to the interests and capacities of the groups involved, in accordance with their own needs, situations and changing contexts.

Experience to date has shown that community networking is a very powerful platform for larger-scale development – a platform that involves a synergy of learning, sharing of experiences, boosting of morale and mutual inspiration. The networks have given urban poor groups enormous confidence. Community networking has emerged at many levels and in many forms, and has become the main community-led development mechanism to support a national-scale urban poverty development process that links with existing programmes through the urban poor communities themselves. The networks have also been critical in helping communities to manage debt repayment problems, drawing on the Miyazawa Community Revival Loan Fund described in Box 2.2. Box 2.4 gives some examples of networks and the work that they do. Lending is now increasingly to networks who then on-lend to savings schemes, depending upon their needs and capacities.

Results and impacts for housing

Returning to the theme of housing, this section explores what has been learned from UCDO's experiences.

General impacts on urban poor community development

At the time of CODI's creation in 2000, activities were taking place in 53 out of Thailand's 75 provinces. Nine-hundred-and-fifty community savings groups had been established (out of 2000 urban communities in the country) and more than 100 community networks had been set up. There are also further networks representing non-settlements-based interest groups. Community networks had been accepted as an important development mechanism by most formal development agencies.

More than 1000 million baht has been provided as various kinds of loans and more than half of the loans have already been fully repaid. Community savings now total more than 500 million baht. These community-owned savings are being used as rapid release revolving funds that circulate among community members. Informal estimates suggest that the assets generated within communities as a result of these savings and loan processes equal 2000 million baht. During 1999–2000, a review of the Miyazawa loans to community networks (provided to reduce the effects of the economic crisis) found that about half of the 240 million baht loaned to communities was being used to repay debts to informal money lenders. Typically, these money lenders charged interest rates of between 10 and 20 per cent a month. Under such conditions, it was almost impossible for borrowers to ever repay the capital. They had to keep making repayments to cover interest charges. The use of Miyazawa loans to reduce the debt burden had immediate and significant impacts. Most networks on-lent the funds to savings schemes at 5 per cent a year. Debts suddenly became affordable and repayments to savings schemes were made on time. With repayments, savings schemes' revolving funds were re-capitalized and could start to offer emergency loans to members. The local development process was re-ignited.

As a result of controlling their own resource base, of links with other groups and of support from the UCDO, communities have developed the confidence to implement their own self-managed activities to directly address their own insecure conditions. With a stronger financial base and greater confidence in their own development capacity, several communities have been able to develop community enterprises, with collective investments in many activities. Several communities have formed groups who contract for work together – for example, with construction contracts from private and public companies, producing school uniforms under municipal contracts, and the ownership and management of petrol stations by taxi driver co-operatives.

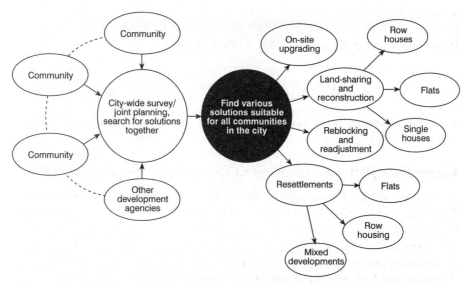

Figure 2.1 *The linkages for a local housing development partnership by city-wide networks with communities and local authorities*

Housing strategies have development as part of this much wider set of development activities. Initiatives include buying existing urban poor community land, resettling on land close to former locations following eviction, improving housing in situ and repairing housing after a crisis. The extremely local nature of networks has meant that they can respond appropriately to need and opportunity regardless of how unusual or fragmented. For example, some private landowners were only prepared to sell 4 or 5 of the 100 plots that they owned. Networks found it easy to respond to the opportunities identified by members of savings schemes, whereas conventional agencies would have struggled to achieve similar levels of flexibility.

As community network processes have grown stronger, several city-wide housing development activities have been introduced within such cities as Nakornsawan, Ayuthaya, Uttraradit and Chiangmai, amongst others. This is an exciting new direction in which local community networks work with city authorities to develop city-wide plans that provide secure land and housing for all urban poor communities in the city (see Figure 2.1). Some cities have great potential for stronger links to be forged between community networks, local government agencies and other civic groups to work on broader city development issues such as planning, the environment and solid waste management within broader city development programmes – for example, the Healthy and/or Liveable Cities Programme (see Box 2.5). The way in which the UCDO works, in practice, is illustrated by the experiences in Uttraradit, a city of 46,000 in the north of Thailand.

Most community networks have developed their own community welfare programmes. These act as flexible, local safety nets as small sums can be made available very rapidly in response to particular needs or opportunities. The

---

BOX 2.5 ADDRESSING HOUSING NEEDS IN THE CITY OF UTTRARADIT

Several years ago, savings schemes in Uttraradit began to borrow money to improve their situation. One leader in the Jarern Dharm community had problems with repayments. Urban Community Development Office (UCDO) staff sought to help resolve this problem. On one trip, the team took a walk around the city and found a large number of squatters living along the canal edge in wooden homes that they had built over the water, the only place where they were allowed to stay. Many of the houses were of poor quality and infrastructure was virtually non-existent. At the time, the people were not part of a savings scheme; but, as a result of this visit, they began to start saving and within a short time there was a network of savings groups.

Together with two young architects, the community undertook a survey of all the settlements and discovered that there were 1000 families in the city with housing problems. In Jarern Dharm itself, there were 30 families living over the canal in acute need of better housing. A local temple offered a long-term resettlement area at a nominal rent and a plan was made for relocation. But there were delays in securing the agreement of different families and it was decided to go ahead with a partial solution for eight families. With the help of the architects, the families considered their options. To attract the interest and commitment of residents, it was decided to build a life-size model house. Within days of the model being started, families were actively engaged in the process. The final agreed house model measured 42 square metres with a ground floor of 30 square metres and a loft area with an extra 12 square metres. The community received a loan of 324,000 baht and the total cost of each house was 40,500 baht. The loan repayments worked out at just 15 baht a day (or 450 baht a month).

The two processes – the house construction and the city-wide survey of low-income settlements – have opened up many processes in the city. The inhabitants of 16 'mini' squatter settlements are being rehoused in a new settlement on land purchased by the municipality with the settlement designed through a community planning workshop. The mayor is supporting a process of urban redevelopment around the idea of Liveable Cities for All (one of the objectives of the Ninth National Plan). Further activities are already planned in three other communities. Within the wider programme of Liveable Cities for All, parks and environmental improvements, together with income-generation activities, are also planned and there is renewed interest in the city's history and culture.

---

programmes also help to take care of the more vulnerable groups – for instance, those who fall sick and the elderly. The existence of these welfare funds allows communities to help each other in ways that make isolated problems become a communally shared responsibility. They also provide security to community members who have never had any form of welfare protection.

In several cities, urban community development forums have developed as a collaborative platform for communities and other development actors working together at city level. Many formal development programmes have formalized partnerships, with community representatives sitting on the highest level committees. Such committees may be concerned with the general development of low-income settlements or with aspects such as health or housing. Increasingly, a culture and belief is developing that communities of the poor should be key development actors and should participate in decisions that relate to their lives. Increasingly, local authorities are assuming a culture of 'inclusion'.

The combined work of the networks and of the UCDO brought about changes in the ways that development institutions operate. Most development institutions (whether local, national or international) claim that they are in favour of decentralization and participation; but the way in which they set up their institutional systems and the way that they plan, administer and implement their programmes are mostly in complete contradiction to their stated preferences. This new approach has helped to demonstrate new development possibilities in which communities are prime actors. As a consequence, it has given much broader and more lasting impacts. The process demonstrates the strength and power of horizontal development against the traditional, expensive and often unsustainable hierarchic vertical system.

Impacts on low-income housing development

One of the constant debates within government concerns the role of housing in development and the interest rate that should be charged for housing loans. Officials and representatives from government organizations reasoned that UCDO loans were similar to social investment funds and were not large enough to address housing problems. In addition, they argued that low interest rates would lead communities astray, encouraging them to apply for housing loans, which – in their view – was not a productive investment. They proposed high interest rates to prevent this problem. But community representatives argued that community organizations had sufficient managerial capacity to implement their own housing development. The urgent needs of communities for more secure housing, especially for those facing eviction, meant that housing loans were more, rather than less, urgent. They proposed lower interest rates for housing loans because larger loans were needed and because housing development is a basic need and develops a long-term asset.

After intense lobbying by community representatives, the board decided that the interest rate for housing should be 3 per cent a year, and it restricted housing loans to not more than 30 per cent of the total fund (to maintain a higher overall return on capital and to reduce the risk of communities overextending their housing debts). In April 1993, housing loans were subdivided into housing (project), with an annual 3 per cent interest rate, and housing (non-project) – that is, housing improvement, with an annual 10 per cent interest rate. The reasoning was that housing projects were used in emergency situations when a community was being evicted. By necessity, costs were high as they involved land purchase and reconstruction. Only in these cases could an interest rate subsidy be justified. Communities who simply wished to improve their housing while remaining on their existing site should do so incrementally through housing improvement loans.

In retrospect, this early debate over housing was important because it demonstrated the responsiveness of the board to community perspectives. Community members felt responsible for the decision that was taken and became actively engaged in decision-making as UCDO's systems began to emerge. This was an early breakthrough in changing community perspectives; through this

Table 2.3 *The different kinds of UCDO-supported housing projects*

Type of project	Number of projects	Number of communities	Families		Loans	
			Number	Per cent	Million baht	Per cent
Buying existing land or land close to former locations	8	7	229	7.3	43.176	12.6
Relocation	20	45	2713	87.0	257.153	74.9
Housing construction on leased land or NHA land	5	5	240	7.7	27.544	8.0
Infrastructure improvement	4	-	-	-	15.456	4.5
Total	37	57	3182	100	343.239	100

process, community representatives grew in confidence. At the same time, those inside and outside of the UCDO began to recognize that this was a process that was different from previous housing programmes because the urban poor themselves were involved in decision-making.

A number of different kinds of housing strategy emerged – and these can be grouped in four categories (see Table 2.3). Some groups bought the land upon which they were squatting (in some cases purchasing only part of the site) or found sites close to their existing location. Other groups relocated, buying land some distance from their original site that required development. A third group built new homes on land purchased and improved by the National Housing Authority or some other authority. Most communities spent all of their loans on land purchase and found that infrastructure improvements required additional funds. For infrastructure improvement projects, unit costs were relatively high in some projects since one reason why the land had been affordable was that it had inadequate infrastructure. With support from the National Housing Authority, some infrastructure improvement projects have been able to secure a grant of 18,000 baht per family.

Loans are also provided for improving housing but where land tenure is not changed.

As Table 2.3 shows, most UCDO housing loans were used to support community relocation projects. These were managed by community organizations or networks. For example, in Thonburi, 56 households purchased land and designed two-storey housing; the cost was 323,000 baht per household and the National Housing Authority provided the infrastructure free of charge. However, many communities managed to find lower-cost alternatives; the average cost for land and infrastructure per plot has been 100,000 to 150,000 baht. The development of new land for housing has cost less than existing land since it is generally more remote; but once the cost of landfill has been taken into account, the cost of new land is similar to that of existing sites.

The high price of land is the main reason why these are often expensive. With regard to location, 31 per cent of projects have been located 10–20

BOX 2.6 PARTICIPANTS IN UCDO-SUPPORTED
HOUSING PROJECTS

- Eighty-three per cent of those interviewed were from urban poor communities; 10 per cent used to live in urban poor communities but had moved out prior to joining the project, although they still retained membership of the group; 7 per cent came from outside the urban poor settlements and may be related to members.
- Before joining the project, 72 per cent owned their houses and 23 per cent rented a house or room. Fifty-four per cent had rented land and 43 per cent had squatted.
- Thirty-one per cent were small traders; 21 per cent had their own business (taxi drivers, construction workers, clothes producers); 12 per cent were labourers; and 11 per cent were factory workers.
- The average household income was 14,767.6 baht* and 40 per cent earned less than 10,000 baht per month.
- Housing expenditure before joining the project was as follows: 42 per cent had no fixed expenditure on land and house rent; 18 per cent paid less than 100 baht per month; 17 per cent paid between 100 and 500 baht per month; and 15 per cent paid more than 1000 baht per month. The average expenditure on infrastructure for households with no fixed housing/land expenditure was 736.5 baht per month.
- The average cost of travelling to work and school was 1615.2 baht per month.

Note: *The urban poverty line in 1996 was 9356.8 baht per month.

---

kilometres from the city centre, with 27 per cent of projects 30–40 kilometres from the city centre. Forty per cent of the projects are relatively small, with 50 or fewer households receiving assistance (some of these settlements may be larger than 50 households; but only a few residents may receive loans.) The largest project included 540 plots, the smallest only 6 plots. The average plot size per family is approximately 80 square metres, although the smallest plot was 20 square metres; larger plots are possible outside of Bangkok where the cost of land is lower.

Most of the organizations that provide loans add a margin of 5 per cent to the rate charged, resulting in an average rate for the final borrower of 8 per cent; some groups add only 4 per cent with a consequent smaller final interest rate. The highest rate charged to borrowers (by one group) is 10 per cent.

A household survey of 249 housing project participants (from a total potential population of 1323) was compiled in 1996 to provide a preliminary analysis of experiences (see Box 2.6). The 1996 survey was important for the UCDO and led to changes within the organization. If people are facing eviction, the obvious response is to find and purchase land; but if the purchased land is too far out or too far from the inhabitants' employment locations, this leads to many problems. The survey found that 71 per cent of those in relocation projects had been unable to relocate to the new area; generally, only those with immediate eviction problems had moved. Twenty-nine per cent of those who had taken part in buying existing land had already settled. Since the majority of those in relocation projects had not yet relocated, this has been less effective in comparison to other strategies. Most of the communities remaining on their original sites were satisfied at having secure land ownership without having to change jobs or find new schools for their children. Some households had started small home-based enterprises, such as producing clothes and selling food, using their own savings, the community revolving loan fund and UCDO loans.

But for those who relocated (often because they had no possibility of remaining where they were) the situation was more difficult. Despite being satisfied at having secure land tenure, conditions on the new lands were often unsatisfactory. The new sites were on the city periphery and journey-to-work times had lengthened, with additional travelling expenses. Some people had rented a room close to their original job or stayed with relatives in the city. Total expenses can be high when new housing had to be paid for, as well as additional rented accommodation. The 1996 survey showed that 49 per cent of those who were planning to relocate but had not done so had housing expenditures of 1001 to 2000 baht per month, whereas 61 per cent of those who had already relocated were paying more than 4001 baht per month for land, housing, infrastructure and travelling expenses. This suggested that the financial implications of relocation needed to be more carefully understood.

Another issue raised at this time was that some residents who had secure land tenure had started to pay less attention to community activities. Most participants take part in choosing the land and in deciding on plot specification, relocation plans, membership rules and co-operative regulations. However, after land has been secured and housing construction completed, levels of community participation decrease. In part, this problem exists because only some of the participants have been relocated and there is not yet a developed community. For those who have relocated, being on a remote site makes it harder to link with other development processes, and this prevents possible learning and sharing between groups. However, in well-established projects with secure land ownership, the level of community participation has also decreased. The community ties that developed in their former site to help cope with the insecurity are no longer there. As houses are built, groups can become inward-looking and it is hard for them to maintain the same level of commitment to other activities.

Regarding savings performance, fixed repayments and increases in housing and travelling costs made it difficult for communities to save. As a result, savings groups found it hard to provide their members with additional loans for housing and some had to apply for 'non-project' housing loans. Designed to fund small-scale housing improvements, these loans attract a higher interest rate. In some cases, this compounded problems, with additional debt-management issues.

In terms of repayments, during the first two or three years following loan release, 76 per cent of repayments were punctual, 6 per cent were occasionally late and 18 per cent were missed frequently. In general, those people with problems were individuals or households who were attracted by the prospect of housing and had overextended themselves. With increased unemployment, they were unable to maintain the previous rate of repayment.

In 1997, most housing projects were affected significantly by the economic crisis. The cases where large extended families had purchased more than one plot were particularly difficult. Some members considered selling their plots back to the co-operative to get the money they needed to pay their debts. Some moved back to their former insecure settlements or to others close by. For these families, the scale of debt was simply too great to manage in a situation of falling incomes. Local savings schemes were not strong enough to support them through these difficulties; in some cases, they lost most of their assets. At the same time, there were a growing number of empty plots in the housing projects, which produces additional difficulties in managing collective loan repayments. A survey in 1998 identified 944 empty plots in housing projects: one-quarter of all new plots that had been created. To address this problem, the UCDO considered allowing co-operatives to find new members who could take over the land and debt burden from the former owner. The viability of the group was at risk because of the inability of the community to support the more vulnerable members. While this problem still exists to some extent, it is considerably less prevalent than during the late 1990s. The growing strength of networks has helped considerably, as groups can benefit from earlier experiences and be warned about the risks that they are taking.

Communities who had taken loans for both land purchase and housing construction also faced repayment problems. Although the UCDO had a maximum loan size of 300,000 baht per family, some communities obtained additional loans from other sources to increase their building capacity. Since 1997, many of these communities have struggled to cope with multiple debts.

There is a definite benefit from the introduction of new funding opportunities. New funds help communities to start again, put their problems behind them and move forward. Stagnant leadership is removed in favour of new and more energetic leaders. Old problems are looked at afresh and new solutions are proposed.

The growing role of networks in housing has been particularly important. There are a number of different kinds of arrangements in housing projects. Some consist of one organization made up of one or two communities (settlements); some have community organizations with multiple communities; and, finally, some are managed by networks in the same city or by the same interest group. Most of these organizations have immense experience in community and housing development processes, including responding to eviction problems; negotiating for compensation; coordinating with government agencies responsible for land and infrastructure development; subdividing land in informal and poorly planned areas; planning housing construction; financial management; conflict resolution; and dealing with policy at a national level relating to squatting, land issues and eviction.

The growing role of community networks

Most community organizations have strengthened their own development capacity through housing development projects. They have developed links with several other development actors and local authorities, such as the National Housing Authority, the Bangkok Metropolitan Authority and many municipalities in activities such as infrastructure improvement, income generation and urban community environment activities.

The emergence of city-level housing activities came about to support communities in developing land and housing. The UCDO found that providing housing loans to needy communities without creating links that enable communities to support each other and learn from each other presented many problems. Urban land that has been settled by low-income families, and the associated housing development process, can pose difficulties for the communities because this is a complicated process that needs connection to, and negotiation with, the formal system – for instance, regarding tenure, land subdivision and house construction. It may be difficult to find a completely legal solution. Communities struggle to merge the informality of their previous lives with the formality that is now required. No single community can achieve its housing development process without support. Each community needs allies from which to learn and gain strength in order to negotiate with government authorities. The UCDO's early experience showed that isolated communities face many problems; the problems of communities choosing distant sites for relocation was noted already. In addition, isolated development can encourage speculation, with community leaders becoming land agents. While the presence of communities as a new agent in land acquisition and development was an important step forward, some problems also became evident.

Community networks emerged as a solution to the difficulties faced by isolated and atomized communities. In a first stage, networks began to offer communities a chance to help themselves and to help each other (what was earlier termed horizontal support). Community networking at city level helped to extend the scope of community housing development. These networks encouraged communities in the same city to broaden their understanding of the situation and extend their vision in order to link immediate problems with structural issues of land and urban management. At the same time, the networks strengthened communities' negotiating power with city authorities. Networks create permanent forums on housing and land at the city level.

Loans to support relocation are no longer seen as the only solution to eviction threats. In many cases, the networks support communities in exploring alternatives with their landowners. Community networks in several cities began to plan housing development activities together at city or district level. Networks have linked similar communities, such as the canal-side community network, the railway community network and the Rama III community network (related to communities affected by major road construction).

Communities have found that solidarity is an alternative strategy to reducing their vulnerability, and one that may be more effective than loan capital. Community networks are now engaged with government agencies and other actors at the city level, with solutions to problems being negotiated and developed in a more proactive way. Thus, the key change is from seeing the fund as the solution to housing and land problems, to recognizing the need for the fund to support community networks that change the ways in which cities are planned and managed.

In the past, the Bangkok Metropolitan Authority and other local authorities involved in the housing development process had done little to address housing problems due to their limited resources and limited understanding. However, once communities began developing their housing initiatives and had their own financial resources (mainly from UCDO loans), many local authorities started to develop partnerships with communities and became involved in community housing development processes.

Expansion, follow-up and the transition to CODI

Moving beyond housing

Despite the focus on housing and the high percentage of initial lending allocated to it, it might be argued that the UCDO did relatively little to address housing needs in Thailand. Only several thousand individuals improved their housing directly through their affiliation with the UCDO. But the UCDO ended up supporting much more than housing – building communities and community networks, building economic activities, supporting savings, and supporting community capacity with regard to welfare. In effect, it demonstrated that collective housing developed by organized communities and housing developed within community and local partnerships – including city-wide development – are the means to solve the urban poor's housing problems. Nevertheless, housing improvements were a major reason why urban poor communities developed links with the UCDO.

The experience with the UCDO (and in other nations) suggests that savings and loan groups and networking activities are an educational process for communities. They start to realize that they can improve their lives in many ways, and housing may not be the main priority. While security of land tenure is critical for those facing eviction, it may make little sense to other communities.

Households participate in all kinds of different strategies to secure their housing without taking loans. For instance, over the last ten years, some communities negotiated for secure land tenure, some reached an agreement to vacate half of the land in return for permission to stay on the remaining part (land-sharing), and some took an income-generation loan – improving their houses incrementally as incomes increased while keeping debts (and debt repayments) low. Some households purchased land outside of their existing settlements in rural areas in order to reduce the uncertainty associated with squatting, while also maintaining a prime city-centre location. Some completed environmental improvements, including upgrading and painting their houses, to reduce public pressure on the local authority to remove them.

Paradoxically, many of the groups who joined to take housing loans found alternative strategies that offered more secure and better standards of accommodation without increasing their debt burden. The processes of reorganization prompted by the 1997 economic crisis have further increased such strategies. Community leaders realized that the management of debt is not an easy process. Households themselves became more cautious about increasing their vulnerability and taking financial risks.

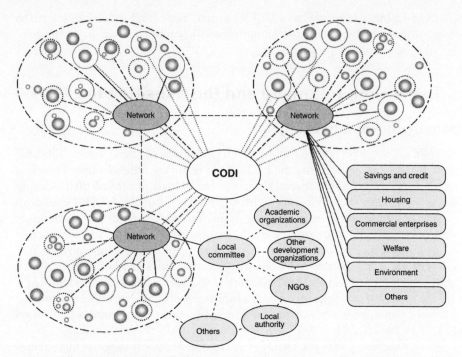

Figure 2.2 *How CODI links groups together and supports networks*

New programmes and directions

In 2000, the UCDO merged with a rural development fund to become a new public organization called the Community Organizations Development Institute (CODI). The royal decree that brought the UCDO into existence allowed developments launched under UCDO to continue, but enabled important changes in how the organization functions and how it relates to the low-income community organizations that it supports. The decree means that CODI has its own legal entity as a public organization, providing greater possibilities, additional flexibility and wider linkages for collaboration between urban and rural groups. CODI can also apply to the annual government budget directly, so that additional finance can be raised to support low-income communities. The emphasis on decentralizing to communities and community networks developed by UCDO will continue. Figure 2.2 shows how CODI, like the UCDO before it, works with community organizations and networks of community organizations.

CODI's board, like that of UCDO, includes representatives from poor communities, government and outside organizations. CODI's 11-member board of directors has one chairperson, four representatives from government organizations, three community organization representatives and two specialists/experts. CODI's director serves as the secretary of the board.

CODI manages various funds for developing community organizations in rural and urban areas. The amount totals 3.3 billion baht and includes:

- 1700 million baht from the UCDO fund;
- 747.5 million baht from the Rural Development Loan Project;
- 247.6 million baht from the Miyazawa fund;
- 80 million baht from the New Elderly Welfare Project; and
- 500 million baht from new government support for the Urban and Rural Community Organization Empowerment Project.

The transition from UCDO to CODI has meant that, as well as adding the management of the rural fund to the other funds that it manages, CODI has responsibility for managing a new elderly welfare fund that supports older citizens in various community networks to link together, determine what they would like to do as a group, and then design and implement their own welfare and development programmes. CODI also added a new mixed fund to the other funds that it inherited from UCDO, which is used to support community networks. This has provided support for provincial linking grants (to allow rural and urban groups in each province to meet, exchange experiences and develop plans); small grants for network-based projects; loans to networks; and partnership grants (to support joint projects by communities, civic groups and NGOs).

In 2003, the Thai government approved a national community-upgrading programme that will support 200 'cities-without-slums' programmes. CODI endorses this, helping local networks and actors to develop these. Upgrading programmes on this scale are only possible if the 'infrastructure' of community processes and networks and their savings schemes are in place. CODI's work has also expanded greatly in comparison to UCDO, as it supports and works with 30,000 communities and their community networks in rural areas. CODI can also support links between rural and urban enterprises, communities and networks. This allows it to move beyond the artificial division between 'rural' and 'urban', including working with communities on the fringes of cities that have both rural and urban characteristics.

During 2003, CODI's work will include the *Baan Mankong* programme to address land and housing problems in ten overcrowded pilot communities and 20 city-wide processes to support cities without slums. The budget for this is 126.6 million baht, with an infrastructure subsidy of up to 20,000 baht per family for on-site upgrading and up to 100,000 baht per family for resettlement and with support for housing loans provided at 1 per cent interest. A further 20 million baht has been allocated to support the city-wide processes in the 20 cities.

Expanding the experiences of community development finance to other countries in the region

Because of the close collaboration and mutual learning among groups in different countries in Asia and Africa, as facilitated by the Asian Coalition for Housing Rights and Shack Dwellers International, the experience of the UCDO has been widely disseminated to other countries. Countries such as Cambodia, Laos, Vietnam, India and South Africa have been able to learn about the role of community development funds. Similar models have been developed in other countries, such as the Urban Poor Development Fund in Phnom Penh; the Pak Ngum Community Development Fund in Vientiane; community development funds in five provincial cities in Vietnam; the Payatas Urban Poor Development Fund in the Philippines; the *u Tshani* Fund in South Africa; the Windhoek Urban Poor Development Fund in Namibia; and the Gungano Fund in Zimbabwe.[5] Extensive exchange visits between groups in Asia have been organized to facilitate and broaden experiences. Many of these funds place a major emphasis on housing and secure land tenure, while also providing loans for enterprise and community activities.

Institutionalizing links between urban and rural community development

The creation of CODI brought considerable changes to the former UCDO structure. Many decisions have been decentralized to the regions (which include a number of provinces), and each region has a management committee made up of community leaders and other development groups to direct activities in that region. There will also be provincial development committees selected from various community networks in the province in order to direct development.

The experience of UCDO and then of CODI shows that it is possible to alter the delivery of development so that the outcomes are more favourable for the poor. What it demonstrates, above all, is the need to support the poor themselves in becoming key players in the development process. The poor must be involved in decision-making, must be able to own the decisions that are taken and must be in control of the activities that follow.

Savings and loan activities are important because, together, they build community management capacity. The capacity of a community to determine its priorities, transparently manage finance, negotiate with other powerful local groups, and plan and reformulate its strategies are all essential attributes of an empowered community. Collectively organized savings activities help by strengthening the links between community residents and by ensuring that leaders are accountable to local members. Collectively managed loan repayments help a community to assess the financial investments that it wishes to make and to ensure that finances are not managed by external groups living outside of the community. What has also emerged from these experiences is that loan management helps networks of communities to understand when accumulating debt is a necessary burden for a community and when it is best avoided. Together, savings and loan activities help communities to prioritize, manage and implement development.

As important as savings and loan activities is community learning. In the UCDO and then in CODI, community learning takes its concrete form through collective engagement in implementation and through community exchanges. Learning cannot be abstract if it is to involve the poor. Rather, it needs to be related in a concrete way to project-level activities. Exchanges help the analysis of experience and the modification of plans.

---

5 See the February 2002 issue of *Housing by People in Asia*, published by the Asian Coalition for Housing Rights (on community funds); see also *Environment and Urbanization* (2001), vol 13, no 2.

Projects cannot be an end in themselves, but need to be integrated within a more comprehensive plan that is driven by the poor. Conventional development systems and processes are not designed for the conditions of the poor, nor are they appropriate to the needs of the poor. The problems when the poor try to fit into these systems are considerable. What is required is that the poor determine the conditions attached to projects – thereby enabling plans and processes to be more favourable. At the same time, the poor cannot resolve their problems on their own. What is needed is an open and inclusive process that engages with the many other groups who are relevant to urban development in ways that are determined and controlled by the poor.

The UCDO and the Urban Development Fund has had no claim over the projects that it has supported. At all times, it sought to open up inclusive processes that are controlled by the poor themselves. The institutional form that is suited to this way of working has, by necessity, to be flexible and dynamic. Moreover, the UCDO and then CODI have chosen to become institutions that have open participatory governance. The creativity with which UCDO responded to the challenges that it faced reflects the diverse and representative nature of the board. During the last ten years, all groups represented on the board have worked to create new kinds of relationship that enable it to effectively address issues of common concern. CODI now looks forward to its increased scale of operation and the opportunities that this brings.

References

Angel, S and S Boonyabancha (1988) 'Land sharing as an alternative to eviction: the Bangkok experience', *Third World Planning Review*, vol 10, no 2, May, pp107–127

Boonyabancha, S (1999) 'The Urban Community Environmental Activities Project, Thailand', *Environment and Urbanization*, vol 11, no 1, April, pp101–115

Boonyabancha, S (2001) 'Savings and loans: drawing lessons from some experiences in Asia', *Environment and Urbanization,* vol 13, no 2, pp9–22

Chapter 3

The Community Mortgage Programme: An Innovative Social Housing Programme in the Philippines and Its Outcomes

Emma Porio with Christine S Crisol, Nota F Magno, David Cid and Evelyn N Paul [1]

Introduction

The Community Mortgage Programme (CMP) is an innovative housing finance programme in the Philippines that allows low-income families, particularly those living on public and private lands without security of tenure, to have access to affordable housing. It is a programme for legalizing and upgrading squatters and informal settlements or for supporting their inhabitants to develop homes on a legal site elsewhere. Between 1991 and 2001, it assisted 106,273 poor families in securing housing and land tenure in 854 communities (CMP, 2001). It is the most responsive and cost-effective government housing finance programme in the Philippines; it also has the highest collection efficiency rate of all government housing loan programmes.

This chapter focuses on three aspects. The first is the institutional and policy context from which the CMP emerged, the form it took and the constraints on its effectiveness. The second is the changing relations and dynamics in the housing sector, after housing functions were devolved to local governments. The third is the socio-economic and political impacts of the CMP on beneficiary community associations.

---

1 This chapter has also been written with the collaboration of Anna Marie Karaos (Urban Research Consortium/Institute of Church and Social Issues); Ma Lourdes Rebullida (Urban Research Consortium/University of the Philippines); Ma Lina Mirasol (Urban Research Consortium/Fellowship for Organizing Endeavor); Napoleon Amoyen (Urban Research Consortium/Ateneo de Davao University); and Francisco Fernandez, Ana Oliveros, Vikki Horfilla and Miriam Quizon (National Congress of CMP Originators of the Philippines).

Institutional and policy context[2]

As in many other low- and middle-income countries, limited access to land in Philippine cities has been the greatest barrier to providing affordable housing to the urban poor. Until the 1970s, the urban poor enjoyed relatively easy access to urban land through spontaneous or organized land invasions that were generally tolerated by government authorities. During this period, squatting or informal self-built housing was the principal means by which the urban poor gained access to urban land and housing. From the 1980s to the present, access has been restricted by increasing urban densities (which reduce the supply of unoccupied land), the rapid commercialization of land markets, rising prices and increased competition. These forces, together with increasingly globalized financial markets and the rapid expansion of real-estate development and construction industries, have denied the poor residential lands near their places of work.

Social housing policies since 1985

Since the mid-1980s, three major policies have shaped the initiatives, performance and relationships of different stakeholders in the housing sector:

1   *Executive Order 90*: Recognizing the magnitude of housing needs and the scarcity of available resources, the Aquino government (1986–1992), through Executive Order 90, initiated a shift in government policy from the direct production of housing units for middle-class families to an enabling strategy that focused on the urban poor. It offered the urban poor access to mortgage finance, and encouraged private-sector and non-governmental organization (NGO) involvement. Mortgage financing was centralized under the Unified Home Lending Programme that offered different loan packages, the lowest of which (then 150,000 pesos, now 180,000 pesos)[3] is classified as 'socialized housing'. Other programmes in this category include resettlement projects, Cooperative Housing, and the Community Mortgage Programme. The adoption of this strategy in 1986 meant that the National Shelter Programme shifted to mortgage finance, and significantly reduced direct production through slum upgrading and sites and services. Market forces, such as land supply/prices and availability of housing credit, increasingly shaped access to housing assistance.
2   *The Urban Development and Housing Act of 1992*: This marked the departure from eviction and relocation to the adoption of a more decentralized approach towards housing and urban development, incorporating housing needs and urban poor participation in land-use planning. Local government units were to establish local housing boards and require developers to comply with a 20 per cent share of social housing within their developments.

---

2 This section is largely based on the Institutional and Policy Context Study undertaken by Anna Marie Karaos as part of the CMP study supported by the International Institute for Environment and Development (IIED).

3 The exchange rate for the peso against the US dollar has varied during the period under consideration from 39 to 50 pesos per US$1. Where figures are given on exchange rates, these reflect the exchange rate at that time.

3   *The Local Government Code of 1991*: This supported the new policy framework
     and made local government units share the responsibility of providing social
     housing and of regulating shelter-related activities.

Complementing these initiatives were the Comprehensive Integrated Shelter
Finance Act of 1994 and the Social Reform Agenda of the Ramos administration
from 1992 to 1998. The short-lived Estrada administration attempted, rather
unsuccessfully, to devote a higher proportion of government funds to social
housing and to enhance local governments' capability in urban planning and
shelter development. *Erap Para sa Mahirap* (Estrada for the Poor) and *Pabahay sa
Mahirap* (Housing for the Poor) were banner statements often heard from
housing officials between 1998 and 2000. But the political and economic crisis
dampened the initiatives of the housing sector, especially those aimed at the
poor. In addition, the administration focused its efforts on resettling
slum/squatter populations under threat of eviction in Metro Manila (including
those beside the Pasig River and canals), ignoring other cities. The
Macapagal–Arroyo administration continued to view CMP and social housing as
central to poverty alleviation of households below the poverty line (current
estimates suggest that about 42 per cent of households are below the poverty
line) and to increase the proportion of government funding that goes to social
housing.
    Despite the more favourable political environment and better legal
framework, cases of eviction were still reported and the announced shift towards
the urban poor has not been realized in financial terms. Between January 1993
and September 1998 only 19.5 per cent of the total expenditure on housing was
allocated to poverty-oriented housing projects (socialized housing) and only 1.33
per cent to CMP (CMP, 1998). Despite the growing gap between land prices (25
to 50 per cent increase per year) and urban real incomes (5 to 7 per cent increase
per year) during the last six to eight years (1992–2000), there has been little state
finance for the urban poor. Between 1995 and 1998, less than 30 per cent of the
12.5 billion pesos allocated in the Comprehensive Integrated Shelter Finance
Act were released. For the year 2000, the CMP had about 2.7 billion pesos
available; but only 7.3 per cent of this was released to assist CMP projects during
the first quarter of the year. In the first quarter of 2001, only 38 million pesos
were released to finance six projects that benefited 819 urban poor households.

The Community Mortgage Programme (CMP)

Formulated after the EDSA Revolution[4] in 1986, the CMP derived its inspiration
from the community organizing and housing experiences of NGO leaders who
came to be within the Aquino government. The programme drew heavily from
the experiences of housing officials who had worked in NGOs and progressive
community-based organizations, which were partly a legacy of the resistance to
the 18-year Marcos dictatorship. During the first ten years (1989–1999), the
implementation of the programme was severely hampered by the government's
heavy dependence upon private pension/mutual funds as sources of finance,

4 Named after Epifanio de los Santos Avenue.

and by a housing bureaucracy that could not respond to the particular conditions and needs of the poor. By 2000–2001, however, the biggest problem faced by the programme was the limited capacity of the National Housing Mortgage Finance Corporation, the government agency that has the task of managing the social housing funds.

The CMP targets squatter communities occupying public and private lands, and offers them financial support for land acquisition, infrastructure development and house construction. It has the following features:

- Target beneficiaries organize themselves into a community association.
- The organized community association can obtain a loan for the purchase of property and land development without having collateral.
- The communal finance/loan must have an NGO, a local government unit or national housing agency as an 'originator', which is responsible for making sure that documentation requirements are complied with and monthly amortizations paid.
- Individual members of the association may obtain loans for house construction and improvement after securing land titles.
- Loan amounts are 30,000 pesos for an undeveloped lot, 45,000 pesos for a developed lot and 80,000 pesos for a house and lot. All loans are charged 6 per cent annual interest, with a 25-year loan term.
- The origination fee is 500 pesos per beneficiary or 2 per cent, whichever is higher.

As of February 2001, the CMP had benefited 106,273 households in 854 urban/rural poor communities. It is relatively cost-effective compared to other Philippine housing programmes, with an overall average loan amount of 27,946 pesos (about US$665) per family. It also has the highest collection efficiency rate (75 per cent) compared to other government housing loan programmes such as the Unified Home Lending Programme, which has a lower collection rate of 54 per cent. Through the CMP, the National Housing Mortgage Finance Corporation has extended a total of 2.99 billion pesos (about US$71 million) to the housing projects of several hundred community-based organizations. Box 3.1 gives an example of the CMP and its impacts.

Box 3.1 illustrates how the CMP can provide the urban poor with one of their most basic needs: access to urban land with security of tenure without the need for collateral. The CMP is a programme for legalizing squatters and informal settlements, with either on-site development or the development of another site (voluntary relocation). NGOs have always had a leading role in formulating the concept and implementing the CMP, especially in terms of organizing the poor to access finance.

Although the CMP has the highest repayment rates among government housing programmes, it has suffered the most significant budget cuts compared to other funds. Between 1993 and 1995, the Unified Home Lending Programme enjoyed the largest subsidy share (74 per cent or about 18.8 billion pesos), about 20 times that of the CMP, and with most of it going to higher-income groups (Llanto et al, 1996).

BOX 3.1 THE CASE OF JANNSENVILLE NEIGHBOURHOOD ASSOCIATION IN CAINTA, RIZAL

An hour and a half's drive from Manila International Airport lies Jannsenville Neighbourhood Association, a community composed of 348 families living on a 9.1 hectare lot. This used to be part of the 36-hectare estate owned by one of the elite families living in the national capital, Quezon City, which is within Metro Manila. Migrants/transients from the rural areas had been squatting on the estate since the early 1970s, having arrived looking for better work opportunities in the metropolis. Residents draw income from factory work, tricycle-driving, construction and collecting, and selling scrap materials.

In 1988, the estate's owners obtained a demolition order from the court. Confronted with community resistance, the estate administrator sought the help of the Catholic Church through Cardinal Sin who, in turn, referred them to an NGO, the Samahang Bagong Buhay Foundation or the United New Life Foundation. The foundation recognized how much the residents wanted to own the land that they had occupied for the past 10 to 15 years and helped community leaders negotiate the purchase of a portion of the estate for the site occupants. Much was accomplished that year, with the residents re-blocking the land and excavating temporary toilets. In late 1988, the beneficiaries were able to transfer to their own house lots and build temporary shelters.

In 1989, the occupants of the land – squatters turned beneficiaries through community-organizing and cooperation with various groups – organized themselves into a neighbourhood association and registered with the Securities and Exchange Commission and the Homes Insurance Guarantee Corporation. Soon after, the association founded other organizations to serve the needs of the community, such as a multipurpose cooperative, a mini-pastoral council, a tri-bike group and a parent–teacher association for a newly opened kindergarten school.

In 1990, the foundation was issued with a development permit and a permit to sell. However, nearly half of the residents had not yet raised enough money to pay for their individual lots. To address this, the foundation linked the community with the Foundation for the Development of the Urban Poor (FDUP), an NGO that assists informal settlers to access Community Mortgage Programme (CMP) housing loans from the National Housing Mortgage Finance Corporation. With the support of the FDUP, the community residents began mobilizing their savings to pay for their loan equity. By the end of 1995, they had submitted all their housing loan documents to the National Housing Mortgage Finance Corporation for securing land tenure; by 1997, their CMP loan was released.

A total of 348 families benefited from two phases of the project. Their land titles were individualized but kept under the association's name. With secure land, they were able to build houses using permanent construction materials. Without pressure to build immediately, they were able build their houses incrementally, according to their capabilities. Since obtaining land security, some residents have created additional sources of income from rental, transport services and buying/selling goods and commodities.

Savings mobilization had several impacts on the residents. It built a strong bond between them and made it easier to mobilize other community resources. In the process of organizing themselves into a well-functioning association, they also created a viable community in which to live. The security they found in tenure and the consequent drop in crime rates allowed them to pay attention to the needs of the community. Their level of organization allowed them to come up with groups that managed transport, parking and co-operative enterprises in the community. What was initially a community of people who did not believe that they could qualify for the CMP programme is now an association of successful CMP beneficiaries. The process of group formation and cooperation gave residents the self-confidence to access other resources, such as day-care services from the local government and livelihood credit from local business groups. The majority of the leaders are women who have, over the years, built their competence in counselling members, explaining policies and collecting payments.

The present community leadership consists of board members elected annually from both CMP and non-CMP beneficiaries. Decision-making remains strongly participative. There is constant consultation and exchange of information within the community regarding issues and policies. The community association is also keen on maintaining and managing its facilities so that members will benefit equally. For instance, delinquencies in payment are covered by the association; but penalties are strictly enforced. Residents continue to attend training seminars and workshops. Meanwhile, the FDUP also supports the community through follow-up monitoring and consultation. The association views the NGO as a symbol of credibility and legitimacy, a fact that leaders maximize when collecting amortization dues and other payments.

Constraining factors to the CMP's effectiveness

The programme's effectiveness has been hindered by the lack of long-term funding sources and by the National Housing Mortgage Finance Corporation's administrative and institutional inefficiencies. Until 1998, CMP financing was under serious threat because government housing finance institutions were experiencing immense financial strain. However, the biggest constraint to CMP access by the urban poor is the sustained increase in urban land prices. For example, most land within Metro Manila is priced way beyond the CMP loan ceiling.

Both state and non-state agencies have lobbied to ensure a steady stream of funds to the government's housing programmes. However, their success has been limited and there are evident bureaucratic constraints. In addition, the CMP may be incorrectly located within the National Housing Mortgage Finance Corporation. Despite its high collection efficiency rate, the CMP has been indirectly 'punished' for the corporation's inefficient performance in other loan programmes. Moreover, the CMP does not fit into its mandate to promote/develop a secondary mortgage market in order to mobilize private-sector funds for housing. The low interest rates of the government's home-lending programmes have discouraged commercial home lending, and for the National Housing Mortgage Finance Corporation to pursue its original mandate, it cannot continue to manage the CMP with its subsidized interest rates.

The corporation has also administered the Abot-Kaya Pabahay Fund, created in 1990 to provide interest subsidies to low-income home-buyers and cash-flow guarantee, liquidity support and interest-shortfall subsidies to government and private lenders to low-cost housing. Unlike the CMP, the Abot-Kaya Fund is under-utilized because very few people buying homes qualify under its stringent requirement that only those with under 5000 pesos gross monthly incomes can receive support. Given a poverty threshold of 10,000 pesos per month, it is hard for families with less than 5000 pesos a month to make use of a housing loan since subsistence and children's education are generally higher priorities. Thus, substantial Abot-Kaya funds remain unutilized every year, prompting CMP originators to repeatedly ask the National Housing Mortgage Finance Corporation to reallocate these funds to the CMP. But the corporation has consistently refused because it has invested the funds in high interest-bearing accounts to get a cash income for the agency (Karaos, 1996).

Other housing agencies are developing their own CMP-type programmes. The Home Development Mutual Fund (or PAG-IBIG) makes available to its members the Group Land Acquisition Programme (GLAD), while the National Housing Authority has the Land Tenure Assistance Programme, which offers group loans at a slightly higher interest rate than the CMP.

Viability of the CMP and its prospects

The government's intention is for the National Housing Mortgage Finance Corporation to concentrate on its primary mandate to develop a secondary mortgage market. Consequently, some moves are being initiated to take the CMP out of the corporation. NGOs are lobbying strongly before Congress to create a separate Social Finance Corporation, devoted solely to the housing finance needs of the poor. But the CMP has failed to obtain the support of some government officials, including heads of housing agencies, because of the perception that it legitimizes the existence of squatters and low-quality neighbourhoods. Limited on-site physical improvements for land purchased under the CMP may hinder its acceptability as a legitimate housing solution. To escape this stigma, most community groups want their neighbourhoods to look like formal subdivisions, mimicking housing characteristics associated with middle- or upper-class housing enclaves. At the heart of this issue are the different perspectives as to what constitutes a valid housing solution and whether incremental housing is an acceptable approach. Records show that over 90 per cent of CMP loans are used only for lot acquisition. Subsequent improvement is through self-help, with resource mobilization from other sources. While this fund-utilization pattern supports the argument that land and security of tenure are the most singular requirements of the poor, the settlements are criticized and land availability is limited.

Given the imminent shift in government home-lending policies towards market-based interest rates and spiralling land costs, home ownership as the prime objective of government housing policy and financial assistance through long-term housing loans might usefully be re-examined.

Decentralization of social housing to local governments: achievements and challenges

The 1991 Local Government Code and the 1992 Urban Development and Housing Act transformed the relationship between local government units and national government agencies. The new decentralized structure devolved the delivery of social services, including housing, to local government units. But the transition from a highly centralized to a decentralized regime has been filled with problems and challenges for local officials, NGO/community-based organization (CBO) leaders, and real-estate developers and contractors because of the proposed additional new institutional roles and arrangements. However, a few local government units have found new opportunities for housing improvements. This section explores the potential opportunities and limitations for social housing with the devolution of housing functions from central state agencies to local government[5] through examining the experiences of selected innovative cities.

The Local Government Code and the Urban Development and Housing Act mandated that local government units are primarily responsible for functions relating to shelter planning and delivery. Local government units have to prepare land-use plans and identify the actual number of poor households and land available for their housing needs. They also have to identify the location and size of land available for socialized housing and to register potential beneficiaries. However, most local government units only started to comply with the code and act requirements after 1994 and, in general, they lack the technical capabilities to follow these requirements. By 1999, only 60 per cent (320 out of 532) had completed the beneficiary listing and only 40 per cent had identified their social housing sites. Aside from the lack of technical capacities, the absence of an effective monitoring scheme and the existence of strict central government sanctions also account for their slow compliance with the act.

Mandaluyong and Muntinlupa in Metro Manila, and San Carlos City in the Visayas region are examples of cities that have successfully begun to address housing problems. These experiences show that enabling conditions have to be present at both the local government unit and NGO/CBO levels for housing initiatives to occur. Legislative instruments (ordinances, memoranda of agreements and resources for housing, including technical and financial capability) have to be created within local government so that local officials can legally respond to the demands of their partner NGOs/CBOs who, in turn, need the organizational capability and maturity to initiate, implement and monitor CMP/housing projects. NGOs must be capable of organizing CBOs, as well as assisting them in accessing land to purchase, helping to mobilize bridging finance for land purchase and, most importantly, fulfilling the documentary requirements for the CMP loan. Moreover, they must be able to assist CBOs in negotiations with landowners and officials, and in the enforcement of CMP rules with recalcitrant community members.

For Mandaluyong City, one of the 17 cities and municipalities comprising Metro Manila, the leadership of Mayor Abalos Senior (1989–1995) built a strong network of NGOs and CBOs who were interested in making housing and other social services accessible to the poor. To a certain extent, these groups also strengthened the mayor's political legitimacy, and he was thus willing to help

---

5 Although there are other social housing funds available from the National Housing Authority, in practice only the CMP has been accessed widely by local government units. These funds are often supplemented from other sources, such as the local government units' 20 per cent development fund.

these NGOs to access financial and fiscal support to help the CBOs obtain land and housing. He used the state's power of eminent domain to force landowners to sell their land to the local government at zonal value rather than at the prevailing land market rates,[6] which were much higher and beyond the capabilities of the urban poor. Several legal cases were filed against him by landowners; but, according to the mayor, local politicians cannot afford to be intimidated by court cases if they want to do something progressive such as initiating a social housing programme. For him, court cases indicate that the local chief executive is doing something worthwhile. In 1996, at the end of his third term, a new administration was elected, led by the mayor's son. Although the housing programmes continued to receive support under the new mayor, the ability of the city to acquire land for the poor was greatly reduced because of increased land prices and a scarcity of land for social housing. Towards the end of the 1990s, as in other rapidly urbanizing areas where land prices were escalating, it became too expensive for the city to support land and housing acquisition programmes for the poor.

Another major factor that has affected the housing situation, especially in cities outside of Metro Manila, is the new pattern of population growth. Since 1994, population growth has been highest in the regional growth corridors (for example, Calabarzon in southern Luzon, SocSargen and Davao City in southern Mindanao, and the Cagayan-Iligan corridor in northern Mindanao). This growth has greatly increased the demand for housing in secondary cities and along the regional growth corridors. In Bacolod City, for instance, the increase in population between 1980 and 1990 resulted in a housing backlog of 47,737 households. In 1995, the master list of squatter families revealed 39,921 families, constituting 51 per cent of the city's households. By 1997, the city was able to provide housing to only 10 per cent of the squatter population, with most of these funds coming from the CMP and the city's discretionary funds (those not regularly allocated in the annual budget).

Local government units' compliance with the Urban Development and Housing Act requirements is far from ideal, and the sample cities in this study are exceptions to the general pattern of non-compliance. For example, Bacolod City allotted 6 million pesos in 1997 for its housing and relocation programme, just 1 per cent of the total city budget. The city planning and development office formulated the Bacolod Shelter Development Project (BASIS), to be constructed on 150 hectares south-west of the city hall. The 70 hectares allocated to social housing is expected to accommodate 14,000 50-square-metre home lots for slum and squatter families. To support the housing programme, the local government unit also reorganized the Bacolod Housing Agency and merged it with the newly created Urban Poor Affairs Office, making it the lead agency for CMP implementation and the first to take out CMP loans in this region.

In general, local government units do not have the ability to mobilize and generate resources to finance social housing. The cities here have innovated in

---

6 Urban lands are classified according to use/zones (eg industrial, commercial, etc) and their values by zones are based on the tax assessment made by the city assessor's office. The zonal value of the land is always lower compared to the market value (determined by the last transaction or sale in that zone or area).

raising and mobilizing housing finance through bond flotation and joint ventures with national agencies, NGOs and the private sector. Bond flotation for housing has been initiated in the cities of Victorias and Bacolod in Negros Occidental, Puerto Princesa in Palawan, and Naga in the Bicol region. Joint ventures with national agencies, NGOs (particularly those affiliated with CMP Congress, a grouping of NGOs within the programme) and the private sector have been undertaken by the cities of San Carlos, Dumaguete, Davao, Mandaluyong and Marikina, to name a few. Crucial in these ventures is the loan guarantee issued by the Homes Insurance Guarantee Corporation that assured stakeholders of the viability of the joint venture.

Tables 3.1–3.3 show the activities undertaken by Muntinglupa City in order to access CMP funds. This was possible because of the progressive leadership of the mayor, who has created partnerships with NGOs/CBOs and the private sector. In 2000, Muntinlupa City had a population of 378,310.

Table 3.1 *Local government assistance to CMP projects: the case of Muntinlupa City*

Name of organization	Total land area (square metres); approximate share per beneficiary (square metres)	Local government unit assistance*
1 Samahan ng Nagkakaisa ng Medina's Compound	8836; 70	2 million pesos for land acquisition
2 Putatan Hillside Neighbourhood Association	11,442; not available	17.133 million pesos for land acquisition
3 Samahang Magkakapitbahay sa Purok 6, Tunasan	2203; 75	30,000 pesos for land acquisition
4 Samahang Nagkakaisang Magkakapitbahay ng Ilaya (SNMB)	14,972; 40	9,634 million pesos for site development
5 Samahang Magkakapitbahay ng Cabezas Compound (SMCC)	660; 35	736,000 pesos for land acquisition
6 Planas Homeowners Association, Inc (PHNAI)	12,420; 40	146,000 pesos for payment of real property tax
7 Villa Arandia Homeowners Association, Inc (VAHAI)	2271; 24	3.7 million pesos for land acquisition
8 Carmina Homeowners Association, Inc (CHAI)	12,515; 50	Technical support
9 Putatan Urban Poor Association	14,930; 50	Project origination
10 Katipunang Anak Pawis Homeowners Association	not available	163,500 pesos for land acquisition
11 Samahan ng Bayanan Ph 1	not available	548,000 pesos for site development

Note: *At this time, US$1 = 42 Philippine pesos
Source: Urban Poor Affairs Office, Muntinlupa City

Table 3.2 *Housing indicators and key events in Muntinlupa City before 1995 and during 1995–1998*

	Pre-1995	1995–1998
Indicators	• 95 CMP beneficiaries per year • 2.9 million pesos in Community Mortgage Programme (CMP) loans taken out per year* • 0.5 million pesos in local government unit loan assistance to communities • no baseline data for housing backlog	• 132 CMP beneficiaries per year • 7.5 million pesos in CMP loans taken out per year • 34.11 million pesos in local government unit socialized housing loans • ten CMP projects in process

Activities and events that contributed to socialized housing

	Pre-1995	1995–1998
Operations	• CMP operations • local government unit as CMP originator • tripartite partnership of local government unit–Municipal Development Fund (MDF)–community-based organization (CBO) formalized (1991) • 9 originators for 12 projects	• CMP operations • implementation of Urban Development and Housing Act requirements (survey, registration, etc) • local government unit pulls out as originator; MDF handles five out of ten projects in process • three originators for ten projects
Finance		• approval of interim financing facility (1995–1997) • Muntinlupa becomes a city; gets additional Internal Revenue Allocation (IRA) from national government
Policy-making, planning and organization	• 1987 Philippine constitution provides for urban land reform and housing • A Vision for Muntinlupa (1987) • MDF-local government unit visioning workshop (1990) • Passage of Urban Development and Housing Act and Local Government Code (1991–1992) • medium-term plan; land code drafted (1992)	• strategic planning workshops; organization of task force on human settlements (1995) • drafting of human settlements plan • Urban Poor Affairs Office organization (1996) • Carmina Homeowners Association, Inc (CHAI) inter-agency task force created (1996) • community-level planning and organization

Note: *At this time, US$1 = 42 Philippine pesos

Pre-1995, the political administration of Mayor Bunye with the local government unit was very active in housing. From 1995 onwards, there was a change of leadership and change of procedures in the local housing with the NGOs/CBOs in the lead role.

Table 3.3 *Muntinlupa City's response to housing problems*

Long-term and short-term problems*	Muntinlupa response
• Limited access to land due to rising land prices and the state's retreat from land-banking and acquisition	• Negotiated outside the market; entered into land-banking; limited by refusal of other constituents and land speculation
• Lack of long-term sources of funds to sustain government's housing programme due to the failure to tap private finance	• Put up interim financing facility; limited by delays in release of funds attributed to insufficient documentation and slow, bureaucratic procedures
• Current policy frameworks that centre on resettlement	• On-site development preferred; resettlement well managed
• Ineffective targeting as evidence of bias by lending programmes towards higher-income groups	• On-site Community Mortgage Programme (CMP) projects ongoing, but prefers medium-rise building construction, which is more expensive
• Inadequate local government capacities for financing and managing social housing programmes	• Available funds; invested city revenues in interim financing; NGO-subsidized social capital formation; use of 20 per cent IRA for development not well monitored

Note: *As identified by the Urban Research Consortium Metro Manila Housing Survey, 1997

Creating an enabling environment for social housing

To some extent, the Urban Development and Housing Act and the Local Government Code have empowered local government units to formulate policies and allocate resources to social housing, and most have set up the appropriate structures and mechanisms to respond to the housing needs of their poor. As with national government housing agencies, the city planning development office that usually takes care of housing is also responsible for many other activities. To overcome this problem, some cities such as Puerto Princesa, Bacolod and Marikina have established a housing department, while the cities of Cebu, Muntinlupa and Naga have created their own urban poor affairs office with a portfolio that includes social housing issues. In addition, these cities have also created linkages with overseas development assistance agencies to provide them with additional support for their housing programmes. The cities of Bacolod, San Carlos, Butuan, Iloilo, to name a few, have formulated their shelter and housing plans with the support of the Local Government Shelter Programme of the Canadian International Development Agency (CIDA).

Table 3.4 shows the enabling conditions that cities have created for their social housing.

In addition to creating partnerships with civil society groups, especially NGOs and CBOs, the enabling environment for social housing includes creating necessary structures (for example, housing offices, urban poor offices and housing committees), passing legislation/ordinances, financial instruments (for instance, tax revenues, incentives and bond flotation) and other initiatives, such as build-operate-transfer schemes.

Table 3.4 *Enabling instruments created by some cities*

City	Creative instruments towards housing initiatives	
	Legislative and financial instruments	*Forging partnerships and building capabilities of non-governmental organizations (NGOs)/community-based organizations (CBOs)*
Bacolod	• Government devoted budget to housing and relocation programme • The Bacolod Housing Agency was created in 1972 • The Urban Poor Affairs Office was created in 1992, which led to the implementation of the Community Mortgage Programme (CMP) • Tax incentives for social housing	• Strong network of NGOs and CBOs or housing associations • Joint ventures with national agencies, NGOs and the private sector
Mandaluyong	• Used the state's power of eminent domain, forcing landowners to sell their land to the government at zonal value rather than at prevailing market rates • Tax incentives for social housing	• Strong network of NGOs and CBOs or housing associations • Joint ventures with national agencies, NGOs and the private sector
San Carlos	• Created structures (eg committees) and mechanisms at the city level to support housing • Tax incentives for social housing	• Joint ventures with national agencies, NGOs and the private sector
Muntinlupa	• Established an Office for Urban Poor Affairs • Tax incentives for social housing	• Joint ventures with national agencies, NGOs and the private sector
Puerto Princesa	• Local government unit financed housing through bond flotation • Established a department of housing • Tax incentives for social housing	• Joint ventures with national agencies, NGOs and the private sector
Naga	• Established an Office for Urban Poor Affairs • Tax incentives for social housing	• Joint ventures with national agencies, NGOs and the private sector

Despite these initiatives, several areas still need further work. NGO/CBO advocacy is required for local officials to create broader revenue sources for social housing. Experiences in cities show that the additional local government unit revenue sources can be tapped for social housing – for example, taxes from idle land and social housing; funds recovered from local government unit housing projects; proceeds from projects with interim financing from bond flotation; and proceeds from the sale of alienable land and titled properties owned by the city, and from the developed properties through the build-operate-transfer schemes.

Meanwhile, the local government unit can assist CBOs to access funds from national housing programmes such as the CMP, Abot Kaya Fund, Local Housing Programme, Resettlement Programmes for Local Government Units, and the Medium-Rise and Public Housing Programme.

NGOs and the decentralization of social housing

Land-use planning and social housing inventories are new functions for local government. The deadline for the first round of submission of plans and documents to national housing agencies was June 2000, yet only a few local government units have done this properly. The delays reflect the contentious nature of the planning process, as well as the administrative work involved. In Cebu City, for example, the basis for zonal values became a very contentious issue between the realtors/business sector and the NGOs and other civil society groups. Businesses and real-estate developers, who often stand to gain from land speculation, favoured high zonal values, whereas civil society groups wanted to keep them low, otherwise there would be no affordable land available for social housing. But one reason why some local government units have not identified land for social housing is because the zonal values of land located nearby would be reduced, thus affecting their tax revenue base.

NGO-related professionals have had, and continue to have, important roles in fulfilling decentralized housing functions. Since the implementation of the Urban Development and Housing Act, there have been increased personal and professional links between NGOs and local government units. Some of the NGOs' community organizers are undertaking consultancy services with local government units in urban planning, land registration and other areas. NGO consultancy services may give them a chance to influence local government units and the local political system, as well as to implement joint projects. This supplements their meagre incomes and fits with their role as mediators between government authorities and people's organizations. This is particularly crucial when it comes to deciding on areas for social housing. Some NGOs have developed strong relations with local governments, which, in turn, benefits their role as advocates for the poor. The Pagtambayayong Foundation in Cebu City, the Julio Ledesma Foundation in San Carlos City, and the Mindano Land Foundation are examples of NGOs that have maintained strong collaborative relations with their respective city governments.

The devolution of housing and land-use functions to local governments presents new opportunities for NGOs, local government units and people's organizations engaged in delivering social housing. Aside from the new policy framework that devolved housing functions to local government units, several other factors have been found to support NGOs/people's organizations at the local level, including:

- political connections/influence of NGO/people's organization leaders with local government units;
- openness of some local chief executives;
- availability of low-cost land;

- manageable size of the urban poor population;
- willingness of local government units to compel developers to fulfill the 20 per cent social housing requirement;
- feasibility of incremental housing models due to lower population densities and availability of cheaper materials; and
- current policy thrust of the Housing and Urban Development Coordinating Council and the National Housing Authority to enhance local government unit capability in housing and urban development.

Currently, only a few NGOs (such as the Pagtambayayong Foundation, the Julio Ledesma Foundation and the Mindano Land Foundation mentioned above) and a few local government units (for example, General Santos, Cebu, Bacolod, Marikina, Muntinglupa, Mandaluyong, Cagayan de Oro and Puerto Princesa) have taken advantage of the opportunities presented by the devolution of urban development and social housing functions. This is due primarily to the slow processing of CMP loans (average time of 1.5 years) and its complicated documentary requirements. Moreover, local government units find central agencies unresponsive to their needs. If they could mobilize alternative sources of funds, they would rather use these than deal with the central government's housing agencies. Local chief executives who are elected only for a three-year term cannot wait for programmes with long maturation requirements such as the CMP.

Many local politicians and businessmen only favour housing and relocation programmes for the poor if they are related to other enterprise plans or real-estate development projects. Many mayors do not want to be seen by the private sector as 'cuddlers' of the urban poor and of 'the criminal elements' popularly associated with slum/squatter communities. In many cases, politicians have treated urban poor communities as election vote banks and support bases for their political agenda. They make promises to, and investments in, local community groups in order to strengthen their political alliances, which are crucial to advancing their political ambitions. This is particularly significant in local government units where local officials are closely connected with landowning interests and also steeped in patron–client politics, and this often complicates the procedures during negotiations for land acquisition and purchase, especially where local politicians and landowners belong to the same kin group or where NGO/CBO leaders are closely allied to certain political parties or personalities.

There are other initiatives at the local level that can support the CMP and other social housing programmes for the poor. These include the Local Government Shelter Plan of CIDA and other housing-related projects, such as the Local Housing Programme or the local government unit *Pabahay* programme. NGO leaders (also members of the CMP Congress) from the three foundations noted above have served as resource persons for these projects. Moreover, the current move towards CMP decentralization and the establishment of local housing boards will provide an institutional framework for a more systematic collaboration with local government units.

It has been suggested that local government units undertake land-banking to ensure viable sites for the CMP. Local government units can be encouraged to do this by making available finance for the acquisition of CMP project sites. Idle government lands can also be used to secure municipal bonds, the proceeds of which can be used for land banking. However, suggestions for land banking have not progressed much because local governments have limited resources to spare for future needs.

Local government units can also help to solve the problems that often arise on CMP sites relating to site development and infrastructure provision. Because of the communities' lack of resources, site improvement remains a challenge once a loan has been taken out. However, local government unit-originated projects seem to have less difficulty in accessing support for site improvements and services after land acquisition. Local officials appear to feel more responsible for local government unit-originated projects because the CBO leaders in these housing projects have links with the local political machinery. In some cases, NGO-originated projects and their leaders feel that they have to struggle hard in order to get equal assistance from local governments (as is the case in Butuan City). Effective collaboration between NGOs, CBOs and local government units needs to be examined systematically because this could have a contradictory effect on the goals of urban poor mobilization and access to basic services. This is especially crucial in areas where clientelist politics are significant.

While the new administrative landscape that empowers local government units has created new partnerships and institutional relationships, it has yet to be addressed systematically by NGOs in their efforts to mobilize resources and promote more effective/strategic interventions. The potential for local tripartite partnerships that involve the community organization, the housing-related NGO and the local government is promising. While local government systems are prone to all kinds of irregularities in relation to land, they tend to be more concerned about, and sensitive to, providing settlements for the poor than the central government. Local politicians are much closer to their constituency and hence face criticism if election promises do not materialize.

Decentralizing CMP operations: experiences from pilot-testing

In June 1999, the CMP Congress submitted a proposal to decentralize CMP operations, and the Housing and Urban Development Coordinating Council undertook a pilot implementation in the regions of Visayas and Mindanao. Preliminary processing of CMP papers was to be conducted at regional level. However, in March 2000, the experiment was abandoned.

The experiences, from August 1999 to March 2000, showed that government agencies have been reluctant to facilitate the completion of CMP requirements. For example, the Bureau of Internal Revenue delayed implementing the local ordinance exempting urban-poor housing associations from paying certain taxes because it decreased their revenue earnings. Furthermore, local bureaucracy has slowed down NGOs' attempts to fast-track the approval of CMP projects. Because of the number of signatures needed from different government offices to approve documents for CMP loans, the urban poor groups find the programme difficult. Approval of a housing development plan or securing a building permit from local government can cost several thousands, if not millions, of pesos in illegal payments to speed up approvals and obtain the necessary signatures. Politicians and government officials often see real-estate development and housing projects as opportunities for raising their own treasury and/or campaign funds.

Aside from corruption, attempts to secure CMP processing are greatly hampered by the property system in the Philippines. In fact, the single most important factor slowing down the implementation of the CMP is the land administration system (titling and other necessary documentation).

The decentralization of housing and land-use functions, in general, and of the CMP, in particular, was promoted based on the assumption that bringing bureaucracy closer to the people would simplify and hasten procedures. The experiences, however, do not seem to bear out these expectations as many of the most basic requirements are not in place. In addition, local government units, in partnership with civil society groups and the private sector, must create an enabling environment for social housing. This includes the creation of enabling legislation and city ordinances, and an increase in the political and technical expertise of both local government units and civil society in implementing social housing programmes, especially with regard to financing.

Local governments and social housing: conclusions and recommendations

Decentralization has increased opportunities for the poor to access housing in local government units that have attempted to implement the provisions of the Urban Development and Housing Act. These local government units, however, are the exception rather than the rule, and this is because their mayors (in collaboration with their local development council and local NGOs) have had the political and financial commitment to formulate and implement social housing programmes.

The housing initiatives of these innovative local government units have highlighted the limitations of the Urban Development and Housing Act and many local government administrations. Moreover, they have shown the relative lack of power of communities compared to local economic/political elites and local government bureaucracy. To be successful, social housing initiatives have to be formulated within the dynamics of local politics, as well as in relation to the politics of central state agencies. The support of local chief executives for the housing aspirations of their low-income constituency changes over time depending upon their political influence and available resources. The strong political support of the mayor does not guarantee the allocation of resources for social housing.

NGOs/CBOs might usefully understand the strategic location and the potential of their housing agenda within the broader context of political mobilization amidst other interest groups who are competing for scarce municipal resources. Members of both local government units and civil society groups do not always have the orientation, knowledge and technical expertise necessary to implement the Urban Development and Housing Act provisions, especially in relation to social housing. Thus, there is a need to build the technical capability of local government units, NGOs and community organizations dealing with housing and housing finance issues. These capabilities include activities relating to community organizing, site development and construction. However, the study also shows that there is a critical need to lower technical costs in relation to land survey and site development.

There is also a need to strengthen the collaboration of local government units, NGOs and community organizations in implementing CMP/social housing projects. This can be done through the creation of local housing boards as provided for in the Urban Development and Housing Act. These boards may have a critical role in promoting the appropriate local housing policies, formulating a shelter and land-use plan, monitoring land-use validation, and raising funds for housing programmes.

The CMP beneficiaries and their communities: socio-political and economic impacts[7]

What social, political and economic impacts have CMP projects had on the beneficiaries and their community associations? Has the CMP programme really reached the poor and has it empowered them? What factors account for the socio-political and economic impacts? This section reports on the socio-economic profile of CMP beneficiaries and the political impacts of community organizing for housing amongst the urban poor in CMP-organized communities. This is based primarily on the results of a nationwide sample survey of 600 beneficiary CMP households located in Luzon, Visayas and Mindanao.

Estimates for 1991 suggested that 35 per cent of urban dwellers had incomes below the poverty line. By 1997, this had fallen to 32 per cent; but the Asian crisis and the lingering political instability may have pushed this figure back up since then. The number of urban poor households is likely to be growing faster than the number of urban households. As well as low-income families, not-so-poor families also live in squatter settlements or in settlements lacking basic services. Karaos (1996) suggests that, in 1991, more than half of the squatter population were 'not poor', based on a simple income criterion. Based on this observation and on CMP survey data, this study suggests that it might be useful to distinguish the 'housing poor' from the 'income poor'. The latter are associated with the poverty threshold, defined as the minimum income needed to buy food and other necessities to support a family of six; the former would

---

7 This section is largely based on the following reports: Ma Lourdes Rebullida (2000) *The Socio-economic and Political Impacts of the Community Mortgage Programme in Luzon*, IIED and Urban Research Consortium (URC); N Mirasol (2000) *The Socio-economic and Political Impacts of the Community Mortgage Programme in the Visayas*, IIED and URC. The CMP study in Mindanao conducted by Napoleon Amoyen of URC-Mindanao was only partially completed because of the peace and order situation. These studies were conducted with the support of IIED and the URC, which comprises NGOs engaged in organizing and/or policy research and advocacy and academics from research institutions based in Ateneo de Manila University, De La Salle University and the University of the Philippines.

include those who do not have housing because of the large gap between their incomes and the cost of housing in the market. This distinction is important in ascertaining the target population of social housing programmes. In 1997, the urban poverty threshold was 6231 pesos per month (about US$160 per month at US1$ = 39 pesos). Using this criterion, most of the CMP beneficiaries seem to fall below the poverty line, although – as described below – most are not among the poorest.

The CMP beneficiaries: a socio-economic profile

NGO-organizing among the poor has been critical to the large number of CMP loans accessed by the 106,273 households in order to obtain housing and security of tenure. The CMP beneficiary household survey shows that CMP/social housing programmes are reaching the upper segment of the urban poor and the lower segment of the middle class as reflected by incomes and occupational profiles. In 1998, 61 per cent of households who took out loans between 1989 and 1994 had monthly incomes of 5000 pesos and above, while only 23 per cent had incomes below 5000 pesos.[8] However, the average incomes of household heads and households at the time of the survey were 5582 pesos and 7932 pesos, respectively. If we consider only household-head monthly incomes, the reach of the CMP to the poor improves, with 41 per cent having incomes below 5000 pesos. If we take the poor to be those with incomes of 10,000 pesos and under, then 77 per cent of the CMP beneficiaries are poor.

Using the 1997 urban poverty threshold (6231 pesos per month), the average current CMP beneficiaries' earnings are below the poverty line. If we use the 1997 income deciles criteria, beneficiaries would belong to the fifth and sixth income deciles (5516 to 6927 pesos). However, at the time of CMP application, the majority of applicants had monthly incomes of between 2000 and 3500 pesos. The CMP survey revealed that there has been a discernible improvement in the incomes of 37 per cent of the CMP beneficiaries after loan take-out due to increased pressure to save for the amortization payment, and the creation of new opportunities to earn (for example, rental and other small business ventures). The physical structures in 'mature' (defined as three years after take-out of loan) CMP communities also show economic and environmental improvements as a result of investments in site development and infrastructure, such as drainage, cement pathways, water systems, chapels and a basketball court. After obtaining the CMP loan for their home lots, the beneficiaries feel secure enough to invest in home/site improvements, as well as in income-generating activities based in the community.

If we take the income level of beneficiaries at the time of CMP application, the programme has reached those from the bottom three income deciles (3178 pesos and under; NCSO, 1994), with the majority coming from the second and

---

8 Income data, however, is not sufficient to determine the housing needs of the urban poor and who should be receiving a subsidy. The more accurate indicator, as argued by some housing officials such as Toby Monsod, past National Home Mortgage Finance Corporation (NHFMC) secretary-general, is the difference between the income/wages of the family/household and the cost of housing in the market.

third income deciles (2600–3178 pesos). Only a small percentage (7 per cent) of the beneficiaries came from the bottom segment or the first income decile (2600 pesos and under). It should be noted that, usually, the beneficiaries from this bottom segment have not improved their physical/environmental structures because of inadequate income/livelihood sources, primarily as a result of their lack of education/skills and opportunities. But despite the lack of physical improvement, CMP beneficiaries from this category asserted that they have more psychological security because the threat of eviction has been removed.

The study highlights how the socio-economic characteristics of CMP communities change. The socio-economic characteristics at the time of application for a loan can be quite different years later because of the substitution for better payers (ranged from 0 to 30 per cent in the survey), in addition to economic improvements among beneficiaries (about 37 per cent). Substitution of beneficiaries occurs when members cannot/refuse to fulfill their duties to the association and decide to forfeit their access rights. The substitution of beneficiaries, through the selling of rights (ranging from a low 5 per cent to a high 35 per cent), has occurred because of the inability to pay the amortization as a result of loss of income due to sickness, death or unemployment. In some cases, the beneficiary has moved to another place because of marital separation, death or job transfer.

Clearly, the poorest of the poor (those with no income or no regular source of income) cannot avail themselves of social housing without substantial subsidies or grants. This is a serious issue because, between 1994 and 1997, the incomes of the bottom income decile decreased by 10 per cent while those of the top decile increased by almost 50 per cent (NCSO, 1994). The fact that CMP beneficiaries do not come from the poorest of the poor is further supported by occupational profiles and income sources. Almost half (45 per cent) derive their income from low-wage work (for example, employee, nurse/teacher, factory worker and services) or from the informal sector (for instance, vending/selling, transport service workers). Most families have several income earners who pool their earnings in order to pay the amortization, as well as to meet their basic survival needs. For the bottom segments of the urban poor, security of housing and tenure is secondary to their immediate needs for food, health, education and employment. Given this situation, NGO housing strategies must be reoriented to focus on the needs of the poor to secure a roof over their heads and, more importantly, to increase their capacity to secure other basic needs. This strongly points to the importance of differentiating between different groups of the urban poor and to formulate a corresponding range of interventions according to their critical needs. For example, families belonging to the first two income deciles are more likely to require livelihood and capability-building interventions rather than social housing assistance.

But overall, both the CMP survey data and field observations indicate that the CMP is the most responsive programme to the housing needs of the urban poor. Llanto et al (1996) also concludes that, of all social housing programmes, the CMP is relatively well targeted and is more efficient than other programmes, such as the Unified Home Lending programme, at reaching its intended beneficiaries.

Poverty alleviation and other CMP impacts

Thirty-seven per cent of beneficiaries have increased incomes, which they attribute to their access to affordable housing through the CMP. Access to housing gives them opportunities for new sources of additional income, such as rental, retailing and other income-generating activities. CMP beneficiaries attest to the fact that becoming homeowners and lot owners has greatly increased their social capital in the eyes of business and retail owners in the area. They feel that businesses now trust them because they are no longer squatters or renters who will move at any time. As homeowners or lot owners, they are more bankable and appear trustworthy and reliable before potential business partners. Beneficiaries said that being a homeowner 'roots' them, and therefore they have higher status in social, economic and political transactions with local businessmen/local retailers.

NGO advocates for housing argue that security of tenure (ownership of land and house) releases the creative energies of the poor for productive activities, resulting in the improvement of their status and that of their communities. The survey data confirmed this assertion. Comparing the incomes of beneficiaries at the time of their application (four years earlier) with their incomes at the time of survey shows that their incomes have increased by at least 10 per cent. Further analysis shows that those in the top income segment increased their incomes by almost 30 per cent. It is also noticeable that in housing associations with high (80 per cent or above) collection efficiency rates, average household incomes were 30 per cent higher than those with lower collection efficiency rates (50 per cent or less). It is clear that those from the top segments of the poor are better able to take advantage of new economic opportunities in the community.

The results of this survey of CMP beneficiaries definitely indicate the positive socio-economic, psychological and political impacts of acquiring housing and security of tenure, and the survey and focus group discussions show that several factors are important in the transformation. The community organizing conducted by NGOs among CMP beneficiaries is crucial in securing tenure among the poor.

The different orientation and training sessions regarding community organizing, CMP housing finance and securing the papers necessary for loan applications, amongst others, can be instrumental in transforming the urban poor beneficiaries' orientation about themselves and their relationship to other poor communities, the government and the rest of society. The majority of the respondents said that their experiences in CMP organizing have transformed their perceptions of themselves and their capabilities. During the focus group discussions among beneficiaries, a constant theme was how the CMP had fulfilled their dreams and changed their lives. Their training and experience in community organizing to access CMP loans also built their confidence to negotiate with landowners, local officials and housing officials. Moreover, this led them to find sources and/or pressure for the delivery of other basic services such as water, electricity and health services. More importantly, their links with the NGO loan originator, housing agency and local officials allow them to access cheaper housing-related services (for example, land survey, land-use and subdivision plans, as well as site development). The CMP beneficiaries argued that without their community organization training and advocacy as a housing association, they would have had a hard time in obtaining these services. However, as Box 3.2 illustrates, there are both internal and external challenges that community organizations have difficulty coping with.

Most of the CMP survey respondents expressed their sense of pride in becoming a lot or homeowner as opposed to being a squatter. They feel that securing legitimate papers showing that the land on which their home is standing is theirs offers a tremendous benefit to them and their children. The removal of the threat of eviction gives them peace of mind and confidence. More importantly, mobilizing their resources/savings for the monthly amortization for the land, as well as for home construction/improvement, gives them the skills to plan their savings and expenditures. According to the beneficiaries, having a home/lot in which to sink or bank your resources and energies gives a different meaning and perspective to their lives other than their day-to-day financial struggle.

For the NGOs and CMP beneficiaries alike, community-organization training and lobbying for their housing needs increases their social and political confidence within their locality. This is especially evident in their struggle to obtain basic services (such as water, streetlights and health centres) and further site development needs from their local governments. Advocacy activities often result in some leaders being elected to leadership positions in their locality.

CMP beneficiaries from the lower economic segments (those with monthly incomes of 2500 pesos or less) still believe that their lives have improved because of their participation in the CMP housing association. Through association activities, they feel more connected to the larger community and do not feel as isolated as before. Thus, according to the beneficiaries, aside from the economic impacts of the CMP on families and households, the more important result of the housing association's activities is the strengthening of community support networks. And, as a result of the housing-related activities of the association, other community concerns (security, drainage, healthcare/day-care services) are also addressed. Traditional activities (for example, fiestas and religious celebrations) in the community have been transformed to become opportunities to mobilize resources for the association's housing-related projects.

CMP as a social housing finance innovation: impacts on poverty and gender relations

In most urban and rural poor communities, women's participation in securing tenure and housing is quite high. Most (70 to 90 per cent) CBO officers and board members are women, and they are highly trusted in resource/savings mobilization, the collection of amortization payments, and other financial aspects of the association. NGO/CBO officers and members who were interviewed in this study asserted that women are more reliable managers, especially in the collection of amortization payments and in 'smoothing out' organizational dynamics. They say that men have little patience for dealing with

---

BOX 3.2 INTERNAL AND EXTERNAL CHALLENGES TO CBOS: THE CASE OF THE HKKI COMMUNITY ORGANIZATION IN SAMBAG, CEBU CITY

Only 2 kilometres from central Cebu City, located on what was previously 5500 square metres of wet and marshy land, lives a community of 110 families. When they were still illegal settlers on the land, the landowner tried to evict them and sell the land to a religious group. In 1987, the settlers organized themselves into a community organization in order to fight the impending demolition. Initially, they were able to link with the Division for the Welfare of the Urban Poor (DWUP) of Cebu City government's Urban Poor Office, which helped them negotiate with the landowner. The sale was settled, with the residents paying 10 per cent of the total cost and the remaining 90 per cent to be paid through Community Mortgage Programme (CMP) loans. The DWUP transferred the CMP origination to the Pagtambayayong Foundation, Inc. This created confusion among the organization and seemed to have affected its operation. By 1989, the community association had embarked on the take-out stage of the CMP.

Several issues influenced the overall situation of this community with regard to housing. Firstly, the change in originator caused a lack of consistency in loan records that adversely affected the management of collection activities. Secondly, the site's location close to the city centre, allied to the general land scarcity, attracted commercial investors and potential residents. Thirdly, there was high unemployment among residents, which was compounded by crisis events such as death, sickness and family separation.

As a consequence, many members were less able to pay the amortization on CMP housing loans and faced increased pressure to sell their rights. By 1998, several beneficiaries had already sold their rights, and they received much more than the original sale price – 1000 to 5000 pesos per square metre compared to 250 pesos per square metre. Beneficiaries capitalized on the CMP and made an immediate profit, as the 1998 land zonal value was 15,000 pesos per square metre. Altogether, there was a high rate of non-repayments and only a small number of residents fully paid for their lot. Eventually, the disparities in the status of beneficiaries caused internal tensions among the residents, as well as with their NGO originator.

The composition and history of the community have created a weak organization with no effective leadership. Much decision-making is left to the president, who has been in office since 1988 and who controls the association's funds. The organizational policies and procedures are not clear to members and have not been effectively implemented. This absence of good leadership and member participation has resulted in self-interest among the residents. Lack of information and communication has promoted rumours, eroding the sense of community and spreading misinformation about the programme. Hence, it has been difficult to access other resources that might benefit the members. Common activities are limited to cleaning the drains and building structures.

Despite gaining access to the CMP, the community is faced by challenges that reflect spatial change and various pressures imposed upon the community (particularly population growth and escalating land prices). These, in turn, are compounded by the internal weakness of the organization and its inability to cooperate with other groups.

---

the cumbersome requirements and precise records of the programme. Thus, gender-related characteristics and the perception that women have more free time have led to women assuming greater responsibilities in CMP projects.

Housing-related activities have highlighted women's participation in 'public' issues and have enabled them to assume key roles in negotiations with landlords, barangay (district council) leaders, politicians and civil servants. Organizing the community and securing the documentary requirements for the CMP have given women members of housing associations the exposure and, eventually, the confidence to assume public roles. The CMP community survey showed that 25 per cent of women leaders/members of CMP housing associations or CBOs have achieved some public status as a member of the *barangay* or community legislative council, or as volunteer/paid health, social or education workers. These increasingly public roles have led women to access livelihood loans or income-generating opportunities. Their confidence and security as legitimate homeowners and lot owners (with ownership and/or tax papers to support it) – reinforced by their community-organizing training/knowledge and engagement with housing institutions and local government unit bureaucracy – have enabled women to take greater advantage of business or entrepreneurial opportunities (such as opening *sari-sari* or merchandise stores, food stalls and other small-scale or home-based enterprises).

Aside from security of tenure and socio-economic opportunities, women have been instrumental in accessing other basic services such as day-care, livelihood, health and sanitation services. According to the women interviewed in this study, their socially defined roles as mothers compel them to deal with these issues. Women assert that it is they who feel and are affected strongly by the basic needs of their children and families.

Box 3.3 reviews the impacts on gender issues in one particular association and illustrates how CMP housing projects have enlarged/transformed women's traditional roles. In addition, they have also added to their traditional roles as spouses/mothers. In some CMP communities, women's groups who are active in savings mobilization have set aside about 10 per cent of their savings to support community projects such as day-care centres and water and sanitation services. According to the women, since these community projects directly affect their domestic obligations, they were more likely to contribute money and other volunteer services for its operation. However, classic 'added burdens' are also evident. While the women have taken on more political and economic responsibilities, there is no commensurate development of new work and economic arrangements that will create a more real partnership between men and women in securing housing and social security for themselves and their families. Women adjust their working hours and activities to accommodate their new 'public/collective' responsibilities, while men have not increased their share of domestic work.

Several issues that bear on the relationships of men, women and their children are often peripheral to NGO and community struggles for land and security of tenure. For example, women's public involvement may result in harassment and violence from their husbands; but these issues have not been discussed in their organizations. Similarly, the impact of eviction and relocation on women and children has not been systematically addressed in off-site CMP communities. Another issue concerns property rights in cases of consensual unions. While the family code recognizes that husband and wife have equal access to land/home ownership, problems have been observed in common-law arrangements or consensual unions. There have been cases where the male

Box 3.3 CMP IMPACTS ON GENDER ISSUES AND BEYOND: THE CASE OF A FEMALE-HEADED ASSOCIATION IN MARIKINA CITY

Aling Lila heads a neighbourhood association in Apitong, Marikina City, one of the cities within Metro Manila. Her track record as president of the association for four years (1996–2000) reflects her leadership and competence in organizing her community and in mobilizing its resources. As a result of her and the other officers' efforts, her community now enjoys security of tenure and livelihood.

During the early 1980s, Aling Lila and her family left their home in Southern Mindanao to escape from poverty and insurgency in the area. They migrated to Metro Manila in search of work and a better life for their three children. Her husband became a tenant in a coconut area. When they first arrived, there was only a handful of families settled there who were also rural migrants. By late 1989, over 100 families were squatters on the estate, which belonged to a big landowner who owned several commercial educational institutions in Metro Manila. The settlers perceived this to mean that the land was not of great importance to the landowner. This gave them hope that they could stay and eventually acquire the land. They established a neighbourhood association, with Aling Lila as one of the board members, and registered it with the Homes Insurance Guarantee Corporation and the Securities and Exchange Commission. The Mondragon Foundation, Inc assisted the organization in organizing its members and familiarizing them with the CMP.

Later, a businessman who owned a nearby factory competed with them in trying to buy the land. Fortunately, the landowner was also a widow and took pity on the plight of Aling Lila and her neighbours. In 1996, she agreed to sell the land to the community, and even loaned them some money to pay for the documentation stamps required for paperwork. The Mondragon Foundation also conducted community seminars and training.

The community association faced other challenges in the course of acquiring land tenure. The engineer whom they had hired ran away with the money that the community had raised to pay for his services. This disheartened the members who then refused to relocate their houses for the re-blocking of the land, a task that was left incomplete with the flight of the engineer. But re-blocking was a requirement for having a CMP loan. Aling Lila convinced the residents to voluntarily relocate to make way for re-blocking – including threats to disassemble the residents' makeshift houses if they did not do so.

At present, community members enjoy the home/home lots that they now own and continue to pay for them. Aling Lila herself monitors the payments made by the members to ensure efficient collection and the fewest non-repayments. She has also facilitated the creation and maintenance of a complete set of records and receipts so that systems are transparent to the members. Thus, the members do not suspect her leadership of fraud. The organization has also started mobilizing savings to prepare for individual titling of home lots. At the same time, the Mondragon Foundation continues to provide support to the community through negotiating the provision of infrastructure (roads, drainage and a multipurpose hall) and through monitoring. In general, the women members have been very active in facilitating these projects. They have started a paluwagan (savings group) for sewing machines and materials that they can use for livelihoods because the foundation had not approved their proposed income-generating project. Each female now earns an average of 200 to 300 pesos (around US$4 to $6) weekly with the rags that they sew out of cloth scraps.

Through the influence of Aling Lila and other women officers, the organization registered the names of each husband and wife as joint owners of the home/home lot. Moreover, the women pushed successfully for the establishment of day-care services and the installation of community water pipes. Despite this, however, Aling Lila accepts that the women in the organization have to work triple time in order to meet their domestic and community duties while trying to earn a living as seamstresses, vendors, etc. But the women members are very proud of their abilities to balance their roles at home, in the community and in their workplaces.

partner was listed as the *bonafide* CMP member, but who later left his partner for another woman. The female partner lost out in benefits during the subsequent adjustment of amortization payments, substitution and selling of rights.

During the research team's field visits, women identified the need for a greater focus on:

- safety and convenience for women and children by setting up streetlights, elevated footpaths/bridges and faucets near the kitchen/laundry areas;
- play/leisure spaces for children, which can be seen from their windows/work areas; and
- a place for livelihood activities in both domestic and public places (such as community halls, chapels and basketball courts).

Some leaders have argued, however, that because they are occupied with the basic issues of land acquisition and shelter, these other issues can be addressed only at a later time.

In general, NGOs belonging to the Congress of CMP Originators (for example, the Guide Foundation, the Foundation for the Upliftment of the Urban Poor and the Pagtambayayong Foundation) and their leaders have been quite sympathetic to women's issues, as most of the community organization leaders are women. Thus, there is no evident discrimination in membership and loan access by women-headed households. In fact, these NGOs have instituted pro-poor women policies in their organizations. But, in general, both NGO and CBO leaders have not paid close and systematic attention to gender issues because they are already swamped with land acquisition and resource mobilization issues that need more immediate attention.

At the heart of the gender issue in social housing is the recognition that because of poverty and the lack of economic opportunities, men's traditional economic and 'protector' roles have been seriously eroded. Women do not mind undertaking a number of community and small and petty income-generating activities (which some men consider beyond their dignity) in order to provide for their family needs; often, this results in domestic violence. Yet, discussions on the rethinking of gendered norms and the crafting of a new paradigm in gender roles that is more closely related to current social realities and the capabilities of men and women have yet to be systematically initiated.

There is no doubt that the CMP housing projects have benefited the women in the community because of their dominance in the housing associations. But central to this vision is a partnership between men and women that involves the creation of new work, social and institutional arrangements. Admittedly, this is quite difficult and remains a big challenge even for NGOs focused on gender empowerment issues.

Conclusions

The potential power of the CMP has not been fully realized because of its heavy dependence upon government finance. The increased state support extended by the past two governments to economic housing and the lack of broad-based savings mobilization for housing among NGOs and community organizations in urban poor communities have exacerbated the problem. But even with funding support, which has been available since 1999, there remains a critical need to develop the institutional capacities of national government housing agencies, local governments, NGOs and the CMP housing associations so that they can effectively support community-based housing projects among informal settlers and low-income segments of the population. Most of these institutions are used to programme approaches and procedures that are suited to clients from the formal sector who receive regular incomes.

The problems of programmes such as the CMP are rooted in the structure of financial markets and the institutional weakness of housing agencies at the macro level, and in the social orientations of NGOs and people's organization mobilization at the community level. The absence of a broad-based movement for savings mobilizations for housing and other self-help initiatives among poor communities such as exists in many other Asian cities (see the case studies from Thailand and India in Chapters 2 and 9) seems to reinforce a widespread but mistaken idea that the poor cannot generate resources for their own housing needs. Most NGOs have yet to realize that housing credit can be achieved by mobilizing the informal credit systems present in urban/rural poor communities. More importantly, government must still recognize the particular housing needs and resource capacities of the poor, the specific resource mobilization roles of NGOs and the private sector, and the need to support informal housing.

Despite these problems, the CMP is the most innovative and responsive social housing finance programme among government housing programmes, responding to the housing needs of slum and squatter communities. It is the only programme that makes possible a legalization of the status of squatters/informal settlers without the urban poor having to provide collateral. To do so, the programme had to instigate new institutional roles and relationships, maximizing the capacities of community organizations, housing-focused NGOs, local governments, financial institutions and central-state housing agencies so that the poor can access housing loans to buy land and acquire security of tenure.

The CMP is most effective in reaching the top segments of the poor because subsistence and livelihoods, not housing, are the top priority for the poorest groups. Similarly, economic improvements are also highest among the better-off and more entrepreneurial CMP beneficiary households. Economic improvements are related to their ability to take advantage of new opportunities such as renting out rooms and providing goods/services in the community. This same ability was also displayed in their efforts to link with the NGOs, local government units and other stakeholders to secure basic services and other resources for their community association.

Access to housing and security of tenure has built community participation and solidarity among the poor. This has pushed housing associations to address community needs beyond housing, such as livelihood and income generation, and savings/resource mobilization to finance other community needs, such as day-care/health centres, kindergartens, parks/playgrounds and sewer systems.

Thus, investment in social housing is efficient and effective because it causes a powerful ripple of positive multiplier effects among beneficiaries, their communities and their NGO and government organization partners.

Accessing CMP housing loans has led to the political-economic transformation of the low-income beneficiaries, as well as a modification of the institutional roles and capacities of NGOs, local government units and central state agencies. In assisting the poor, NGOs and the government agencies have had to adjust their institutional practices to respond more effectively to the needs of the poor. Creating new ways of providing sustainable direct/indirect subsidies to the poor, making scarce technical assistance affordable, and instituting new procedures are prime examples of these changes among innovative government agencies and NGOs/CBOs. This has also forced both NGOs and government personnel to increase their political and technical capacities. But much still needs to be done as this situation exists only among innovative sectors of government and civil society.

Various challenges remain. While several institutional reforms have been initiated during the past decade to support the efforts of the poor in obtaining housing and security of tenure, the institutional and policy context of the CMP still needs adjustment. The lack of institutional capacity on the part of government agencies to respond to the particular housing needs of the poor, especially families with irregular or inadequate income sources, is reflected in the delays in processing CMP projects. To respond to this, NGOs have proposed that the CMP should be organized as a relatively autonomous social housing corporation with minimum bureaucracy. More importantly, a large part of the CMP processes need to be decentralized, at least to the regional level. At the community level, several challenges continue to confront NGOs/CBOs, local government units that are project originators and local officials. Housing associations are confronted with issues such as non-repayment, selling of housing rights and the substitution of beneficiaries, accessing basic services that need large capital outlay, and lack of affordable technical assistance in site development plans. But in the final analysis, the positive impacts of the CMP far outweigh these problems and challenges.

References

CMP (1998) *CMP Bulletin*, January

CMP (2001) *CMP Status Report*, Community Mortgage Group, Project Assistance, Evaluation and Accreditation Committee, March

ICSO (1996) Occasional Paper no 1, May

Karaos, A M A (1996) *An Assessment of the Government's Social Housing Programme*, Occasional Paper #1, Institute of Church and Social Issues, Manila

Llanto, Gilbert et al (1996) 'A Study of Housing Subsidies in the Philippines', report submitted to the Housing and Urban Development Coordinating Council (HUDCC), Office of the President, Philippines

NCSO *1994/1997 Survey*, Government of the Philippines, Manila

Chapter 4

The Mexican National Popular Housing Fund

Priscilla Connolly

Introduction

The Mexican National Popular Housing Fund (FONHAPO) was created in 1981 to provide housing loans for low-income households. It achieved significant results between 1982 and 1998, reaching low-income families who were too poor to benefit from existing housing loan schemes. During this period, with 4 per cent of the investment, FONHAPO financed 23 per cent of all new housing financed by public housing funds. It also achieved many of the criteria that would become policy goals: it *enabled* the initiatives and effort of the target population; *harnessed* resources by operating in *partnership* with the public, private and non-profit sectors; and achieved an unprecedented degree of geographical and administrative *decentralization*. Although heavy subsidies were involved, these were relatively transparent and the recovery rate was high compared to other Mexican public housing schemes. The programme was considered a success by national and international observers from the non-governmental sector and by left-leaning academics. However, those responsible for Mexican housing policy after 1988 did not share this positive appraisal. FONHAPO's operational principles were modified, and it has ceased to offer a housing option for the urban and rural poor.

This chapter discusses the causes for the demise of the FONHAPO model in order to better understand the contemporary realities of low-cost housing finance programmes. An easy explanation would be to blame the 'neo-liberal' economic policy, with reductions in public expenditure and the subordination of social needs to market forces. This is not only a grossly simplified interpretation but it leads to an ideological cul-de-sac. If the FONHAPO experience is to contribute to future housing policy, both inside and outside Mexico, there needs to be a critical look at the programme itself, from the basic premises of its operation to its real impact on housing conditions.

The next section examines FONHAPO's basic philosophy, its aims and objectives, including the fundamental idea of a housing policy to support *'popular'*[1] or *social* housing processes and an exploration of what inspired it. FONHAPO's impact is then discussed with regard to the results of the housing projects and their political significance for grassroots organizations, specifically in the consolidation of the concept of 'popular' or community-managed housing development (autogestión popular in Spanish). This chapter also considers how the changing political context meant that these approaches to housing policy went out of favour with the Mexican government. At the same time, it shows how the formation of effective opposition parties, electoral struggles and electoral success at local government levels altered the meaning and scope of 'popular' organizations' involvement in housing development.

The FONHAPO vision and its context

The story line [2]

The Mexican constitution recognizes the right of every family to a decent home.[3] FONHAPO was created in the understanding that this implies the state's obligation to guarantee this constitutional right. Specifically, it was set up to provide loans for families whose economic situation excluded them from existing housing finance programmes. This essentially defined a target population of 'non-salaried'[4] workers and those whose incomes were less than 2.5 times the minimum wage: an estimated 60 to 70 per cent of Mexico's total economically active population. FONHAPO's beneficiaries were thus identified as the low-

---

1 The Spanish word *popular*, while sharing some of the meanings of 'popular' in English, should be strictly translated as 'of the people' or 'of the common people' (originally, as opposed to the nobility). In a social or political context, however, *popular* is laden with connotations, ranging from the folkloric and traditional (*culturas populares*) to low cost (*a precios populares, vivienda popular*) and, in general, to denote lower social classes (*las clases populares*). These include a much wider segment of society than those within incomes 'below the poverty line' (however defined) – the majority of the population, in fact – with a further connotation of the 'masses' (*las masas populares*). In the Mexican and other Latin American contexts, this majority is poor by standards in high-income nations, particularly with regard to housing conditions. In relation to housing, *popular* is also used to denote a residual category (like marginal or informal), defined not for what it is, but for what it is not (that is, not public, private or well to do). Finally, throughout the Spanish-speaking world, a wide array of political parties and movements of all denominations also claims to be *popular*. This extraordinary richness of meaning defies translation; hereafter in this chapter 'popular' is placed within inverted commas.

2 The following paragraphs are based on the written testimony of one of the FONHAPO's main proponents and general director from 1984 to 1988 (Ortiz, 1996, pp17–25).

3 After constitutional reforms to Article 4 in February 1983, which were brought about under the same arguments that gave rise to FONHAPO's creation.

4 The term 'non-salaried' workers used to denote what in Mexico is understood as the *población no asalariada*. This refers to a wide spectrum of employment situations in which the worker cannot prove employment and income, such as casual labour, self-employment and informal wage labour. These types of employment do not carry social benefits, such as access to health services, pensions and the right to loans from payroll housing funds.

income majority rather than a minority, however large, of the extremely poor.[5] FONHAPO loans were designed to cover only a part of the houses' final cost: the plot of land with (or sometimes without) services, a minimum first stage home, and/or investments in home improvement.

FONHAPO projected the concept of *social housing production*, harnessing the organized collective effort of people to solve their own needs for shelter. Social housing production was premised on the conviction that satisfactory housing solutions for low-income groups are incompatible with the free market and commercial housing production and is supported by the fact that most Mexicans live in houses that are not the product of formal market processes. Recognizing that individually produced informal housing may be of poor quality, FONHAPO sought improvements. It was hoped that government support, in the form of land, loans and technical assistance, would procure better-quality housing for more people, using less public funds and maximizing individual and collective endeavour. FONHAPO sought the more effective participation of different levels of government, housing developers and other private-sector actors, 'providing the latter changed their profit-making outlook and adopted a more socially orientated approach' (Ortiz, 1996, p24).

The FONHAPO story line does not end here. The idea of organized social production of housing was not strictly limited to one-off projects, but extended to include a much wider notion of *community control over urban affairs (autogestión comunitaria)*,[6] including access to land, house-building and the introduction and running of public amenities and services, including health, education, retailing and recreation facilities. Both in practice and in theory, the concept of 'community control' meant substituting traditional top-down clientelistic mechanisms with more democratic procedures. Providing financial and technical support for alternative ways of building and administrating urban development to empower the poor tacitly forms part of the FONHAPO story line. In the context of a one-party state, 'community control' and the 'social production of housing' became potentially subversive and were easily assimilated into opposition politics. How, then, in the single party state that was Mexico until very recently,[7] did this story line become incorporated into official federal housing policy? To answer this question it is necessary go back a couple of decades to uncover FONHAPO's origins.

---

5 The definition of what constitutes extreme poverty is a matter of debate, as is the calculation of how many people are in extreme poverty at any moment in time. Boltvinik (1999) estimates that in 1996, 43 per cent of households, equivalent to about 54 per cent of the population in Mexico, live below a poverty line defined as twice the basic food requirements.

6 This term was possibly coined in Coulomb and Sánchez (1992).

7 Although political reform began during the 1970s, it was not until 1988 that the PRI (Revolutionary Institutional Party) was seriously challenged in presidential election. In 2000, the PRI lost the national presidency to Vicente Fox, candidate for the right-wing PAN (National Action Party).

The 1960s and COPEVI: community development, co-operatives and student protest

Perhaps the most important conceptual input in the design of FONHAPO was the experience of COPEVI (Centro Operacional de Vivienda y Poblamiento AC, or the Operational Centre for Housing and Human Settlement), a non-governmental organization (NGO) that was the first of its kind in Mexico (Ortiz, 1996). COPEVI was founded in 1965 by a group of young professionals, mostly architects and social workers, to improve housing for the poor by promoting experiences that would contribute to democratic housing and urban development policies. Its functions combined research, networking and planning studies with technical assistance, training and the development of concrete housing projects. Some key FONHAPO concepts, such as the organization and attention of *groups* (not individuals), including *co-operatives*, are present in COPEVI's original statutes.

The emphasis on collective action and grassroots organization may be understood in the light of housing provision and its relation to the Mexican political system during the late 1960s. At that time, Mexican housing policy had provided a limited number of high-profile and mostly high-rise good-quality apartments and housing estates to be rented or sold at subsidized rates to middle-income public- or private-sector employees. Access was usually controlled by the unions, contributing to the clientelistic mechanisms upon which the Mexican corporativist state depended (Padget, 1966; Cockroft, 1983; see also Connolly, 1990, with regard to housing). There was little commercial middle-class housing, while the burgeoning low-income urban population housed themselves in irregular settlements. Like the public housing projects, one important feature of housing provision in irregular settlements was its contribution to political stability guaranteed by the virtual monopoly of political power exercised by the ruling party, the Revolutionary Institutional Party (PRI). Along with the wide array of instruments for political domination, including electoral fraud and, if necessary, repression, the supremacy of the PRI in irregular settlements was secured as access to land and services were conditioned by allegiance to organizations affiliated to the party (see, for instance, Cornelius, 1975; Ward, 1986; and Eckstein, 1990).

Two further points must be mentioned. Firstly, an important feature of the irregular settlements then, as now, was their ostensible poverty. Although they tend to improve over time, the process was little understood during the 1960s. This was a decade in which an unprecedented number of irregular settlements were just being started, in Mexico City and other larger cities, and were still in the stages of extreme environmental deprivation. Secondly, there were two important Latin American influences on COPEVI's early work that would eventually be reflected in FONHAPO: the ideas about marginality and community development elaborated by Centro para el Desarrollo Económico y Social de America Latina (Centre for Social Development – DESAL) in Santiago that were inspiring a number of organizations and projects, especially in Chile, Colombia and Peru (DESAL, 1969; 1970); and the experience of the Uruguayan Housing Co-operatives by Mutual Aid programme of the late 1960s and early

1970s. This Uruguayan example supplied at least three basic principles that would inspire the FONHAPO experience: the use of co-operative ownership to promote social cohesion and to prevent the houses being sold; an 'advisory organization' to guide the co-operative through the project, including design, financial arrangements and construction supervision; and laws that defined the state's role in housing provision (Carvajal, 1998).

Early prototypes of the FONHAPO model: COPEVI during the 1970s

This post-1968 context allowed COPEVI to develop a handful of projects in Mexico City that would later inspire the FONHAPO model. In particular, the Palo Alto Co-operative, a medium-density development on the outskirts of Mexico City, had immense symbolic significance. The project involved a group of very low-income ex-quarry workers and their families, mostly rural immigrants, who previously inhabited caves on the same site occupying a piece of land surrounded by Mexico City's most exclusive residential neighbourhoods. Co-operative land ownership guaranteed that members could not be bought out individually. The group was organized and 'conscienticized' by radical Christians and sponsored by an upper-class Catholic organization. COPEVI provided technical assistance in layout, house design, construction, materials, supervision, finance and negotiations with the authorities, but was not involved in the more educational and political organizing work.

About the same time, COPEVI advised *vecindad* (central slum) tenants who were being organized by a group of Jesuits operating from the local parish church. Apart from substandard and overcrowded living conditions, there were frequent evictions as landlords got rid of tenants enjoying frozen rents since the 1940s. At that time, the city government was offering loans for new public housing projects on the outer periphery to tenants who were evicted from buildings demolished for public works and, in some cases, to victims of private evictions. Most tenants, however, could not meet the loan requirements and few wanted to live on the outskirts. COPEVI proposed new housing in the inner city at affordable prices to the existing population. An initial project of 74 flats for the Colonia Guerrero Co-operative finished in 1977 and received international acclaim (Turner, 1988; Connolly, 1986).

It was increasingly accepted that the organization of low-income population groups around housing problems was becoming an important factor of political mobilization.[8] By the mid-1970s, the early endeavours of radical Christian activists, student political organizations and incipient political parties were beginning to bear fruit. The organizations that would a few years later converge to form a self-proclaimed Urban Social Movement were in the process of

---

8 While certain sectors of the traditional left dismissed political struggle around such issues as 'reformist', there was growing adherence amongst left activists of their revolutionary potential as propagators of urban social movements. These, in turn, were invested with academic legitimacy as serious political forces by such publications as Borja (1975) and Castells (1974), who were widely read (and listened to) in Mexico at that time.

formation and consolidation in Mexico City and other cities of north and central Mexico. An important factor enabling such organizations to operate in the open was the *apertura democrática* (democratic opening), initiated in 1973, followed by more concrete steps towards political reform later in the decade. This created a more permissive atmosphere for political organization and facilitated the registration of political parties.

Government housing policy during the 1970s: credit and land

The COPEVI experiences, such as Palo Alto and Colonia Guerrero and their replicas during the following years, were matched by developments in Mexican state housing policy. Public housing finance began to provide credit for middle- and lower-income households. During the early 1970s, three federal payroll housing funds were constituted out of a new obligatory 5 per cent tax on wages and salaries by the public, private and military employers: the Housing Fund of the Health and Social Security Institute for State Employees (FOVISSSTE); the Institute of the National Workers' Housing Fund (INFONAVIT); and the Military Housing Fund (FOVIMI and ISSFAM). At the same time, the mortgage funds from the banks, subsidized by the central bank to reach middle-income sectors, expanded their operations. The number of houses financed by the public sector escalated from an average of 7219 a year between 1965 and 1970 to 67,134 a year the following decade.

However, this met a tiny fraction of effective demand, while the lowest income brackets, non-salaried workers and people who could not prove their incomes were disqualified. To nominally address their problems, the existing National Housing Institute was transformed in 1970 into the National Institute for Community Development and Popular Housing (INDECO). Like its predecessor, INDECO was not a financial institution and its housing projects were financed by other agencies. However, it built up a solid institutional experience regarding the social realities of housing for the poor in urban and rural situations, including building technologies, core housing and sites and services. Equally important for FONHAPO's performance a decade later was INDECO's constitution of publicly owned land reserves for low-cost housing development.

The Mexican government's land policy during the 1970s covered two closely related processes: the constitution of land banks by the major housing institutions on an unprecedented scale (see Table 4.1) and a radical change of government action in irregular settlements. Well over half of the land reserves in hand at the beginning of the 1980s would be available for projects financed by FONHAPO. Most were acquired by INDECO through the new policy to regularize irregular urban settlements. These settlements had developed on both publicly and privately owned land, including communally owned agrarian properties (*ejidos* and *tierras communales*).[9] A main source of the illegality of the

---

9 The *tierras comunales* are those communally owned properties, originally granted by the Spanish Crown to Indian communities, some of which survived, wholly or partially, the 19th-century liberal reforms. The *ejidos* are lands that were expropriated and redistributed to local communities by the agrarian reform following the Mexican Revolution of 1910–1917.

Table 4.1 *Land banks acquired by different government organizations, 1973–1980*

Organization	Land (thousands of square metres)		
	Available in 1973	Total acquired 1973–1980	Available December 1980
INFONAVIT		83,274	46,374
FOVISSSTE		15,271	4282
FOVIMI/ISSFAM		1214	452
BANOBRAS	14,386	21,038	
INDECO	658	136,592	87,253
Others		2073	4366
Total	15,044	259,462	142,727

Source: Comisión Intersecretarial de Planeación, Programación y Financiamiento de la Vivienda (1982)

land subdivision is the fact that this kind of property cannot be legally sold or rented, although this happened frequently (Varley, 1985; Azuela, 1989). By the early 1970s, special measures were created to regularize and upgrade these settlements in Mexico City and Monterrey, including the creation by the Mexican government of AURIS (Instituto de Acción Urbana e Integración Social, or the Institute for Urban Action and Social Integration) in 1969. In 1974, new procedures for regularizing urban settlements on *ejidos* and a national agency were established. Usually, the quantity of land expropriated exceeded that which was occupied and the remainder was handed over to INDECO. INDECO also acquired land by purchase and other kinds of expropriations. In 1982 INDECO was replaced by local housing institutes, usually state government dependencies, to which the land reserves were transferred. These institutes and their land reserves played an important role within FONHAPO. The institutes in Mexico State and Nuevo León not only regularized settlements and built up land reserves, but also implemented innovative housing projects, such as home improvement schemes, serviced sites and core housing. The expertise gained by certain individuals in AURIS was also a crucial input to FONHAPO's creation.

Vancouver, the new urban planning apparatus and the National Housing Programme

The first United Nations Human Settlements Conference in Vancouver in 1976 was an important milestone in Mexican housing policy. The exceptionally large Mexican delegation and the event's high profile in Mexico may be explained by the fact that the outgoing Mexican president was angling for the job of UN secretary-general – although unsuccessfully. The conference gave many academics, planners and housing activists, including COPEVI's director, an opportunity to exchange ideas and consolidate a common platform with non-governmental organization (NGO) representatives from other countries (Ortiz, 1996). It also provided the international background for the first comprehensive urban planning legislation enacted in Mexico. A new ministry for urban planning, the Secretariat for Human Settlements and Public Works (SAHOP), was created

---

BOX 4.1 GUIDELINES OF THE NATIONAL HOUSING POLICY PROPOSED BY SAHOP, 1976–1982

Guidelines for the National Housing Policy proposed by the Secretariat for Human Settlements and Public Works (SAHOP) comprise the following:

- wider access to housing for the highest possible number of beneficiaries;
- government acquisition of land banks for low-cost housing to avoid speculation with urban land;
- coverage of the credit institutions extended to ensure more resources for loans to non-salaried workers, marginal urban populations, peasants and middle-income sectors;
- compatibility between housing actions carried out by different levels of government and by the private and social sectors;
- active participation of the social and private sectors in collaborative actions and incentives;
- improvements to the housing stock to benefit family welfare;
- improvement to housing production processes and the promotion of construction systems that can be socially appropriated;
- promotion of housing within urban planning and permanent improved housing for rural populations in their environment;
- support for organized community participation in service and infrastructure provision;
- support to building materials production and distribution to reduce costs;
- integration of housing with the environment;
- promotion of solidarity among the population for housing development and aid to organized self-build programmes and to the social movement for co-operative housing.

Source: Ley Federal de Vivienda, Article 2, 1993

---

whose responsibilities combined the more traditional role of a public works ministry with setting up the normative framework for planning, as well as the design of a national housing policy. This produced a National Housing Programme in 1979 and the Federal Housing Law of 1983. The main objectives of these policy documents, summarized in Box 4.1, are important precedents to FONHAPO.

Key individuals in the secretariat's housing team included two members of COPEVI and several architect-planners who had gained experience in INDECO experimenting with low-cost solutions, such as serviced sites, core housing and integrated programmes. These people had first-hand knowledge of how the urban poor secured their livelihoods and their housing. The fact that public-sector housing finance programmes had practically nothing to offer most of the population was well understood, as was the need to devise more accessible credit schemes and other policy measures. Importantly, the way that the practical experience of these professionals was rationalized in the discursive content of the housing policy documents was also strongly influenced by a particular interpretation of the housing problem. This interpretation, which this chapter calls the 'tripartite vision', is perhaps responsible for some major fallacies in the assumptions underlying the FONHAPO 'story line' as a housing policy.

Conceptual confusions: the tripartite vision of housing production, the popular sector and markets

Increased government preoccupation with human settlements has been accompanied by an upsurge in academic endeavour to understand the problem. COPEVI's own studies were largely inspired by John Turner's vision of the more positive aspects of 'self-help housing', drawing from his observations of the slums in Arequipa, Peru, during the late 1960s (see, in particular, Turner, 1969) and Althusserian Marxism, in its applications to urban sociology by writers such as Castells, Topalov and Lojkine.[10] From the Turner model came the idea of irregular urban settlements and 'self-help housing' as a *solution: an architecture that works*, and the equally important idea of *housing as a verb* – that is, an incremental form of housing production, the *popular housing sector*, which is distinct from both *public-sector* and *private-sector* housing. The heated discussions and disagreements with Turner were mostly about whether this form of housing provided a 'good' or a 'bad' solution (see Ward, 1998, for a summary of the debate in relation to Mexico City). But they seldom questioned the conceptual weaknesses of what was rapidly becoming established as the *popular or social housing sector*. Before examining these methodological weaknesses, it is worthwhile recognizing some of popular housing's strengths. Firstly, reconceptualizing 'slums' as a form of housing provision was a marked improvement to the 'deficit' approach that either led to slum clearance policies or to total inaction regarding irregular settlements. Secondly, the tripartite classification of housing production corresponds to the spatial segregation of most Latin American cities. Thirdly, following this basic morphological approximation, the tripartite classification represented a genuine attempt to equate housing conditions with the social relations that produce them. But the way in which this developed incurred some problems.

Conceptual problems of the tripartite classification are reflected in the difficulties of quantifying each category of housing production. The SAHOP team calculated 'public' housing from records of the housing institutions; 'private' production, lacking operational definitions, was imputed on the basis of dubious assumptions; 'popular' housing was then calculated residually from total increase in dwellings registered in consecutive censuses. As a heuristic tool, the exercise throws some light on how the housing production system is roughly structured, although important housing forms such as rural dwellings and cheap rental accommodation are ignored. As a prescriptive model for a housing policy it has more serious flaws. The ideal of housing that is neither commercially produced nor sold, and not even privately owned, does not really reflect the needs and aspirations of the poor. 'Popular' housing production would seem to respond to a target population comprised of eternally poor, eternally young families, who live in the same place or at least never have to sell their house.

The tripartite classification system confuses forms of housing provision (production) with forms of commercialization (the market) and obscures their

---

10 These authors were published in Spanish, specifically in Mexico, long before English translations became available: Castells (1974; 1976); Topalov (1979); Lojkine (1979). But even before these publications, there were strong personal contacts between Latin American researchers and these Paris-based urban sociologists.

relation to the structure of effective demand for housing. These aspects are intimately related but need to be tackled separately. The National Housing Plan model put priority on housing provision, particularly the state's role as a provider, while neglecting the housing market. The problem of finance for secondary markets was not addressed in the National Housing Plan or by FONHAPO. Neither was the question of how to distribute intrinsically scarce benefits (in this case, subsidized housing loans that could be individually capitalized via the market) without resorting to clientelistic practices, lotteries or the black market. A tremendous amount of faith was placed in the capacity of social organizations, and the 'popular sector', in general, to carry out social justice in assigning these benefits, while resisting market pressures, political expediencies and personal interests. The Mexican government's performance as housing provider greatly improved after 1982; but the market struggled: real-estate values fell, housing funds disappeared instead of revolving, cities expanded at even faster rates into the surrounding countryside, and political clientelism in the distribution of housing benefits was seen to flourish.

FONHAPO's aims and achievements, 1982–1988

Mexican housing policy during the 1980s and FONHAPO's role in housing provision for the poorer population

The 1980s have been termed 'the lost decade' for Latin America, including Mexico. Between 1982 and 1998, annual inflation ranged between 52 and 106 per cent; gross domestic product (GDP) growth was stationary; and GDP per capita decreased dramatically by more than minus 6 per cent in 1983 and 1986. There was a corresponding increase in the number of people living in poverty and extreme poverty. But, more noticeably, there was also impoverishment among the middle classes, unemployment (open unemployment registered in official surveys increased from 4 per cent to 17.8 per cent between 1981 and 1989) and an increased informal economy. Improvements slowed for many social indicators, such as the infant mortality rate and education and health indicators. Housing was the exception and actually improved during the 1980s, especially in quantitative terms (see Table 4.2). One set of reasons is demographic: fertility rates dropped from over 5 during the 1970s to 2.2 during the late 1990s (resulting in falling average household size, especially in urban areas).

Further reasons for the relative improvement in housing are related to the increased participation of the state. Between 1983 and 1988, 45.6 per cent of the net increase in housing stock may be attributed to publicly financed housing. Workers' housing funds are collected and administered independently of national finances, so these were relatively stable. More importantly, as workers' salaries decreased, so did their ability to pay for housing; as a result, a proportionately larger number of cheaper, smaller units were built. More impressive was the increase of new housing financed by the banks. After their speculative behaviour prior to Mexico's financial crisis in 1982, private banks had been nationalized. This facilitated the interest in social housing. Indeed, the proportion of all the

Table 4.2 *Housing indicators in Mexico, 1970, 1980, 1990, 1995 and 2000*

Housing indicator	1970	1980	1990	1995	2000
Average household size	5.82	5.50	5.02	4.67	4.44
Average number of occupants per room	2.57	2.24	1.93	*	*
Per cent homeowners	66	71	78	*	*
Per cent with brick walls or similar	24	44	56	*	79
Per cent with inside piped water	39	50	50	54	58
Per cent with sanitation/drainage**	41	48	61	72	75

Notes: * Data unavailable
** During 1980, 1990 and 1995, this means drainage or septic tank.
Source: Population censuses for 1970, 1980, 1990, 2000 and the National Population Count of 1995

banks' operations applied to this kind of mortgages, at subsidized rates, had already increased following regulatory changes in 1978. As important was the introduction of the refinancing system of mortgage repayment that took account of inflation. Until 1988, the system was successful as it enabled the financing of more houses with less funds, while maintaining the target population within the 2.2 to 11 times minimum wages range. However, an increasing proportion of this housing was built for the higher income brackets within this range (see Barragán, 1994). During the difficult 1980s, the scale of public investment in housing did not greatly increase, but the number of units built increased substantially.

Another reason for the increase in public housing provision was that land banking and regularization facilitated housing programmes and opened up a new and cheaper kind of housing programme: sites and services (and sites without services). The main implementer of this 'doing more with less' was FONHAPO (see Table 4.3).

Just over 10 per cent of all new dwellings, including core houses, financed by the public sector from 1982 to 1988 may be attributed to FONHAPO using 4 per cent of the available funds (see Table 4.3). FONHAPO had been set up explicitly to fulfil the state's role as housing provider to a target population whose lower income or non-salaried employment excluded them from existing housing programmes. This was accomplished through giving a high priority to smaller credit packages for core housing and sites and services, providing exclusively collective credit to public and private housing organizations, and providing credit for technical assistance (and even for establishing new NGOs as required). Between 1982 and 1994, FONHAPO financed 203,657 core housing units, 115,870 sites and services, 179,661 home improvement loans and 1730 finished houses (see Figure 4.1). As Figure 4.1 shows, it continued to provide credits from 1995 to 1998, although much fewer in number compared to the years between 1986 and 1994 and with no breakdown available as to what kind of unit was financed. Box 4.2 shows the main features of FONHAPO's operations from 1982 to 1988.

Table 4.3 *FONHAPO's participation in public-sector housing credits, 1982–1994*

	1982–1988	1989–1994
Finished dwellings		
All public-sector organizations	903,287	1,103,565
FONHAPO	1730	0
Per cent FONHAPO	<1%	0
Core housing		
All public-sector organizations	111,876	239,284
FONHAPO	109,089	94,568
Per cent FONHAPO	98%	40%
Sites and services		
All public-sector organizations	76,643	138,918
FONHAPO	72,640	43,230
Per cent FONHAPO	95%	31%
Improvements*		
All public-sector organizations	178,871	904,487
FONHAPO	62,541	117,120
Per cent FONHAPO	35%	13%
Other credits**	123,814	282,723

Notes: * Improvements cover everything from a coat of paint to the addition of several rooms or services.
** This includes credits or secondary market, mortgage repayment and other types of credit not provided by FONHAPO.
Source: Presidente E Zedillo (1998) 'IV Informe de Actividades', quoted in Puebla (1997)

FONHAPO as a financial institution

FONHAPO was funded by three sources: internal resources, federal government budget allocations and loans from other financial institutions. Its internal resources were made up of one-off amounts, originally belonging to the housing fund of BANOBRAS (Banco Nacional de Obras y Servicios Públicos – the National Bank of Public Works and Services) that FONHAPO took over in 1981, profits accruing from its own properties and loan repayments. The relative importance of the different sources of finance varied over 18 years of FONHAPO's operation (see Tables 4.4 and 4.5). FONHAPO 'inherited' the federal budgetary allocations of direct investment from INDECO, receiving comparable amounts to those gained by that agency during the oil boom years of 1978 to 1981 (Puebla, 1997).

The other main source of FONHAPO financing was two World Bank non-concessional loans. The first was for US$150 million, negotiated in 1985, with interest payments paid by the federal government. Apart from one previous loan for self-build housing in a new steelworks town during the early 1970s, this was the first World Bank loan for housing in Mexico. It would be followed by a series of further loans, not only for FONHAPO, but also for other Mexican

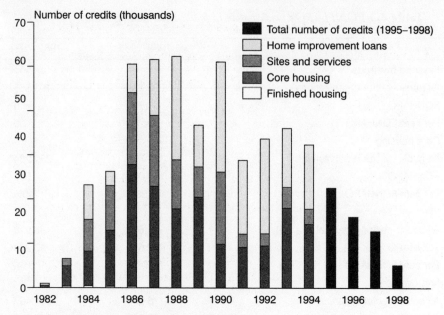

Source: Puebla (1997), with data added for 1995–1998

Figure 4.1 *FONHAPO: number of credits by type, 1982–1998*

housing organizations.[11] The significance of World Bank lending emerged slowly. Firstly, World Bank housing dogma began to permeate Mexican housing policy. According to Enrique Ortiz, director of FONHAPO at the time of the first loan, it was possible to negotiate 'an adequate level of subsidies' and 'with the contribution of Mexican government resources, finance for the purchase of land for housing projects was allowed' (Ortiz, 1996). Such heretical principles were not permitted in the second loan; since then, loans for land and financial subsidies have been removed from FONHAPO's programmes. A second effect of World Bank lending was that, instead of increasing FONHAPO's total resources, it essentially substituted for the federal government contribution, which declined from 1987 onwards (see Table 4.5). A third implication was the financial strain of the 1990 loan, whose debt service had to be paid by FONHAPO rather than the federal government. By 1994, these interest payments constituted 20 per cent of FONHAPO's total budget, equivalent to 40 per cent of its investment in housing (see Table 4.5). Table 4.5 also shows how FONHAPO's running costs were extremely low initially; but after 1990, costs greatly increased, partly as a result of the relative reduction of the total budget.

---

11 In 1985, a US$400 million World Bank loan was negotiated by FONHAPO for housing and urban development in the Istmus zone to the south-east of Mexico; but following the 1985 earthquakes, this was reallocated to Mexico City's housing reconstruction programme, which was administered independently of FONHAPO. Apart from the second World Bank loan to FONHAPO in 1990, two other loans 'in support of the Mexican housing market' were subsequently granted to FOVI.

Box 4.2 FONHAPO'S OPERATIONAL PRINCIPLES, 1982–1988

- The target population consisted of individuals, preferably non-salaried workers, earning less than 2.5 times the minimum wage and with dependants (spouse, children), who, except in the case of home improvement loans, are not in the possession of another property.
- FONHAPO did not provide the loans directly to individuals, nor was it responsible for the planning and execution of the housing projects. It financed intermediate organizations that could be either public (belonging to the federal, state, municipal or quasi-state sector), private (such as financial institutions and development trusts) or social (co-operatives and other legally constituted social organizations). In this way, it promoted the decentralization of the housing bureaucracy.
- Five types of housing project were financed: sites and services; incremental housing; home improvements; finished dwellings; and production and distribution of building materials. FONHAPO, in contrast to the other housing institutions, favoured financing partial housing solutions over finished dwellings.
- These projects were supported by five types of loan corresponding to different phases of the projects: up to 95 per cent of the cost of studies, projects and advisory centres; up to 95 per cent of the cost of land; 100 per cent of the costs of urban development (street layout and public services); 100 per cent of construction costs; and up to 90 per cent of the costs of assistance to self-build housing (packages of building materials). In this way, FONHAPO was the first institution to offer a flexible range of credit packages, including small loans, on a large scale.
- The value of the loans was expressed in terms of multiples of the local daily minimum wage, the maximum value being 2000 minimum daily wages (about US$6000 in 1988). The amount of money loaned depended upon the income of the head of household. Those earning less than the minimum wage could be loaned up to 1200 daily minimum wages (about US$3700 in 1988); those earning between 1 and 1.5 minimum wages could be loaned up to 1600 (US$4900); and those earning between 1.5 and 2.5 minimum wages could receive up to the maximum loan of 2000 minimum wages. The credit limits for sites and services, incremental housing, home improvements and finished housing were 600, 2000, 1150 and 2000, respectively (US$1847, US$6157, US$3540 and US$6147 in 1988).
- A down payment of between 10 and 15 per cent had to be paid by the final beneficiaries.
- An initial subsidy of between 15 and 25 per cent was offered on the value of all loans. Additionally, a further 15 per cent would be offered for prompt repayment. That implied a direct subsidy of 30 per cent of the loan value for the larger loans for incremental or finished housing, and up to 40 per cent of the loan value for smaller loan packages.
- On the basis of a maximum payment of 25 per cent of the beneficiary's monthly income, the amount and number of repayments were calculated in terms of percentages of minimum wages at the time of contracting the loan. For example, a 2000 daily minimum wage, or US$6147 loan, would require 96 monthly payments (seven years), each equivalent to 52 per cent of the current monthly minimum wage, or US$48 in 1988. These payments would escalate according to the increase in minimum wage. In this way the real value of loans repayment was maintained approximately in line with inflation.
- In all, it was estimated that the total subsidy to the beneficiaries would average at 50 per cent – that is, the repayments from two loans would finance one more of a similar amount.

Source: FONHAPO (1987)

Table 4.4 *Sources of FONHAPO housing investment, 1982–1994*

Year	Total investment	Own resources	Fiscal resources	IBRD loans
1982	417	284	134	0
1983	398	282	115	0
1984	892	224	668	0
1985	932	313	619	0
1986	739	107	406	225
1987	909	154	341	415
1988	847	312	193	342
Total 1982–1988	5133 100%	1676 33%	2476 48%	982 19%
1989	881	283	211	388
1990	1228	291	365	573
1991	923	212	305	407
1992	896	149	331	417
1993	856	322	184	349
1994	764	292	114	358
Total 1989-94	5548 100%	1548 28%	1508 27%	2492 45%

Note: Millions of 1974 pesos deflated according to the national social-interest housing construction cost index.
Source: Puebla (1997); FONHAPO (1995), Tables 16, 24 and 25

The third source of FONHAPO funding – loan recovery – brings us to the crucial question of its financial efficiency and the feasibility of its direct subsidy policy. It was originally thought that the 30 to 40 per cent outright financial subsidies described in Box 4.1 would effectively mean a 50 per cent overall subsidy to FONHAPO beneficiaries. Table 4.6 shows that this goal was not attained after nine years – although FONHAPO's performance in this respect is certainly not bad by Mexican standards.[12] Loan recovery has steadily grown in absolute terms, at least until 1991, and has provided about one-quarter of total investment during FONHAPO's peak years of 1989 to 1992. This is in spite of the effective devaluation of the loans themselves (which are expressed in multiples of minimum wages) given that the value of the minimum wage has itself devalued relative to real average wages, construction costs, cost of living indexes and dollars (Schteingart and Graizbord, 1998).

FONHAPO's subsidy policy should be considered in relation to Mexico's other housing programmes, especially from 1983 to 1988, when annual inflation was running at between 60 and 160 per cent. Workers' housing funds (or 'payroll' funds) were providing their affiliates with 100 per cent mortgages at an annual interest rate of 4 per cent. As wages rose with inflation, these mortgages were paid off in three or four years with monthly payments equivalent to 18 or 20 per cent of the worker's wage. The beneficiary was then free to sell or rent his or her house. This system clearly implies a high degree of subsidy and resulted in the acute decapitalization of the funds. To overcome this, after 1987 the workers' housing funds adopted the FONHAPO model of indexing the value of the mortgages to minimum wages.

---

12 For instance, loan repayments to INFONAVIT were equivalent to as little as 13 per cent of investment during the inflationary 1980s, reaching a high 25 per cent by 1995 (Puebla, 1997).

Table 4.5 *FONHAPO's budget, 1982–1994: investment, running costs and debt service*

Year	Investment in housing credits	Other investments	Running costs	Debt service to World Bank	Total
1982	417	50	50	0	517
1983	402	28	33	0	463
1984	901	39	50	0	991
1985	951	38	56	0	1044
1986	759	15	41	0	815
1987	941	9	31	0	980
1988	886	17	48	0	951
Total 1982–1988	5257 91%	195 3%	309 5%	0	5761 100%
1989	939	18	58	0	1015
1990	1262	33	127	43	1465
1991	941	4	140	122	1207
1992	912	4	136	140	1193
1993	869	2	127	187	1184
1994	779	2	122	230	1133
Total 1989–1994	5702 79%	63 1%	710 10%	722 10%	7197 100%

Note: Millions of 1974 pesos deflated according to the national social-interest housing construction cost index.
Source: Puebla (1997); FONHAPO (1995), Tables 16, 24 and 25

The subsidies provided by the Housing Finance Programme through the nationalized banks are of another order. The financial subsidies consisted of the difference between the low interest rate offered for social interest housing loans and the commercial interest rate, which, by 1984, was at least four times as high (Barragán, 1994). This subsidy was reduced, though not eliminated, by the new refinancing system introduced in 1984 (the World Bank lamented an estimated US$670 million in 'revenue losses' to the banks in 1986). Following the re-privatization of the banks in 1989, restrictions on credit operations were lifted, for the first time opening up mortgages for residential development. Financial mismanagement, inflation and finally the crash of December 1994 led to the accumulation of bad debts. These included between 550,000 and 863,000 mortgages to middle-income families facing unpayable debts, combined with acute negative equity as the market plummeted. In 1996, a special programme to restructure mortgage debts was set up as part of the more general scheme to bail out the banks. At that time, the cost to the taxpayer of enabling the banks to go on collecting 600,000 or so mortgage repayments was estimated at US$5300 millions (Poder Ejecutivo Federal, 1996).[13] This could be compared to FONHAPO's annual investment budget of US$111.4 millions in its peak year of 1984.

Thus FONHAPO's financial strategy would never have constituted a self-sustaining revolving housing fund. Neither could it have provided housing loans on a scale that would benefit the majority of lower-income households. Its funds would always be limited to budgetary allocations from federal government,

13 In 1996, the entire bank rescue programme was estimated at US$26.5 billion, equivalent to 8.5 per cent of total Mexican GDP.

Table 4.6 *FONHAPO's loan recovery compared to total investment*

Year	Total investment in housing credits	Loan recovery	Loan recovery as per cent of total investment
1986	259	148	19.5
1987	941	198	21.1
1988	886	236	26.7
1989	939	252	26.8
1990	1262	274	21.7
1991	941	282	29.1
1992	912	311	34.1
1993	869	312	36.0
1994	779	297	38.2

Note: Millions of 1974 pesos deflated according to the national social-interest housing construction cost index.
Source: Puebla (1997), Table 28

supplemented by World Bank loans. FONHAPO's function was to channel subsidies from Mexican taxpayers to selected groups of the lower-income population. These subsidies were substantially less than those channelled by the other housing finance agencies, such as to payroll tax beneficiaries, and far far less than those from Mexican taxpayers to the banks.

The impact of FONHAPO

Who benefited from housing loans?

Available sources and studies[14] provide fairly detailed information about FONHAPO's beneficiaries and their housing conditions. Information is also available on the nature of the intermediary organization that handled the loans. FONHAPO's primary function of providing housing loans for the 'non-salaried' working population appears to have been fulfilled in the case of just under half of the beneficiaries between 1982 and 1988 (Ortiz, 1996). This proportion dropped to 45 per cent in 1989 and 26 per cent in 1993, rising to 40 per cent in 1994 (Duhau and Schteingart, 1999). However, the definition of a non-salaried worker is ambiguous: many 'salaried workers' earn very low wages and are not eligible for other housing loan programmes. The second objective to provide loans for people with incomes of under 2.5 times the minimum wage seems to have been met in terms of the average incomes of heads of families. For the most expensive FONHAPO loans (sites and services and core housing), this indicator rose from a minimum of 1.2 minimum wages for sites and services in

14 The primary sources for this section are annual evaluations undertaken by FONHAPO in 1983, 1984 and 1985, and from 1991 to 1994; housing statistics generated by Secretaría de Desarrollo Urbano y Ecología (1982 to 1998) and the Secretaría de Desarrollo Social (1989 to 1994). Secondary sources include Duhau (1988), Duhau and Schteingart (1999), Puebla (1997), Monterrubio (1998) and CENVI (1997).

1992 (Duhau, 1988) to 2.5 minimum wages in 1994 (Puebla, 1997). For the cheaper home improvements loans, the average rose from 1.3 in 1983 to 2.1 in 1984 – an insignificant increase considering that the value of the minimum wage relative to real incomes and prices has decreased over this period.

These figures need to be interpreted cautiously. Firstly, they are based on answers to official questionnaires by people well aware of FONHAPO's rules and priorities. Secondly, the income of the family head does not necessarily reflect family income. In 1985, it was found that one-quarter of family heads had a second job, while nearly half of the families had more than one breadwinner. Drawing on the same surveys, the average *family income* of FONHAPO beneficiaries with more than one breadwinner in 1985 ranged from 3.5 to 4 minimum wages (Duhau, 1988).

Additional information about beneficiaries indicates that behind the statistics are a wide variety of situations. For instance, the 1985 FONHAPO internal evaluation shows that 5 per cent of beneficiary family heads were illiterate, 39 per cent had primary education and 17 per cent had professional qualifications. The percentage of professionally qualified people among FONHAPO's beneficiaries rose to a national average of 45 per cent in 1993, although this figure dropped to 30 per cent in 1994 (Puebla, 1997). The average participation of female-headed households receiving FONHAPO loans was less than 30 per cent until 1991, although the percentage then increased to 36 per cent (FONHAPO, 1985; Puebla, 1997). The average family size seems to have been fairly constant over two decades, ranging from 4.5 members for sites and services to 6 members for home improvements loans. This is substantially higher than the national average.

FONHAPO primarily benefited the middle to poorer sections of the working-class population. It has not, and could not, do much to help the extremely poor, who are mostly without regular employment and/or may live outside a structured family environment. It seems likely that there are some beneficiaries whose higher income would theoretically exclude him or her from access to FONHAPO loans.

Impact on housing conditions

The systematic evaluations carried out by FONHAPO provide some surprising findings. Surveys in 1984 and 1985 showed few short-term advantages of living in a FONHAPO-financed home. The new core houses or dwellings built on sites and services schemes tended, on average, to be smaller and more poorly equipped in terms of basic services, bathrooms and kitchens than the beneficiaries' previous home. They also tended to be built of more makeshift materials and offer considerably less accessibility to amenities and workplaces (FONHAPO, 1984; 1985). For instance, in 1985, 30 to 40 per cent of beneficiaries were without inside bathrooms, 25 to 30 per cent were without drainage and 25 to 40 per cent were without piped water. There was no access to public transport in over 55 per cent of the projects (compared to 14 per cent in the previous dwellings), while garbage collection was lacking in 46 per cent of FONHAPO projects. People were also paying considerably more for their housing than before. Surveys between 1991 and 1994 also show that FONHAPO projects generally provided smaller, more expensive, housing with worse service levels and access than their occupants' previous dwelling. By the 1990s, FONHAPO housing had shrunk from an average of 46.1 square metres in 1983 to 35 square metres in 1988, rising again to about 42 square metres thereafter as the programmes became more expensive. Average plot sizes also decreased from over 150 square metres between 1982 and 1989 to 115 square metres after 1990 (Puebla, 1997). At the same time, FONHAPO projects tended to be located increasingly on the periphery of cities, as land banks became depleted and land prices soared. Access to suitable land became a growing problem as FONHAPO progressively withdrew its credit line for land purchase after 1986 and suspended it in 1994.

Despite these apparent drawbacks, FONHAPO offered one important advantage: security of tenure. It also provided many families with the opportunity to have a home of their own. For the years 1984 to 1995, the majority of households (between 47 and 60 per cent) had been tenants, as many as 23 per cent had been living in 'loaned' accommodation, up to 20 per cent had been sharing and the rest had been living in their owner-occupied housing. Moreover, these comparisons refer to the situation of FONHAPO beneficiaries soon after occupancy. FONHAPO housing is designed to *improve* over time, allowing for the house to grow according to the families' possibilities and needs. Although there is no comprehensive data available, there can be no doubt that FONHAPO housing projects – like most of the spontaneous irregular settlements that they seek to replace – do improve over time and, unlike most spontaneous self-built houses, they improve very quickly.

Behind this summary of national averages is a wide variety of situations, of success stories and relative failures, and also a strong regional differentiation in almost all aspects. Compared to other government programmes, FONHAPO was decentralized. Between 1982 and 1988, only 18 per cent of the loans went to the Mexico City area. However, a disproportionate amount of loans went to a few localities and little or no participation by some states. For instance, Aguascalientes, a prosperous and fast-growing city in central Mexico, received over 11,000 loans (5 per cent of all loans) between 1982 and 1988, and a further 16,248 between 1989 and 1992. This means that approximately 16 per cent of this city's population (of 862,335 in 1995) lives in a house or plot financed by FONHAPO, while scarcely 5 per cent of the city's urbanization is unauthorized or 'irregular' (Jiménez, 2000). Twelve out of 32 states accounted for 80 per cent of all of FONHAPO's loans for sites and services, 41 per cent for core housing and 38 per cent for home improvements.

Three major (related) factors explain FONHAPO's relative success in certain states and cities: the availability of land reserves; the capacity of state–government housing institutes to negotiate and implement FONHAPO-financed programmes; and the effectiveness of grassroots (popular) organizations, aided by non-governmental agencies, in obtaining FONHAPO loans. Land is perhaps the major issue, but this is also related to the effective action of state. FONHAPO was most effective in cities located in states whose local governments had built up land reserves.

Between 1982 and 1994, 76 per cent of all FONHAPO loans went to public intermediate agencies (Puebla, 1997). Of these, 84 per cent were state government institutions; the rest were federal or municipal agencies. It can rightly be claimed that FONHAPO contributed to the decentralization of public housing practice. In the more prosperous, more urbanized, states with more effective political opposition parties, particularly in the north, local housing institutes have been able to continue independently with low-income housing developments (CENVI, 1997). However, in the more rural states such as Oaxaca, Guerrero and Michoacán, the action of the local housing institutes was totally dependent of FONHAPO resources.

FONHAPO, the Popular Urban Movement and community housing development

As noted above, the relative concentration of FONHAPO loans in certain cities and regions was linked to the capacity of popular grassroots organizations to successfully negotiate and carry through the appropriate programmes. Support for the 'social housing sector' was the prime objective of FONHAPO and 23 per cent of its loans from 1982 to 1994 seem to have been managed by 'social-sector' organizations (Puebla, 1997). Of these, slightly less than one-third were housing co-operatives, slightly less than two-thirds were 'civil societies and associations', 6 per cent were rural organizations and 1 per cent comprised trade unions.

A large proportion of these were in Mexico City. But FONHAPO also supported popular housing organizations in other cities where the urban social movement and/or NGOs working on human settlements or habitat issues encouraged neighbourhood associations to apply for FONHAPO finance: Jalisco, Chihuahua, Puebla, Oaxaca and Tlaxcala. The main experiences would be associated with 'independent' (in opposition to the governing political party from a leftist stance) grassroots organizations. However, the official party was quick to learn and soon many popular organizations affiliated to the PRI – and other political groups – joined in FONHAPO programmes.

Regardless of the political leanings of the local organization concerned, FONHAPO came under increasing criticism for reinforcing traditional clientelistic methods of political mobilization: the allocation of state subsidies in exchange for support for a particular party or a particular candidate. Remembering that FONHAPO was designed to combat this kind of practice, it is necessary to examine what the model of 'social housing production' really implied in order to see whether these accusations were true or to what extent this really represents an innovative step towards structural improvement in housing provision for the poor.

It was in Mexico City that FONHAPO's experience with community organizations made the greatest contribution to establishing the paradigm 'popular housing production' or *autogestión comunitaria*. The basic condition was the combined presence of the growing coalition of local organizations that made up the urban popular movement and a group of habitat NGOs.[15] Between 1982

---

15 By the 1980s, COPEVI had split and multiplied into a series of similar NGOs, such as CENVI (Centro de la Vivienda y Estudios Urbanos), Casa y Ciudad and FOSOVI (Fondo Social de la Vivienda), which mainly operate in the Mexico City area.

and 1987, personal contacts between FONHAPO officials, community activists and supportive NGOs played an important role in initiating the projects. As a result, by the mid-1980s, the main actions of the urban movement had shifted substantially from defensive measures, such as resisting evictions, opposing land tax and regularization charges, or simply getting rid of corrupt community leaders, towards much more active demands. *Protesta con propuesta* (protest with proposal) became the dominant theme, a position whose logical conclusion was the realization of housing and urban development projects, controlled by community organizations themselves. The combined efforts of the aspiring beneficiaries, the community leaders and organizers, the NGO professionals and FONHAPO finance, among other factors, effectively gave rise to a considerable number of projects that both fulfilled and recreated the FONHAPO story line.

The aims and achievements of many projects went beyond solving immediate housing needs. Employment, health and education, women's organizations, communal facilities, alternative technologies, ecology and integral neighbourhood development were strong on the agenda. So were new visions of community democracy: decision-making in assemblies and obligatory participation in the commissions set up to solve all the project requirements, from finding a plot of land to organizing the fiesta. The success stories are numerous and some have been documented.[16] Few self-critical appraisals have been undertaken. Whatever else, the importance of these experiences should not be underestimated for their local, national and international influence *as models in moulding political demands for government action.* By the end of the 1980s, the major task of most factions of the Popular Urban Movement in Mexico City was the development of popular or community housing projects (Moctezuma, 1993; Coulomb and Herrasti, 1993a; 1993b).

The aftermath of the 1985 earthquake was as significant a factor as FONHAPO in transforming community organizations into housing developers. After the devastation of many buildings in central Mexico City, there was an upsurge in inner-city community organizations. Initially, this mobilization was to resist possible evictions from damaged property. Later, in response to the government reconstruction programme favouring the re-housing of the affected population in situ, the community organizations promoted housing projects. The main thrust of the Popular Urban Movement in Mexico City shifted from tackling the problems of peripheral irregular settlements to building houses in the inner city. New political organizations were consolidated. After the initial reconstruction programme was completed, these political organizations demanded more finance for housing projects in central and intermediate areas. In addition to FONHAPO, Mexico City's federal district government set up a succession of housing finance agencies to build low-cost houses in central areas. These were generally medium-rise buildings of three or more storeys and loans were an absolute necessity. This process represented a small, but significant, attempt to counteract the depopulation of central areas. It was enthusiastically recorded as 'poor people against the state and capital: successful community mobilization for housing in Mexico City' by Eckstein (1990).

---

16 Based on Suárez Pareyón(1987); Herrasti (1996); Moctezuma (1999).

Ironically, most of these projects, including those financed by FONHAPO, were not carried out between 1983 to 1988, when housing policy was in tune with the aims and objectives of popular organizations. Between 1983 and 1987, only 782 FONHAPO loans (out of a total of 3954 in the federal district) went to social-sector housing projects. Over the following four years, this number increased to 2793 (out of almost 27,000 FONHAPO loans in the whole Mexico City area). FONHAPO's efforts represented slightly less than 10 per cent of all social-sector projects financed in the federal district. After 1992, FONHAPO investment in social-sector housing in the federal district practically dried up.

The time lag here is significant. The impact of FONHAPO's initial policies on community housing development was not instantaneous. It took several years for the communities, NGOs and, most importantly, other public-housing finance agencies to assimilate the model. By this time, those elements of FONHAPO's loan packages that had been initially designed to support community housing development, such as loans for land purchase and NGO technical assistance, had been withdrawn. The FONHAPO model for supporting community housing projects was being increasingly criticized for being 'clientelistic' and anti-democratic and for interfering with free-market processes.

While it is not possible to analyse FONHAPO's political impact at a national level because of the immense differences between one region and another, and also because of the lack of information, this is not the case for Mexico City. Here, the evolution of the general political climate over the last 20 years and of the Popular Urban Movement, in particular, is well documented and understood.

FONHAPO and politics

The switches from periphery to centre and from protest to housing project were not the only major changes running through the Popular Urban Movement during the 1980s. The loose agglomeration of community-based organizations that made up the movement was influenced by the general tide of political reform. Initially, these mostly Maoist-inspired 'mass-line' organizations had steered away from party politics. The hierarchical structure of traditional Marxist–Leninist parties were anathema to popular organizations who preferred open assemblies and commissions. Participation in electoral campaigns seemed pointless when there was no chance of winning. However, as the opposition parties expanded and mobilized around electoral campaigns, it became increasingly difficult for the Popular Urban Movement to remain on the margins. Their allegiance and, very often, their leaders became absorbed within electoral politics.

In 1988, for the first time in more than 50 years, the governing Revolutionary Institutional Party faced serious opposition in the presidential elections. The competition came from both sides; but the broad left coalition, the Frente Democrático, posed the major threat. It is clear that the Mexico City vote favoured the Frente candidate Cuauhtémoc Cárdenas, and it is widely believed that the PRI candidate, Carlos Salinas de Gortari, only won with electoral fraud. There were three consequences for community organizations and their relationship with FONHAPO. Firstly, the opposition coalition re-organized into various leftist parties, the strongest of which was the broad-based left-of-centre Party of the Democratic Revolution (PRD), headed by Cárdenas. The PRD became the natural political option for a large section of the community organizations. Secondly, there was gradual political reform within the federal district itself, leading to the establishment of a local congress and elections for its head of government in 1997 for the first time in 70 years. Thirdly, the PRI government took energetic steps to overhaul and modernize the popular support system for its party base, including radical reform of the federal social expenditure system.

The fact that party politics began to permeate community-housing production – the so-called 'social sector' – is reflected in the political affiliation of the organizations that received housing loans. This would not have been the case for projects before 1988. Although not comprehensive, the data painstakingly assembled by Anavel Monterrubio (Monterrubio, 1998) on projects within the federal district shows the increasing political significance of housing loans. As long as housing loans are a scarce commodity, it is virtually impossible to stop them from being used to muster support for local organizations affiliated to one or other political party: clientelism, in short. It could be argued that clientelistic practices that legitimize a one-party state are different from the type of clientelism employed by competing political parties. However, the differences need to be examined further, a task which goes beyond the scope of this chapter.

It was known that the 1982–1988 FONHAPO team was particularly sympathetic towards independent organizations. It is, therefore, more than possible that the PRI regarded the FONHAPO model as a real threat to their political hegemony over urban affairs – contributing, perhaps, to their disastrous election results in Mexico City in 1988. On the basis of the quantitative evidence, this seems unlikely because, as we have seen, FONHAPO funding for the social sector was fairly limited until then. Furthermore, the information suggests that after 1988, more than half of FONHAPO's client organizations whose political preferences are known were affiliated to the PRI. In fact, FONHAPO seems to have supported a higher proportion of PRI community organizations than the other housing finance agencies operating in the federal district. Moreover, the greater part of FONHAPO loans did not go to grassroots organizations but to local government housing institutions in states such as Aguascalientes, Baja California and Quintana Roo, which – during the 1980s at least – were in the hands of the PRI. However, it might be that the impact of the FONHAPO story line regarding its support for popular housing production, with all the political connotations that this implied, far exceeded its concrete results. From the point of view of the PRI, FONHAPO's bark may have posed more of a threat that its bite.

FONHAPO's demise during the 1990s: housing policy versus poor relief

FONHAPO's performance, 1988–1997

The first and most fundamental aspect of the emerging differences within FONHAPO from its original model concerns who was in charge of it and how this was reflected in the way that it operated. The year 1988 marked the transition from a FONHAPO run by housing professionals tuned in to the realities of Mexican housing poverty to one administered by career politicians coming from the ruling party's government bureaucracy. As the ex-director himself has suggested, this transition was accompanied by the introduction of a more authoritarian or vertical internal structure for decision-making, as well as important changes in the relationship between FONHAPO and community organizations. For these, access to credit became increasingly dependent upon their capacity to mobilize as pressure groups, an activity that substituted the previous more horizontal type of negotiations between FONHAPO officials and community representatives (Ortiz, 1996). Another effect of the administrative changes was the noticeable increase in FONHAPO's administrative costs after 1990 (see Table 4.5).

A crucial factor behind many of the changes in FONHAPO's processes was the increasing dependence upon World Bank financing noted earlier, which implied compliance with World Bank housing philosophy. In operational terms, this meant the withdrawal of explicit subsidies on the value of loans, increased effort in loan recovery, the suppression of FONHAPO's previous land banking policy and the elimination of loans for land purchase. Of all of these changes, those affecting access to land in built-up areas were seen by activists and NGOs as the greatest setback to the original FONHAPO community-housing production model.[17]

The second World Bank loan enabled FONHAPO to continue operating after 1990, albeit at diminishing levels and with a significant redistribution of priorities. There was a steady increase in the proportion of 'home improvement' loans of diminishing unit value. This probably reflects the use of FONHAPO mini loans in electoral campaigns. The proportion of loans for core housing remained fairly constant, while their unitary value increased. In other words, the housing solutions financed by these loans were increasingly expensive and, therefore, less accessible to the lowest-income population. Lastly, sites and services loans occupied a decreasing proportion of FONHAPO resources after 1990, while they also became increasingly expensive.

Although the information on recent trends is unreliable and contradictory, it would seem that Mexican government commitment to core housing, sites and services and home improvement loans did not fall with the demise of FONHAPO's popular housing policy. Instead, resources for these have been

---

17 This is reflected in discussions amongst the largely Mexico City-based NGOs and community housing developers who, as a concerted group, repeatedly demanded that FONHAPO should 'go back to the original model and (among other things) provide credit for land'. See, for example, the resolutions of the *Foro Permanente de Vivienda* (1991–1992) and the *Pacto de Guadalajara* (1995).

distributed through other channels. Housing policy for the 60 to 70 per cent of the population who cannot buy or rent a house on the open market or have access to subsidized loans from payroll funds is now a question of poverty relief.

New formulas for social and housing investment

Much has been written about the changes in Mexican social welfare policy introduced by President Carlos Salinas de Gortari after taking office in December 1988 (*El Cotidiano*, 1992; Cornelius et al, 1994). These affected the administration of federal social welfare investment. A widely publicized programme called the National Solidarity Programme (PRONASOL) was ostensibly aimed at compensating for the negative social effects of the structural adjustments prescribed by the International Monetary Fund (IMF) and the World Bank without interfering with the free market (Gordon, 1999). In 1992, it represented 20 per cent of all federal government investment, or 45 per cent of social investment. In sharp contrast to previous policies that, in discourse if not in practice, had been geared at stratified universal coverage, PRONASOL was highly focused, ostensibly to benefit those in most need. The programme covered a wide range of areas: social expenditure such as health services; urban infrastructure; education (subsistence grants to schoolchildren, repairs and maintenance to schools); food supplies; employment generation; and productive activities. Significantly, urban infrastructure included water and drainage provision, electricity supply and paved streets, and home improvement loans based on *crédito a la palabra* ('no need for collateral'). Thus, PRONASOL programmes overlapped with those of FONHAPO.

FONHAPO's function of channelling federal housing benefits towards the poorer sectors of the population has been gradually taken over by successive versions of decentralized federal poverty-relief programmes – first PRONASOL and, more recently, the Programme to Combat Poverty. Superficially, these programmes seem to share many of FONHAPO's aims regarding support for community initiatives. The fundamental differences between FONHAPO and PRONASOL's social housing policy have more to do with the intent behind their respective 'story lines' and their practical effects than with their discursive content.

Changes in housing policy directives, decentralization and the transformation of Mexico's federal social-investment policy expenditure, together with more general political changes, help to explain FONHAPO's transformation from 1989 onwards. The development and consolidation of a new brand of private housing developers further reduces the possibility of a return to FONHAPO-style federal housing policy. The liberalization of mortgage funds from commercial banks in 1989, closely followed by the radical reforms to the payroll funds that privatized all development operations, gave an additional boost to the housing development industry, which has increasingly expanded from the contracting business, landed property and the financial sector. The larger firms now integrate land banking, promotion, design, construction and commercialization. Most act locally, although some extend their operations to various cities all over the country and internationally. In 1994, the National

Federation of Industrial Housing Promoters (PROVICAC) had over 900 members, which, according to Barragán (1994), by then were responsible for almost all formal housing production in the country.[18]

These developers are now building at scale, often with projects for over 10,000 units, in most of Mexico's major cities, usually on the outskirts. Quality is questionable, as is the impact on the urban and rural environment. Catering initially for the middle-income market, they now mainly produce housing paid for by subsidized loans provided by a low-income housing trust fund, Fondo de Operacion y Financiamiento Bancario a la Vivienda (FOVI) (with World Bank loans), and the payroll housing funds. At the lower end of their market, households with around four times the minimum wage, there is an overlap between the effective demand for developers' housing and what used to be the upper ranges of FONHAPO's target population and the irregular market. However, none of the housing loan schemes in operation can offer a completed dwelling to a householder with much less than four times the minimum family wage, although the developers are trying their utmost to reach this market. The poorer half of the population is still obliged to resort to new, and perhaps more impoverished, variations of the 'self-build' syndrome of the irregular settlement.

Conclusions

Many conclusions are to be drawn from the FONHAPO experience:

- FONHAPO's actual performance shows important discrepancies with FONHAPO's main 'story line' concerning the promotion of community housing development and what happened. This is true for the initial period; but the divergence increased drastically from 1988 onwards. Ironically, as FONHAPO's actual performance moved further away from the original story line, this acquired increasing acceptance at a national level through the demands of popular urban organizations, NGOs and certain critical academic texts. At the same time, the model was propagated internationally, mainly via the Habitat International Coalition, where it has received wide recognition and applause.
- One important aspect of this discrepancy is that FONHAPO never was, and never could have been, about solving the housing problems of the very poor in Mexico. Rather, it involved improving the housing conditions of the poorer, and not so poor, sectors of the working population.
- FONHAPO's 'story line' may have been much more successful in that it has had more profound and far-reaching consequences for the conceptualization of housing finance policies than its concrete achievements in Mexico.
- The discrepancy between what was intended to happen and what did happen should not detract from some very real achievements, even though these

---

18 After 1995, unlike the rest of the Mexican construction, the housing development industry has flourished under government housing policy to the extent that, in 2002, PROVICAC was transformed into the National Chamber of Housing Developers, independent from the National Chamber of the Construction Industry.

were not necessarily envisaged beforehand. FONHAPO programmes helped to consolidate provincial government housing institutes, including those operating within the federal district (Mexico City). Some of these agencies have now decentralized to the municipal level. In some regions, especially the more prosperous ones, they were successful in tackling some of the problems associated with irregular settlement formation within the framework of planned urban development and political decentralization.

- The FONHAPO story highlights the importance of the individuals involved – not as 'ideal types' of social actors but as particular people. The primary people in this story are the professionals who set up FONHAPO in the first place, the leaders of the Popular Urban Movement who took on board the FONHAPO project and the NGO members who acted as intermediaries in the process and helped to propagate the model.

- By emphasizing the role of the particular individuals involved, it becomes clear that the strength of FONHAPO's 'story line' lies in providing the vision for others involved at the level of local government, community organizations or NGOs. In particular, the FONHAPO vision concerning improving housing for the poor has been wholly or partially assimilated within local government housing practice in many areas. This is in sharp contrast to the mindset currently dominating Mexican federal house-building policy, inspired as it is by much more mythical 'story lines', such as free-market mechanisms and cost recovery.

- Although Mexican housing policy and practice until the 1980s can be, and has been, highly criticized, World Bank interference in the process did not improve options available to the poor and the very poor, while Mexico's incursion into free-market mortgage finance during the early 1990s had disastrous consequences, bringing financial ruin to thousands of middle-income families, not to mention the banks themselves.

- One criticism of the FONHAPO story line is that it is based on a very particular set of geographically localized experiences. The FONHAPO model needs to be adapted to local conditions, and demands (or suggestions) regarding housing policy also need to be adapted. For example, for the popular organizations in Mexico City and for the NGOs who advise them, access to centrally located land is vital. Building medium-density low-cost housing on brownfield sites makes sense environmentally as it uses existing services and avoids urban sprawl. However, these priorities need not necessarily apply in other cities.

- It is highly unlikely that the FONHAPO model will be reinstated as Mexican housing policy in the near future at federal level. For this reason, and considering the previous points, demands (and suggestions) regarding these matters should perhaps insist less on the return of generalized 'FONHAPO-type measures'; rather, they should emphasize localized needs in the context of municipal development and planning, concentrating on the availability of existing funding sources. Furthermore, in the light of what has been suggested about the importance of individuals, it is clear that demands specifying who should implement the programmes might be just as important as what programmes should be implemented.

- There can be no unified evaluation of FONHAPO. From the point of view of the federal government policy-maker (or the World Bank), FONHAPO was questioned in terms of its subsidy policy or medium-term economic viability. For the community activist, to the extent that FONHAPO provided grist to her or his political mill, the immediate problem was the disappearance of vital resources. For the NGO professional, whose work and even whose rationale had begun to depend a great deal upon the FONHAPO projects, keeping the model at any cost became extremely important.
- Finally, even though FONHAPO's 'story line' is beginning to wear thin, it continues to inspire some localized housing processes, individuals working within these processes and those who aspire to a better home.

References

Azuela, A (1989) *La Ciudad, la Propiedad privada y el Derecho*, El Colegio de México, Mexico

Barragán, J I (1994) *100 Años de Vivienda en México. Historia de la Vivienda en una óptica Social y Económica*, Urbis Internacional, Monterrey, Mexico

Boltvinik, L (1999) 'Medio siglo perdido', *La Jornada*, 25 June, p22

Borja, J (1975) *Movimientos Sociales Urbanos*, Ediciones SIAP, Buenos Aires

Carvajal, S (1998) 'Política habitacional en Uruguay', in Ma E Herrasti and J Villavicencio (eds) *La Política Habitacional en México y América Latina*, Universidad Autónoma Metropolitana, Azcapotzalco, Mexico, pp181–194

Castells, M (1974) *Movimientos Sociales Urbanos*, Siglo XXI, Mexico

Castells, M (1976) *La Cuestión Urbana*, second augmented edition in Spanish, Siglo XXI, Mexico (first edition in Spanish, 1974; English version: Castells, M (1977) *The Urban Question*, MIT Press, Boston)

CENVI (Centro de la Vivienda y Estudios Urbanos) (1997) *México: Programas de Vivienda para Población de Bajos Ingresos. Un Estudio de Iniciativas al Nivel Estatal,* Unpublished report, CENVI

Chávez, A M and F Rodríguez (1998) 'El programa Solidaridad y la organización comunitaria en el estado de Morelos', *Estudios Demográfico y Urbanos*, no 38, pp379–405

Cockcroft, J (1983) *Mexico. Class Formation, Capital Accumulation and the State*, Monthly Review Press, New York

Comisión Intersecretarial de Planeación, Programación y Financiamiento de la Vivienda (1982) *Estadística Básica de Vivienda 1973–1980,* cuadro 7, Mexico City

Connolly, P (1986) 'The Guerrero Housing Cooperative: Mexico City', in R May (ed) *The Urbanization Revolution: Planning a New Agenda for Human Settlements*, Plenum Press, New York

Connolly, P (1990) 'Housing and the state in Mexico', in G Shidlo (ed) *Housing Policy in Developing Countries*, Routledge, London and New York

Cornelius, W (1975) *Politics and the Migrant Poor in Mexico City*, Stanford University Press, Stanford

Cornelius, W, A Craig and J Fox (eds) (1994) *Transforming State–Society Relations in Mexico: the National Solidarity Strategy*, Centre for US-Mexican Studies, La Jolla, California

Coulomb, R and C Sánchez (1992) *Pobreza Urbana, Autogestión y Política*, Centro de la Vivienda y Estudios Urbanos, Mexico

Coulomb, R and Ma E Herrasti (1993a) 'Espacios y actores sociales de la autogestión urbana en la Ciudad de México', in R Coulomb and E Duhau (eds) *Dinámica Urbana y*

Procesos Socio-Políticos, Universidad Autónoma Metropolitana/Centro de la Vivienda y Estudios Urbanos, Mexico

Coulomb, R and Ma E Herrasti (1993b) 'Elementos para una sociología de la autogestión urbana en la Ciudad de México', in R Coulomb and E Duhau (eds) *Dinámica Urbana y Procesos Socio-Políticos*, Universidad Autónoma Metropolitana/Centro de la Vivienda y Estudios Urbanos, Mexico

DESAL (1969) *Marginalidad en América Latina: un Ensayo de Diagnóstico*, Editorial Herder, Barcelona

DESAL (1970) *Marginalidad, Promoción Popular e Integración Latinoamericana*, Ediciones Troquel, Buenos Aires

Duhau, E (1988) 'Política habitacional para los sectores populares en México. La experiencia de FONHAPO', *Medio Ambiente y Urbanización*, vol 7, September, pp34–45

Duhau, E and M Schteingart (1999) 'Nuevas orientaciones en las políticas sociales para los pobres en México y Colombia', in M Schteingart (eds) *Políticas Sociales para los Pobres en América Latina*, Miguel Angel Porrúa, Mexico

Eckstein, S (1990) 'Poor people versus the state and capital: anatomy of a successful community mobilization for housing in Mexico City', *International Journal of Urban and Regional Research*, vol 14, no 2, pp274–296

El Cotidiano (1992) Special edition dedicated to *Solidaridad*, July–August, vol 8

FONHAPO (1984) *Programa de Evaluación*, Mexico City

FONHAPO (1985) *Programa de Evaluación*, Mexico City

FONHAPO (1987a) *Gestión Financiera en Apoyo a la Vivienda Popular. Memoria de Actividades*, Fideicomiso Fondo Nacional de Habitaciones Populares, Mexico

FONHAPO (1987b) *Reglas de Operación y Políticas de Administración Crediticia*, Mexico City

FONHAPO (1994) *Programa de Evaluación*, Mexico City

FONHAPO (1995) *Evolución Estadística 1982–1994*, Mexico City

Gordon, S (1999) 'Del universalismo estratificado a los programas focalizados. Una aproxiación a la política social en México', in M Schteingart (ed) *Políticas Sociales para los Pobres en América Latina*, Miguel Angel Porrúa, Mexico

Herrasti, M A (1996) 'A revolving fund for access to land and the promotion of self-managed popular real estate in Mexico', *Trialog, Zeitshrift für das Planen und Bauen en der Dritten Welt*, no 4, pp43–46

Jiménez, E (2000) *El Principio de la Irregularidad. Mercado del Suelo para Vivienda en Aguascalientes, 1975–1998*, Universidad de Guadalajara/Juan Pablos Editores/Centro de Investigaciones y Estudios Multidisciplinarios de Aguascalientes, Aguascalientes

Lojkine, J (1979) *El Marxismo, el Estado y la Cuestión Urbana*, Siglo XXI, Mexico

Moctezuma, P (1993) 'Del Movimiento Urbano Popular a los movimientos comunitarios', *El Cotidiano*, no 57, pp3–16

Moctezuma, P (1999) *Despertares. Comunidad y Organización Urbano Popular en México1970-1994*, Universidad Iberoamericana-Universidad Autónoma Metropolitana, Mexico

Monterrubio, A (1998) *Autogestión y Política Habitacional en el Distrito Federal –19831997*, Master Dissertation in Planeación y Políticas Metropolitanas, Universidad Autónoma Metropolitana-Azcapotzalco, Mexico City

Ortiz, E (1996) *FONHAPO Gestión y Desarrollo de un Fondo Público en Apoyo de la Producción Social de Vivienda*, Habitat International Coalition, Mexico

Padget, L V (1966) *The Mexican Political System*, Houghton Mifflin Company, Boston

Poder Ejecutivo Federal (1996) *Alianza para la Vivienda*, México DF

Puebla, C (1997) *La política de vivienda en México (1972–1994). Los Casos de INFONAVIT y FONHAPO*, Masters dissertation in Urban Development, El Colegio de México, Mexico

Schteingart, M and B Graizbord (1998) *Vivienda y Vida Urbana en la Ciudad de México. La Acción de INFONAVIT*, El Colegio e México, Mexico

Suárez Pareyón, A (1987) *El Programa de Vivienda del Molino*, Centro de la Vivienda y Estudios Urbanos, Mexico

Suárez Pareyón, A and G Romero (1997) (eds) *Estudio de Seis Casos de Autogestión en Proyectos Habitacionales Asesorados por Organizaciones no Gubernamentales*, Presented in the V Assembly of the Network 'Viviendo y Construyendo', programa Ineramericano de Ciencia y tecnología para el desarrollo, CYTED, Lima

Topalov, C (1979) *La Urbanización Capitalista*, Ediciones Edicol, Mexico

Turner, B (1988) (ed) *Building Community. A Third World Case Book*, Habitat International Coalition/Building Community Books, London

Turner, J F C (1969) 'Uncontrolled urban settlements: problems and policies' in G Breese (ed) *The City in Newly Developed Countries*, Prentice Hall, New Jersey, pp507–534

Varley, A (1985) 'Urbanization and agrarian law: the case of Mexico City', *Bulletin of Latin American Research*, vol 4, pp1–16

Ward, P (1986) *Welfare Politics in Mexico: Papering over the Cracks*, Allen and Unwin, London

Ward, P (1998) *Mexico City*, John Wiley (revised edition), Chichester

Chapter 5

Participation and Sustainability in Social Projects: The Experience of the Local Development Programme in Nicaragua

Alfredo Stein

Introduction

This chapter describes the work of the Local Development Programme (PRODEL) in eight cities in Nicaragua, where it provided small grants for infrastructure and community works projects executed by municipal governments and community organizations, as well as loans for housing improvement and micro-enterprises. The external funds provided by the Swedish International Development Cooperation Agency (Sida) were matched by municipal, community and household contributions. Between 1994 and 1998, more than 38,000 households benefited and both loan programmes achieved good levels of cost recovery. The chapter describes these programmes and the micro-planning workshops and other methodologies through which households and communities were given more scope for participation. It explains how local governments and the bank responsible for managing the loans learned to work in a more participatory way, and it outlines the measures taken to ensure that the needs and priorities of women and children were addressed.

Background[1]

Nicaraguan society experienced major changes during the 1990s. From a situation of war and political polarization, progress was made in the process of national reconciliation and democratization. From a collapsed, centrally managed economy with record levels of hyper-inflation and the highest foreign debt in the region – 700 per cent of its gross domestic product (GDP) – it was

1 This section is based on PRODEL (1997a).

transformed into a market economy with incipient growth, relative financial stability and a significant reduction in the fiscal deficit. This economic transformation required a series of structural adjustment measures that had a negative impact on the poorest sectors of society. Unemployment and under-employment increased. Between 1990 and 1995, the government reduced the number of public employees from 284,800 to 95,600, including a reduction of 84,000 in the armed forces (Villalta, 1997). Wages, which already had little purchasing power, were frozen and access to basic services and infrastructure was reduced.

In this context, the governments of Sweden and Nicaragua signed a cooperation agreement in 1993 for the implementation of the Local Development Programme (PRODEL). The two governments were interested in creating a decentralized, participatory and sustainable programme that would contribute to mitigating the negative impacts of structural adjustment policies, especially in urban areas, and facilitate the process of national reconciliation and democratization.

During PRODEL's first phase (1994–1997), it operated in three mid-sized cities (León, Chinandega and Estelí) and two small cities (Somoto and Ocotal). These cities had experienced serious problems associated with rapid population growth as a result of the internal displacements caused by the civil war and the return of refugees from neighbouring countries. They also faced increased levels of unemployment and poverty and a lack of basic services and infrastructure. During PRODEL's second phase (1998–2001), two new mid-sized cities (Matagalpa and Jinotega) and one small city (Chichigalpa) were incorporated. The total population of these municipalities represented 15 per cent of Nicaragua's total population and 19 per cent of its urban population.

With regard to unsatisfied basic needs, except for León, the cities in the first phase were below the national average in terms of the availability of drinking water, sewers, roads, electric power and waste collection services (see Table 5.1). More than half of the population in the Phase 1 cities had incomes below the cost of a basic food basket and more than one basic need unfulfilled (chronic poor) and another 30 per cent were classified as 'recent poor' and 'borderline poor'.[2] The proportion of 'chronic poor' and 'recent poor' within these cities' populations was higher than the national average and well above the figures for the national capital, Managua.

The poverty indicators highlight the type of urban population that PRODEL was working with:

- large segments of population lacking basic services and with incomes below the cost of the basic food basket;
- many households with income levels above the cost of the basic food basket but living in neighbourhoods that lack one or more basic services;

2 The 'recent poor' are primarily those who have experienced a recent deterioration in income; they have incomes equivalent to one to two times the cost of a basic food basket but are not lacking basic needs such as drinking water, sanitation and electricity. The 'borderline poor' are households with incomes equivalent to more than twice the cost of a basic food basket but with one or more unfulfilled basic needs.

Table 5.1 *Conditions in the cities where PRODEL operated during Phase I (1994–1997)*

City	Number of communities	Communities served by PRODEL	Percentage of communities served	Percentage average coverage of basic services per city				
				Potable water	Sewers	Streets	Electricity	Waste collection
León	126	30	24%	90	60	70	85	75
Chinandega	52	32	62%	74	38	75	75	51
Estelí	54	30	56%	78	35	15	75	55
Somoto	22	12	55%	72	43	60	85	30
Ocotal	18	9	50%	80	10	45	78	65
Total	272	113	42%					
Average coverage in urban areas at the national level, including Managua				90	44	37	93	78

Source: PRODEL (1997b) and Social Action Ministry (1995)

• households in inner-city areas where all of the services may be available but with income levels below the cost of the basic food basket.

Some of these neighbourhoods have a mixed population consisting of professionals with higher levels of education who live next to unskilled labourers, self-employed workers and families employed in the informal economy.

The absence of effective housing policies and programmes aimed at these sectors means that the majority of housing has been constructed by the population on its own initiative. Most housing does not meet minimum standards with regard to health, safety and environmental quality. These municipalities were also particularly affected during Hurricane Mitch in October 1998. About 10 per cent of the housing stock in the eight cities was damaged or destroyed. Much of the damage occurred in poor neighbourhoods that lacked basic services.

The Local Development Programme (PRODEL)

Objectives and strategy

Since it began operations in April 1994, PRODEL's development objective has been to improve the physical environment and the socio-economic conditions of the poor population in the cities where it operates, with a special interest in ensuring improvements for women and vulnerable groups, and that the improvements can be sustained. To achieve these goals, the following components were developed:

• Infrastructure and community works, which included the introduction, expansion, repair and improvement of infrastructure and community works through small-scale projects costing up to US$50,000. These included potable water, sewers and storm drains; treatment plants; pedestrian and vehicular road systems, including sidewalks, roads, gutters and pedestrian by-passes; public and household electrification; health centres, day-care centres, multi-use centres, school rooms, playgrounds and sporting facilities; and sites for the collection, disposal and treatment of waste.

- Housing improvement: small loans targeted at poor families who could afford to repay. Loans were used to enlarge and improve houses, including the construction of additional rooms; repair and replacement of roofs; repair and reinforcement of outdoor walls; the construction and/or improvement of floors and interior walls; the installation of indoor plumbing and sewage facilities; electrification; and upgrading kitchens.
- Financial assistance to micro-enterprises in the neighbourhoods from small short-term loans (between US$300 and US$1500) for fixed and working capital, as well as for the creation of new micro-enterprises for services, trade and manufacturing. These loans were directed to micro-enterprises owned and operated by women.
- Technical assistance and institutional development to strengthen the capacities of local governments in the administration and management of social investments with community participation, as well as encouraging financial institutions to become involved in non-conventional lending programmes for housing improvements and micro-enterprise loans to poor families.

Main actors

Implementation was based on the formation of broad, but clearly defined, cooperative alliances between various institutions. The system of incentives and co-financing supported the participation of all local actors in management, contribution of resources and decision-making. The reason for this combination was to have flexible responses to the urgent basic social problems in the predominantly low-income neighbourhoods and, at the same time, to stimulate longer-term development processes. Thus, PRODEL supported the decentralization process by promoting citizen participation, assisting local governments and creating a financial and institutional framework that is sustainable over the long term. The principal entities involved in these processes were the following:

- *The Instituto Nicaragüense de Fomento Municipal* (INIFOM), or the Nicaraguan Municipal Development Institute, is a central government institution that administered the funds provided by Sida and was responsible for PRODEL's execution and supervision. INIFOM formed a central executive unit to promote and coordinate actions at a central and local level with a national coordinator, an infrastructure coordinator, a housing and micro-enterprise coordinator and four people responsible for coordinating activities in the municipalities where the programme operates.
- *The municipal governments* were responsible for administering the infrastructure component and providing technical assistance to households with housing

improvement loans. Each city created an executive technical unit made up of personnel from the municipal government (a technical person, a social promoter, two technical experts in housing construction and one administrative/financial specialist). Each municipality signed a framework agreement with INIFOM for the implementation of the programme.

- *The consultative council*: the eight mayors, the executive director of INIFOM and one representative from Sida formed a consultative council responsible for defining the strategic guidelines and supervising implementation.
- *Banco de Crédito Popular*: this state commercial bank was responsible for screening, approving and disbursing the loans and supervising their use. The bank was also responsible for collecting payments for the home improvement and micro-enterprise loans.
- *Non-governmental organizations (NGOs)*: PRODEL supported new financial intermediaries to create more competition in non-conventional lending. In November 1998, the programme expanded the use of non-conventional financial intermediaries to allocate loans to poor sectors of the cities where it operates that were severely affected by Hurricane Mitch. Two NGOs, ACODEP and Nitlapán-FDL, were selected after a tender and bidding process to manage loans for housing improvements and micro-enterprises. The NGOs were interested in diversifying their portfolio and both were recognized as having among the best performance for NGOs working with micro-enterprises. In early 1999, they started operations in the eight cities, primarily in neighbourhoods where the bank was not operating.
- *The families who participate in the definition, execution, financing and maintenance of the infrastructure projects and who receive the housing and micro-enterprise loans*: the principal benefit that they derived from their participation was the improvement in their living conditions and the acquisition of new skills in negotiating with public and private sectors to identify solutions to their problems. The families participated either directly or via community project committees established for the organization and internal representation of the neighbourhoods who were responsible for the administration, execution and maintenance of the infrastructure and community projects. Community meetings elected the commissions, and their representatives were members of the municipal commission that the municipal government established for the coordination and supervision of the components of PRODEL.

Achievements

The achievements and limitations of PRODEL's participatory model must be understood in the context of a society that for years was politically polarized, and which only took its first steps towards national reconciliation and reconstruction during the early 1990s. PRODEL also had to face changes in local and central governments. In January 1997, there was a 90 per cent turnover in personnel in the institutions directly involved in the administration and execution of the components, including the PRODEL management.

Infrastructure and community projects component

Between April 1994 and December 1998, 260 infrastructure and community projects were carried out in 155 different neighbourhoods, benefiting more than 38,000 families. The total investment was US$4.4 million (an average of US$16,972 per project or US$22 per person), of which 43 per cent came from contributions from municipal governments and beneficiary communities (in kind, cash, materials, tools, labour, administration and supervision), with the other 57 per cent coming from the programme.

Of the projects, 35 per cent consisted of improvements to roads, gutters and sidewalks; 10 per cent related to the improvement and expansion of potable water and sewage systems; and 14 per cent related to rainwater and storm water drainage projects. Another 18 per cent went to electrification (public lighting and/or household connections) and 23 per cent to community infrastructure (including construction, improvement, expansion and repair of primary schools, day-care centres, health centres, parks and playgrounds). In these 260 projects, the communities contributed some 132,000 days of work, both volunteer and paid, using their own resources.

The infrastructure components were concentrated in the poorest neighbourhoods in the five cities. Their scale was nearly twice that originally planned. The reasons for this are closely linked to community participation. Initially, the plan was to support 64 projects in Phase 1 to be completed in three years at an average cost to PRODEL of US$20,000. In response to the requirement for local matching funds, the municipal governments decided to expand the coverage of the programme to more neighbourhoods. The result was a greater number of lower-cost projects that mobilized more people and resources in each community and required fewer funds per project from central and municipal governments. In addition, the responsibility displayed by families in repaying house improvement and micro-enterprise loans made it possible to refinance new loans and reduced the need for new funds. This allowed a re-allocation of funds to finance more infrastructure projects.

Housing improvement and micro-enterprise loans

In five years, more than 4168 loans were given for housing improvements (total disbursed funds reached US$2.7 million). These loans reached approximately 4000 families (by 1998, around 5 per cent of beneficiary families have taken a second loan). Families also contributed with their own resources, construction materials, labour, transportation and project administration (equivalent to at least 15 per cent of the value of the labour, transport and building materials). Of the families who took on loans, 70 per cent had monthly incomes of US$200 or less, including many with monthly incomes below US$100. This indicates that there is a sector of the population who, despite a low income, can afford to make monthly payments.

More than 12,451 loans were provided for micro-entrepreneurs. Almost US$5.5 million was disbursed, benefiting approximately 2400 existing families. 70 new micro-enterprises were created, which gave jobs to some 210 people. In this component, too, the final results exceeded the initial targets.

Women received more than 60 per cent of the housing improvement loans and 70 per cent of the micro-enterprise loans. Approximately 30 per cent of loans were allocated to women-headed households. One reason for this high participation of women was the approach that PRODEL developed with the bank that managed the loans. Information meetings, credit analysis and loan collection were done in the communities where women lived and worked. So, too, was the technical assistance for the design and budgeting of the housing improvement loans.

With more than 6500 borrowers, the default indicators for the loan programmes make PRODEL one of Nicaragua's most successful programmes. Levels of cost recovery show that there is a real possibility that the funds would become financially sustainable. In spite of two critical factors that affected the programme during 1998 – Hurricane Mitch and the process of privatization for the Banco de Crédito Popular – the default risk or portfolio at risk rate was around 18 per cent in the housing improvement loan component and 10 per cent in the micro-enterprise component.[3] An external evaluation of PRODEL's housing and micro-enterprise loans in 1998 showed that only 1.5 per cent of total loans had more than three payments in arrears or were at risk of being lost and never recovered.

After five years of operation, the funds recovered through interest payments to the revolving fund covered the bank's direct costs and a good part of the costs of PRODEL personnel, who are directly involved in monitoring the loan components. In 1998, accumulated interest recovered from loan portfolio totalled US$382,507 and annual payments to the bank for the administration of the portfolio totalled US$251,386. A provision for those loans that were are not recoverable totalled US$43,268. Thus, the sustainability indicator measured as income generated by the portfolio divided by the commission paid to the bank and provision for unrecoverable loans equalled 1.16. The revolving fund was able to generate a surplus of 16 per cent in 1998. Over four years, the overall profit was 12 per cent.

This success is particularly noteworthy in light of Nicaragua's economic crisis, which includes high levels of unemployment and a lack of experience with credit. It also shows the priority that poor sectors give to repaying their debts. The results also show that this is not simply an isolated project but a pilot experience with lessons to be learned. There is the potential of the programme to be replicated in other cities in Nicaragua (and elsewhere). The government of Nicaragua and Sida decided to continue financing the programme for a second phase in the cities where it has been operating and to expand the programme to three additional cities. Some of the lessons from the PRODEL model have also started to be applied in other countries. *The ultimate goal is to define and institutionalize a participatory model for the provision of services, infrastructure, housing and income generation that will be sustainable on a national level.*

---

3 The method that the bank and PRODEL agreed for measuring the default rate is as follows: the total of the outstanding capital of those loans that are in arrears divided by the total outstanding capital of the whole portfolio. A loan is considered to be in arrears the day after payment is due but not complied with.

The community participation model

The PRODEL community participation model is based on the premise that families who participate in decision-making processes and the administration and execution of infrastructure and housing improvement have an increased commitment to co-finance and maintain the projects. This ensures the sustainability of the social investments over the long term. This section describes and analyses the process of participation in the infrastructure, housing improvement and micro-finance components.

Infrastructure component

INIFOM signs a framework agreement with each municipal government, defining the incentives, responsibilities and contributions of each party to the execution of the different components. It then transfers funds to the municipal governments if certain conditions are met: there must be community participation in the identification, execution and maintenance of projects; there must be a commitment from the municipal council to allocate resources to the infrastructure projects; municipalities must provide technical assistance to those families who are entitled to a housing improvement loan; and municipalities need to form an executing technical unit to manage the projects.

The municipal council, under the leadership of the mayor, forms a municipal commission with representatives of the main entities involved in the programme (INIFOM, the municipal government, the bank and other public service institutions). Every year, based on a set of criteria established by PRODEL, the municipal commission defines and selects the action areas of the programme in the city. Those communities with the highest levels of poverty, the lowest levels of basic services and social infrastructure, and with organized communities, are usually selected.

Community representatives can attend the municipal commission's monthly meetings. Once it has been decided to include a community in the programme, the municipal government holds a micro-planning workshop with the participation of at least 20 members of the community (the majority being women). Usually, an existing community organization coordinates and makes arrangements for the workshop (finding a location, sending invitations and arranging refreshments). During the micro-planning exercise, the participants (the 20 community members and the technicians from the municipal government and from other government institutions) visit the community in small groups to talk with the inhabitants and to acquire in situ impressions about the community's concerns. Special emphasis is placed on interviews with women and children. Then a group exercise is conducted to identify and prioritize the main problems of the community. Priorities are assigned, proposed solutions are discussed and negotiated, and the potential project to be financed by PRODEL is identified. Clean-up actions are also planned – in particular, those related to waste collection. At the end of the workshop, the representatives of the municipal government and the community organization sign an agreement that includes the principal results of the micro-planning exercise.[4]

---

4 PRODEL has adapted the micro-planning method described in Goethert, Hamdi et al (1992) to the Nicaraguan context.

A general assembly of the community is then organized to which the report on the results of the workshop is presented. Technical personnel from the local government explain the procedure for implementing the projects and define the contributions by both the municipal government and the community. Decisions are made regarding the community contributions to the various activities described in the budget. This information must be annexed to the project profile presented by the municipality to PRODEL for approval.

In this general assembly, a formal structure consisting of seven people from the community is elected: the Community Project Administration Committee (CPAC). This committee has to review the budget and design prepared by the municipal technicians, particularly the general characteristics regarding the location and dimensions of the project. CPAC also coordinates the management of the project and administers the stocks of materials, equipment and labour supplied both by the municipal government and the community. The committee reports back to the community on progress and on the use of the funds. It also participates in the financial and physical audit of the project, which is conducted by the municipal government and PRODEL.

CPAC organizes the rest of the community in the physical execution of the project. Depending upon the type and complexity of the project, the municipal government makes an initial proposal for the organization that can be done by block or by house. The municipal government's social services office trains the committee in the management and administration of the building materials warehouse and the methods used to manage the people employed in the project. The committee and the municipal technicians select the area where the materials will be stored. When the contribution is monetary, they initiate the collection among the community.

Once the project has been approved, PRODEL signs a specific contract with the municipal government and disburses the funds to a special account to allow project execution. This contract stipulates the contributions by the parties for each construction activity. PRODEL pays up to 60 per cent of the total project costs. The rest comes from local contributions (in the form of investments in materials, skilled and unskilled labour, machinery and tools, administration and cash) from the community and from the municipal government, and may generally not be less than 40 per cent of total project costs. PRODEL will not finance the project unless the community is prepared to make its own contribution. When the project starts, the CPAC manages the warehouse, the materials, tools and equipment, and the community's labour contributions. The community contributes to project execution in the form of skilled and unskilled labour, depending upon the type of project, either as volunteer labour or as contract labour hired by the community.

The general procedure by which the community participates in project execution depends upon whether the infrastructure being built is for public or private (household) use. For the installation of on-site infrastructure, each family participates individually. In the improvement of schools, skilled labour is hired. In the construction of sewage systems, each family excavates the section in front of its house. When gutters are built, teams are formed that work weekly.

Combined teams carry out projects that involve the construction of a sewage system, the excavations and installing manholes.

The CPAC and other community members work with technical staff from the municipal government and employees of PRODEL in auditing the project. They prepare an inventory of the existing materials and tools at the warehouse (entries and withdrawals), comparing them with the purchase vouchers from the municipal government. They also keep track of the total amount of labour provided. The purpose of this activity is to increase social control over the utilization of the funds and to establish a routine and more direct procedure for the municipal government to report directly to their constituency.

Members of the CPAC and other community members also take part in project evaluations carried out by the municipal commission. These evaluations analyse the experience, the level of organization and the community participation achieved, as well as the quality of the completed project. This process can also be used to identify other requirements related to the project, to resell any surplus materials and to transfer any surplus funds to the municipal accounts for use in other projects. In some of the cities, the organizational experience that was acquired helped the subsequent management and administration of other projects by the communities.

Evaluation of the participatory process in the infrastructure component

The infrastructure component shows that limited amounts of external finance can generate benefits for tens of thousands of households in low-income neighbourhoods. PRODEL has succeeded in meeting its original objectives in terms of working with the poorest groups, mobilizing local resources and establishing a participatory methodology that has been replicated in eight cities.

PRODEL's ability to mobilize matching municipal and community contributions is the key to this process. The reason for introducing participatory financial and administrative procedures was to improve efficiency and transparency in managing funds by municipal governments and to improve their relations with communities. *The community participates throughout the project cycle, from defining the areas of action and identifying problems and projects to managing and administrating funds.* This has created a significant capacity to target resources and to identify and plan infrastructure and urban projects.

Municipal commissions

The participation of community representatives in these commissions has been more formal and relatively passive, and other members of the commission have, in general, made the decisions. Nevertheless, the presence of representatives has legitimized the actions of the municipal government vis-à-vis the communities. It has also given the community representatives the opportunity to learn about (and contribute to) the process by which the municipality establishes annual operating budgets and general development work plans. The community leaders also had an opportunity to become acquainted with the most important factors

---

BOX 5.1 CHANGES IN PRIORITIES ARISING FROM MICRO-PLANNING IN ESTELÍ

As part of its urban development plan, Estelí's local government wanted to build a children's playground in *barrio* 'La Union'. The micro-planning exercise revealed that the community had different priorities. Many inhabitants of the *barrio*, disabled as a consequence of the civil war, urgently demanded the construction, upgrading and repair of the streets that would allow them to move in their wheelchairs without fear of getting stuck in the mud during winter. Street repairs in the neighbourhood and the construction of a 1-kilometre-long pedestrian sidewalk that connects the centre of the city with the community were carried out. With community participation from residents of *barrio* 'La Union' and other communities, the access road was improved and the sidewalk is currently being used by hundreds of families who live in the adjacent neighbourhoods.

---

involved in the decision-making process within the central and local institutions responsible for providing infrastructure and urban services.

Micro-planning workshops

Participation by community leaders and other community members is more active and intense. The mechanism allows participants to gain a greater understanding of their problems, the solutions to these problems and the type of infrastructure and community projects that can be carried out. Communities understand the criteria for assessing projects, such as the urgency, cost of the solution, sequence of work required, time required for the design and execution of the construction work, the technical complexity and the contributions from each party. On more than one occasion, there have been serious discrepancies between the urgency assigned to a problem by the municipal government and by the community (see Box 5.1). The micro-planning methodology helps to create consensus so that the technicians can gain a thorough understanding of the real problems facing the community, and the community understands the financial and technical complexities of a project.

The micro-planning workshop and its subsequent report to the general assembly meeting provide an opportunity for the community to earmark their contributions for the design phase, the execution and subsequent preventive maintenance. On some occasions, these contributions exceed the minimum required by the programme.

The negotiation of community contributions also depends upon the attitude of the municipal government's project manager. If the signals that he or she sends to define the involvement of the community counterparts are unclear, people tend to expect greater contributions from the programme and from the local government. This problem has been exacerbated in recent years as a number of social infrastructure projects have been funded by foreign aid and did not require any active participation from beneficiaries. In some local governments, and also within central government, this has generated the notion of a paternalistic government with citizens as clients, resulting in a passive 'wait and see' attitude in many communities. One of the *barrio* leaders of a community in Chinandega was asked to explain why the community did not want to take part in the PRODEL projects. He stated: 'Why should we get into something so complicated when we know that there are other programmes which have a great deal of money and we can get them without requiring anything in exchange and effort!'

Experience shows that the low levels of income are not an impediment to obtaining substantial financial contributions from very poor communities. When confronted with the limited alternatives that result from the scarcity of tax revenues and from budget cuts, the communities have demonstrated an ability to overcome habits and traditions of paternalism without necessarily threatening their low family incomes. The low income levels of the residents in the *barrio* Mauricio Cajina in Somoto, one of the poorest areas of the city (60 per cent of its economically active population is unemployed), did not prevent them from providing labour and making financial contributions to the development of their project. In four months, US$5000 was collected through the organization of raffles, community dinners, parties, dances and other activities all over the city. The money was used as their contribution to the construction of 285 metres of sewer line, one of the key projects to prevent floods.

Project design and preparation for project execution

Participation is intense at the level of the project committee but not necessarily in the rest of the community. The advantage of the process is that the community and leaders gain a better understanding of the technical and financial complexities of the design, and preparation for the execution, of the infrastructure projects. An awareness of the local factors that affect the residents assists the technical staff in overcoming the obstacles that are generally encountered when public services and infrastructure are introduced to existing squatter areas, and which can slow down the development of the project. Participation in the design phase is greater in the case of schools, parks and recreational facilities. For projects that involve the introduction or expansion of roads, electrification, sewers and water, the participation is less and the municipal technical staff must work harder to explain the aspects of the design and operation of the service. Participation in these phases means that local authorities must develop negotiating capacities to arrive at practical solutions to concrete problems that cannot only be solved by the municipal government. This requires a willingness to empower local communities to assume certain functions, giving the communities more space to participate in the decision-making process, and a transfer of more control in the administration of the resources provided by the municipal government.

In addition to optimizing resources, participation is an important vehicle of social communication to improve neighbourhood relations. This was the case in an electrification project financed by PRODEL in three communities in Ocotal. During the early 1990s, these communities were formed by ex-Sandinista soldiers, former soldiers of the Nicaraguan Resistance (*contras*) and refugee families who returned from neighbouring countries. The level of mistrust between these groups was high. As part of the project, the groups formed a single community project committee that managed and completed the project with a high level of participation from all three communities.

Project execution

This is the most delicate phase and requires considerable training and empowerment within municipal government. Tensions are frequently generated and are related to the fact that the technical and financial officers from the municipality believe that the empowerment process is something that is done exclusively by social workers, and that they do not become involved in the process of transferring know-how to the community. On more than one occasion, this phase has also rekindled acute conflicts within the neighbourhoods, which affects the ability to prioritize the problems, define possible solutions and form the project committee. On average, 3 per cent of the families in each neighbourhood do not want to contribute and this can generate obstacles to project execution.

If project approval is not rapid, and if the municipal government is not prepared for physical execution, the enthusiasm of the Community Project Administration Committee can decline. The community organization may turn out to be problematic if the time required by PRODEL, the municipal government and the community are not compatible. Projects that take longer to complete can also reduce the level of participation by families. Such projects require effective channels of promotion, communication and an understanding of the complexity of administering the organization and community participation in established squatter areas.

Participation in project execution and administration

This allows improved control of municipal resources. By combining the information managed by the municipal government with the information available in the community, it becomes possible to determine how and where the resources are being used, which gives greater transparency to managing the project by the local government. Concerns by local governments that they may not be able to meet the objectives set in their annual construction plans can lead them to limit the participation of the community and training for the execution. Consequently, this phase requires clear methods to minimize any conflicts with the traditional ways in which the municipal government makes decisions and administers resources. The auditing procedure, in the presence of community members, has also increased the level of trust between the community and the local government (see Box 5.2).

The administration of a project with community participation also results in decreased loss and waste in the use of construction materials. This is one of the areas where the building costs of projects carried out directly by municipal governments probably increase without community participation or under the terms of contracts, with construction companies hired through public or private tender offers. Although the costs for projects carried out with community participation are not necessarily lower, they are more realistic and some of the

---

BOX 5.2 MUNICIPAL LEARNING WITH REGARD TO PARTICIPATION

We previously had an erroneous idea of what community participation was. We knew that it was a key element with a great deal of economic and human potential for municipal development; but, in fact, we were not providing any space in which it could take place. We are now convinced that it is essential to have community participation in all possible processes and all stages of the projects. This participation has facilitated the creation of coordinating committees and the identification of opportunities between the communities and the local government, which has been beneficial to both sides. Involving the communities has given the barrios greater confidence in the management and transparency of the funds by the municipal government. There is now improved communication and understanding between the members of the communities and the municipal government, and a higher level of satisfaction on the part of the population with the projects that have been carried out (Manuel Maldonado, mayor of Somoto).

Previously, participation by the communities was limited to the public sessions of the city council. These are generally merely informative and requirements are planned in a very general context. PRODEL's methodology has made possible a more active participation by the communities, their leaders and the families in the decision-making process, and has created a forum for negotiation between the municipal government and the community for the prioritization of problems. The communities have also participated in solving their problems by a more direct involvement and by the contribution of resources. This process has changed attitudes on both sides. Previously, the community thought that the solution to problems was exclusively the obligation of the local government. For its part, the municipal government thought that the community only knew how to make demands and did not have the capacity to co-administer projects and to contribute resources for project execution (Marlon Oliva, former coordinator of the Ocotal Technical Unit).

---

resources saved can be used for physical extensions of the project. The costs for project supervision, if shared, are minimal. Administrative and supervisory costs for projects carried out using PRODEL's methodology are between 3 and 5 per cent of total project cost. Depending upon the type of project, at least one-quarter of these costs are contributed by the community and the remainder by the municipal government. The low cost of project supervision is due to the fact that one or two municipal engineers can supervise five projects at a time, which can result in greater efficiency in each project. A comparative analysis between paving projects carried out with and without community participation in the city of León shows that the cost of the project carried out by a private company was 23 per cent higher than the cost of the project carried out using the PRODEL methodology.[5] The reduction in the cost per square metre in the paving project

---

5 The longer document on which this chapter draws contains a more detailed account of this analysis; see Stein (2001).

with community participation arises from those activities where the contribution in labour and administration by the community can be more intensive. Such activities include moving earth (hauling selected material, cutting, filling, landscaping and compacting, and removing the excess dirt from the excavation), laying cobble stones, compacting pavements, cleaning, and the administration and supervision of the project.

Participation in executing projects also requires clear signals that help to establish the links between the community infrastructure or services introduced and the increase in the value of each home. This helps the families to appreciate the benefits that they receive from their contribution to community projects. For instance, support for community projects for laying sewers is increased as households know that this will also increase the value of their homes.

The type, amount, urgency and complexity of the project are obvious factors that municipal governments must take into consideration when determining participation procedures. Project managers are often reluctant to promote participation because they think that it delays the correct and timely completion of projects. The need for compliance with the municipal technical unit requirements, and continuous supervision and control of the implementation of the programme, have made municipal government department employees realize the variables involved in participatory projects.

The project approval and contracting methods generally employed by local governments or by state entities for works that require private tender offers can lead to significant delays in their execution. The joint execution of the project with the community involves the families in negotiations with central and local government entities, which helps to speed up the approval process as well as the disbursement of funds for project execution. Sometimes, the absence of reference costs means that local governments and community members do not have any criteria to determine whether the costs in the bid are realistic. At least in Nicaragua, the unit costs are high even if the costs of supervision remain hidden. Moreover, those who award the contract generally invite the bidder, which means that the process can be manipulated. Finally, the traditional methods of issuing calls for bids and awarding contracts entail additional costs that can reduce the amount of money available for investment in the project. This does not mean that bidding and tender processes should be eliminated, but, rather, that transparency in the bidding process can be greater if communities are also involved.

Operation and maintenance

When project construction has been completed, it is expected to leave behind a community structure with the ability to manage and negotiate with the municipal government. PRODEL, the municipal government and the communities evaluate the community contribution, the organization that has been established during the execution, and the quality of the work and any unresolved needs that are indicated in the micro-planning workshop and address them accordingly. In terms of post-project preventive maintenance, PRODEL's experience is relatively recent. Yet, it has produced important lessons that were used in establishing a national preventive maintenance fund by the Nicaraguan Social Investment Fund for the maintenance of the primary health and educational systems. As in the case of PRODEL, the goal is to create a fund with resources that promotes local and community contributions.

The communities pay for the water, sewage and electric power services provided, and make additional contributions in the form of labour for the preventive maintenance of schools, roads, health facilities, recreational facilities and parks. The link with the Sistemas Integrales de Salud (SILAIS), or the Integrated Health Systems, has made possible the development of landfills for garbage collection and the cleaning of sewers, which has resulted in improved project maintenance. In Phase II, the municipal governments and communities will contribute *ex-ante* resources to create a preventive maintenance fund before the completion of a project. One of the critical problems that has been identified in terms of the operation and maintenance of the services relates to the connection of households to the established systems, particularly when there is no financing for this process. PRODEL has established information campaigns and incentives for the municipal governments so that, together with the community leaders, they can promote the process of connection by means of a home improvement loan or with the families' own resources.

Women's participation

This has been successful because measures were taken to promote their involvement in all phases of infrastructure project cycles and to encourage their participation in the two loan components. PRODEL also gave preference to projects that addressed women's needs and involved women in the process of evaluating their needs and making decisions, as well as in the planning and administration of projects. The methodology increased the role of women not only as physical builders of projects (some 25 per cent of unskilled labour are women, although no progress was made in the incorporation of skilled female workers), but also in administrative and supervisory capacities. More than half of those attending the micro-planning workshops were women; in management and supervision, 50 per cent are women. Women also make up three-quarters of all team leaders.

> The role played by women in other programmes has changed since PRODEL gave them equality in participation in the various stages of the project, something which had never been done before. Previously, women's role was to prepare coffee, cold drinks and food. PRODEL represented a major change because women were present at every stage, from the identification of projects to their completion. The tasks performed by the women in our city included warehouse managers, finance managers and even carrying building materials in the various parts of the project. It has been shown that a woman can do anything a man can, which has allowed women to assume a new role (Manuel Maldonado, mayor of Somoto, and Osmín Torres, coordinator of the technical unit of the Somoto municipal government.)

Housing improvement and micro-enterprise loans

In the neighbourhoods in which the loan programmes are active, the municipal government, PRODEL's local coordinator and the loan officers from the bank prepare a joint strategy for the promotion of housing improvement and micro-enterprise loans. For micro-enterprise loans, the bank's loan officers visit the houses where the (generally family-owned) businesses and workshops are located. Loans are available if the business is financially viable in accordance with a cash flow statement that is discussed between the loan officer and the micro-enterprise owner. Loans are for between US$300 and $1500 and are recovered over a maximum of six months. Interest rates are high (up to 36 per cent per annum), plus maintenance of value (the indexing of the local currency to the US$ – about 12 per cent per annum). The average loan is about US$400.

Information on housing loans is disseminated through informal meetings at community centres or schools. Representatives of the bank, the municipal government and PRODEL explain the loan terms, the technical assistance provided by the municipal government and the commitments that families must assume in terms of the use of the loan and the repayment. Interested families complete a preliminary application, giving basic information on the location and condition of the home, the employment status of the potential borrower, and the socio-economic characteristics of other family members. Loans are for between US$200 and $1400, repayable over four years at interest rates of 12 per cent per annum, plus an adjustment for inflation (the indexing of the local currency compared to the US$), which gives an effective annual interest rate of 24 per cent on the outstanding balance. The average loan is for US$650.

The bank's loan officer visits each family's home and conducts a preliminary credit analysis to determine the need for improvement and the family's borrowing capacity. The loan officer takes into consideration the monthly family income and expenses and also analyses the land tenure situation, the type of collateral the borrower can offer (mortgage, goods and even title to construction materials) and the sources of income. The loan officer informs the municipality's technical housing assistance office of the potential maximum amount approved for each borrower. In some cases, the bank's loan officer and the municipal official visit the house together. The technical consultant inspects the house, identifying any potential structural problems and assesses the need for expansion, repair and/or improvement. The consultant also identifies problems and establishes priorities for solutions with family members. In general, the household head and his or her spouse or living companion are present during the inspection along with their children. The idea is to take into consideration the problems, needs and priorities of all the people living in the house – in particular, those of the women and children. The technical assistance helps to guide the family so that they can give priority to solving problems of overcrowding and environmental hazards. Emphasis is given to kitchen stoves close to the children's bedrooms, unventilated rooms, absence of drinking water and sanitation, improper disposal of grey waters and waste collection. Ultimately, it is the family who decides upon its priorities and requirements, but in an organized manner, and the decision is subject to a weighting system applied by the technical consultant on the basis of criteria such as urgency, cost, sequence and time required to effect the improvements. The result is the identification of the type of improvement that has the highest priority, and the development of a plan of action for the gradual improvement of the house. The technician takes into consideration the costs that can be covered by the loan and the resources that the family already has (accumulated construction materials, volunteer labour, project supervision tasks and money available to pay for skilled labour and the transport of the materials). The technical consultant prepares a budget, a schedule of activities and a brief report describing the current situation and the type of improvements that can be made. The budget also describes what activities the loan and the family contributions can cover, and the plan defines the possible improvements to be made, supported by the loan. The borrower agrees to carry out the improvements defined with the technical consultant and signs the budget.

With the prepared budget, the beneficiary requests the loan from the bank, providing the collateral and submitting the forms required. The bank generally issues a single cheque that the borrower uses to buy materials and, in some cases, to hire labour. The invoices for the materials remain in the borrower's file at the bank. Five to ten days after the loan has been made, the bank's loan officers visit the home to verify whether the family has bought the materials and begun the construction process. The technical assistance department makes at least one more visit to supervise the construction process and to provide guidance to the family and/or to the masons who are working on the project. In general, projects do not take more than 30 days.

One month after receiving the cheque, the borrower begins to repay the loan over a period of up to four years. The bank services the loan and monitors the placements and collections of the rotating fund. If the loan is not repaid and the normal administrative collection procedures have failed, legal action is taken. Although loans are individual, on some occasions the bank has had recourse to the community project committees to ask their assistance in collecting payments from defaulting borrowers.

Evaluation of participation in housing improvement loans[6]

The housing improvement loans recognize that most poor families build their houses in an informal way without any support or assistance from central and local governments or from formal housing finance institutions. They usually achieve this through a long, difficult and complicated process, using savings and mobilization of family and inter-family contributions. PRODEL has sought to provide these families with access to resources from the institutionalized financial system. It also sought to provide them with technical assistance in a rapid and easy manner that allows them to accelerate their housing consolidation process. The programme is based on the fact that much of the population in the eight cities own a plot of land or are in the process of legalizing land tenure.

---

6 This section is based on Morales and Herrera (1997).

The programme has created healthier environments, a reduction in overcrowding and improvements in the standards and systems of construction in at least 4000 houses, which represent approximately 4.5 per cent of the total housing stock in the cities and 14.5 per cent of the households classified as poor. A sample of 69 houses studied in the five cities in PRODEL's first phase showed that the creation and improvement of healthy environments and attending to the problems of overcrowding in the houses were the users' first priority. In second place was attention to the structural safety of the houses and the security of the house perimeter to protect against external theft and crime. Finally, attention was paid to improving the levels of comfort in the building.

The assisted self-help construction and access to credit provided a major impetus to the local economies, mobilizing more than US$2.5 million in purchases in construction materials, many of them produced locally in small micro-enterprises (cement and clay blocks, adobe, cement tiles and bricks). The housing improvement loans also generated indirect employment for some 270 persons in the construction sector. Family contributions, which add 15 per cent of the value of labour and transport, may represent up to 36 per cent of the actual cost of each housing improvement.

The technical assistance is a new service that gives local governments the opportunity to learn how to support housing improvements. This required a major effort by PRODEL to train municipal technicians and the bank's loan officers and other employees so that they could understand the complexities of the loan operations and work with households in the design, planning and definition of solutions.

Some of the programme's main weaknesses relate to the manner in which the financial and technical/construction aspects must be defined simultaneously with thousands of user families. The informal introductory meetings are often not enough to develop the work plan and for the household to understand the complexities of the loan's financial terms. Sometimes, the incorrect preparation of project plans, budgets and schedules can affect the progressive development of the home. In all of the cities, supervisory site visits have been insufficient, late or have even caused errors in the construction itself. Nor was sufficient effort made to train the staff. At times, the beneficiary families do not see the link between the technical assistance and the opportunity to obtain a better-quality house design and construction at a reasonable cost, and to repay the loan in accordance with their capacity to pay.

These problems relate not only to the existing capacities of municipal technicians and the bank's loan promoters, but also to the difficulties of administering a portfolio of thousands of small loans and coming up with technical solutions for a large number of small and very varied on-site improvements scattered over a wide geographical area and carried out individually by the families or by construction workers. The possibilities of control are, therefore, more complex. Nevertheless, like the infrastructure component, the housing improvement component shows that the urban housing problems faced by the urban poor are not necessarily a lack of financial resources. Making institutionalized financing systems and technical assistance accessible to poor families stimulates their internal savings, mobilizes significant family resources and improves the overall housing situation. The repayment levels are acceptable, in spite of the non-conventional collateral provided, and the rotating funds system is close to achieving financial sustainability. Good financial performance depends less upon the families' collateral and more on the pre-loan analysis and approval, the type of information given, the follow-up by the bank and the administrative procedures for cost recovery.

Lessons learned

This case study shows that there are methods and processes that serve poor people and that may help to lift them out of poverty. It also illustrates how external funding can support this. The experience with PRODEL has also provided important lessons regarding the potentials and limitations of community participation and of institutional and financial sustainability in social programmes that are aimed at providing infrastructure, services, housing improvement and income generation, especially for the urban poor.

The experience suggests that community participation has been a determining factor in:

- Improving the quality of life of the poor. More than 38,000 poor families (representing 47 per cent of the population in the eight cities) improved their access to basic infrastructure and services by participating in the definition, execution and maintenance of 260 infrastructure and community works projects. In addition, some 4168 houses were improved or expanded and some 2400 micro-enterprises were supported.
- Targeting and focusing social investments on the poor. The involvement of community leaders in the municipal commissions allowed more accurate identification of the geographical areas where there were higher levels of poverty and a greater need for infrastructure and services. Participatory micro-planning exercises conducted in 150 different communities made it easier to identify the type, amount and scope of projects required by each *barrio*. These two mechanisms helped to increase the efficiency and accuracy of the assessment measures and of the proposals prepared by the municipal governments for the annual social investment plans and the longer-term municipal development plans.
- Making more efficient use of public resources. As local governments developed projects with communities through micro-planning workshops, public investments (including those provided by central government via the municipal government and the municipal government's own tax revenues) reflect the priorities and preferences of the users and the actual capacities of the municipal government in providing and financing services. Experience shows that these preferences are not always for new services, but also for the improvement, expansion, repair and maintenance of existing services and systems. The micro-planning workshops have a positive impact on the costs of the solutions and optimize the use of the municipal government's scarce resources for this type of work.

- Improving accountability and transparency. The participation of beneficiary families in different phases of the operation and management of the infrastructure projects helped to establish new systems of control within municipal governments and better reporting to, and joint responsibility with, the communities. It also improved communities' understanding of the role of the municipal government, including the real limitations in the technical and financial resources available to address the problems of the poor.
- Mobilizing internal savings. Contributions from communities in kind, labour and materials exceeded 10 per cent of the direct costs of the infrastructure projects and exceeded 15 per cent of those for housing improvements. Municipal governments were encouraged to improve the tax collection processes in response to the programme requirement to come up with local matching funds. The resources mobilized over four years totalled US$10.5 million: 53 per cent from the central government (with the foreign aid financing provided by Sida) and 47 per cent from local governments, the communities and the user families (including loan repayments).
- Reducing the costs of the projects. Technical solutions defined with the direct participation of the end-users can cost up to 20 per cent less than projects carried out by local government (either directly or through contracts to private companies), primarily due to the contributions from the beneficiary families in the administration and supervision of the project, as well as to their contributions in terms of skilled and unskilled labour.
- Increasing social and gender equity. The experience shows that community participation can help to direct the benefits of projects towards the poor and vulnerable sectors of society. The participatory methodology employed also facilitated the ability of women to secure access to loans and other project benefits.
- Improving national reconciliation. The relations between local governments and communities are now based on incentives and the structuring of concrete alliances founded on tangible plans and solutions, not merely on simple social demands and false promises and expectations. The participatory methodology also helped to facilitate communication between antagonistic groups and to coordinate positive actions for the improvement of living conditions in neighbourhoods between groups who might appear to be politically and ideologically irreconcilable.
- Making programmes sustainable. The system of incentives established for the contribution of national, municipal and community resources, and the involvement of beneficiary families in the management and administration of the project cycle, have created a solid basis for an increased commitment and division of responsibilities between participants. This facilitates the maintenance and sustainability of projects. Our experience also suggests that sustainability of social programmes can best be achieved when there is a clear division of labour between financial institutions and those organizations that give technical and social assistance. The fact that the bank operated at the level of the community was also critical for a good cost-recovery record for loans.

Certain external factors facilitated the design, organization and implementation of PRODEL:

- Non-partisan programmes. In spite of the political changes in Nicaragua between 1994 and 1998, authorities from the central government institution responsible for promoting the programme and the local governments (regardless of their political tendencies) made it possible to create alliances and to use methodologies that provide incentives for the participation of poor families, without discrimination on the basis of political, ideological or religious factors. All governments are tempted to make use of scarce resources for partisan purposes. But if the rules between the funding agency and the recipient government regarding the misuse of funds are clear, the problem is more likely to be avoided.
- Programmes with limited resources. The deficiencies in infrastructure and services in informal settlements is not only a problem of a lack of financial resources. It also relates to the methods that promote (or exclude) the involvement of communities. (Limited) resources need to be used to stimulate and provide incentives for community contributions. By quantifying the real and positive contributions of participants (in terms of money, materials and labour), municipal governments gain an understanding of the importance of cooperating with and involving communities.
- Work with existing institutions. It was important for PRODEL to identify and utilize the institutions at local level that were closest to the demands and needs of the users of the services, and which could facilitate the process of community participation. The different institutions were able to establish overall agreements and rules. Thus, local governments and a commercial bank were able to promote different types of participatory solutions in the areas of infrastructure, housing improvement and income generation. These activities obviously required a major effort in terms of training and the development of methodologies.
- Streamlined and flexible mechanisms. It is important to recognize that communities are heterogeneous groups of people in which there are potential beneficiaries for different forms of technical assistance and financial services. Participation in upgrading or installing urban infrastructure and services requires the communities to have more information and a greater understanding of the technical, physical, social and financial variables that influence a construction project. At the same time, they must have rapid decision-making mechanisms and access to resources. If not, the scepticism and mistrust of external agencies that usually prevails in poor communities is not broken.
- Division of functions and responsibilities. PRODEL was able to recognize each institution's particular interests and clearly define what was expected from community participation in each component. INIFOM's primary interest in the programme was the possibility of establishing innovative methods to promote and enhance local government capacities through decentralized processes. The PRODEL participation model has been used by INIFOM to promote additional decentralization programmes using

resources from other international funding agencies. Municipal governments were interested in involving communities in co-financing the projects and in contributing to the maintenance of the infrastructure and community assets. Municipalities have also used the PRODEL participation model for initiatives, drawing funding from other sources. The commercial bank sought to increase the commission it earned from managing the portfolio of housing improvement and micro-enterprise loans, and to accumulate capital for the rotating funds. The relationship and the coordination between participants have been more effective when the sequence of the components of the programme has been discussed and planned with the community and its leaders.

- Adequate social organization of the community. It is common for projects of this type to have unrealistic expectations of what can be accomplished through community participation. Actions may be based on models of community organization that have very little to do with the requirements of the construction processes. When providing infrastructure in established communities, it is important to strengthen the participation and organization of the beneficiaries by territorial divisions appropriate to the neighbourhoods. The different commissions and committees formed must be in line with the complexity and nature of each project. These have been effective instruments in the programme's ability to accomplish its physical and social goals.

- Empowerment of, and technical assistance to, beneficiary families. Community participation requires effort to provide families with new options, capacities and skills in different areas. This primarily relates to the identification and analysis of problems (micro-planning workshops); project planning (design, scheduling and budgeting); mobilization of internal and external resources; specialized physical execution; the administration and supervision of the projects (inventories, audits, etc); the evaluation of projects (impact and efficiency in the use of the resources); and project maintenance (cleaning campaigns, security and protection of the project constructed, and management of resources for preventive maintenance tasks).

Even with its successes, PRODEL must be further consolidated if it is to have a greater long-term impact. The first five years tested various hypotheses concerning schemes of participation and administration at the local level. The results obtained for the three components in eight cities indicate that it is not simply a pilot project and that community participation is a determining factor in the processes of introduction, improvement and maintenance of urban services and facilities. The goal of PRODEL for the next few years is to replicate the system in other municipalities. It will also demand an improvement in the capabilities of the local participants so that they can define and structure the permanent fora and places for negotiation that will ensure the financial and institutional sustainability of the efforts to promote community participation in a socio-political environment that changes every four years.

PRODEL will also have to deal with the issue of its institutionalization and face difficult questions regarding the type of legal structure that it needs for a longer-term perspective.[7] Should it continue to be a governmental programme or should it try to mix the nature of private and public perspectives that will enable the programme to avoid the difficulties posed each year because of elections? How will it retain the staff whom it has trained to promote community participation? These are some of the challenges that the programme has to face in the near future.

References

Goethert, R, N Hamdi et al (1992) *La microplanificación. Un proceso de programación y desarrollo con base en la comunidad* (*Micro-planning. A community-based planning and development process*), IDE of the World Bank, FICONG, Washington, DC

Morales, N and E Herrera (1997) *Evaluación: prestación de servicios de asistencia técnica en mejoramiento habitacional en cinco municipios* (*Evaluation of technical assistance services in home improvement projects in five cities*), Programa PRODEL, Managua, December

PRODEL (1997a) *Documento de proyecto para la segunda fase de PRODEL* (PRODEL Phase II project document), INIFOM, Managua

PRODEL (1997b) *Proyecto de la segunda fase* and reports from the municipalities served by PRODEL, Managua, Nicaragua

Social Action Ministry (1995) *Medición de la pobreza en Nicaragua* (*Measurement of Poverty in Nicaragua*), MAS/UNDP, Managua

Stein, A (2001), *Participation and sustainability in social projects: the experience of the Local Development Programme (PRODEL) in Nicaragua*, IIED Working Paper 3 on Poverty Reduction in Urban Areas, IIED. The entire text can also be downloaded at no charge from http://www.iied.org/urban/

Villalta, L (1997) *Proceso de modernización*, UCRECEP, Managua

---

7 Unfortunately, the Nicaraguan government, under pressure from international financial organizations, closed the Banco de Crédito Popular in the year 2000. PRODEL decided to bid and tender its housing and micro-enterprise loan portfolio. Private banks were invited to participate. Although two of them showed interest in managing PRODEL's portfolio, their internal financial situation was not sufficiently solid. Thus, it was decided to transfer the portfolio to the two NGOs that started working with PRODEL funds after Hurricane Mitch.

Part III

Civil Society Initiatives

Chapter 6

The Work of the Anjuman Samaji Behbood in Faisalabad, Pakistan[1]

Salim Alimuddin, Arif Hasan and Asiya Sadiq

Introduction

This chapter describes the work of a local non-governmental organization (NGO), the Anjuman Samaji Behbood (ASB), in Faisalabad, one of Pakistan's largest cities. The experience shows the possibilities of supporting community-built and financed sewers and water supply distribution lines in the informal settlements in which most of Faisalabad's population lives. The work of ASB suggests a model where provision for water, sanitation and drainage could be much improved in the city despite deficiencies in the existing infrastructure and institutions and the limited availability of local government resources. ASB also manages a successful micro-credit programme for local businesses.

ASB has used the model developed by the Karachi-based NGO Orangi Pilot Project (OPP), although it has also adapted it. The model requires that each lane within a settlement that wants improvements in water and sanitation has to organize and work out how to pay for the immediate cost of the water supply and sewer infrastructure, as well as the connection charges. This case study describes the difficulties encountered in developing a piped water supply and sewage network for individual households in an area with a high water table and the lack of slope. Despite the difficulties, a self-financing piped water supply and underground sewer system were developed between 1995 and 1999, with 253 houses benefiting from in-house connections to water and 1300 houses with sewers. Many communities are now asking ASB for technical assistance in laying

---

1 This chapter is drawn from a more detailed report: Alimuddin, S, A Hasan and A Sadiq (2001) *Community Driven Water and Sanitation: The Work of the Anjuman Samaji Behbood and the Larger Faisalabad Context*, IIED Working Paper 7 on Poverty Reduction in Urban Areas, IIED, London. The text can also be downloaded at no charge from www.iied.org/urban/.

BOX 6.1 EXCHANGE RATES AND UNITS USED IN THIS CHAPTER

The exchange rate between the rupee and the US dollar or UK pound sterling obviously varied during the period covered by this case study. To get an idea of the value of the different amounts mentioned in rupees, the exchange rates are around 55 rupees to US$1 and 88 rupees to UK£1.

Linear measurements are presented in inches and feet in this chapter, since these are the measures used in Pakistan. One inch is equivalent to 2.54 centimetres; 1 foot is 0.348 metres.

---

sewage lines, and a second phase of the programme is underway, developing a new collector sewer to serve 1000 households.

Now that the model has been shown to work, ASB is being offered support from international donors (most of which it is refusing because of its commitment to developing a model that does not depend upon external funding). Like OPP, ASB also feels that development has to take place at a pace dictated by the commitments and priorities of the local inhabitants, rather than according to an externally imposed timetable from international donors. ASB is also having to re-evaluate its role; given the demand for its advice, it is shifting towards working more as a trainer and a provider of services. Maintenance is a particular problem, so the organization has set up a maintenance unit that can clear blocked trunk sewers and pump water from plots, and which should become self-financing.

Background

In 1998, Faisalabad had close to 2 million inhabitants. There has long been a wide gap between the growing population's need for land for housing with piped water, sanitation and drainage services and the capacity of the government agencies responsible for such provision. Two-thirds of Faisalabad's population live in areas with little or no official provision, and most new housing and land developments take place without official approval. Less than half the city's population have piped water and less than one-third are connected to the sewer system.

The Faisalabad Development Authority is the main policy-making body and is responsible for supervising development; the Water and Sewerage Authority (WASA) comes under it. Funding shortages have meant that projects to improve water and sanitation have consistently not been completed. WASA has a serious financial crisis and large deficits. Its operating costs are increasing (especially for electricity, which is needed to power water and sewage pumps), whereas its revenues (drawn mainly from water and sewerage charges) are not. Its very limited investment capacity also means that uncoordinated investments in water, sanitation and drainage are made, often by other institutions. Most new housing developments are undertaken informally (outside of any master plan) and each neighbourhood seeks to improve its water, sewers and drains. Due to WASA's limited capacity, they often seek funding and develop projects independently.

Many local investments in water, sanitation and drainage are supported by the 'grants-in-aid', funding that each national and provincial assembly member has to spend. Each politician identifies and funds schemes that are implemented in their constituency but on an ad hoc basis, with no reference to any larger plan and no coordination with larger public works programmes. Municipal councillors also have similar funds, although on a smaller scale. The grants-in-aid controlled by different politicians support many investments in drains and water supplies; but the work is often unnecessarily costly and of poor quality, with drains that do not work and water supplies that do not reach the outer areas of the settlement. New sewers and drains often empty their effluent into neighbouring streets. There is little coordination between WASA and the different projects supported by these grants from national, provincial and municipal politicians. Most settlements have WASA trunk sewers close by; but local sewers and drains are often not connected to them.

The Faisalabad Development Authority is not elected and comes under the provincial government. An elected council and mayor head the Faisalabad Municipal Corporation; but there are few links to the development authority. The municipal council comes under the provincial government executive (which has the power to overrule the decisions of its council). Revenue collection is very deficient and revenue shortfalls make the city increasingly dependent upon provincial government funds – but these have also proved uncertain.

This provides the context in which there has been a search for new ways to improve water, sanitation and drainage that can serve the settlements that develop informally, and can also integrate within the system of water mains and trunk sewers managed by WASA.

The development of the Anjuman Samaji Behbood's work in Dhuddiwala

Dhuddiwala is one among many informal settlements in Faisalabad. Its population increased from 500 in 1947 to 8080 in 1999. Refugees settled here at the time of partition, along with a few families who came from the rural areas. These families were allowed to settle freely for humanitarian reasons by the leaders of the clan who owned this land. According to senior citizens in Dhuddiwala, their settlement grew after 1955 as rural–urban migration to Faisalabad responded to the setting-up of industries, and two large industrial units (a silk mill and a textile mill) were established nearby. As a result, mill workers and their families started acquiring land from the clan leaders, initially with leases or rented, and, later, purchased (with payments in instalments).

Groundwater in Dhuddiwala was brackish; but the clan leaders arranged for a deep well to be dug and were lucky to find potable water. A tap, fitted to the bore, provided water free of charge and encouraged more migrants to settle here. The clan leaders sold the land and laid out the main streets with the settlers organizing the lanes, plots and open spaces. There were no middlemen involved in this development. Hasanpura and Rasool Nagar are two settlements that developed on the Dhuddiwala agricultural lands.

Until the early 1960s, there was no provision for sanitation and the inhabitants used open fields as latrines. Water came either from the deep bore or from irrigation channels. As the settlement's density and size increased, using the fields was no longer convenient, especially for women. Water from the irrigation channels was also increasingly polluted. By the late 1960s, over half of the households had installed hand pumps in their homes and built soak pits. But the water table kept rising and soon the soak pits started overflowing into the streets and diseases and environmental degradation increased. The government's anti-waterlogging programme (installing deep tube wells along the main irrigation channels and pumping water back into the canals) caused water levels to fall drastically during the late 1960s and most of the hand pumps became inoperative.

There were also other problems in the new settlements, relating to health, education and funerals. In 1968, Dr Naseer, a medical practitioner, formed an organization (or *anjuman*) with his friends. The *anjuman* identified ten persons with secondary- and intermediate-level education, and who were comparatively well off, and asked them to spare one hour each evening to teach 35 students who had completed their primary education. The *anjuman* also helped the successful students to gain admission to high school. In 1970, the *anjuman* took on the responsibility of upgrading the school in Hasanpura, and with the help of a member of the district council from Dhuddiwala, the primary school was upgraded to a middle school and then to a high school in 1986. The *anjuman* also purchased land in Hasanpura and established a space for holding funerals. The inhabitants contributed 150,000 rupees for the construction of its boundary wall.

By 1999, Dhuddiwala, Hasanpura and Rasool Nagar had 1010, 1000 and 200 households, respectively. According to the residents, about 60 per cent of the working population are employed in the formal industrial sector or on looms.

The formation and development of ASB

Another welfare organization was formed in 1964, the Anjuman Samaji Behbood (ASB), by Nazir Ahmed Wattoo. He was born in 1944 in Dhuddiwala, where his family have been farmers since 1882. But he did not follow his family profession and obtained a diploma in electrical works from the local polytechnic and then worked as an electrician. He supplemented his income at different times by working as a stationery supplier, a general contractor and as editor of a magazine. At present, apart from being the coordinator of ASB, he has shares in an automobile workshop.

ASB was founded with a few like-minded young people, including four of Wattoo's primary school friends, a high school graduate and a tailor. The organization was registered and the tailor's shop was used as offices. Stationery, postage and registration expenses were met through donations from team members. The fund soon proved inadequate and the team started to depend upon donations from prominent local people. These funds were used for arranging receptions for political representatives and influential government officials. At these receptions, speeches were made in their honour, they were garlanded, food and beverages were arranged, and they were presented with requests for a water supply, sewerage, drainage, electricity and social-sector facilities. The dignitaries promised these facilities and more; but nothing concrete came of it. However, the practice became a habit and encouraged the ASB team to rely on funds from local politicians to run their organization, in return for support for a political candidate or party. In Pakistan, thousands of *anjumans* operate in this manner.

Since this lobbying was unsuccessful, ASB also undertook development work with community funds. This included solid waste management, street cleaning and the construction of open drains. It was from these experiences that ASB identified sewage disposal and water supply as the most urgent local problems. However, ASB's development work was never successful because it was expensive and did not function properly, and this created distrust between ASB and the inhabitants. Much of ASB's time was spent on organizing political rallies, campaigning for elections and spreading propaganda against their actual or perceived political opponents. This caused poor relations between ASB and other NGOs and civic agencies working in Dhuddiwala. Mr Wattoo also stood for the elections to the municipal council, first in 1979 and then again in 1984; but he lost both times.

Although Mr Wattoo's work with ASB and his political career were failures, this experience brought him into contact with community-based organizations (CBOs) and national-level NGOs. In 1987, he met the principal consultant to the OPP in a seminar in Islamabad. The OPP consultant was impressed by Mr Wattoo's clarity and outspokenness and invited him to visit OPP in Karachi and to consider replicating OPP's work in Dhuddiwala. As a result, Mr Wattoo visited OPP for the first time in December 1987 (see Box 6.2 for details of the OPP).

When Nazir Ahmed Wattoo visited OPP in 1988, he expected OPP to fund ASB's plan to build infrastructure in Dhuddiwala and was disappointed when he learned about the OPP model with its support for community-investment and management and its transparent manner of working, since it was so different from the way in which ASB had worked since 1964. However, the concept intrigued him and he often came back to OPP to learn more about its work. After many meetings with inhabitants of Orangi who had worked on sanitation systems and had received micro-credit, he felt that the programme could be replicated in Faisalabad. But he was hesitant because he felt that people would not be willing to make investments in development on his advice due to his past record. He even doubted that communities, given their psychological dependence upon politicians and civic agencies, would accept the model. These were issues that he debated at great length with the OPP team over a period of six years.

In February 1993, a technical adviser to the UK charity WaterAid and the OPP consultant visited Dhuddiwala. They surveyed the situation and discussed the possibility of initiating a water and sanitation pilot project in the area with ASB involvement. Mr Wattoo agreed and he and other social activists from Dhuddiwala came to OPP for formal training.

In September 1994, a social organizer from OPP visited Dhuddiwala and introduced OPP as a loan-giving agency that promoted 'self-help' development.

BOX 6.2 THE ORANGI PILOT PROJECT (OPP)

Orangi is Karachi's largest informal settlement (*katchi abadi*), extending over some 4160 hectares. By the late 1990s, its population was 1.2 million. Most of the 113 settlements within Orangi have been accepted by the government and land titles have been granted. Most inhabitants built their own houses and none received official help in doing so. When Orangi developed, there was no public provision for sanitation.

The Orangi Pilot Project (OPP) was established by Dr Akhtar Hameed Khan in 1980. In 1988, the project was reorganized into four autonomous institutions: the OPP Research and Training Institute (RTI); the Orangi Charitable Trust; the Karachi Health and Social Development Association; and the OPP Society, which channels funds to these institutions. OPP considers itself a research institution whose objective is to analyse Orangi's problems and, through action research and extension education, find viable solutions. These solutions can then be applied, with modifications where necessary, to other settlements and can become part of government policies. OPP does not fund development; but, by providing social and technical guidance, it encourages the mobilization of local resources and the practice of cooperative action. Based on these principles, OPP has evolved a number of programmes, some of which are described below.

The Low-cost Sanitation Programme

This programme enables low-income families to construct and maintain an underground sewage system with their own funds and under their own management. OPP provides social and technical guidance (based on action research), tools and implementation supervision. OPP's work has shown that people can finance and build underground sanitation in their homes, their lanes and their neighbourhoods (what OPP terms 'internal' development), but cannot initiate 'external' development, consisting of trunk sewers, treatment plants and long secondary sewers. This can only be provided by the state. In Orangi, the inhabitants have invested 78.8 million rupees (equivalent to more than US$1.4 million) on internal development (including 405 secondary sewers) in 5987 lanes consisting of 90,596 houses (there are 104,917 houses in Orangi). It would have cost the state more than six times that amount to do the work. The programme is being replicated in seven cities in Pakistan by non-governmental organizations (NGOs) and community-based organizations (CBOs), and in 49 settlements in Karachi by the Sindh Katchi Abadi Authority. The OPP concept has been accepted by the Karachi Municipal Corporation and is being applied to its development plans.

The Family Enterprise Economic Programme

With funds borrowed from commercial banks, the Orangi Charitable Trust lends to small family businesses that have no collateral to obtain loans from other financial institutions. Loans are usually provided to people who have expertise in what they plan to do or who are already operating businesses. Interest on the loans is charged at the current bank rate of 18 per cent. At present, there are 6555 units that are supported by loans totalling 123.7 million rupees. The recovery rate is 97 per cent. The World Bank has given support to the revolving fund for the programme.

OPP's Low-cost Housing Programme

This programme provides loans and technical assistance to building component manufacturing yards so that they can mechanize and increase their production, improve their products and train their staff. The programme also trains masons to use the new technologies and components being developed at the manufacturing yards. House builders are given advice on how to relate to the manufacturing yards and masons, and advice on design, lighting, ventilation and other hygiene-related design aspects. OPP is training para-professionals to provide this advice, drawn primarily from young unemployed youth from the Orangi communities who are paid by house builders or those who want improvements to their homes.

Health Programme

This originally consisted of developing women's organizations at the lane level, where the sanitation system has been built. A mobile team of experts gave advice to such organizations through discussions and meetings on the most common serious diseases in Orangi, their causes and ways of preventing them. The team also advised on hygiene, immunization and family planning. However, this method could not increase its scale sufficiently and a new model was developed with the health programme, imparted through training to local women teachers, managers of family enterprise units and doctors in private clinics, thus anchoring the programme institutionally in schools, private clinics and family enterprise units.

OPP's Education Programme

This provides social and technical guidance and loans to improve and upgrade the physical conditions and academic standards of private schools in Orangi. These private schools cater to the needs of the vast majority of Orangi school-going children.

Significance and new directions

These programmes have provided NGOs, CBOs and government agencies with successful models for overcoming the physical, social and economic problems faced by low-income settlements and communities. They have been successfully tested through government–OPP–community participation projects, but still have to become official policy. The infrastructure development models, in particular, reduce capital costs, ensure good quality work (since communities acquire skills for building internal infrastructure, for maintaining it and for supervising government work for external infrastructure) and create a more equitable relationship between government agencies and poor communities.

Increasingly, OPP is involved in policy issues and in promoting macro-level solutions, based on its models. For instance, it developed proposals to improve Karachi's sewage system, which showed a cheaper, more easily implemented, model than was recommended by the Asian Development Bank. OPP has also prepared detailed documentation of conditions in 189 *katchi abadis* in Karachi and put forward physical and economic proposals for upgrading the drains (*nalla*) of Karachi, through which most of the city's sewage flows. For this purpose, OPP trains young people from low-income settlements who, after their training, become an asset to the community to whom they belong and part of a larger movement to create self-reliance, freedom from foreign loans and grandiose projects, and a more equitable relationship between low-income communities and government agencies.

The four barriers

OPP has identified four barriers that prevent communities from taking responsibility for internal infrastructure and other social sector initiatives:

---

1   *Psychological barrier*: communities feel that building a house is their responsibility, but that the development of infrastructure and of the lane is the responsibility of the government.

2   *Social barrier*: people have to come together to form some sort of organization to build infrastructure and take over the lane and open spaces. The organization should be large enough to be effective but small enough to be cohesive. In Orangi, the organization has been lane-based and consists of 20 to 40 households.

3   *Economic barrier*: the cost of developing infrastructure should be low enough for people to afford. This requires technical research and the development of cost-effective community-based building procedures.

4   *Technical barrier*: people do not have the technical expertise or tools to design, build and supervise underground sewage and water supply systems. To do this they need tools, technical advice and managerial guidance.

ASB and OPP agreed to initiate a small credit programme to help establish a relationship of trust between ASB and the community. Mr Wattoo identified the loans; but the money transactions were kept under OPP's control to avoid any misunderstanding between ASB and the community, since Mr Wattoo felt that people would not trust him. WaterAid also supported ASB surveying, documenting and mapping existing water and sewage facilities in the areas in and around Dhuddiwala, as well as developing a pilot project for replicating the OPP infrastructure model. OPP supported this with training and on-site advice.

The beginnings: the Micro-credit Programme

The credit programme started with three loans, and only when these were successful were two more released. ASB carefully monitored these loans and gave regular progress reports to OPP. Trust developed between OPP and ASB, and ASB's credibility within the community grew. Many businesses approached ASB for loans, agreeing to follow the procedures that OPP had laid down. By March 1999, 277 credits had been provided to a value equivalent to around US$79,000 with a recovery rate of 88.5 per cent (see Box 6.3).

In September 1995, a team of activists was formed in Hasanpura. Initially, they talked to individuals about the programme in order to gauge their reaction while maintaining a low profile so as not to build up false hopes. Once it was felt that the community would support the idea, a meeting was organized in November 1995 to present the OPP concept and stress that this was a 'non-political' project. The meeting was attended by 48 residents. The community accepted the proposal for a people's committee to organize and undertake the development work, with ASB working as a teacher, adviser and liaison between OPP and the Hasanpura residents, and a ten-member Water Supply Committee was chosen.

The Water Supply Committee felt that it needed funds to lay the main pipeline to the WASA water mains. Individual lanes could then lay their own distribution lines and households would connect to them and pay their share of the costs so that the project costs would be recovered. A loan for 200,000 rupees for a revolving fund was received from WaterAid to cover the cost of laying

Box 6.3 OPP–ASB Micro-credit Programme

Credit is obtained from Orangi Charitable Trust (OCT), Karachi, at 0.5 rupees (50 paisas) per 1000 rupees per day and given to clients at 0.6 rupees (60 paisas) per 1000 rupees per day.

Credits

277 are provided (232 to men, 45 to women) with 166 repaid and 111 ongoing.

Financial position

4,351,500 rupees are loaned with 3,376,495 rupees repaid. Overheads until March 1999 are 110,000 rupees. There are no defaulters, a recovery rate of 88.5 per cent and four cases of death.

Credits provided

Bakery	01	Consumer stores	62	Cloth shop	10	Clinic	07
Crockery	03	Cosmetics	02	Carpets	01	Decorators	01
Dairy cattle	17	Electrical store	13	Embroidery	11	Garment factory	08
Hotels	04	Hardware	02	Junk dealer	05	Leather works	03
Medical store	04	Moulding	01	Printing press	01	Repair shop	01
Stationery	07	Spare parts	05	Small business	42	Stitching	10
Supplier	05	Shoemaker	02	Steel works	02	Taxi motor	04
Thela	13	Typing institute	01	Water land		Workshop	17
Home school	01	Hairdresser	01	development	04	Video shop	04

The beginning of the water project

The success of the credit programme gave ASB confidence in the OPP approach and in their capacity to manage programmes, so it initiated a pilot water-supply project. Hasanpura was chosen as the pilot area because of its severe water problems. Most households had installed hand pumps ,but many were inoperative as the water table had been lowered by the government-installed tube wells. Mr Wattoo, with help from OPP, identified a WASA water main 1100 feet from Hasanpura, from which water could be drawn. WASA permission was needed, so a formal application to WASA was made. WASA responded by saying that Hasanpura could not be treated as an individual case as it formed part of a larger WASA water supply plan that would be implemented in 2008 and that this depended upon the availability of funds. Another problem was that the pipeline would have to pass under a major road and this required permission from the municipal corporation.

ASB calculated that Hasanpura residents incurred costs of more than 9 million rupees a year due to the non-availability of potable water. If no water supply was installed until 2008, the community would spend 100 million rupees by then – the equivalent of nearly US$2 million (see Box 6.4). A water and sanitation system could save them this expense. It was therefore decided that the community should be informed of these figures and presented with the OPP alternative.

1100 running feet of main pipeline. The Water Supply Committee was responsible for collecting payments for water connections, keeping accounts, purchasing construction materials and supervising the construction of the main line and the distribution lines in the lanes.

Box 6.4 THE COSTS OF INADEQUATE WATER PROVISION IN HASANPURA

Hasanpura residents obtained drinking water from outside their settlement using donkey-cart vendors. For other uses, underground water was extracted from shallow bores by electric pumps. Each household was purchasing around 35 litres of water each day at a cost of 5 rupees so the total expenditure for 1000 houses was around 5000 rupees per day or 1.8 million rupees per year. Since almost every house had an electric pump for extracting ground water, around 730,000 units of electricity were consumed annually, costing 1.46 million rupees per year. Additional community expenses were incurred for washing clothes using saline water – including an estimated additional 4800 kilograms of laundry soap used each year at a cost of 960,000 rupees. The consumption of around 96,000 pieces of bath soap had an estimated cost of 672,000 rupees. The use of saline water, the dearth of clean water and poor sanitary conditions were also responsible for various diseases. It was estimated that residents spent about 2.4 million rupees annually on medicines and doctors. Open drains were also causing waterlogging and were damaging housing, and each house was spending an estimated 2000 rupees per year dealing with this problem. Taking into account all of the above factors, it was estimated that the community was spending 9.292 million rupees annually.

The committee applied to the managing director of WASA for a 'no-objection certificate' to make the connection to a government water source. The application was passed to the deputy managing director, who then passed it on to the engineer in charge of the area who, after giving his approval, sent it to the deputy director of the Planning and Development Department. The whole process took over three months and, at every stage, ASB had to apply pressure on WASA staff and give informal payments to junior staff in the department to keep the file moving. Finally, in January 1996, the no-objection certificate was given with the proviso that the 4-inch main pipeline that had been proposed by ASB should be increased to 6 inches. However, the committee decided not to wait for the certificate and began work.

After the formation of the Water Supply Committee, an OPP team visited Dhuddiwala and trained the ASB team in mapping, surveying, estimating and planning. A purchase committee was formed that included Mr Wattoo, a WASA fitter (not in his official capacity), and three members of the committee. The WASA fitter was included because he was a Hasanpura resident and had technical expertise. The committee was made responsible for buying and storing materials until the work could be started.

There was disagreement within the committee, with some members feeling that the 4-inch diameter pipeline proposed by OPP engineers was insufficient for 1000 households and insisting on at least a 6-inch diameter. This was resolved by the proposal that a 6-inch pipeline should be laid under the paved road in Hasanpura and the rest of the line should be 4 inch.

The Water Supply Committee decided to begin work by laying the water line under the road. This required permission from the municipal corporation. The committee contacted junior staff in the corporation, who told them that getting permission would take a long time and would also require illegal payments. They suggested that the committee should lay the line across the road and subsequently pay any fine; the committee also discussed the matter with the area councillor and he, too, backed the suggestion. This work had to be done clandestinely and completed before being noticed; this could only be achieved after dark.

On 24 November 1995, the laying of the pipeline was inaugurated by Hasanpur's oldest resident. Excavation began at 9 pm and the 110 running feet were laid across the road in one night. The excavation was then refilled and the road repaired. WASA would have needed three days to carry out this work. Throughout the night, committee members and the municipal councillor remained on site to deal with any possible interference with the work. However, it was only in the morning that an opposition group in the area reported the laying of the pipeline to the area magistrate. But the case came to nothing because of support from the councillor and municipal corporation executives, and WASA had no objection because only a pipeline had been laid and no water connection was involved.

Connecting the new pipe to the water mains could only be done if the mains was emptied. To do this, a pump was required. The Water Supply Committee asked WASA officials for a pump but was refused. The problem was overcome when a pump was acquired informally from WASA pump operators for a payment of 2000 rupees, and two WASA fitters were informally hired to work on the connection. All of the work was done clandestinely and executed in six hours in the freezing cold. After the connection was made, the line was extended into the project area by 400 running feet within a few days and the first tap was installed at the ASB offices. The community was ecstatic when they saw clean water coming from the tap.

Connections to lanes only took place when the inhabitants were organized and approached ASB for a water connection. Each household wanting a connection had to pay 20 rupees to cover the costs of stationery and the forms used to register the request. ASB then contacted WASA and each applicant household had to pay WASA connection charges of 1175 rupees. Originally, this was 1363 rupees; but it was reduced by WASA in July 1997. A design for laying the water line was then developed by ASB, executed by the lane community and supervised by the ASB team. The average connection cost per house was 600 rupees (the actual cost is influenced by the length of the pipe and the excavation necessary to make the connection), and this payment was made to the Water Supply Committee, along with an additional payment of 1300 rupees per household for the cost of the lane line and the water main that had already been laid with funds from WaterAid and 100 rupees as a service charge. Thus, the total cost of acquiring a water connection was 3195 rupees per household.

The water system is designed for 1000 houses in 84 streets, although the actual number is 829. The extra 171 households were included in the estimate as it was expected that they would join in from neighbouring settlements. The number of beneficiaries was calculated at 700 households and the total project was calculated at 910,000 rupees, or at 1300 rupees per household, excluding connection expenses.

Problems and conflicts

Soon after the connection to the WASA water mains, differences arose within the Water Supply Committee. Two committee members began maligning ASB's work and told the local provincial assembly member that ASB and the committee were using the water project to build a constituency for themselves and that they were his political opponents. They also informed him that water connections had been provided in violation of WASA rules. The provincial assembly member then called WASA for an explanation and was told that the committee was not making illegal connections because it had acquired a no-objection certificate and it was paying WASA connection charges.

The provincial assembly member then started laying his own water line in Hasanpura, promising free connections for the community – this inevitably slowed down progress on the water project. ASB pointed out to the community the substandard nature of the new initiative (which was visible to all) and the fact that WASA could not provide any more water to the area. This generated considerable debate in the community; but the initiative fizzled out within a couple of months.

This highlighted the need to build the community's spirit. A member of the Water Supply Committee decided to organize his lane as a demonstration model. The community was organized and a design drawn up following ASB procedures. A connection charge of 3195 rupees per household was requested. People said that this was too expensive, so ASB requested an exemption from WASA connection charges. However, three months later it was refused. After this, the community decided not to waste any more time and collected 22,000 rupees from six houses and, with this, they laid the first lane.

Opponents of ASB struck back in August 1996 when Mr Wattoo was in Karachi for a training session. With support from the political party in power, they managed to make 65 unauthorized connections to the water lines laid by the Water Supply Committee and paid no charges either to the committee or to WASA. This generated a lot of anger in the community, who wanted to take revenge on the opponents of the water project. However, ASB asked the community to keep calm and to take legal action against the illegal connections. An application requesting their disconnection was made to WASA; but it took three months before WASA approved the request. Meanwhile, this new conflict slowed down work.

WASA issued disconnection orders in November 1996. Those who had made illegal connections were fined 500 rupees each and the connections were made legal only after the WASA connection charge of 1175 rupees had been paid. However, those with illegal connections refused to pay an additional 600 rupees to the Water Supply Committee, so ASB filed a petition with the senior civil judge in Faisalabad requesting him to order that no water connections could be acquired without ASB's approval and a payment to the committee. The petition was accepted and households who had made illegal connections were forced to pay. In September 1997, 13 Hasanpura residents approached the area's municipal and provincial assembly members, informing them that ASB's activities in Hasanpura were a threat to their political standing and claiming that

ASB was extorting money from the poor. When the committee became aware of these events, it arranged a meeting with the political representatives and explained ASB's water and sanitation work; this cleared up any misunderstandings. As a result, the provincial assembly member decided to give support to the ASB programme and issued a directive to WASA that no new connections should be issued to anyone unless they made the required payments to the committee. However, despite this and the civil judge's order, WASA continued to issue connection notices to people who had not paid the ASB/Water Supply Committee charges. As a result, ASB filed a petition against WASA in the Punjab High Court and also complained to the WASA board. This led to a meeting at WASA in December 1997, where the vice chairman of the WASA governing board directed WASA that no new connections would be provided from the community's line without first consulting ASB. After this meeting, WASA officials became very cooperative and work progressed smoothly. In January 1998, ASB withdrew the petition.

Details of work done and loan recovery

Between 1995 and 1999, water pipes were installed in 36 streets with connections to 253 houses.

Table 6.1 summarizes the costs involved and shows how the project was financed. The community invested 1,028,367 rupees in this work (around US$18,700) – under the original ASB estimate of 1.3 million rupees and only one-third of the cost of WASA estimates for this project (3.2 million rupees). 73,500 rupees have been recovered from the WaterAid loan (300 rupees per household). The recovery has been slow, as slightly more than 30 per cent of households are connected to the system. The reasons for this relatively low take-up include:

- People who make a connection share it with their neighbours, who therefore do not feel the need to make a connection themselves.
- Uncertainty regarding the programme as a result of opposition from within the community and from the politicians has prevented people from making connections.
- Water lines were laid in the lanes once enough money had been collected to lay them, irrespective of how many households were willing to connect. This procedure is now being revised by ASB; in future, only lanes where over 70 per cent of the households agree to participate will be supported and given permission to connect to the main line.

ASB's sanitation project

While the water supply project was being planned, ASB began investigations into sanitation and drainage issues in Dhuddiwala and adjacent settlements with OPP assistance. Most households were disposing of their sewage into open drains in the streets. As a result, damp and erosion had affected the foundations and walls of houses. Furthermore, many of the drains were blocked and only

Table 6.1 *Cost of ASB's water supply project in Hasanpura, 1995–1999*

Expenses incurred	Expenses (rupees)
Main lines: 1925 running feet, 6 inches and 4 inches in diameter	194,901
Lane lines: 4414 running feet, 3 inches in diameter	284,395
Miscellaneous	56,000
Payment to WASA for connection fee of 1363 rupees and 1175 rupees (two rates prevailed during this period)	333,371
253 house connection charges at 600 rupees per house	151,800
ASB service charges	7900
Total cost until 30 June 1999	1,028,367

Source: ASB Progress Report (1999) ASB, Faisalabad, June

cleaned when there was a major crisis. It was therefore decided to adopt the OPP model for sewerage.

Both OPP and ASB had established their credibility within the community through the credit programme and the initiation of the water project. Social organization and mobilization of the community were easy, as contacts had already been established for the water project and activists had been identified. A number of people volunteered their help and Dr Naseer, a member of the Water Supply Committee, offered to organize his lane as a demonstration model.

In OPP's work in Karachi, the disposal points for sewage were the natural drains; but in Faisalabad this was not possible because there is almost no slope. The sewage system could only be built if it could be connected to WASA trunk sewers, which were a considerable distance away. So, ASB decided that laying a collector sewer to connect with the trunk was the first priority as this would motivate the lanes to connect to it. It was also decided that households would not contribute to the construction of this collector sewer but would pay for it when the lanes were connected. Since, at that stage, there was no money to lay a collector sewer, it was decided that one lane should be developed that could be connected to an existing WASA trunk sewer in order to demonstrate what could be done.

The cost of the collector sewer was to be borne by a revolving fund, with funds recovered from households when a lane connected to it. So far, the average cost per household for the collector sewer has been about 600 rupees. Lane inhabitants would construct the lane sewer at their expense and under their supervision and management. The cost per household has worked out at between 700 and 900 rupees. Installing a latrine pot and P-trap in each home costs 750 rupees. Thus, the average cost per household for the entire system is between 2050 and 2250 rupees (US$37–$41).

It was decided that during the connector sewer construction, work would stop when it reached a lane intersection. At that stage, the lane inhabitants would be asked to lay the lane sewer and connect to the collector sewer. A connection would not be allowed once the collector sewer had been built beyond the intersection. It was further decided that every household would have a small one-chamber septic tank, whose main purpose was to prevent solids from entering the sewage system and choking it up.

Laying the first lanes

In Hasanpura, the open drains from 35 lanes discharged their sewage into a canal that had originally been used for irrigation purposes, but had become blocked with waste and silt. In 1989, the municipal corporation built an open drain parallel to this canal and connected it to a WASA trunk sewer; but this drain, too, was often blocked so the lanes were often flooded. Whenever there was a crisis, households collected money and hired scavengers to clear the drain and make it functional again. Dr Naseer's lane was one of the 35 lanes that connected to the municipal corporation's open drain.

Once the organization and mobilization of Dr Naseer's lane had begun, ASB requested technical help from OPP. An OPP technician and social adviser provided on-the-job training to the ASB team in documenting, estimating, levelling, shuttering for manholes and laying pipes. Construction work on the lane began in January 1996. Dr Naseer was unable to continue his work due to differences between himself and some of the lane members, so a new social organizer was chosen and the community started to lose interest in the project. ASB panicked; in order to motivate the community, it gave them a loan of 5500 rupees to finish the work from WaterAid's water supply fund.

This provision of a loan for work at lane level was against the OPP's philosophy; but it meant that the work gained pace and 534 running feet of underground sewage line serving 32 houses was completed. However, people hesitated to make individual connections as they were unsure whether the system would work. Eventually, one young man took the risk and by-passed the old open drain to connect to the new system, building a one-chamber septic tank. People saw that the system worked and other houses started to make their connections. At the same time, other lanes approached ASB for technical assistance in laying their sewage system.

Five lanes were completed in the following five months and all fed into the municipal corporation's open drain; but due to the condition of the open drain, they did not function well. ASB decided that if the system was to function, this drain should be cleaned and replaced by a collector sewer, which would connect to the WASA trunk sewer. In addition to the 35 lanes, the Jalvi market shops also used the open drain and it was decided to involve shopkeepers in the project, as well. Jalvi market is a commercial area in Dhuddiwala, developed by an informal developer. It has about 700 shops that disposed of their sewage into the open drain, also known as the Jalvi market drain. Since the drain constantly overflowed, it adversely affected environmental conditions in the market. Mr Wattoo informed the developer of plans to replace the open drain by an underground collector sewer and asked him to participate in the work. The developer initially refused, afraid that his money would be misused. However, when he saw the work being undertaken in the lanes and the building of the water supply system, he changed his mind. He recognized that improved environmental conditions would increase the value of the shops. He offered to

Table 6.2 *ASB's low-cost sanitation project*

Location	Number of lanes	Length (running feet)	Number of houses	Total cost (rupees)
National Colony	3	582	38	81,680
Dhuddiwala	27	3573	161	415,781
Hasanpura	51	7664	540	1,211,580
Niamat colony	6	1600	64	173,126
Rajada town	4	635	37	83,235
Al-Najaf colony	1	160	16	32,720
Jalvi market	14	2591	97	266,484
Jalvi TR line	2	1820	41	334,705
Factory area	1	310	10	42,670
Abdullah town	3	1668	48	190,742
Daruslam colony	2	300	12	30,600
Iqbal Nagar	2	418	22	48,774
Mujahid town	5	680	30	77,330
Bilal colony	18	3232	178	520,000
KTM Chowk	2	210	6	21,000
Total	141	25,443	1300	3,530,427

Source: ASB Progress Report (1999) ASB, Faisalabad, June

pay half of the estimated costs of the underground collector sewer (150,000 rupees); but on OPP's advice, ASB declined this and, instead, asked him to purchase the materials for the sewer line. The reason for refusing a cash donation was that he could later claim that his funds had been misused.

With OPP's help and training, the Jalvi market collector drain was installed and, in four months, 1700 running feet of trunk sewer were laid. The laying of the sewer was not an easy task. Cleaning the drain, diverting the water and laying the sewer all involved intensive and dirty work. Four teams of labourers quit, refusing to complete the work, with a fifth team completing it but at higher wage rates. The work went slowly; but the community was impressed with the work of the fifth team and awarded its members a 5000-rupee bonus. The completion of the collector sewer was a major boost for ASB and it motivated more communities to mobilize and request ASB support for their lane sewers. ASB identified further connections to existing WASA trunk sewers as disposal points and the programme expanded. To finance the collector sewer, ASB used materials provided by the Jalvi market developer and funds recovered from the WaterAid loan for the water project. In addition, individuals from the community made contributions as loans.

Table 6.2 shows the work done in the lanes. In addition to the lane sewers listed here, 1820 running feet of collector sewers have been laid at a cost of 277,305 rupees. Thus, the total cost of the work undertaken so far is 3,807,732 rupees (equivalent to around US$69,000), and the proportion of investment in the collector sewers compared to the lane sewers works out at 1:13.7.

Repercussions of the water and sanitation programmes

Requests from other communities and future plans

After the completion of the Jalvi market collector sewer, numerous communities applied to ASB for technical assistance for laying their sewage lines. These have now been included in ASB's Project Area Phase 2. By early 1998, ASB completed the surveying, mapping and planning of these settlements and identified the need for a 3300-running-feet collector sewer to connect to a WASA trunk sewer. This would serve 1000 houses in 52 lanes, who would build 12,000 running feet of underground lane sewers. According to the plan, each lane would have its lane organization and there would be three committees, each building the different lengths of the collector sewer. It was estimated that work on the collector sewer would take four months and that the lane sewers would require two years. For the trunk sewer, ASB applied to WaterAid for a revolving fund of 500,000 rupees, which would be recovered from the lanes as and when they connected to the collector drain. The fund was made available in the 1998–1999 financial year.

Work did not begin immediately on the collector drain. This is because plans were often changed due to insufficient and often inaccurate information regarding WASA disposal points and future plans. Furthermore, OPP was reluctant to begin work since it felt that ASB did not have the technical expertise to survey and implement such a large project. Mr Wattoo therefore underwent extensive training, first at OPP and then on site in Faisalabad, and the plan's feasibility was tested by OPP's engineer through an on-site survey and cost estimate. Communities from eight new settlements, which were created through the informal subdivision of agricultural land, have also applied to ASB for assistance. In all of these settlements, the developers did not provide any infrastructure. ASB has visited three of the settlements to present its programmes and it has prepared documentation, designs and estimates. Reaction from the communities is awaited.

Offers of collaboration and funding

A number of national and international NGOs and agencies have offered financial support, including the Canadian International Development Agency (CIDA), the Asia Foundation and the Trust for Voluntary Organizations. ASB has not accepted funds because it feels that (as it has demonstrated, alongside OPP) low-income households in Pakistan are capable of financing infrastructure collectively. Furthermore, ASB and OPP feel that development has to take place at the pace of the people and most external funders apply pressure to complete projects rapidly. Mr Wattoo has accepted invitations to workshops and seminars, where he has presented his work and delivered the message of self-reliance; like OPP, he feels that ASB is not a consultant or a contractor but, rather, a teacher who guides people to make them self-sufficient.

Action Aid sent a group of 26 people belonging to two union councils from the Faisalabad region for orientation to ASB and six applied to ASB for work to be conducted in their villages. Action Aid has also sent a group of activists, councillors and staff from a district in North-West Frontier Province for orientation, along with people from a neighbouring village. Caritas Faisalabad sent a group and, after being shown how sewers were laid, they borrowed three sets of manhole shuttering from ASB and sought their advice. The group went back to their settlement and laid their sewer lines at their own expense. Many other NGOs have shown interest in ASB's work and Anjuman Falah Behbood (AFB) from Rawalpindi, which is replicating the OPP model with WaterAid funding, has visited Dhuddiwala with its staff, area councillors and activists for orientation and training, as have groups from Multan who are in contact with OPP.

Changed attitude of government agencies and politicians

The Pakistan government's Social Action Programme offered ASB a grant to expand its development work. However, when ASB instead asked for a loan, this was refused. In September 1998, the Punjab Social Welfare Department invited ASB to Lahore to present its work to 25 social welfare officers from the district. In addition, undergraduate and post-graduate students from the University of the Punjab have visited ASB in groups. Various government officials and staff from international agencies have visited their work and Mr Wattoo also made a presentation of ASB's work to senior civil servants at the National Institute of Public Administration in Karachi.

Three councillors from Faisalabad visited ASB in September 1998, and ASB convinced them not to invest in water supply or sewerage at the lane level, but to spend their funds on building collector sewers and paving lanes where water supply and sewage lines have been completed. The councillor from the ASB project area has already started following this advice and has paved six lanes in which water and sewage lines have been laid by the community.

WASA's relationship with ASB has also changed. At the neighbourhood level, there is considerable interaction between WASA area staff and ASB activists and staff. ASB monitors their work and, since it now has an understanding of water- and sewage-related issues, there is growing acceptance of its role. At the WASA head office, too, ASB contacts have developed into mutual understanding and respect. Since WASA does not have area plans, it has on more than one occasion used the plans prepared by ASB to help it design area sewage and water-supply proposals.

Improved physical and social conditions in the project areas

Lanes in the project area show enormous physical changes. Waste water and sewage have disappeared, and lanes that have been paved are now clean and full of people. Children play there, women gather there and residents have started planting trees in the streets. Residents have also come together to arrange for the collection and disposal of solid waste and for lane cleaning. There is collective pressure on councillors to install street lights and this is working. Dr Naseer reports that the incidence of water and sanitation-related diseases has fallen by over 60 per cent. He says, in good humour, 'Doctors are losing money. They will have to shift to settlements where water and sanitation do not exist or they will become broke and homeless.' In the many meetings that have been held between the residents and the authors of this chapter, community members have said that water- and sanitation-related quarrels that were common between neighbours have now disappeared and the value of their properties has gone up. They also said that they were making considerable savings on medicines and doctors' fees, which they could now use to improve their homes.

Emergence of new needs

With the development of sewerage and water-supply systems in the ASB project area, requests from communities, and changed attitudes of government and donor agencies, ASB had to reassess its future needs and directions. Firstly, it was assuming the role of trainer, for which it required better-trained staff and training materials. Secondly, the infrastructure that it had helped to develop needed maintenance and, for that, equipment, funds and staff were required. And, thirdly, an expansion in its work meant covering a larger area; to do that effectively, transport was necessary.

With regard to documentation, ASB decided to hire a commercial video-maker to make a video of its programme to help in training other CBOs and NGOs. Hiring the equipment was very expensive, so ASB applied to WaterAid for funds to purchase video equipment; the equipment was also made available to other CBOs and NGOs for recording their work and for training purposes. WaterAid granted them funds and a film was completed and is now being used for motivation and orientation. Four more films are planned, relating to motivation techniques; surveying and mapping techniques; material purchasing and accounts; and on-site work.

The need for more staff members is being addressed by training local staff as this seems to be the only way that the non-availability of technical staff can be overcome since external professionals have shown little interest in working with communities. To address the issue of maintenance, especially the continuous blockages in WASA trunk sewers that adversely affected the functioning of the community-built sewers, ASB set up a maintenance unit in August 1997. This consists of a de-sludging pump, a safety kit (a diver's suit and mask so that someone can enter the trunk sewer safely) and two sweepers, hired as manual labour. Usually, when a sewer gets blocked, communities collect money, hire sweepers and clean the line. Sometimes, WASA provided a pump for doing this and the approximate cost to the community for removing the sludge worked out at 800 to 1200 rupees. WASA was informed of ASB's new unit and the equipment was made available to any community who has a sewerage committee. WASA sewers serving the community-built sewage systems have been de-silted at three locations; but no charge was made as this work is in the experimental stage. However, in future, ASB intends to charge 200 rupees per hour for its services, which will cover the cost of fuel, transport, operation and labour and is less than one-third of what communities spend at present. ASB has also responded to requests for the removal of water from open plots, which are being used to dispose of sewage for a number of houses, and has recovered costs.

With the increase in the size of the project area, ASB needed a vehicle. A pick-up was purchased in 1999 for 400,000 rupees. Before this, manhole shuttering and construction materials were transported by donkey carts, and the community was charged between 20 and 40 rupees for a one-way trip. ASB intends to charge the same price and the profits will be used for the repair and maintenance of shuttering. A removable sewage-collecting tank and pump have been purchased that can be mounted on the pick-up and can be used for cleaning the one-chamber septic tanks and for carrying away sewage when WASA trunk sewers have to be de-sludged. At present, WASA staff charge 300 rupees for cleaning a one-chamber septic tank. However, they do not complete the task and usually dispose of the silt that they remove into the lane. Having the vehicle has also enabled ASB to visit neighbouring rural areas to present their work. Previously, they had to hire a van for carrying their staff, activists and equipment.

Results of OPP replication projects outside Karachi

To date, ASB is the most successful of the OPP replication projects outside Karachi. Several attempts to replicate OPP-like water, sanitation and micro-credit programmes have been tried, most with support from WaterAid. Two projects supported by WaterAid and OPP training never materialized. The first was the Okara Development Programme; but here the support NGO who had requested OPP assistance faced certain operational and staffing problems. The second was in Sialkot and here, too, the local NGO who requested OPP support found it difficult to take on the new roles needed for successful community-based water and sanitation, over and above its fairly successful human rights lobbying. Two sanitation projects were not sustained. The first was a partnership with a Lahore-based NGO, who developed a sanitation and micro-credit programme with OPP support. However, it then shifted its focus to education and health when support for this became available from the government's Social Action Programme. An NGO in Muzzaffargarh sought OPP help to develop a sanitation programme but then suffered serious internal problems. The Organization for Participatory Development in Gujranwala successfully adopted the OPP micro-enterprise credit model and also took on the OPP sanitation model with OPP support. Although initially successful, the work started to decline after mid-1997. After an internal evaluation, the organization decided to close down its sanitation programme, feeling that this could be better done by motivating the local authorities and by collaborating with them. It also found that almost 50 per cent of the households in its project area could not afford the cost of the OPP model. The organization's priorities are now education, credit and health, for which it is operating successful programmes, and it keeps in touch with OPP.

ASB Faisalabad and AFB Rawalpindi are two projects that have consolidated their sanitation and water supply projects. In both cases, their success is a result of being able to adapt the OPP model to local conditions rather than simply adopt it. In addition, in both cases, constant contact with OPP has been maintained and there has been no internal conflict within the organizations. Also, they have shown no impatience for quick results or for acquiring large funds.

As a result of these experiences, OPP has decided to be more careful in choosing partners. To begin with, only a small start-up grant is provided to NGOs and CBOs for a sanitation programme. If they show signs of promise, only then is an agreement between them and WaterAid finalized. It has been observed that CBOs relate to the OPP model better than NGOs, whose staff and leadership belong outside the project area. This is now an important aspect that OPP looks into when deciding with whom to collaborate. OPP has also learned that the CBO or NGO with whom it works must have a team of social and technical people with whom it can relate. Such a team is not always available and needs to be built up. The methodology for building up such a team from within the community has now evolved and, as has been demonstrated by many OPP replication projects, social organizers and technicians from outside the community are not a viable alternative.

Reasons for ASB's comparative success

Adapting rather than adopting the OPP model

ASB adapted the OPP model to its context. Changes were made in the methodology regarding motivation, financing external development and taking on service provision for maintaining infrastructure. ASB, unlike OPP, did not begin by holding meetings to motivate communities. It identified 'respectable' community elders with whom it held individual dialogues; they, in turn, spoke to people whom they could influence. It was only when this process had been completed that a meeting was called. Even then, the elders decided on where and when to hold the meeting. Development work was converted into an event – for instance, the inauguration of the water line by an elder, complete with banners and a gathering. Muhammad Naseem, a famous populist artist from Faisalabad, was invited to inaugurate a sewage line in the settlement, although he lives in a formally planned middle-income settlement. Through him, ASB has been able to lobby for support from government agencies and to get him to design their literature and posters. Since he has numerous visitors, Muhammad Naseem is able to spread the ASB message. These innovations in motivation reflect the reality of Faisalabad, as opposed to Karachi. In Faisalabad, ASB deals with a homogenous and cohesive society, which has its roots in the soil. Karachi, on the other hand, has a migrant population and is a city where traditional values and organizations no longer exist. This also helps to explain ASB's effective interaction with area councillors.

ASB's decision to build external infrastructure with a loan and then recover it from the beneficiaries is also a departure from the OPP model. Again, this decision was taken after a careful examination of local conditions and a firm belief that social pressure could be exerted to recover the loan. The decision to lay the external infrastructure first was proposed by OPP and was followed by communities in Karachi, Sukkur and Hyderabad – all areas where a disposal point was not available.

The decision by ASB to organize the maintenance of the sewer system and to provide a service for it is, again, a major departure from OPP work. OPP has always asserted that it is not a service provider and that this work should be organized, undertaken and financed by the communities themselves or by entrepreneurs. It will be interesting to see how the ASB maintenance model works out and what administrative and financial pressures it puts on the organization.

The role of Nazir Ahmed Wattoo

Mr Wattoo's personality and experience has been pivotal to the achievements in Faisalabad. He had the advantage of having spent 25 years interacting with politicians, government agencies and communities before becoming involved with OPP. As a result, he knows the nature of the government institutions, their procedures, the manner in which one has to deal with them and the relationship between them and the politicians, on the one hand, and communities, on the other. He is familiar with legal processes and has access to courts and lawyers. Since he has interacted with various elements of society, he knows how to motivate them and use them for his cause. Because of his failures in lobbying for development and in politics, he was willing to try a new approach, which is why he accepted OPP philosophy and methodology and realized that there were no shortcuts to improving the conditions in low-income settlements.

Mr Wattoo took his time getting to know OPP. Both here and in the course of his work on ASB programmes, he showed no impatience. He also recognized that development does not occur as a result of money, but through teaching people how to look after themselves and how to hone their skills for this purpose. Because of this, he rejected various offers of grants, which would have forced him to expand his work and staff, increasing his dependence on unreliable funds and external people. The most important element in ASB's work is that all decisions are taken collectively and with the involvement of community members. In addition, unlike many NGOs and CBOs, the ASB's accounts are transparent and available for community members to examine, and this builds trust and confidence.

Low cost, culturally compatible

ASB has also managed to keep down overheads and manage with a small staff. This makes management easy and also creates greater understanding between ASB and the communities with whom it works. The three members of staff are also drawn from the community, strengthening these links. The health and credit programmes are kept separate from the water and sanitation programmes, both financially and organizationally. In addition, there is no conflict between the organizational culture of ASB and the communities with whom it works.

Table 6.3 *Total funds received by ASB from WaterAid for water and sanitation projects*

Financial year	Description	Amount received (rupees)	Actual expenses (rupees)	Balance (rupees)
1995–1996	Amount received for annual budget, plus 200,000 rupees as revolving fund for water project	405,160	458,622	–53,462
1996–1997	Amount received for annual budget	301,251	291,928	+9323
1997–1998	Amount received for annual budget	251,470	155,708	+95,762
1998–1999	Amount received for annual budget	434,327		
1999–2000	Amount received for annual budget*	379,000		
	Total received for budget and revolving fund	1,771,208		
	Deduct 200,000 rupees for revolving fund	–200,000		
	Subtotal 'A'	**1,571,208**		
1997–1998	Amount received for video and sewer maintenance unit equipment	305,002	305,002	Nil
November 1998	• Video-making	320,280		
	• Trunk sewer revolving fund	500,000		
	• Transportation (truck and equipment)	705,000		
	• For video-making project	116,710		
	Total for equipment, video and revolving fund	1,943,992		
	Deduct 500,000 rupees for sewer revolving fund	–500,000		
	Subtotal 'B'	**1,443,992**		
	Total 'A' plus 'B'	**3,015,200**		

Note: * Of this, 234,000 rupees are for staff salaries, 39,000 rupees are for operational costs and 106,000 rupees are for equipment.
Source: ASB reports, ASB, Faisalabad

Against a total investment of 1,571,208 rupees (approximately US$28,500) for staff salaries, operational costs, office equipment and training, the community has been able to invest 4,558,794 rupees (approximately US$82,900). In addition, capital expenses for sewer maintenance unit equipment, the truck and related equipment, the video camera and the making of a video film amounted to 1,443,992 rupees. As the work expands, the ratio of ASB expenditure to community investment is bound to fall.

Relevance, constraints and future directions

The ASB Model consists of the following:

• community-built and financed sewers and water supply distribution lines in the lanes;

- ASB-built collector sewers and neighbourhood main water lines, financed through a revolving fund and recovered from the community; and
- WASA-developed trunk sewers and disposal points and water-source development and main lines.

Given the financial and technical constraints of government agencies, Faisalabad cannot acquire a conventional water and sanitation system for its existing and rapidly expanding population for at least the next two decades. The ASB model points a way out if it can become part of official planning policy. Lateral and collector sewers and water distribution lines account for a major part of the funds required for water supply and sanitation development.[2] The funds required for an ASB-type model are very modest. The model also increases knowledge about local infrastructure-related conditions and creates opportunities for community organizations and activists. These community organizations and activists do not arise because of pressure from ASB or through promises of a subsidy, but because people need water and sanitation. As a result, the programme is entirely demand driven. The model, through support from OPP, also develops technical skills within the community, promotes self-reliance and creates a more equitable relationship between government agencies and local communities.

Constraints

The ASB model has depended upon the personality and competence of Mr Wattoo. In order for the model to grow and become sustainable, new people or existing activists need to be trained to take over his roles and responsibilities. ASB has to become an institution if its work is to survive and flourish. ASB needs more technical people to be able to deal with demand. When work begins in areas other than Dhuddiwala, Hasanpura and Rasool Nagar, individuals who can undergo this training should be identified and supported. Dialogue with WASA will also be necessary – and, for this, documentation and an understanding of existing infrastructure and its condition are essential.

Recommendations for future directions
Documenting infrastructure

To meet communities' demand for sewers and water supply, ASB will need to identify the location of WASA water mains (for supply) and trunk sewers (for sanitation). Settlement surveys are required to integrate existing neighbourhood infrastructure within its planning. Visits to various settlements indicate that if existing infrastructure and its problems can be mapped, then the whole approach to infrastructure provision in Faisalabad can change. A similar exercise in Karachi carried out by OPP has resulted in new policy directions. This documentation may take two to three years to prepare. The data should be analysed and the analysis shared with WASA and development authority staff.

---

2 See longer report upon which this is based, as described in note 1.

Further study on informal development

Faisalabad will continue to develop housing through the informal development of agricultural land because, firstly, formal development as it is currently structured is not affordable by lower-income groups and, secondly, because the development authority has no funds or land for it. The authority can direct this informal development through the appropriate expansion of trunk infrastructure; but a further study on informal development patterns and locations is required. Furthermore, work is needed on developing small, decentralized and affordable sewage treatment facilities for informal schemes as it will be difficult and very expensive to integrate them within the city-wide sewage master plan.

Links with academic institutions and the Faisalabad Area Upgrading Project

The documentation of existing infrastructure, continuous research on informal settlements – relating WASA plans to community realities – and the integration of informal development within a larger city plan can all be aided by linking ASB work to the research work of an academic institution. The possibilities of doing this are being explored with various local institutions. The possibility that the Faisalabad Area Upgrading Project might develop missing trunk and secondary infrastructure, and that ASB might help to develop neighbourhood infrastructure, has already been explored.[3]

Lessons from the case study

- It is possible to develop good-quality provision for water and sanitation in low-income settlements in Faisalabad, funded by what low-income households are able or willing to pay.
- It was possible to draw on the OPP model developed in Karachi; but it was necessary to adapt it to local circumstances.
- The solution needed time to develop and to work out how to overcome local difficulties (including those posed by households in the community who were seeking to obtain free water and by local politicians hostile to the scheme).
- The local NGO was able to develop and fund secondary sewers (it is often assumed that this is not possible).
- Solutions that do not depend upon donor funding (especially grants) are more suitable and sustainable; but many donors find this difficult since they need to spend their money.
- The work of ASB, like the work of OPP in Karachi, demonstrates the great potential for improving water and sanitation in low-income areas through partnerships between community organizations and local NGOs (who can

---

3 The original report from which this chapter draws included a discussion of how staff from this upgrading programme and from other government organizations viewed the work of the ASB.

work together to install and pay for the water and sewer pipes within the settlement), as well as municipal authorities (who can provide the water and sewer mains to which these pipes connect).

On broader issues:

- Development does not occur as a result of available funds. It takes place through the development of skills, self-reliance and dignity – the three are closely inter-linked. These factors make relationships within communities, and between communities and government agencies, more equitable, and this change in relationships brings about changes in government planning procedures and, ultimately, in policies.
- 'Capacity and capability-building' of government agencies can never be successful without pressure from organized and knowledgeable grassroots groups. Such groups can only be created by local activists, who need to be identified, trained and supported financially; formally trained professionals and technicians are no alternative to such activists. The formation of such groups forces government agencies to become more transparent in their functioning. The most important aspect of transparency is the printing of accounts and their availability to community members.
- One of the main reasons for the government's very poor urban planning record is that plans are often idealistic; finance is then sought to implement them, and often the funds do not materialize. Much more could be achieved if planning was based on a realistic assessment of available funds; if an optimum relationship could be developed between resources (financial, technical and other), standards and demands; and if planning recognized and accommodated the fact that all three are dynamic and can change over time.
- Low-income communities do not own programmes developed by 'others', however participatory these programmes may be. It is government agencies that must learn to participate in people's programmes and in their existing processes, rather than seek to incorporate them within public programmes.
- The role of NGOs and support agencies is primarily to educate; but for this, they must, above all, have a knowledge and a sympathetic understanding of the context in which they are working.

Chapter 7

Municipal Programme for the Reform and Extension of Homes: Casa Melhor/PAAC Cearah Periferia, Brazil

Débora Cavalcanti, Olinda Marques and Teresa Hilda Costa[1]

Introduction

The Better Home and Programme of Support for Self-building (Casa Melhor/PAAC) was developed initially in the city of Fortaleza in the north-east of Brazil, where it sought to improve the living conditions of socially excluded families. Within six years, the programme has been replicated in a number of other cities and 4400 families had benefited. Variations of the programme are being implemented in Maracanaú and Sobral in the state of Ceará, Belém (capital of the state of Pará), and Maracaibo in Venezuela.

The first part of this chapter describes the programme and its evolution. The second section assesses its effectiveness in addressing housing need. The final section draws together the emerging lessons, especially in relation to the impact on poverty, the institutional relationships and the programme's sustainability.

Background

In Brazil, around 80 per cent of all households live in urban areas. In some regions, the increase in the level of urbanization accelerated during recent decades; in Fortaleza, for example, the urban population increased by 129 per cent between 1970 and 1996. In 1950, Ceará (the state in which Fortaleza is

1 Translated by Christopher William Scott and with field-work and data analysis by Andréia Teixeira, Cristiane Faustino, Cristina Carvalho, Cristina Frota, Elisabete Serra, Fábio Leão, Gleyciana Antunes, Isabella de Albuquerque, Mairton Bernardo and Maria Ester.

located) was predominantly agrarian, with only 25 per cent of the population living in urban areas; by 1996, the level of urbanization had risen to 74 per cent, with the greater part of the urban population concentrated in its capital, Fortaleza.

Brazil has very considerable problems of inequality and poverty. In 1999, it had the highest concentration of income among 174 nations (UNDP, 1999). The monthly per capita income of the poorest 40 per cent of Brazilians is 125 Brazilian reals (US$70), while the average monthly income of the richest 10 per cent is 2478 Brazilian reals (US$1380), equal to 19 Brazilian minimum salaries.[2] The average income of the richest 20 per cent is 32 times that of the poorest 20 per cent. In countries with greater social justice this ratio is less than 10:1 – for example, in Canada the figure is 7:1.

Large numbers of urban dwellers live in very poor-quality homes in dangerous or high-risk areas – for example, along the margins of polluted water courses, on slopes, in waterlogged areas (including mangrove swamps) and without access to minimum basic services. In 1999, around 57 million Brazilians – 35 per cent of the population – lived in conditions of poverty.[3]

Low-income households are obliged to find or develop their own housing without government or private support. The result is very low-quality homes developed in informal settlements, generally located on the periphery of the city and lacking in services and infrastructure. The poor cannot obtain loans to help finance their housing because they cannot meet any of the conditions of the formal banking system: their income is low and it generally comes from work outside of the formal sector. They also have no assets to use for guarantees and they occupy land informally.

The housing finance sector in Brazil has concentrated on those with higher incomes, as in most other nations. The low-income housing programmes of the Brazilian federal government are officially targeted at families who earn up to 12 minimum salaries. However, the interest rates used for loans in official housing projects do not distinguish between the different income levels or livelihood situations of households and, therefore, loans cannot be afforded by many. Hence, the formal financial institutions mainly serve better-off families as they are better able to meet the demands of the banks. The consequences for the poor are illustrated in Box 7.1.

Paradoxically, and in spite of this lack of finance for low-income families, the poor are prolific builders: 4.4 million housing units were constructed in Brazil between 1995 and 1999. Of this total, only 700,000 were produced by the formal housing market. Thus, 3.7 million homes were constructed, under difficult

---

2 One minimum salary corresponds to approximately US$75 per month. It is the official minimum value that a Brazilian worker may receive; but, in reality, there are many workers, in the informal sector, who receive less than this minimum. The minimum wage had been established in 1936 and each year its value is adjusted for inflation. From the year of its creation until today, it has been readjusted 133 times. Almost 70 per cent of the population of the north-east survives with one minimum wage or less, including many pensioners. The fight of the workers, currently, is to get a minimum salary that is differentiated by region.

3 Instituto de Pesquisa Econômica Aplicada (IPEA) considers the poor to be those with a monthly per capita family income of less than half the legal minimum salary, which is insufficient to meet basic nutritional needs and to pay for housing and transport.

BOX 7.1 THE CASE OF A FAMILY ON THE PERIPHERY OF FORTALEZA

Ângela lives with her five children in a shack of *taipa* (long straight branches that are woven together to form the structure of the dwelling and then plastered with mud) and plastic. Her husband moved away and the family was left with 'nothing, only a gas cooker...we can't even pay for the gas, we cook with charcoal and bits of wood.' The family is extremely poor, surviving from day to day: 'I have no one, only Jesus,' says the mother. They all live in the one-room shack with an improvised bathroom in one corner and a little kitchen in another. Hammocks and cardboard on the floor are the beds of this woman and her children.

The whole family moved from Ocara, a poor municipality in the dry interior of Ceará to Fortaleza after a period of drought. Today they are threatened with eviction as they are unofficially occupying a plot where there is no sewerage system and water only arrives in a nearby pipe at night during the week. The refuse truck doesn't pass by because there is no road and rubbish lies scattered everywhere.

The little children study in community schools in the neighbourhood; but the older ones have stopped studying because there is no secondary school nearby and they don't have money for the bus. To go to the doctor the mother needs to leave the house at 4 am to attend the state health service clinic. Because of the miserable housing conditions, they suffer constantly from diarrhoea and breathing problems and from endemic diseases such as dengue, cholera and calazar (a kind of leishmaniasis).

---

conditions, by socially excluded families without access to any additional finance. Millions of families reduce their already low levels of consumption to subsistence levels in order to have the money to buy the materials that they need to construct their own homes, brick by brick, and bag of cement by bag of cement. They undertake the construction during the weekends, even though their tired bodies and often poor state of health demand rest. Their homes are the fruit of their own 'savings'. To be more correct, and realistic, they are the fruit of under-consumption, and of their and their children's hunger.

Instead of diminishing, this permanent tragedy is increasing. In 1970, only 1 per cent of the population of Greater São Paulo lived in *favelas*. By 1995, this figure had leapt to at least 20 per cent. In other state capitals, the picture is even worse: 25 per cent in Belo Horizonte; 28 per cent in Rio de Janeiro; 33 per cent in Salvador; more than 50 per cent in Belém; not to mention the *favelas* of *palafitas* (houses built on stilts on the margins of the river) in Manaus, to cite only some examples (Instituto Cidadania, 2000, p9).

Households earning less than three minimum salaries, 450 Brazilian reals (approximately US$250) have three options to obtain a home:

1   They can occupy unused land, facing permanent illegality and the risk of eviction.
2   They may rent accommodation, paying rents that are generally high and frequently sharing space with other families.
3   They can purchase a land site in a subdivision that is not officially recognized (an illegal subdivision), without infrastructure, and generally in areas unfit for human habitation.

The World Health Organization (WHO) suggests that 15 square metres is the minimum space standards in which a person should live. The housing deficit can be considered to be quantitative when there is such a lack of homes – entire families living underneath bridges, in streets and squares, in improvised or overcrowded accommodation. It can be considered qualitative when the homes are in poor condition, with inadequate water and/or electrical systems and without other infrastructure and services. The João Pinheiro Foundation in Belo Horizonte estimates that, in 1995, the Brazilian housing deficit was around 5.6 million housing units. If access to infrastructure is included, the deficit rises by an additional 4.6 million homes. According to the foundation, 85 per cent of the housing deficit is to be found among families with a monthly income of less than five minimum salaries.

Residents' associations search for solutions to these social problems. These associations are formed by the residents, both in informal settlements and in other areas. Normally, the inhabitants organize around the common interests of the community and form the associations of inhabitants to make demands to the government.Through an assembly general meeting, where a board is elected, the residents become members of the organization. After its creation, it must be registered at a notary's office to have a legal status. In Fortaleza alone there are more than 2000 such associations. In Brazil, these are generally well organized; but they often have a confrontational attitude to the state, lobbying for more and better support. In partnership with non-governmental organizations (NGOs), universities and other support agencies, these social organizations have been seeking improvements in urban policy, land ownership and land distribution.

The four case studies

This is the context in which Casa Melhor/PAAC emerged as an alternative strategy to improve the housing conditions of those with an income of less than three minimum salaries. The analysis in this chapter considers the implementation of this evolving programme in four cities: Fortaleza, Maracanau, Sobral and Icapui. Table 7.1 provides some statistics for these four cities to highlight their diversity. Fortaleza, as capital of the state of Ceará, is the seat of the state government and the place where the most extensive urban services and infrastructure are found. It is the fifth largest Brazilian state capital and the most important development pole in the northern zone of the north-east region of Brazil. It is a port city, with extensive tourist and commercial sectors. Small household enterprises have contributed to the success of the textile industry. In spite of its dynamic economy, Fortaleza is an extremely segregated city. There is a rich city with high-quality services and infrastructure, and there are low-income areas lacking in infrastructure where the urban poor live. There are 630 *assentamentos irregulares* (irregular settlements) where land is occupied unofficially; 67 are considered to be high-risk locations.

Maracanaú is a dormitory town for lower-grade workers. Although it has an important industrial district, most of the higher-paid employees of these industries live in Fortaleza. The lower-income residents of Maracanaú work in

Table 7.1 *Background data and conditions in the four cities*

Indicator	Fortaleza	Maracanaú	Sobral	Icapuí
Area (square kilometres)	312	98	2120	428
Total population	1,965,512	160,065	138,565	15,666
Proportion of population who are urban %	100	100	84.8	49.2
Population density (persons per square kilometre)	6300	1633	65	37
Child mortality rate (per 1000 live births)		58	107	48
Female heads of household (per cent)	27.5	18.6	19.0	17.0
Family income: percentage with				
Up to 2 minimum salaries	74.3			
2–5 minimum salaries	15.8			
5–10 minimum salaries	8.2			

Fortaleza. There are serious infrastructure problems in the peripheral areas of the town; for example, one in five houses does not have a toilet.

Sobral is one of the industrial poles of the north-east of Ceará; but the industrial workers do not live in the city. Hence, a large part of the income earned from the industry is spent in other municipalities of the region. As in Maracanaú, families excluded from the economic development process live in high-risk conditions in areas considered unsuitable for human occupation. Icapuí is a small town in the north-east of Ceará. Most residents are landless and earn their living from fishing or as farm labourers. Those with small plots of irrigated land produce tropical fruits; but they have difficulty selling their products on the commercial markets. The majority of land around the city is owned by two families.

History and description of the programme

In 1987, after the fall of the dictatorship that had ruled Brazil between 1964 and 1984, and with pressure from the urban social movements that had an important role in the re-democratization of the country, the federal government launched a housing programme. The programme was based on the idea of mutual help known locally as *mutirão* (see Box 7.2). It offered subsidies to enable community organizations to buy materials and collectively build their own houses. Although the programme started well, the initial objective of achieving 400,000 units was never reached and the national programme abruptly ended in 1990. However, in a number of cities including Fortaleza, the programme continued with local funds.

During the late 1980s, the Mutirão Housing Programme was supported by the provincial government of Ceará and by the municipal government of Fortaleza. The result was 10,000 more houses. However, this number was insufficient since the housing deficit in the city was an estimated 150,000 housing units.

BOX 7.2 MUTIRÃO

The word *mutirão* has its origins in the native Tupi language, and was initially used to mean 'free help', in which workers assist each other through collective work to address individual needs. During the 1960s, the idea of working in groups to reach a common objective was transferred to the urban context. Today the interpretations and forms of *mutirão* are varied; they include, for example, cleaning the neighbourhood through collective initiatives.

Through *mutirão*, it was intended that the construction of houses for families with limited financial resources would be undertaken by the residents themselves. Technical and financial help would be provided by the public authorities.

At the beginning of 1990, a number of issues came together: the end of the federal support for the Mutirão Housing Programme, the increased recognition of corruption and the collapse of the Banco Nacional de Habitação (National Housing Bank), which had financed 4 million housing units in 22 years (1964–1986). At a local level, there was an awareness of the deficiency in the scale of the programme in Fortaleza. Moreover, for housing improvements to operate within the Mutirão programme, it was necessary to set up SCHPs (Sociedades Comunitárias de Habitação Popular, or Community Societies for Popular Housing). This was in spite of already existing neighbourhood organizations in most low-income residential areas. There was a further concern that the programme sought to undermine existing organizations and weaken mass movements by ensuring that local grassroots organizations existed for no other reason than to support the mutirão. This was the context in which hundreds of community organizations in Fortaleza began a process of reflection on the provision of low-income housing in the city.

A community fund for popular housing

This reflection was supported by an NGO that had just been created, Cearah Periferia. Cearah Periferia had been founded with the intention of supporting the reconstruction of the housing programme in Fortaleza. At the end of 1992, a seminar was organized that brought together more than 100 leaders of 30 community organizations. A commission of 21 representatives, elected during the seminar, began to meet regularly to draw up proposals and identify activities. In March 1993, the leading local newspaper published a special edition of its supplement 'Open University' on low-income housing. The preparation of the supplement was coordinated by Cearah Periferia and it included a proposal for a popular housing fund. The fund subsequently became an important catalyst for the mobilization of many local organizations.

The communities in Fortaleza organized themselves, and, among many other activities, some members travelled together by bus to Brasilia, the seat of the federal government, 2200 kilometres from Fortaleza. Their intention was to present the project for a national housing fund to the recently appointed minister of housing (who came from Fortaleza). In spite of a lack of concrete outcomes, the communities gained experience from their negotiations with the public authorities. At the same time, their relationship with the NGOs who supported them became much closer because of the amount of time that they spent working together.

In 1993, an international seminar on financing alternatives[4] created an opportunity to share experiences and ideas with NGOs from South Africa, Namibia, Mexico, Colombia, Thailand, the Philippines, England and Brazil. The idea of creating an alternative funding system to facilitate the access of low-income families to loan finance began to take shape. Soon after the seminar, one member of a Belgium foundation called SELAVIP (Latin American and Asian Service for Low-Income Housing) visited Fortaleza. In cooperation with the community organizations and Cearah Periferia, SELAVIP further examined the possibility of a financial system that would draw together grassroots organizations, NGOs and public authorities.

This 'system' planned to incorporate three basic elements that had been little used in development projects for low-income families in Brazil: savings, subsidies and loans. The practice of saving in Brazil is not common, especially among low-income groups. For 15 years, hyper-inflation of up to 4000 per cent a year had made saving meaningless. Frequent changes in currency made it even harder to see the value in saving. At that time, subsidies were being eliminated by the federal government with the end of the *mutirao* programme, and loan finance was only available for those earning more than five minimum salaries.

A further factor was also important in supporting the growth of new ideas. Since 1988, the municipal authorities in Fortaleza had established a working relationship with GRET (Groupe de Recherche et d'Echanges Tecnologiques, or Group for Research and Technology Exchange)[5] to implement (on a limited scale) innovative projects for urban development and income generation with community organizations. A channel for new ideas and projects had been opened with the municipality in spite of the limited tradition of cooperative work between NGOs and government in Brazil.[6]

As a consequence of these different activities, it was agreed that the municipality and NGOs would establish a fund to provide low-income families with access to small subsidized loans to improve their housing conditions. The negotiations took time because the idea was innovative and because of its central principle that the fund should support a housing development process based on joint management. This was not part of the tradition of Brazilian municipal government.

The important points of the final agreement were that:

• Loans should be made available to workers in both the formal and informal sectors.

---

4 Organized by the International Institute for Environment and Development (IIED) and sponsored by HIC (Habitat International Coalition) and Misereor (a German NGO).
5 A French NGO with a team of professionals based in Fortaleza since 1991.
6 When Cearah Periferia and GRET began their partnership with the municipality and the state government, their strategy was not fully understood by the other NGOs, who were used to much more confrontational strategies.

- A title of land ownership would not be necessary; the *posse* or the right of use of the land would be sufficient.
- The residents' associations should have an active role in the process.
- Although the repayments were to be made at the bank by individuals, the process would be collective and the formation of savings groups would be a pre-condition for loan finance.

In May 1994, an agreement was signed for the implementation of the financial system Casa Melhor.

The programme was not universally accepted. One federation of residents' associations linked to the radical left objected that the programme involved a relationship of partnership with the municipal government, used loan finance and was not directed at families in a state of absolute poverty.

Implementation

During 1994 and the first half of 1995, an intense campaign was mounted in the low-income settlements to explain and motivate interest in the programme. There was a lack of confidence in the public authorities; but there were good relations between the neighbourhood associations and the two NGOs, Cearah Periferia and GRET. Local leaders, municipal employees and Cearah Periferia staff (some of whom were community leaders) organized meetings in the favelas and neighbourhoods almost every evening and weekend to explain the programme and address concerns. The local groups quickly understood and accepted the basic principle of financing with equal amounts of savings, loans and subsidies – in other words, what they saved would be tripled by equal amounts of subsidies and loan finance.[7] It was agreed that the loan would be for 600 Brazilian reals (then equivalent to around US$600).

The programme received a further impetus when there were outbreaks of dengue fever in the southern part of Fortaleza. There was a widespread recognition that improvements needed to be made. The Casa Melhor programme started in six neighbourhoods in that part of the city to construct bathrooms and install water supply and sewerage systems. In January 1995, the first group received its finance.

The piloting of the programme in six neighbourhoods resulted in a slow pace of implementation and caused a number of problems. Hence, in June 1995, as a consequence of the Casa Melhor programme, the Better Home and Programme of Support for Self-building (PAAC) was initiated by Cearah Periferia with some additional features. This programme drew on a strong and trusting relationship between the NGO and a small group of well-organized communities. PAAC was created to extend the reach of the Casa Melhor programme, to provide greater flexibility and innovation, to assist in the consolidation of the programme, and to help counterbalance some bureaucratic difficulties created by the municipality. Table 7.2 summarizes the differences between Casa Melhor and PAAC.

---

7 Until 1996, the three contributions were equal: city hall = subsidy of one-third; family = savings of one-third; and NGO = credit of one-third.

Table 7.2 *Casa Melhor and PAAC compared*

	Casa Melhor	PAAC
Origins of resources		
Savings	People	People
Subsidy	Local authority	External donors
Loan	External donors	External donors
Value		
Maximum saving	US$200	US$100
Maximum subsidy	US$200	US$200
Maximum loan	US$200	US$300
Duration	Maximum 12 months	Maximum 10 months
Types of guarantee	Personal collateral	Solidarity and mutual
Loan use	Building materials	Building materials
Types of works	Kitchen, bathrooms, shops, enclosure wall, additional rooms	Kitchen, bathrooms, shops, enclosure wall, additional rooms

By September 1995, more than 1800 families had attended meetings and 1000 had expressed an interest in joining a programme. The families belonged to many diverse types of community organizations (community housing societies, residents' unions, popular councils, community associations, social philanthropic unions and groups of community crèches). All of the groups were located within low-income settlements in the southern part of the city.

Casa Melhor was managed by an administrative council and management unit. All changes to the programme had to be approved by the council, whose initial members were GRET, the municipality's Institute of Planning (IPLAM)[8] and a community leader, elected as the representative of the associations involved in the programme. When GRET wound up its activities in Fortaleza, Cearah Periferia became a member of the council. In order to reinforce the space given to civil society, a local NGO, Cáritas (Arquidiocesana de Fortaleza), also became a council member to represent the organizations[9] that financed the loan fund managed by Cearah Periferia. The participation of community representatives in meetings of the administrative council led to the gradual incorporation of other neighbourhoods within the programme. The programme has operated in 49 neighbourhoods.

Shortly after receiving a 'best practice' award at the United Nations (UN) Habitat II Conference in Istanbul, the municipal authorities suddenly withdrew from the programme. Not even the publicity and the recognition associated with the UN prize was enough to secure their continued involvement. The reason for their withdrawal was primarily political. Delays in the release of subsidy funds began to prejudice the continuation of the programme, and there was political polarization between the municipality in Fortaleza and the Ceará state government.

8 Instituto de Planejamento do Município de Fortaleza
9 Secours Catholique, an organization of the French Catholic church.

The programme carried on functioning with already allocated resources. However, the ambivalence of the municipality made it difficult to secure international development support for the loan fund. Donor agencies wished to support a programme that received a municipal subsidy to ensure its affordability. To counter this difficulty, the staff of Cearah Periferia directed its efforts at the development of PAAC–Interior. Activities were targeted on municipalities of the interior of Ceará who were interested in responding to their housing problems through participative strategies that reinforced local community organizations.

The expansion of the programme

In 1998, in an attempt to counter the delays in providing subsidies for the Casa Melhor programme by the municipalities, Cearah Periferia and the community organizations decided to implement PAAC–Fortaleza. PAAC–Fortaleza was a modification of the original PAAC. Faced with the pent-up demand for financing from the neighbourhood organizations, it was decided to present the families who had been saving with an alternative financing scheme. PAAC–Fortaleza compensated for the absence of the municipal subsidy with a longer loan period and more time for repayment. When the commitment of the municipality returned in September of the same year, the two programmes became integrated.

The implementation of PAAC–Interior was taken up rapidly. In general, it has been more successful in municipalities committed to participatory development. For example, PAAC–Interior was part of the participatory budget[10] discussions in Icapuí. It is also one of the most important programmes of the Housing Management Department of Sobral municipality, which used its own resources to create the Fundo Municipal de Apoio à Habitação Popular (FUMHAB, or Municipal Fund for the Support of Popular Housing), which is managed by a municipal housing council.

In 1999, a new challenge presented itself. Programme staff became conscious that as new and greater demands emerged, there was a danger that the scale of the programme would grow but quality would be sacrificed. Further worries were how to finance the expansion and which type of resources would enable the programme to maximize its impact. At the same time, the worsening of the financial crisis in Brazilian municipalities caused the poorest municipalities to give priority to emergency programmes rather than ongoing development initiatives.

By January 2000, in spite of the municipal funding crisis, Casa Melhor/PAAC was being implemented in seven municipalities in Ceará: Fortaleza, Maracanaú, Sobral, Icapuí, Maranguape, Eusébio and Independência. Programme staff had also advised the Programa Morando Melhor (Living Better Programme) in Belém in the north of Brazil, and the Programa Vivienda Digna (Living Decently Programme) in Maracaibo, Venezuela.

---

10 The participatory budget is a way of drawing up the local government budget in which the use of part of the investment resources for public works is defined by the inhabitants themselves, through meetings with the council created for the purpose.

Tools and mechanisms

The programme that has emerged has a number of characteristics. It brings together the capacity of families to save, the right to a municipal subsidy and a loan that must be paid back in 12 months. The municipal government provides subsidies for the fund and technical assistance (through a programme technical team). The grassroots organizations direct the process in the neighbourhoods and represent the interested families who provide resources through savings groups. The NGOs provide technical assistance and participate in the management unit and the technical team.

The programme has four objectives:

1 Make families aware of the importance of savings.
2 Strengthen the interaction between grassroots organizations and member families.
3 Support grassroots organizations in their other activities by encouraging community and citizen participation.
4 Improve housing and, consequently, the health conditions of low-income families.

One-sixth of the amount given to the family is through savings, one-third is the municipal subsidy and half is a loan drawn from the donor funding. The donor funding is rotated as each part loan is returned invididually by each family. Another part of the donor funding goes to support maintenance of the team and Cearah Periferia's operational administrative costs. The money collected from families through loan repayments is then available for reloaning. The proportion that comes from savings is lower than was originally the case and this was done following a request from the families. The programme strengthens community organization through supportive interventions. Technical assistance is provided through support for project development and expenditure estimates. The acquisition of greater financial skills is encouraged through the loan process.

Grassroots organizations are highly involved. They spread information and awareness about the programme, form savings groups, complete forms giving information about the socio-economic status of the applicants, take part in inspecting the improvements, accompany the teams during field-work and ensure prompt loan repayments. The savings groups themselves are made up of 10 to 30 committed families with family incomes of between one and three minimum salaries.[11] They should be homeowners or have the legal right to occupy their home[12] (in the case of mutirões, the contract of real right of use,[13] which is

---

11 Although initially the programme reached families with incomes of 1.5 to 3 minimum salaries, the minimum value was lowered as the programme sought to serve lower-income families.
12 Families must have lived in the house for more than five years, without their occupation of the house having been legally challenged during that time.
13 A form of contract with a community association in which a person who was involved in the construction of a property may live in the property but may not sell it until after the expiry of a period defined by the association (for example, ten years). During this time, the person must pay a very small monthly contribution to the association. At the end of the period, the person becomes the full owner of a property that has, in fact, been heavily subsidized by the state through the intermediary of the community association.

signed by the community group), and they must live in the house that is to be improved. The community group must be legally recognized with a constitution, elected board and registered with the Cadastro Geral de Contribuintes (General Register of Tax-Payers).

Loans are for a maximum of 12 months. No interest is charged; but repayments are adjusted upwards in accordance with inflation-related increases in the minimum wage (this is revised annually by the federal government, generally by less than the rate of price inflation). The loan can be used to improve or extend any room or aspect in the house (such as the bathroom, bedroom, kitchen, water and electrical installations). Each beneficiary needs to provide a guarantor from within the savings group.

A grassroots organization can have one or more savings groups functioning at the same time. A group can apply for second and subsequent loans; but the subsidy is reduced to half its value in the first loan, and in further loans it disappears altogether. If a second group of 15 to 30 families is formed within the same association, loans will only be released if the first group is up to date with its repayments. This requirement works as an additional incentive, using social pressure to speed up the repayment process.

One of the most innovative aspects of the programme is the mix of institutions that make up the programme and their joint responsibilities. Although collaboration between state and civil society is common in some countries, in Brazil such relationships have taken a long time to develop. At the beginning of the 1990s, NGOs were little-known institutions, few in number and with a very limited degree of interaction with the formal public powers. During the dictatorship, many had specifically designed their projects to operate at the margin of governmental activity. Despite the advent of democracy, there remained a considerable distance between the public sector and civil society. With no accepted channel for communication between the excluded population and the government, NGOs acted as intermediaries. NGOs facilitated contact by advising both the grassroots organizations and the public sector about the preparation, implementation and evaluation of participatory development projects.

Moreover, the NGO community in Ceara is not as large as in many parts of Brazil. In PAAC–Interior, for example, NGOs are simply not present and so Cearah Periferia trains the municipal governments to provide technical assistance.

The administrative council of Casa Melhor was designed to reduce the influence of the local authority and political parties. In Fortaleza, the present council is made up of two representatives of the municipality, two representatives elected by the community groups involved in the programme, one representative of Cearah Periferia, and one representative of the Cáritas Arquidiocesana of Fortaleza. A management unit has been created for the technical and operational management of the programme. This unit has one representative of the municipality and one representative of Cearah Periferia. A technical team is linked to the unit and is made up of technicians, engineers, architects, social assistants, trainees and community activists.

Technical support covers many aspects of the programme. In some cases, one meeting is enough for the constitution of a saving group, while in others it is necessary to hold two or three. The process of constituting a savings group takes from one to three months, depending upon the rhythm of the community (that is, if the interested people already have a degree of minimum cohesion with the community or association, if they live next to one other, etc). However, the methodology of conscientization adopted by the team is an important factor: the one, three or four meetings with the families and the social visits to each house to better understand the reality of each family. As well as an approach with this communitarian dynamics, a good relationship is needed between professionals from NGOs, the municipality and the community. The constant contact between the community representatives and the families who are saving is important for the groups' success in saving and in ensuring good repayment records.

These variations make it difficult to precisely quantify the inputs required and to evaluate their costs. Administrative expenses include the operating costs of the three support teams (salaries, communication, and office equipment and materials), transport costs and office rent. The costs are shared between the local authority and the NGO.

Financial aspects

Families have to save to be part of the programme. Saving requires the family to create a surplus by reducing its expenses, working more, or selling something that it owns. A savings contribution is linked to citizenship, self-esteem and collective action. Programme staff now believe that such additional factors may be of greater developmental importance than the monetary value of the savings.

Development associations or savings groups are not allowed by Brazilian law to receive money from individuals and to hold that money on behalf of the individuals as savings. The Brazilian Central Bank only allows formally constituted banks to receive savings. Partly because of this legislation, the community finance sector in Brazil is very new. While existing community organizations have a very relevant social role, until a few years ago they did not directly involve themselves in neighbourhood economic development. They lobbied for the provision of public services and infrastructure. There are few examples of organizations who have supported the development of financial activities in their communities. Rarer still are those organizations who have some form of relationship with the formal financial sector. Today, however, because of the absence of the formal financial sector in low-income settlements, and because of the growing conviction among grassroots organizations that the control of resources is critical, alternatives are beginning to emerge.

However, the relationship between the community finance sector and the formal financial sector is not a comfortable one. The Central Bank imposes many unrealistic rules, and there are currently very few possibilities for interaction with the formal sector. Although the Central Bank has not modified the rules that govern financing, BNDES (the National Bank for Economic and Social Development) is now beginning to finance NGOs and community organizations. A law currently being considered by the federal legislature will facilitate the development of community-based financial operations.

Analysis of the programme

The assessment

To understand the impact of the programme, a detailed assessment was undertaken in 2000. Available studies were augmented with structured interviews with families participating in the programme. Open interviews were held with key informants (members of the administrative council and staff from the Fortaleza municipality), the technical, social and financial teams of Cearah Periferia, officials and politicians from Maracanaú, Sobral and Fortaleza municipalities and the director of a private-sector social housing company. Focus groups were held with various organizations who have participated in the programme and with active community leaders.

The selection of neighbourhoods and communities was based on several criteria. There had to be two existing savings groups, some families that had dropped out of the savings scheme or whose repayments were overdue; and the neighbourhood had not previously been included in a research programme. In total, 121 interviews were carried out in four areas of Fortaleza. Each area represented one of four broad categories of high-risk, low-quality settlement in which the programme is operating: illegal land occupations, unfinished housing estates, low-income neighbourhoods and *mutirão* construction. Twelve interviews were carried out in three savings groups in a low-income neighbourhood and *mutirão* group in Maracanaú. In Sobral, 12 families from two savings groups within the same association were interviewed. In all, 145 interviews were completed.

Who benefited

Who has benefited from the programme? In summary, the beneficiaries are families with five or more members and who live in houses of 40 to 60 square metres. Most of them only have the legal right to use the house that they occupy. Of the families interviewed, 46 per cent had already received funds, 1 per cent had given up seeking loans because they had failed part of the registration phase, and 43 per cent were in the savings phase.

The 11 per cent who had given up emphasized the difficulties associated with savings and the difficulties of loan repayments:

- 'I couldn't save.'
- 'I felt I couldn't pay because my salary is small.'
- The person registered, or someone from the family, lost their job.
- 'It [the slowness in the release of the credit] was taking a long time.'
- 'I got sick and was only getting one [minimum] salary, so I was afraid to take on a commitment.'
- The sum of money involved wouldn't have been enough to carry out the work planned.

Of those interviewed, 58 per cent came from the interior of Ceará, an example of the migration flows from the towns in the interior to the major centres.

Table 7.3 *Employment status*

Do you work?	Quantity	Percentage
Yes	89	73.6
No	26	21.5
Retired	3	2.5
Receive pension	1	0.8
Unemployed	1	0.8
Did not reply	1	0.8
Total	121	100

However, almost 80 per cent had lived for more than eight years in the locality. These families are stable and have an urban lifestyle. But, at the same time, factors such as the media can distort their perception of need and some believe that it is more important to have a television than a bathroom in the house.

It appears that the programme appeals to families who are interested in consolidating their homes and improving their quality of life in an area that they have come to regard as a permanent home. Most live in families of less than four persons, although about 38 per cent of respondents live with between five and eight family members. In cities in the interior, family size is larger, with an average of six family members.

Sharing housing is not as common as it is among many poor families. In 81 per cent of cases, only one family lives in the house. In 18 per cent of cases, two or more families live in the same house (this situation of overcrowding demonstrates the qualitative housing deficit, as young couples and families with an unemployed wage earner are obliged to share space with parents or friends).

Although the families interviewed live in peripheral neighbourhoods with high indices of unemployment, the majority of those questioned are working (see Table 7.3). Many of these do not have a formal job contract, but are street sellers or have other occupations in the informal sector.

Almost all of the respondents work in the tertiary sector (services and commerce), with only 4 per cent working in industry. Table 7.4 shows that half of the families receive up to two minimum salaries and 17.3 per cent state that they receive more than three minimum salaries. This is above the programme's permitted limit; hence, either salaries improved since they registered for the

Table 7.4 *Respondents' income levels*

Income Level	Quantity	Percentage
0–1 minimum salary	15	12.4
1–2 minimum salaries	46	38.0
2–3 minimum salaries	37	30.6
3–4 minimum salaries	13	10.7
About 4 minimum salaries	8	6.6
Did not reply	2	1.7
Total	121	100

Table 7.5 *Respondents' use of credit*

Previous purchases on credit	Quantity	Percentage
Yes	82	67.8
No	39	32.2
Reasons for not taking credit:		
• fear	1	2.5
• don't like to	9	23.0
• name in SPC*	2	5.2
• small salary	19	48.8
• prefer to buy for cash	2	5.2
• other	6	15.3
Total	121	

Note: * Serviço de Proteção ao Credor (SPC or Credit Protection Service) blacklists those who have debts.

programme or there is some problem with the information. The latter is the more probable because the majority of the families are involved in activities in the informal sector with very variable earnings.

The programme was designed to reach the lower-income families (with between 1.5 and 3 minimum salaries), and not to meet the needs of the poorest families. However, the programme hopes to reach the most excluded who have few other possibilities to obtain loan finance. Through the interviews, one can see that those at the lower end of the target salary range were not being reached.

Just under 68 per cent of those interviewed already had previous experiences with the use of credit (see Table 7.5). One-third had never done this, with the main reasons being linked to the low level of salary (48.8 per cent).

The responses differed greatly between municipalities. In Sobral, 83 per cent had already taken loans due to a credit network established to make the inhabitants' lives easier. In Maracanaú, 66 per cent of those interviewed did not buy on credit. This is a dormitory town experiencing rapid growth, in which families do not have the links and trust that make access to credit easier.

Effectiveness in reducing poverty

The impact of the programme on poverty reduction can be measured through the changes that occur in relationships within the family, between neighbours and in community organizations.

From the names of the programme's registered title holders among those families interviewed, it can be seen that the participation of women is greater than that of men. Of those interviewed, 61 per cent had the title registered with the woman. This reflects the leading role of women in managing the house. The considerable number of men recorded as the title holder is explained by the fact that this is a financing programme, and that common belief is that men are better negotiators than women. The focus groups suggest that even if the man is the title holder, it is the woman who participates in the process of meeting, registering and visits. The construction is generally the responsibility of the man.

Table 7.6 *Who was motivated to join the programme?*

Motivated to participate	Quantity	Percentage
Woman	73	60.3
Man	32	26.4
Couple	7	5.8
Children	6	4.9
Sister/brother	2	1.6
Mother	1	0.8
Total	121	100

According to these focus groups, there is no difficulty that prevents women from participating in the programme. The workshop itself was the proof of a greater female participation: 5 men were present and 47 women. Table 7.6 shows that it is women who are motivated to join the programme.

Of the 121 interviewees: 88 were members of the community association before the programme and 32 became members as a result of the programme; 80 per cent participate in association meetings, while an overwhelming 97 per cent believe that it is important to pay the membership fee; 85 per cent note that their association is very well organized; 97 per cent believe that the Casa Melhor programme has strengthened the association. This finding is supported by the technical support staff in the municipalities of Sobral and Maracanaú, who suggest that, in their experience, '[the programme]…strengthens and increases participation. Families who have difficulties in participating because they are not organized in associations are encouraged to found associations. The programme restores the role of community associations… interactions between associations begin to take place.'

Families who had never participated in community organizations and who were initially very sceptical have begun to participate and involve themselves in the associations. For some, the experience was more than simply participating in the association to benefit from the programme. One beneficiary described her attitude to the association: 'I didn't know that there was such an important thing in the neighbourhood…I entered and I'm taking part.' Thus, it appears that the programme has helped to build and strengthen community associations. Before the formation of the groups, 31 per cent of the community said that they did not know each other and 21 per cent had little contact with each other.

However, the representative of the participating families on the administrative council is concerned that families are only looking to the associations because of the programme. Half of those interviewed say that they had little contact with each other, even through the programme (the remaining half had good contact and some have participated actively in other community programmes). Once the lending activity is over, 42 per cent have no further contact, 32 per cent maintain good relations with their community and 26.7 per cent have slight contact and attend meetings. Of those interviewed, 67 per cent state that there is solidarity between the neighbours, while 25 per cent do not believe that this is the case. It appears that there is potential for participation and mutual support that needs to be more widely emphasized.

Table 7.7 *Changes in frequency of visits to doctors*

Frequency of visits to doctor	Quantity	Percentage
No change in frequency	20	30.3
Very few visits to the doctor	18	27.3
Reduced frequency	17	25.8
Maintained same number of visits	10	15.1
Only go once a year	1	1.5
Not yet benefited from improvements	55	–
Total	121	100

Health improvements

The main improvements were the construction of bathrooms, water and sewerage pipes and wastewater pits. Those who had been involved in the programme were asked about how the programme had improved their lives. Forty-three per cent said that there had been conflict over space previously, while 56 per cent said that this had not been the case. Beneficiaries made a number of comments, such as:

- 'There are less insects [scorpions, spiders, cockroaches].'
- 'The rats have gone.'
- 'It's cleaner.'
- 'The tiled floor is more hygienic, healthier.'

Turning to health conditions, 69 per cent said that there had been an improvement in health conditions with 30 per cent not being able to identify any improvement. Table 7.7 reports on the changed frequency of visits to the doctor.

Local health volunteers are able to confirm the improvements mentioned in the questionnaires and reaffirmed the importance of improvements. They emphasized that respiratory diseases, diarrhoea and other gastrointestinal complications, especially in children, are related to the lack of cement floors, plastered walls, bathrooms and other unsanitary conditions.

Beneficiaries were not asked about the physical improvement of the neighbourhoods; but there are many stories from community leaders and families that provide evidence of the transformation achieved in areas included in the programme. The programme assists the community to grow stronger and address local conditions.

Economic well-being

Of those interviewed, 54.6 per cent did not have a bank account. Most did not know of or did not use unofficial money lenders. For the 15 per cent of respondents who did use unofficial money lenders, interest rates varied from 20 to 50 per cent a month. Two-thirds of the sample did not save, with the main reason being the low level of income.

Table 7.8 *How families managed to save*

How did you make your saving?	Quantity	Percentage
Reducing spending	42	50.0
Working more	23	27.4
Selling something	2	2.4
Taking a loan	11	13.1
Holiday or compensation payment	6	7.1
Not that far into the programme	37	
Total	121	100

The 'savings' required by the programme were generally seen as a down payment. Families used a number of strategies to secure the amount (see Table 7.8). Ninety-five per cent of interviewees stated that the programme helped them to plan for the future and offered them an incentive to improve their living conditions. Despite the problems with savings, the families' representative on the administrative council noted the important position of savings within the programme: 'One of the secrets and the principal features of the programme is saving, as it brings a concern with saving into the heart of the family and is one of the main contributions of the programme to the development of the community.'

While some focus group members argued that the savings requirement should be reduced, none argued that there should be no savings component. All agreed that the family should contribute and thereby indicate that they really want to take part.

With regard to the benefits of the programme, just over half of the families suggested that there was no change in the incomes of the family or of others as a result of the programme. However, 6 per cent of improvements are undertaken to start or advance a business.

Almost all of the families use local labour; as a result, the programme has a beneficial effect on local employment. Ninety-six per cent use labour and construction materials from their immediate neighbourhood. However, in general, there was no specific strategy to promote local enterprises.

The views of participants highlight what was important about the programme for them:

- greater comfort for the family (38 per cent);
- greater security (16.5 per cent);
- increased value of the house (14.9);
- improved relations inside the family (10.8 per cent);
- improved relations with neighbours and the group (9.9 per cent);
- contributed to bring those involved closer to the association (9.9 per cent).

The focus groups emphasized that the improvements to the house were worth much in terms of self-esteem and a renewed sense of determination for self-improvement.

Table 7.9 *Impact of programme on family life*

How is family life after the improvements?	Quantity	Percentage
Very well, united, happier	25	37.3
Better, much better	30	44.8
More comfort and space	9	13.4
Just the same	3	4.5
Total	67	100

Poverty reduction

Although many of the families are satisfied with the programme, others believe that it is limited in its contribution to poverty reduction. The representative of the families on the administrative council argues that the programme does not reach the families who experience the worst conditions. More generally, there is a feeling among the community members consulted through the focus groups that the programme improves the quality of life, but does little specifically to address poverty. This view was broadly supported by a comment from one of the staff members of the municipality in Fortaleza: 'You only reduce poverty with economic development.' The NGO team involved in the project was very enthusiastic arguing that 'It is the first programme that gives the excluded access to the banks.'

Relationships between institutions

Many of the families involved in the programme have a general knowledge about the partners, structure and function of the programme. However, there is limited knowledge of the specific contribution of the partners among some of the families, reflecting the extent to which families are not involved in decision-making. Although families contribute 25 per cent of the programme funds, only 3 per cent of the families consider themselves to be a partner in the programme. However, 98 per cent of the families consider that the community associations have an essential role in the programme. The municipal officials and NGO emphasize the importance of the associations.

Although there is limited understanding by the families of the work undertaken by the administrative council, the community representative on the council considers that it is important. She believes that it is more democratic and transparent than other projects carried out by the municipality. The administrative council is seen as important in a number of ways:

* It provides for continuity of projects and programmes when the councillors change at four-year intervals.
* It ensures that the families themselves have a knowledge about the programme.
* It helps to create a new kind of relationship between public power and the community that is based on partnership, and not on providing assistance in exchange for votes.
* It helps to create a sense of responsibility among the families.

Table 7.10 *Families' financial contributions*

Families' financial contribution	Quantity	Percentage
400–600 Brazilian reals	3	4.5
601–800 Brazilian reals	42	62.7
801–1000 Brazilian reals	5	7.5
1001–1200 Brazilian reals	6	8.9
1201–2000 Brazilian reals	4	6.0
More than 2000 Brazilian reals	7	10.4
Total	67	100

In Sobral, the programme has evolved to create a Municipal Fund for Popular Housing with a council for housing, in which all parties have equal representation.

Financial issues and financial sustainability

As noted above, savings are considered to be one of the most important elements in the programme. However, in addition to the required savings contribution, families add their own funds. Table 7.10 summarizes the extent of these funds. In reality, the programme acts as a catalyst for housing investment.

With regard to the loan itself, two-thirds of respondents considered that the value of the loan was insufficient and that more was needed. However, the focus groups with community associations suggested that the loan was sufficient (given the problems families experienced when making repayments). The programme, overall, has good repayment rates; but these aggregate figures hide the realities faced by some families. For many years, loan repayment was between 95 and 97 per cent. In recent years, late repayments have increased to 17 per cent, although unrecoverable losses are still only 5 per cent.

Many families struggle to repay their debts, given the multiple demands on their incomes. The associations, in particular, were concerned that there was a lack of strategies to secure repayment. If groups have bad debts, the association cannot put forward more savings schemes for loans and therefore the community leaders feel under pressure to secure the repayments. The current structure of the programme means that much of the responsibility for debt collection falls onto them. There was a general belief that the programme needed to rethink debt collection and develop ways that involve greater solidarity between the members of the savings scheme. For example, the members of the group could define among themselves the penalties and forms of assistance that they wanted to use when there were repayment problems.

For the subsidy, the funds in Fortaleza are 3 per cent of the taxes collected by the municipality (no charge is made by the municipality for technical assistance). The NGO raises funds from international development assistance and the community organizations carry out a series of unpaid activities (part of their costs are covered as the association receives 2 per cent of the loan value). The community representatives on the administrative council believe that the subsidy should be increased. The municipal officials note that this depends upon the perspective of the leader of the council.

NGO administration costs are estimated to be about 60 Brazilian reals for each loan released, or 10 per cent of the final value of the money received by the families. The municipality estimates that it spends a similar amount, of which half are direct costs.

Financial viability

The revolving fund that has been set up with donor finance does not charge interest; therefore, over time, it is being eroded. The issue of interest rates has never been fully explored. In general, the charging of interest was not felt to be appropriate as Cearah Periferia and the federations of community organizations believe that the state should be subsidizing families, helping them to secure adequate accommodation and facilitating access to loans for those who can pay.

However, due to the erosion of funds, the fund managers are now beginning to explore the possibility of charging interest in certain situations. The research team has calculated that:

- An interest rate of 2 per cent a month would have enabled the same amount of financing to support almost 50 per cent more improvements.
- However, interest charges of 2 per cent would cover only 65 per cent of the real costs of high-quality technical assistance.
- At present, with low rates of inflation, the loss in the value of the fund is very small – although inflation is now rising again.

It is not clear that charging interest is the best option and an alternative might be to charge families for some of the costs of technical assistance.

While there are many financial advantages in the growth of funds, there are increasing concerns that the current flexibility of fund management will be difficult to maintain as the programme expands. At present, the programme is very flexible. For example, when the municipality temporarily stopped providing subsidies, it was possible to have an alternative means of financing with PAAC–Fortaleza using only loans and savings. However, as the programme grows it may be necessary to formalize the administration, making it harder to amend terms and conditions as circumstances change.

There is a need to make a stronger case for the value of such funds as development tools. The community financial sector has been a subject of discussion in Brazil recently. Grassroots organizations were always active in issues of social development and social justice; but traditionally they have been reluctant to enter the financial field. Today, however, with the recognized absence of the formal financial sector in low-income settlements, and with a widespread conviction that managing resources is key to the development of community organizations, there has been interest in new experiences and alternatives. As noted earlier, while the Central Bank is not interested in amending its rules and regulations, the National Bank for Economic and Social Development (BNDES) has begun to finance NGOs. Generally, the context is one of exploration and openness.

Construction method and its financial implications

The need to reduce construction costs continues to be a challenge for the programme. The type and origin of the construction materials need to be carefully considered. The cheaper the costs of construction, the more the family can do with limited resources.

In order to reduce costs, it is necessary to explore several alternatives for low-cost technologies, producing building components through collective effort and/or using local materials. However, staff from building companies consulted during the research explained that commercial construction material companies do not permit public bodies to approve the use of non-conventional materials to ensure that the market for cement, steel and aluminium remains intact. While the families and neighbourhood construction workers are familiar with traditional building techniques, lack of expertise and time among the technical team mean that such techniques are not widely used.

At present, only 9 per cent of the families undertake the improvements themselves, with 61 per cent paying others and 25 per cent using family members. Generally, families prefer to do the work themselves if they can.

There was a widespread appreciation for the technical assistance provided through the programme. The families found this to be important through the plan and the associated budget. A gap was perceived with regard to monitoring the works themselves. This was, in part, related to the individualism of the programme. While the loans and savings were organized through the collective organizations, the building improvements themselves were carried out by individual families.

Support for the programme

Table 7.11 summarizes the opinions of respondents to the programme, overall. In particular, the following points were noted:

- The programme is credible and serious.
- There are clear criteria for allocating loans.
- Learning and reflection are built into the programme.
- There is no clientelism.
- The associations are serious in their participation.

Many of those who had recently started the programme were unwilling to make a judgement about the quality of the activities, and this explains the large number who did not reply. However, some of the families struggled to take part (see Table 7.12).

The programme staff anticipated that securing savings would be difficult because it is difficult for families to accumulate funds due to an absolute lack of income and the lack of experience in saving. What is of concern is the number who mentioned bureaucratic problems and the time taken to secure funds. Some

Table 7.11 *Respondents' opinion of the programme*

Opinions of the programme	Quantity	Percentage
Excellent	41	34
Good	41	34
Regular	0	0
Bad	0	0
Very bad	0	0
Don't know	2	2
Did not reply	37	30
Total	121	100

of this perspective may be accounted for by the lack of experience in securing loan finance. Thirty per cent have had no similar experiences. What has been recognized is the small size of the loan in relation to the work involved. The associations believe that it is necessary to make the operation of the programme more efficient so that larger numbers of people can secure the loans quickly.

Families commented on their experiences in the programme. Many of those involved mentioned that they had learned the value of union, mutual respect, solidarity, participation and collective activities. A number of suggestions were made for improving the programme and these are summarized below:

- Increase the loan and reduce the repayments (15 people).
- Have less bureaucracy (14 people).
- Leave as it is (7 people).
- Remove or reduce the savings component; failing that, give more time for the funds to be raised (6 people).
- Increase the size of the group (5 people).
- Ensure all repay so that other group members are not penalized (4 people).
- Provide finance for the community labour (4 people).
- Have more meetings to spread information (3 people).
- Expand the programme (2 people).
- Enable the association to act as guarantor (1 person).

Table 7.12 *Difficulties in participation*

Difficulties in participation	Quantity	Percentage
Bureaucracy, slow speed	19	23.2
Savings and affordability	25	30.5
Need for guarantor	7	8.5
Need for proof of income	2	2.4
Small value of loan	5	6.1
Formation of groups	3	3.7
None	21	25.6
Total	82	100

Many more individual proposals were related to the savings component and this reflects a broader concern in the community. The families' representative on the administrative council suggested that there needs to be a 'social agent' from the association paid for by the programme to support the families.

Conclusions

The Casa Melhor/PAAC has moved through a number of phases, influenced particularly by the political realities. This concluding section summarizes its successes and difficulties.

Effectiveness of the programme in reducing poverty

The initial hypothesis of the programme was that housing improvements for the poor require improvements in the social relationships between families. This programme uses the process of savings and loans, combined with improving and extending houses as a catalyst for changes in social relationships. The programme recognizes its limitations in poverty reduction. Nevertheless, through the relationships that it promotes, the nature of activities and the material products, staff believe that the programme is effective in addressing some of the consequences of poverty.

The programme facilitates housing improvement. As noted above, there are benefits for health and for family well-being from additional space. Besides a general improvement in living conditions, there are improvements in incomes for many families (and sometimes others in the community). New businesses are opened, there is more work space in the house, construction workers are employed, people learn new occupations as they help to improve their own houses, and they learn about their capacity to mobilize resources and bring about improvements for their family and for the neighbourhood. The device of saving and improving the value of the house has positive consequences for the neighbourhood economy. Learning to save helps families to plan their lives, and accumulating assets through improving the value of their house lessens risk and offers more security. Casa Melhor appears to result in a positive change in the community organizations as they became more practical. Women have participated actively in all phases of the programme, especially within the stronger communities.

The programme represents a qualitative jump in relation to other poverty reduction programmes because of its impact on citizenship and self-esteem. The efforts of the family are rewarded when they receive a subsidy two times more than savings and a loan three times more than their initial contribution. This is a programme that recognizes that the contributions of households are essential to the struggle against poverty.

However, there are a number of limitations. Improvements in infrastructure would strengthen the effectiveness of the intervention. The links between programme activities and strengthening of the residents associations are an important aspect of poverty reduction; however, families have struggled to undertake all of the communal activities. There is little to suggest that savings groups and grassroots organizations achieve the degree of political maturity required to address the needs of their members. In a very few cases, the associations have gone on to secure improvements of infrastructure, such as piped water and sewage facilities.

Institutional positioning and sustainability

The programme's institutional form seeks to promote participation and democracy. One of the programme's most significant aspects with regard to institutional strengthening has been savings. Without savings groups, the programme could not have secured its achievements. Savings groups have comparative advantages in relation to the other grassroots organizations: the families have a common objective; they are generally small groups; and they look beyond the political perspective of most residents' associations. It is important to balance the need for housing improvements with the associations' main objectives to improve the quality of life of everybody in the neighbourhood. In PAAC–Casa Melhor, the number of people in the savings group was small enough to work together for housing improvements and to fight for better conditions in the neighbourhood.

However, there are questions that remain with regard to community organizations. Should community organizations seek to strengthen general activities? In the beginning of the programme there was an increase in activities; but this is not seen after the third or fourth savings group receives loans. Is there a need to introduce modifications and innovations to encourage more participation? Despite savings, the programme struggles to ensure that families own all activities. Families do not demand more involvement in either administration activities or decision-making. The communities may lack a social space in which the interests of everyone are respected, enabling them to negotiate outcomes that are acceptable to all and not imposed by rules.

The sustainability of the programme is more than just a financial issue. The financial design seeks to secure political redistribution with a municipal subsidy for housing improvements. The current subsidy is large and the loan fund requires new contributions to continue in its present form. To improve the political and financial sustainability of the fund, the programme seeks to increase the communities' managerial capacity, thereby reducing administrative costs. At the same time, there is a need to ensure that the programme is understood as a poverty reduction initiative, rather than as a financial intervention or as a housing programme.

Critical components for success

What has been shown to be fundamental to the success of the programme is *the existence of a good organization*. Grassroots structures need to be sensitive to adapting the programme to family needs. Training opportunities, meetings and the development of new skills and capacities have helped to strengthen local processes.

It was important to have a municipality *committed to addressing the needs of the poor*. This contributes to trust and confidence in the partnership. A related element is a support group within the staff and the councillors responsible for by-laws, regulations and municipal budgets so that the necessary legal framework can be put in place.

A *representative city-wide organization* that is both strong and engaged in the programme is also important. In the case of Casa Melhor, the Federação de Bairros e Favelas de Fortaleza (Federation of Neighbourhoods and Squatter Settlements of Fortaleza, or FBFF) had a fundamental role. The federation took on public debates on the subject of the programme and gave legitimacy in the eyes of the associations. Moreover, it mobilized many families and lobbied the municipality when the subsidy was delayed.

The programme's team needs to be prepared and flexible in order to cope with the inevitable changes that will be necessary during the programme's development. Technical knowledge and a willingness to listen are fundamental attributes for the staff who participate in the team.

A few final suggestions

Other studies suggest that families should buy materials through their groups to obtain bulk discounts. A further possibility is the formation of a materials bank from which families could obtain construction materials on credit. In particular, there is a need to consider the more effective use of centralized purchasing and distribution of construction materials.

There is an ongoing discussion about the restructuring of technical assistance. The families say that when they need assistance, during the execution of the works, the technicians are absent. Hence, there is a need for more assistance later on in the process, not simply during the design stage.

A better definition of income criteria that regulates access to the programme is also required. Many families are excluded because they have income above three minimum salaries; but their housing needs are acute because they have a great number of children or other dependants. However, there is a strong argument in favour of introducing programmes for lower-income families. This will involve new challenges, particularly if the programme is also to consider working with the landless.

The programme in its two parts, Casa Melhor and PAAC, is now ready to be restructured. Today, the programme is being implemented bureaucratically, rather than as processes capable of transforming community development. The capacity of the programme is too small to meet current needs. Growth requires both simplification and new alliances. In particular, there may be a need for another agency able to support programme activities, especially in the area of loan management. A second area of support is in finance. There is also still a need to better understand the informal financial circuits in low-income settlements.

Cearah Periferia's role in the review phase of the programme should be to:

- Consider how to transfer ownership of the programme to community organizations.
- Rethink the development aspects of the programme and continue to drive learning and experimentation.
- Play the founders role, absorbing the concerns and frustrations of other parties.
- Provide technical support for the municipal teams.
- Lobby and mobilize national resources.

However, with its many positive aspects, the programme Casa Melhor and PAAC continue to be one of the most innovative of housing finance programmes, with a proven effectiveness. Hopefully, they will continue to make a contribution to poverty reduction and social development.

References

Instituto Cidadania (2000) *Projeto Moradia*, Instituto Cidadania, São Paulo
UNDP (1999) *Human Development Report 1999*, United Nations Development Programme, New York

Chapter 8

The Age of Cities and Organizations of the Urban Poor: The Work of the South African Homeless People's Federation[1]

Ted Baumann, Joel Bolnick and Diana Mitlin

Introduction

This chapter describes how the South African Homeless People's Federation and its support non-governmental organization (NGO), People's Dialogue on Land and Shelter, have sought to develop approaches to housing that meet the needs of low-income households. It describes what has been achieved in physical terms – the houses and neighbourhoods developed, the savings mobilized, the income-generation schemes supported. But, as the chapter stresses, the ways in which these are done have as much importance for poverty reduction as what was constructed. It describes the ways in which these were achieved – rooted in community learning, experimentation, control and management – and how the alliance of this federation and the support NGO has sought to demonstrate to national, provincial and local governments and international agencies that there are more cost-effective approaches to housing improvement and development for low-income groups that are also more inclusive, participatory and sustainable.

1 This chapter draws on a longer report; see T Baumann, J Bolnick and D Mitlin (2001) *The Age of Cities and Organizations of the Urban Poor: The Work of the South African Homeless People's Federation and the People's Dialogue on Land and Shelter,* IIED Working Paper 2 on Poverty Reduction in Urban Areas, IIED, London. It can be downloaded from www.iied.org/urban/. For more details of the work of the South African Homeless People's Federation, see www.dialogue.org.za/pd/index.htm.

The challenge and the opportunity

The rapid integration of national economies that is part of globalization has widened the gap between wealth and poverty. On both a material and a cultural level, an increased overall level of wealth and sophistication has been accompanied by an increase in the absolute numbers of the poor, as well as an increase in the distance between their living standards and those of the rich. Recent instability in global financial markets shows how fragile this process may be. Swings in international currencies may bear little relation to economic fundamentals.

Even in those low- or middle-income nations that have enjoyed economic success, rarely has economic development matched the massive growth of urban populations. Export-oriented or speculative, contemporary economic growth has not provided most of their urban population with secure, formal jobs or adequate incomes, and a high proportion survive in the informal economy. Unlike Europe or North America during the periods when they urbanized rapidly, today's developing economies exist in a highly globalized economy, increasingly shaped by large multinational corporations and financial systems that are not constrained by government. Unconstrained flows of financial capital, in particular, limit national governments, who fear that they will suffer capital flight, exchange rate collapse and economic crises if they adopt unconventional economic policies. It is increasingly difficult, if not impossible, for governments to regulate economic development to ensure that the benefits are more evenly distributed or to redistribute its product when they are not.

In spite of these problems, globalization is not all bad news for the urban poor in the South. On a purely demographic level, it is swelling their ranks through urbanization. At the same time, processes of social liberalization and democratization have been accelerated by globalization's imperative for stability, no matter how flawed and incomplete. The globalized economy dislikes nothing so much as social and political conflict. Significantly, the increased political and social openness linked to globalization has enabled organized (and socially reconstituted) communities of the urban poor to engage the state and private sector in new and substantively different ways. Open conflict and impassioned contestation have given way to a new energy of critical cooperation.

Such processes have enabled shack dwellers of the South to contest political space and struggle for resources as never before. There is the possibility for the urban poor to secure some redistribution in return for pragmatic and effective strategies that enable cities to compete in the global economy. As a consequence, low-income communities have been pushed to explore and develop new systems of internal organization and governance. In some situations, pressure on traditional practices mean that social relations are changing within their communities, especially regarding the role of women and the poorest amongst them.

As importantly, the global economy with its rapidly advancing communications technology has given organized communities of the poor some of the opportunities available to politicians, corporate leaders and financiers. It has enabled them to exchange knowledge and share resources across international boundaries. In the process, organizations of the poor have consolidated their knowledge and capital, offering opportunities to the poor and excluded to move from the political and economic periphery to the centre of the modern city.

Like most social transformations induced by the global economy, this one is moving with stealth and intent. Globalized capital accumulation has spawned a dictatorship by money markets and, with the help of international regulatory agencies, forced politicians in the South into ever-deeper compromises. However, it has also spawned the antithesis of this process: self-managed local initiatives of the urban poor who link together by means of a loosely knit international federation.[2] It is to this low-key but profound development, and its local manifestations in the informal settlements of South Africa, that we turn to in this chapter.

South African poverty and homelessness

There are now some 15 million people squatting in shacks in the towns and cities in South Africa. Across the country, there are huge inequalities in housing provision. In 1989, it was estimated that the median floor area was 11 square metres per person. For the white population, the average was 33 square metres per person; for the black population living within the informal sector, the average was 4 to 5 square metres per person. There is little to suggest that substantive change has taken place since then. In addition to the approximately 3 million new housing units needed to meet the existing housing deficit, an estimated 150,000 units a year are required to keep up with need.

When the African National Congress (ANC) government took up office in 1994, it recognized that housing was a priority for those living in South African townships and promised to build 1 million houses in five years within its Reconstruction and Development Programme. The government introduced a capital subsidy programme for land purchase, infrastructure and housing to achieve this aim. This subsidy of up to 15,000 rand[3] was available to low-income households. But this was not a subsidy to the household; instead, it was offered through a subsidized housing unit built for them by a commercial developer. By 1999, some of the difficulties were apparent. Most of the 680,000 new houses that had been produced were very small – usually a single core room and a latrine. Moreover, a high proportion of them were badly designed, poorly constructed and located far from jobs or other possible income sources. In response, many residents sold their newly acquired Reconstruction and Development Programme Houses (or core units) at low prices because they were simply not

---

2 For more information on Shack Dwellers International, see www.sdinet.org/ and www.achr.net; see also *Environment and Urbanization* (2001) vol 13, no 2; the on-line edition is available at www.ingentaselect.com/09562478/v13n2.

3 The exchange rate for the rand against the US dollar and UK pound sterling varied during the period covered by this chapter – from 10 to 16 rand to UK£1 and 7 to 11 rand to US$1.

homes. This is creating a new homeless class in South Africa since those who sold the units that they had received under the housing subsidy programme had no entitlement to another housing subsidy. They joined those who cannot realize their entitlement to subsidies because they cannot obtain land (to apply for a subsidy, a family requires a plot and most of the housing built within the subsidy programme has been within existing settlements). Such an outcome repeats the familiar story of many site-and-service or core housing schemes throughout the world. Low-income households value the cash that they can get from selling the core house or site provided to them through a public programme because this is more useful to them than the unit, with its poor location, poor quality construction and inadequate infrastructure.

In order to support community-driven, often self-build, activities, the South African government later developed a People's Housing Process. However, it remains marginalized within the housing department. It is difficult to see why government has not taken this more seriously since a true people's housing process is more effective as a means of creating housing. With an average subsidy per house of 10,000 rand, the South African Homeless People's Federation can consistently construct a good-quality four-room house, whereas a contractor constructs a serviced site or a single-room (and often poor-quality) core house. Only a very small proportion of the government housing subsidies have been allocated to people's organizations such as the Homeless People's Federation – probably less than 3 per cent; the rest has gone to a fund for private developers to spend 'on behalf of low-income families'. As one federation member commented, 'The money goes to the developers and they build us wardrobes, not houses.'

Origins of the Homeless People's Federation

The South African Homeless People's Federation (which calls itself *uMfelandaWonye*, meaning literally 'we die together') is a national network of organizations from informal settlements around South Africa. It is formed by over 1500 autonomous local organizations of urban poor households who have developed savings and credit schemes and are seeking to develop their own housing schemes. Working in alliance with the People's Dialogue for Land and Shelter (its NGO partner), it is engaged in a process through which the urban poor reclaim their power to choose. By coming together and comparing their experiences, the poor are able to see that they have options, and that their collective resources can help them to make better use of those options.

The process that led to the development of the federation and its support NGO began in March 1991, when the Southern African Catholic Development Association organized a five-day conference for South African shack dwellers. Over 120 community leaders came together to share ideas and experiences within a conference that was called the South African People's Dialogue on Land and Shelter. The year of 1991 was a time of much agitation and expectation. The liberation movements had been unbanned during the previous year. Political prisoners had been released and exiles had begun to return. The conference organizers also extended invitations to well-known development practitioners from other Southern nations. After decades of sanctions and with apartheid in its death throes, the foreign delegates were keen to participate. They came from many backgrounds: housing rights activists from the Philippines and Hong Kong; researchers from Kenya, Zambia and Colombia; grassroots networkers from Thailand and Japan; community leaders from Zimbabwe and India. Contributions by overseas delegates made apparent the differences between old development paradigms and practices and ones that, at the time, were struggling to be born. On the one hand, there were the service-providing NGOs who mobilized communities around abstract 'human rights' and generally maintained confrontational postures towards government and the private sector. For those who did work directly with poor communities, they tended to adopt a few settlements as pilots and to work painstakingly towards upgrading them in terms of their professional image of what 'development' should be. On the other hand, there were those who were struggling to re-invent their role. They saw their function as support organizations for the urban poor in their efforts to design and sustain their own institutions, through which they could determine development priorities and contest political space and city, regional and national resources.

This distinction was neatly replicated among the community participants from South Africa. The majority insisted that as soon as political rights were secured, a new non-racial government would deliver social and economic rights to the poor. They perceived any effort to organize autonomous institutions of the urban poor as reactionary and counterproductive. A significant minority was less convinced that political liberation would bring social and economic emancipation. They felt that a democratic society would not guarantee a better life for the poor; it would simply open space for the poor to contest power and resources within broader society. Box 8.1 outlines how the contribution of Jockin Arputham, the president of the National Slum Dwellers Federation in India, helped to provide a focus for this minority opinion.

The conference put the issue to the vote. Thanks, in part, to convincing interventions from Jockin, the conference organizers were mandated to sustain a network of those communities whose leaders wanted to explore different ways of working together. As a result, People's Dialogue on Land and Shelter became a registered voluntary organization (NGO), established in 1991 as a vehicle to explore ways for non-racial South African governments to work with poor communities through partnerships. The Homeless People's Federation was formed in 1994 by community leaders who emerged from the networking process that came out of the 1991 conference.

People's Dialogue has offices in Johannesburg, Cape Town, Queenstown and Durban and a technical staff of three building and finance specialists who work together with a small number of consultants and field officers. Together, these professionals have helped the South African Homeless People's Federation to manage over 45 million rand in loan finance and to build 8000 houses. Operating this programme with a small professional team is possible because the vast majority of federation activities occur without its support. The role of People's Dialogue is to facilitate the interface between formal institutions and

---

Box 8.1 Who can you trust?

The Indian Congress fought the British for independence and one person one vote. They promised the people that when the British were gone there would be milk and honey for all. The British have been gone for 44 years; but all the poor get from their government is shit. A change in government does not mean a change for the poor and the homeless (Jockin Arputham, president of the National Slum Dwellers Federation).[4]

---

the poor; to assist in designing and developing strategies and mechanisms that federation members learn and practise; and to work with external agencies to create space for people's organizations.

The work of the federation

The federation represents its member organizations – autonomous local organizations that develop savings and credit schemes, and develop their own housing schemes. By April 2000, there were 80,600 active savers and 5.2 million rand saved.

The federation provides communities with a feeling of ownership of development processes and a feeling of identifying with a national programme. This creates confidence and reduces the sense of marginalization that low-income communities feel when dealing with city officials to find solutions to their problems. The federation process empowers communities to take charge of their lives, demand their entitlements and find sustainable, sensible solutions to the problems that they face.

The organizations that are members of the federation share a common mobilizing strategy around savings and loan activities. All members of the federation are encouraged to start saving daily. In the early days of federation activities, this was a difficult process. Now there are hundreds of groups with successful savings schemes. Through the federation, women's savings collectives are able to gain recognition in their settlements and are empowered to play key leadership roles. These savings collectives manage community processes in cooperation with the traditional male leadership in order to strengthen their joint capacity to face the outside environment.

Savings and credit is the basic element (or the 'glue') in the development strategy. The process starts with a consumer, production and crisis credit fund, established by a savings group. Treasurers visit each member daily to collect their contributions. Women who are interested are drawn into the training process and are shown how such crisis credit funds work in other communities. Within three months, most settlements are able to understand, agree and manage the rules and regulations to make the crisis credit fund operational.

---

4 See Chapter 9 on the work of SPARC and its partners *Mahila Milan* and the National Slum Dwellers Federation for details of the programmes that they developed to address this.

The savings groups are encouraged to cover as many residents as possible in the settlement. If many women in each settlement wish to be involved, it is proposed that they divide into groups of about ten households. Within each of these groups, one woman is identified as a treasurer and the savings groups are linked to one another through these treasurers. Although most of the women are illiterate, they have very good oral memories. Through working with school children, the treasurers learn sufficient skills to be able to keep written records of savings and loans.

Within the federation networks, there are three kinds of savings schemes: schemes for crises, for income generation and for housing. Each community begins with crisis credit. Women save very small bits of money, kept aside from change from daily purchases. The poorest women in the community often set up this process. Even when the savings fund is very small, women begin to borrow small amounts. This could be for medicines, to purchase a bus ticket to find work, or for children's schoolbooks. These small loans are repaid very quickly. Women are encouraged to make their own rules about this fund. This consolidates the women's collectives. Although small, the fund fulfils crucial crisis needs, and women get community acknowledgement for having created these resources. These crisis credit schemes can develop into schemes that organize the construction of homes for their members.

Box 8.2 gives the example of the Victoria Mxenge Housing Co-operative, which developed from a savings scheme and through which its members (most of them women) developed 140 good-quality homes in a new neighbourhood with infrastructure and services.

The federation has used community-driven data gathering and mapping to build communities' skills for developing or dealing with physical development interventions. Surveys are an important tool in educating communities to question themselves and in creating a capacity for communities to articulate their knowledge about themselves to those with whom they interact. The alliance assists communities in undertaking surveys on various levels: listing all of the settlements in a city and enumerating all households within specific settlements, as well as intra-household surveys. In all instances, questionnaires and other survey methodologies are discussed with communities and people are given an explanation of why data is being gathered. Initially, crude tables are prepared with communities and families check household registers. Later, a database is created out of the information collected. The most important aspect of the surveying process is to help communities understand how the aggregation of information becomes the basis of choices that policy-makers use to decide entitlements. Once communities understand this, they can use the aggregate information that they have created in their negotiations with state institutions. They also begin to understand the importance of data gathering when others come to do it.

The alliance also works with communities to build their skills to create their own maps of services, settlements, resources and problems so that they can get a visual fix on their situation and understand how the present physical situation relates to them. This is part of the qualitative aspects of the surveying and data-gathering process, and becomes especially useful in building community skills to

---

Box 8.2 VICTORIA MXENGE HOUSING SAVINGS SCHEME:
WOMEN CONTROLLED, NOT JUST WOMEN CENTRED

The Victoria Mxenge Housing Savings Scheme was formed in 1991 by Patricia Matolengwe and some of her neighbours. Patricia had been an active member of the African National Congress (ANC) Women's League for many years. At first, the other residents laughed at their efforts. How could the few cents that they were able to save result in new homes? When they understood that this was a self-build initiative, they mocked it again. How could women build their own homes!

Just five years later the Victoria Mxenge Housing Co-operative had become a flagship housing development within the Western Cape, with visitors from all over the world. Most of the builders who had constructed 140 good-quality houses in the settlement were women and the development had been managed by women from start to finish.

For the federation, the most important visitors to Victoria Mxenge are the residents from nearby settlements. Every day, poor women come to the community centre to find out how they can build their own homes. Working with Victoria Mxenge and other federation groups, by 2000, 78 housing savings schemes were building houses in the Western Cape. Federation members have constructed over 1500 homes in this province alone and this number is growing all the time. Every Tuesday, Victoria Mxenge's community centre is packed with conveners from housing savings schemes who come together to share experiences and report on progress. Almost uniquely in South Africa, women make up 85 per cent of the members and the leadership of these housing savings schemes:

> *In 1992, I heard about the federation. At that time, no one trusted it in Khayelitsha. They all said it was those crazy women. Then they did not like the fact they should make their own bricks. It was too hard they said. And it was all women. They did not trust it* (a member of the Victoria Mxenge Housing Savings Scheme, Western Cape).

> *There are many organizations claiming that they are women centred. But, you know, often it is just a desk. The ANC Women's League is autonomous, but it is the framework of the ANC. The federation, as far as we know, is the only one that is truly controlled by women* (Patricia Matolengwe, national chairperson, South African Homeless People's Federation).

---

deal with physical developmental interventions, where they have to look at maps and drawings prepared for improving their settlement.

Community-to-community exchanges have been a powerful mechanism for spreading knowledge – for instance, how to set up a savings scheme, how to manage it and how to develop it into a housing savings scheme. As Box 8.2 notes, every week, convenors of housing savings schemes come to Victoria Mxenge to see what they have built and to share experiences. These exchanges bring together ordinary residents to tell their stories and develop new ideas. The benefits are immense. If savings provides the glue to bring community members together, exchanges provide the confidence to overcome problems, the insight to abandon traditional solutions and the knowledge to address critical issues. At any one time, there are several communities within the federation that are taking part in community-to-community exchanges. Sometimes these are just within cities; often they are between cities; on occasion, they are between countries (see Box 8.3).

The Federation and People's Dialogue seek to bring together communities who are doing similar work. At the same time, communities who are involved in different processes are also encouraged to meet. When they get to meet, the learning process initiated at the community-specific level deepens and helps them to develop confidence and determination to seek out city officials, government departments and other resource-providing organizations. It helps them to initiate a dialogue on how solutions can be undertaken jointly. Exchanges inspire and support local groups. Nothing is more powerful than the experience of sharing experiences, options and solutions.[5] A further advantage of an approach that emphasizes strengthening local leadership is that it establishes lasting and effective organizations in communities. The approach is useful when the process has to multiply. Community leadership reproduces itself faster than committed activism; community leaders, because they belong to their respective communities, remain in place long after project implementation is complete.

What has been achieved?

Savings and loans

Savings schemes have spread throughout the country; but the greatest concentrations are in areas in which the federation began its organizations, the cities of Cape Town, Durban, Johannesburg and Port Elizabeth. As noted earlier, by April 2000, there were 80,600 households who were active savers and 5.2 million rand had been saved.

Table 8.1 *Savings activities*

	July 1993	July 1994	April 1995	April 1996	January 1998	July 1998	July 1999	April 2000
Savings schemes	58	137	198	316	1000	1100	2000	1288
Active savers	2178	7002	9627	17,280	40,000	50,000	70,000	80,600
Total savings	34,000 rand	165,000 rand	272,000 rand	453,000 rand	2.5 million rand	3 million rand	3.5 million rand	5.2 million rand

5 This has an important implication. The capacity to share experiences, options and solutions suitable for the poor is necessarily restricted to those who have had such experiences, which excludes the middle-class professional. This methodology relegates professionals to the role of facilitators of processes rather than implementers of solutions. Because the solutions are organic and experiential, training by outsiders cannot diffuse them successfully.

BOX 8.3 LEARNING BY DOING

A common language

When I asked the technician (who works with us in Dakar) to show us how layout plans are designed, he used such a sophisticated jargon that I barely understood a word he said. In Protea South [Gauteng uFunde Zufe, South Africa] during our last evening, we asked a woman to draw us a plan. When she explained house modelling, I understood and felt that I, too, could do it (Aminata Mbaye, Senegalese Savings and Loan Network, communicating with the South African federation through translation).

The art of the possible

I was so impressed with the houses. Now I really believe that women are doing it. It helped me see that this is possible. Of course, I knew the women did it; but it was good to see it. As I said, now I really believe it is possible that we can do this. What really surprised me were the technical skills of the house plans. I brought one back, one of the house plans. It was drawn by one of the women (Elizabeth, member from a new housing savings scheme after visiting Protea South).

Building each other

We have to recognize our need to build one another. We all have problems; we are here to recognize them so that we can build one another through the federation. We need to work together. Here we need to have leaders who lead by example, who can go and show their members their own loan books and let them see that the leaders do repay, and that their leaders are the first names on the yellow forms. We should build a leadership who understand how to manage in difficult circumstances, and who were willing to really support the federation. Then we can all learn from them (Susan, federation leader in the North-West Province on an exchange to strengthen loan programmes).

Together we are strong

The federation is a university. Although we are uneducated, professionals and experts come to us to learn. Me, like many, I came for a house; but I got an education (federation member in Gauteng).

Housing development (subsidies and loans)

The construction of housing by federation members has been supported by housing subsidies from the government and by loans from the *uTshani* fund, a revolving fund for housing loans that the federation established to support community-managed housing schemes. The savings schemes get the funds from the subsidy programme (where possible) and from the *uTshani* fund for an agreed list of members. Although federation members were eligible for the government housing subsidy, they did not wait for housing to be delivered to them. While the government officials were still drafting the detail of the housing subsidy programme, federation members had their first meeting with Joe Slovo, then minister of housing, in June 1994. They asked him to make a contribution to the *uTshani* fund and, in October 1994, the minister responded with a commitment of 10 million rand. The *uTshani* fund is now supported by government funds and donor contributions. By October 2000, total capital invested in the fund was 45 million rand.

Housing construction has been undertaken with a combination of loans and subsidies. Table 8.2 shows how the 8026 new housing units that were constructed by July 2000 were financed: nearly half by loans; 36 per cent by subsidies; and 16 per cent by a combination of loans and subsidies. In some cases, members augmented the loan finance with existing materials (doors, windows or corrugated-iron roofing sheets) taken from their shacks and incorporated within their new homes or with new material bought from their savings. The maximum loan provided by the *uTshani* fund for any individual unit is 10,000 rand, which originally was enough to fund the construction of a four-room house, but which now is barely sufficient for three rooms. In some cases, *uTshani* loans are used as bridge finance, allowing a household that is expecting a housing subsidy to begin construction, and then to (mostly or fully) repay the loan when the subsidy is released.

Table 8.2 shows the large differences between provinces in the amount of houses constructed with support from government subsidies. Different provincial administrations have very different attitudes towards supporting people's self-managed housing; in some administrations, no support was provided. Despite continuous attempts by the federation and the People's Dialogue to obtain subsidies for their members, they have remained out of reach in some provinces. By July 2000, over 47.7 million rand had been released by the *uTshani* fund in loan finance.

Table 8.3 summarizes repayments to the uTshani fund that have been made by members directly and through the receipt of subsidy funds. It is difficult for federation members to fund a new home through a loan – but many members are unable to receive the subsidy to which they are entitled due either to bureaucratic delays or to a dislike of self-help initiatives on the part of the politicians or provincial officials.

Table 8.2 *Housing construction with loans and subsidies (as of 31 July 2000)*

	Houses built with loans and subsidies	Houses constructed with loans only	Houses built with subsidies only	Total houses built
Eastern Cape	226	392	839	1457
Free State	70	141	30	241
Gauteng	0	978	0	978
Mpumalanga	0	60	0	60
Natal	99	1537	432	2068
North-West	81	96	62	239
Western Cape	774	702	1507	2983
Total	1250	3906	2870	8026

Table 8.3 *Members' repayments and subsidy-related repayments (rand)*

	Total loans	Federation repayments	Subsidy repayments related to loans	Total repayments
Eastern Cape	5,951,659	2,002,587	1,742,085	3,744,671
Free State	1,479,218	359,919	686,000	1,045,919
Gauteng	8,929,209	2,274,118	0	2,274,118
Mpumalanga	499,534	148,980	0	148,980
Natal	14,997,676	2,907,334	977,346	3,884,680
North-West	1,426,673	462,027	595,350	1,057,377
Western Cape	14,392,752	2,788,297	7,255,737	10,044,034
Total	47,676,722	10,943,262	11,256,517	22,199,780

The housing subsidy system was designed to support housing constructed by commercial developers on new (greenfield) sites that were allocated to low-income households. It was not designed to support the people who are meant to be the primary beneficiaries. Although government support is available to not-for-profit categories, the federation does not fit neatly into these categories. It neither wishes to be a housing association (renting properties to those in need), nor a housing co-operative (with collective ownership of land and housing).

Apart from the difficulties or delays in acquiring subsidies, another of the major problems faced by federation members is that housing subsidies will only be made available to those with legal tenure of a housing plot. During 1996 and 1997, the federation and People's Dialogue worked with the Department of Land Affairs to try to address the issue of urban land tenure. Eleven test sites were identified in which, it was agreed, the federation would try to obtain security of tenure through existing channels. The department would seek to learn from these experiences and, through following these struggles, to better understand the obstacles within the current system preventing legal tenure from being secured. In return for this action research, the department gave a commitment that it would act to ensure that these pilot communities obtained legal tenure. However, not one of the sites has received title deeds and the projects were gradually abandoned because the scale of bureaucracy appeared insurmountable.

Federation groups that are in need of land have few choices. They can build without land title; invade land (public or private) and negotiate for a title; buy land on the private market; or buy state land. All of these tactics have been used – although the federation is clear that invasion is a last resort. Land title is not required for a *uTshani* fund loan; but the housing savings scheme that applies for the loan must demonstrate that tenure is reasonably secure or that building will help the community to negotiate for more secure tenure.

Millions of people in South Africa live in 'backyard' shacks – shacks built in the backyard of households who have legal tenure. They either pay rent for the shack or rent for the land upon which they build the shack. They generally share water and toilet facilities with the landowner. These people cannot get secure, better accommodation by upgrading their existing homes, so they need new land sites for housing. The federation has a 24-point plan for land development that

---

BOX 8.4 AGRINETTE HILLS

We started to plan to invade. On 19 March [1997] we had a meeting. I spoke to the people. By then there were 516 members. I asked them if we should wait. All the members said no, we should not wait. I asked the federation leaders and People's Dialogue. Mama asked me if I was scared. I said I was only scared of God. Then they said I should do it.

So, on the night of the 20th [March], I moved onto the land. My boyfriend said that he should stay behind with the children. So it was just me and the plastic. I put up a plastic. This first night, there were three women and four children. Just us alone. The next day some others came. There were maybe 20 of us. The others, they were scared that the police would come with guns and dogs. Although there were many members, they waited to see what would happen.

The council came to see us. They said that we should get our things and go to Everton, where they have sites. We said that we would not go there because the houses are too small. Then I told them that I would not go back to a shack. My mother had died in a shack. There was a fire. All the shacks were burned. I lost my family. Then they were silent. They had nothing to say (Agrinette Hills, convenor, Housing Savings Scheme, Gauteng).

---

requires groups to seek state and private alternatives and to negotiate before confrontation. However, frequently, backyard shack dwellers feel that they have no choice (see Box 8.4).

All of the housing savings schemes within the federation are autonomous groups. The federation respects their right to make decisions for themselves, while strengthening their effectiveness through collective action. In the case of the invasion described in Box 8.4, the local government (council) tried to persuade the squatters to accept an alternative site that was being developed through commercial contractors. The community refused to go there. The land was poorly situated and the houses were much smaller than those that the federation could build for themselves. The strength of the community convinced the council that they should be allowed to stay.

Only strong local groups can resolve the many and varied internal disputes that emerge as any development process gets underway. There are members who are nervous, those who are self-interested and those who are misled. *Savings provides a means of reconstructing the social relations that exist within a community as savings activities bring people together to collectively manage their finance.* Women frequently participate in savings groups and women leaders emerge. Local organizations become more representative and grow in capacity. Through their own efforts, the community of Agrinette Hills secured well-located land.

Estimating how many landless have received land though invasion and/or negotiations with local authorities in the federation is a difficult task because federation activities have grown in scope and complexity. Federation groups act autonomously, calling on assistance as required. Some land tenure struggles may never be heard about by the broader federation. There are 21 groups that

People's Dialogue knows about and has worked with; by October 2000, these groups had secured land for 13,500 households.

In a number of places, savings schemes have turned to the market to buy land. The *uTshani* fund now has dedicated loan finance for land purchase. In Cape Town, three sites have been purchased by the federation. Together they have plots for 500 families. An option to buy has been taken on for a further 14 hectares, with space for more than 1000 families; this land will be bought as soon as the required subsidy funds are secured. In Gauteng, housing savings schemes, frustrated by the slow pace of government action, have also been looking to buy land.

Thus, federation-related activities have helped to secure land for over 10,000 families who represent some of South Africa's poorest urban citizens. But the federation, along with many other groups concerned with equitable urban development, has failed to change the distribution of land within cities planned and constructed under apartheid. Land for low-income housing development is invariably located around existing concentrations of the urban poor. They never obtain better located land close to the central business districts or to wealthier suburbs with better employment prospects.

Income generation and employment

The federation and People's Dialogue have long sought to respond to the needs of their members for better incomes and employment opportunities. Housing savings schemes were encouraged to lend capital for income generation; but this was slow and lending was generally for emergencies and consumption purposes. In 1998, federation members agreed to establish regional funds called *Inqolobane* ('the Granary'). Savings schemes are encouraged to contribute about half of their savings capital to these funds. The purpose of the *Inqolobane* is to enable larger income-generation loans to be provided.

In 1999 and 2000, job-creation and income-generation activities took a further step forward as greenfield developments undertaken by federation members enabled the addition of commercial facilities for both formal- and informal-sector activities to housing developments. Two pilot programmes for enterprise development with government departments were also initiated, one with the Department of Welfare to provide small loans and develop commercial areas with retail units and market areas, and a second with the Department of Water Affairs, with the federation working as social development advisers to the department's national Working for Water programme. This is an employment programme that recruits people to clear alien vegetation (trees and bushes) in order to increase the water table, allowing more water to be drawn and reducing the need for dams.

Unpicking the change processes

The People's Dialogue/Federation Alliance experience has shown the importance of three distinct but linked change processes.

1 Organization for empowerment: creating organizational capability within low-income settlements and the links between the community and their peers

This change process is realized primarily through the federation network and through savings and loan activities. Community groups need to develop democratic internal organizational capabilities. They need to explore relationships based on equity, which ensure inclusiveness. These features are essential for sustaining the participation of the poor in demanding change, both within their communities and with external organizations. For too long, grassroots organizations have been neither accountable, nor representative of the poorest and most vulnerable members of their communities. An investment in strengthening democratic organization within low-income communities has many long-term implications, and if undertaken with care and patience, is the most powerful legacy of any developmental intervention. It also becomes crucial in ensuring the long-term sustainability of any process that is introduced.

2 Community-based problem-solving: building skills and locating and building resources within and outside communities

People's Dialogue and federation experience has shown that the difficulties that low-income communities face often require them to reflect collectively on deconstructing problems and identifying solutions. Communities need time and space to explore all possible choices. They need to examine the feasibility and implications of each available option, and to understand the degree of control, which they, as communities, can have over different 'solutions'. It is, therefore, important for communities to examine the internal resources that they can use when they design alternatives at the initial phase of the problem-solving process.

The People's Dialogue/Federation Alliance often provides grant funding to communities for pilot activities through which they can seek to solve a problem, develop innovative decision-making and resource-allocating processes, test their solutions, and even fail and try again. Mistakes and failures are viewed by the alliance as sound investments in the evolution of sustainable change processes, and are considered more effective learning mechanisms than workshops or study tours. As described earlier, community exchanges provide a critical supportive context in which learning can take place.

3 Learning to negotiate: the development of communities' abilities to negotiate with city governments, state governments and other actors

Arriving at long-term solutions requires that communities negotiate with city and state governments and other groups. Often, institutions such as municipalities, state institutions and even developmental organizations do not know how to work with poor communities in order to arrive at solutions. The usual approach is for external agencies to get communities to 'do something', which they – city officials – believe poor people need to do.

The experience in South Africa has shown that this does not work. Communities have to redesign government programmes if they are to be useful in poverty reduction, and negotiations are an essential part of this. Successful negotiations are about getting to know the government and its priorities, building personal relations and identifying and developing possibilities.

Locating the alliance's approach

The philosophy and practice of this approach can be contrasted with the more conventional approach to housing development and urban poverty reduction to highlight some distinctive differences in the federation's way of working. While the change processes discussed above focus on the delivery of tangibles, they are actually entry points for mobilization, rather than organizational goals in themselves. This is an important distinction. Many development organizations (especially government agencies) seek to produce things that address the problems that people face because of their poverty. These can be material things, such as piped water, houses or improved sanitation, or non-physical things, such as knowledge of rights or improved skills. The common thread is that the development organization seeks to produce and deliver, and gears itself to achieve this goal in a way that seems efficient and effective from the perspective of those who run the organization. Along with many modern organizations, their measure of success is their efficiency in doing so – converting a given quantum of inputs into so much output.

In the experience of People's Dialogue and the federation, this is usually an ineffective way of addressing poverty. Many housing programmes around the world have delivered hundreds or thousands of new structures that do not help to address poverty, but, rather, increase the consequence of poverty through concentrating areas of deprivation. In some cases, poverty is actually worse and more intractable – as has been discovered with many inner-city high-rise housing projects in high-income nations, as well as in low- and middle-income countries. Dealing with poverty requires interventions that are multifaceted and adaptive. Box 8.5 describes the frustration of women in one low-income settlement in Durban, when faced with a conventional upgrading programme in their settlement. This group built on their frustration to become one of the strongest groups in the federation.

The 'delivery' approach can be profoundly disempowering for communities. Given the emphasis on 'producing outputs' and its implicit quantitative measures of efficiency, addressing the problems of poverty is seen as a job for technically skilled and specialized professionals. Designing houses, installing infrastructure and managing credit are seen as *products that people need, not things they necessarily need to know how to do*. Poor people may be consulted about their problems; but perceiving, conceiving, organizing and implementing solutions are left to professionals.

BOX 8.5 PIESANG RIVER: FROM PROJECTS TO HOMES

I thought the government wanted to develop people. Now I find that all they want to do is develop roads (housing savings scheme member, Piesang River).

Piesang River is a settlement of 1600 households on the outskirts of Durban. During the early 1990s, a local non-governmental organization (NGO) started an upgrading process using government finance. The improvements, designed and planned by professionals, concentrated on infrastructure. The involvement of community leaders was restricted to commenting on proposals, rather than determining the content of the programme.

The residents knew that they did not want this upgrading programme. Roads were not a priority for them. What they wanted was better, safer and more secure homes. But they did not know how to change the minds of those who controlled the resources and they had little idea that they could themselves control their own development.

When the women of Piesang River heard about savings schemes, they decided to set up their own. Gradually, their savings scheme grew in numbers and in confidence, and the women found themselves with a forum to discuss their priorities and needs. They began to realize that there was an alternative. When they challenged the NGO and the community leaders about the development that was taking place, they received an angry response. But the women were determined that the government funds to improve their neighbourhood would not be wasted. They succeeded in stopping the upgrading programme. The women learnt how to build their own houses and how to manage loan finance. In Piesang River today, there are over 600 federation houses, all built from brick and each measuring over 50 square metres in size.

Development professionals have become increasingly concerned about the inability of these activities to have long-term impacts on poverty reduction. Development agencies talk about 'sustainability', by which they generally mean how the improvements that they helped to fund will be maintained when the external intervention is completed. The main alternative to 'delivery' approaches to development is a 'process' approach. Instead of acquiring material objects, emphasis is placed on the development of local capacity in the knowledge, skills and practices of the poor themselves. It is vital that, in the long run, communities of the poor, as the main group seeking social justice and equity, own their development process and become central to its expansion and growth.

Some process projects focus on 'claim-making.' Such approaches strengthen social activities and organizations so that they are better able to make claims on the state and hold government agencies accountable. In an urban context, claims are generally made around issues such as land tenure, water supplies and waste collection. Communities are organized around campaigning to secure these rights, either through lobbying and petitions or through more direct action. But the major focus of this process is on acquiring what is needed from the state, through the use of existing legislation or the enactment of new rights.

People's Dialogue decided against this approach for many reasons. Such interventions seek, for the most part, to bring formal-sector solutions to development closer to low-income groups. Local communities do not have a chance to design water systems or to set up systems that allow them access to cheap basic goods, education or health services in ways that work for them. The emphasis is on ensuring that formal conventional approaches to urban development are accessible to lower-income groups. However, in many cases, they do not work for the poor, especially for the lowest-income families. Furthermore, because of their design by outsiders and because they do not work well for the poor, success and failure in claim-making frequently bring about a reduction in social organization. At the same time, the often confrontational approach towards government tends to appeal to the better organized and sometimes better-off among the urban poor. Women and the poorest members are habitually not involved, either because they cannot afford to risk what they have or they do not believe that their efforts will be successful in improving their lives.

This is not to say that the state does not have responsibilities. The federation and People's Dialogue believe that the state does have a redistributive responsibility, as is described in the concluding section. However, if solutions are to work for the poor, they need to be redesigned and redeveloped by the poor. The federation seeks to use processes that enable the poor to be involved in designing solutions that work for them, and then negotiating with the state to obtain the required support. Such solutions seek to strengthen long-term community capacity in management and implementation. Before claim-making, community processes need to be concerned with asset-building, developing a knowledge of community priorities and how they can best be met, accumulating resources for independent activities, and establishing community confidence and capacity in their own endeavours. Central to the process of asset development is a strong local organization, able to carry out a local development agenda and linked together to successfully engage the state.

The federation seeks to build the self-reliance of the poor in order to better enable them to address their needs. An important component is to work with the state in improving policies and practices regarding poverty reduction and to ensure redistribution. People's Dialogue and the federation work with all levels of government to demonstrate an alternative practice and to encourage pro-poor community approaches (see Box 8.6).

Conclusions

People's Dialogue approach to development begins by recognizing that very few existing approaches to poverty reduction work for the very poor. At the same time, poor people generally find options that work best for them. Hence, People's Dialogue started its development strategies by recognizing that the most effective solutions to the problems of poverty are likely to have their origins in the practices of poor communities; the challenge is to improve them and scale them up.

This contrasts with many professional approaches to development that assume that the only way to survive is through formal systems or jobs, and, accordingly, seek to produce more of them for the poor. Professionals tend to see development as a process of 'upliftment', in which the poor 'develop' by making their lives more like those of the middle class. This ignores that fact that

---

BOX 8.6 JOE SLOVO VILLAGE: STATE RESOURCES FOR A PEOPLE'S AGENDA

At Joe Slovo Village in Port Elizabeth, support for the South African Homeless People's Federation has enabled local savings schemes to grow in skills and knowledge. *uTshani* loan finance has enabled the community to undertake housing and to pre-finance infrastructure development. The squatters have demonstrated their skills and capacities, and have negotiated a positive response from government. The settlement arose from a land occupation of privately owned land when families living in Veerplus (Port Elizabeth) were threatened with flooding in November 1996.

City council

Once the community occupied the site, the municipality at Port Elizabeth provided the first water connection. The municipality has since worked with the community to modify infrastructure standards, helping to reduce costs. It has also supported the settlement through the planned provision of bulk services.

Provincial government

The Eastern Cape Provincial Housing Development Board has provided subsidy funds to enable land development. The federation agreed that Joe Slovo should be a pilot programme for community infrastructure development. Current cost estimates are 3000 rand per site for water, sanitation and gravel roads – half commercial-contractor costs.

National departments

The Department of Land Affairs provided pre-financing to enable the community to purchase the land upon which Joe Slovo Village is located before the release of subsidy funds. This provided a critical supportive intervention soon after the land invasion.

The federation helps housing savings schemes to negotiate with the different levels of government. At all three levels, earlier networking by the federation meant that the housing savings schemes at Joe Slovo Village could build on existing relations in their struggle to secure state support. Donor funds have helped the community exchanges that have played a crucial part in strengthening the group and enabling it to hold onto the land and strategize about directions to take. They have also assisted in pre-financing the infrastructure costs, enabling the group to employ an innovative engineer able to demonstrate how costs can be saved. Special grants have resulted in a community centre at Joe Slovo that acts as a building materials yard and a crèche, assisting some of the poorest members and those most in need.

---

most people survive through strategies, systems and processes that are not part of the formal world. Moreover, as noted above, the 'delivery' approach to development often actively undermines the informal world by devaluing the skills of the poor and dividing their communities. It also assumes that the formal world can be expanded without any recognition of the structural constraints. An analysis based on an assessment of current pressures within globalization suggests that this is unlikely. Looked at another way, an approach based on integrating the poor within the formal world suggests that there will always be a proportion of people who will 'fail' – creating a class of chronic poor.

At the same time, simply using existing solutions that communities have developed is not sufficient. Community-based solutions have not dealt adequately with poverty and solutions need to be improved. One reason for the inability of low-income groups themselves to address poverty is that they are not only materially poor, but also socially and politically disempowered. To achieve lasting poverty reduction, poor people must be organized, confident and determined. They need to develop solutions that work for them, drawing on a knowledge and experience beyond their immediate boundaries. They need to innovate again as the context changes, and as other opportunities become available and threats emerge.

Hence, an important part of the development process is to identify, try out and further develop new solutions. As important, identifying and adopting new solutions is the indispensable starting point for organizing communities and creating situations in which they can recognize and tap into their capacity to take control of development. The key role of community-to-community exchange programmes in helping to spread innovation and learning was described earlier.

Communities must set development priorities

The fundamental reason why poor communities must set priorities is not that they are always correct. It is, rather, that the poor are much more committed to the solutions if they see that change is possible using their own strategies and processes, aimed at priorities that they have set themselves. But having solutions is only part of the answer. In order to implement them, poor communities also need the support – or at least the acquiescence – of those in power. No matter what they may achieve, micro-communities often cannot demand resources and/or policy changes effectively. The federation, as a national movement, provides a critical component to a people-centred approach to priority-setting, option identification and practical experimentation.

Beyond a reliance on government delivery

Throughout the post-colonial world, political parties have tended to seek to capture state power in order to transform society. Almost invariably, once in power, such political movements – heavily dominated by the middle class, and often educated in the West or the former communist countries – adopt a 'delivery' approach to development. They see their mission as delivering what the previous government failed to do as quickly and as 'efficiently' as possible. Because they see themselves as *comprehensive* liberators, successful political movements do not regard empowerment of the poor as something that needs to be supported; it is assumed to have been achieved by virtue of their ascendancy to power.

The wholesale attempt to implement development usually ends, to be replaced by a more gradualist approach, in which failure to deliver can be blamed on lack of money rather than will (or on elitist political systems). Over time, however, under pressure of reality, spaces emerge within which organized communities of the poor can advertise their success in meeting their needs by using their own systems. These demonstrations can be very attractive, especially to mid-level bureaucrats who seek new ways of achieving their development targets, as well as a popular constituency. Without local support they cannot persuade more senior staff to adopt more radical policies. All too often, forces for change within the bureaucracy are ignored. Sometimes alliances form between low-income communities and their local bureaucratic benefactors in order to make the formal systems work better. Frequently, these solutions are more concerned with the self-interest of those in charge, rather than the needs of the low-income citizens.

Whatever the quality of the solutions, they remain fragmented and restricted in scope as long as there is widespread acceptance of the state's claim to be the sole authentic arbiter and implementer of development. Even in the face of the state's obvious failures, many people cannot imagine an alternative and tend to accept that lack of money is the problem; their mobilization is based on demands for *improved delivery*. This may lead to a 'second phase' of development efforts, in which there are renewed attempts to find new agencies to implement development.

As long as communities practising organic solutions are few, isolated and unaware of the existence of similar communities, they tend to remain unsure of themselves, and are therefore unable to demand resources and policy changes that could help them to scale up their efforts.

Mobilization and development

The alternative is to mobilize the poor into grassroots networks (or federations) of empowered communities practising similar options. Where there is weakness in isolation, there is strength in numbers. Developing a sturdy and self-aware network of organized communities engaged in similar activities is essential if these processes are to be deepened and maintained. The experiences of the South African Homeless People's Federation show some of the benefits that the poor can achieve if they have a truly self-organized presence in the *political sphere*. The federation decided not to operate as a political party, although it wanted a political presence. Of course, this approach has its own difficulties. Politicians may see it as a threat. A further threat and one of the biggest problems is the dynamic of political power itself. With the emergence of 'leaders' from amongst the poor, there may be individuals who see themselves as a privileged elite. The federation and People's Dialogue seek to institute mechanisms of accountability and transparency to reduce these problems. But with a decentralized style, there are always some groups that remain dominated by a small number of individuals.

To achieve the required political presence requires a constant emphasis on the mobilizing aspects of the networking process that is manifest through community-to-community exchanges. Just as the solution process cannot be effective in isolation or in ignorance of its broader context, the need for collective strength means that every solution must contain a corresponding emphasis on community organization, commitment, democracy and transparency, together with an awareness-raising element of the broader context. In the experience of the People's Dialogue and the federation, it is the

BOX 8.7 100,000 LIFE STORIES

There are 100,000 members of the South African Homeless People's Federation. 85 per cent of them are women. About 6 per cent have secured improved housing through the federation. A further 10 per cent have secured legal land tenure. There is no single life story that can represent what the federation offers to its members. But these three women speak for many others when they recount what the federation has meant to them:

> *I joined the federation in 1992. What is important is that now I have my house. You have seen it. It is up the hill. When I slept the first night in my house, I could not sleep. I touched my husband in our bed: this is our house, this is our house, I told him. I was too excited. I lay awake all night.*

I had a shack, down here on this land. Just here, close by. There was a toilet outside. In that shack, when it rained, the water came in under one side and went out under the other. I have a boy, with a chest, you know, no not asthma, just an infection, he could never stop coughing. This is all gone now. When I left the shack, I let someone else take it. It is not worth much. I just let them have it.

Now I spend all day with the federation. One day, you know, I was too tired to come and do this stuff. I just stayed in my house. But they came to get me, you must come to the *uFunde Zufe*, they said. There are people waiting who need you to explain how housing loans work to them. I do the book-keeping, you see, I explain the books. So then I came down the hill and then I carried on (Angelina, Win Housing Savings Scheme, Kleinskool).

I joined in 1996. In 1985, we had left Gugulethu. I could stand it no longer. We moved to Khayelitsha. I was on the same road as Maso (a leader in the Victoria Mxenge Housing Savings Scheme). In 1992, I heard about the federation. At that time, no one trusted it in Khayelitsha. My husband, he did not let me join. He said, why do I need a house? He will buy me a house in Tempani where his brother is living. Then in 1994 I divorced him. [The violence] was just too much.

After my husband, I was for the federation. I was federation. Then I went to Maso and she said, 'Find ten others and I will come to talk to you.' That was December 1995. That is when I joined. In February last year I started building. The house, it took a long time. A lot was stolen. We were the first houses to build in this part. I had to buy it all again. We finished it, just the outside walls, in May.

So in August I took an income-generation loan. It was for 2500 rand. I spent 1000 rand on the machine, the rest on materials. I had made money sewing before. Now my daughter, she has also joined the federation (Kofie, Housing Savings Scheme, Cape Town).

Before the federation I belonged to the congress, the ANC. My husband, he belonged to the congress. We worked together there. Now I belong to the federation. The federation, it means more to me than the ANC. Here are my sisters. Now take Nongazi. She is a sister to me; we are here to help each other. She brings me her problems; then she is like a daughter. Sister, daughter, I do not know what she is.

They really helped me, you see. When my son sold my home, the house I was living in, I went to a friend. Join the federation, they told me. So I did. And I got my loan. I built my house, I was there mixing concrete. It is hard at my age [76]; but I wanted a house. Now, you see...I am for the federation. It is more than the house. Now we are together. I still carry on saving. This pill container, it has all my change. The cents that I bring home, I put them there for the *ntsuka zonke*.

I tell the others, my neighbours, about the federation. They do not want to work hard. They see me laying the bricks, they think it is too hard. They do nothing. But they will come to the federation, wait and see (Mama Jonga, Housing Savings Scheme, Queenstown).

inseparable duality of education and mobilization that implies the need for networks of empowered communities practising similar options, and for horizontal exchange programmes as the principal method of building them (mobilization) and diffusing information throughout them (education).

The networking process in South Africa's informal settlements started by the People's Dialogue conference has yielded some important results. This includes not only the projects and processes described in this chapter, but also changes in government housing policy at the national and state levels. Changes in the national government housing policy towards supporting 'people's housing processes', and away from contractor-delivered 'housing solutions' for the poor, were certainly influenced by the federation – although much still needs to be done to ensure that this is implemented and to change approaches in many provinces that give little or no support to these processes. And even where local politicians or bureaucrats are supportive of these new approaches, it is difficult to get formal institutions to support informal solutions.

All of the activities of the federation are built on one solid foundation: a vision that recognizes that the cities competing within the global economy are largely being built and developed by the poor, with little support from competent authorities. This points to an alternative vision and form of urban development practice in which self-organized communities of the urban poor are given the space and scope to instigate change.

Ultimately, any assertion about the relative merits of development solutions depends upon an understanding of what 'effectiveness' means, as well as a recognition of poor people's subjective feelings. But it is clear that poverty remains a major problem throughout the world. Given the failure to address poverty in recent decades, many development agencies recognize the need to change. If existing solutions are inadequate, it makes sense to look for alternatives. The federation model turns the process of identifying and trying out new solutions into the indispensable starting point for organizing communities. In turn, these organizations learn from one another how to create situations in which they can recognize and tap into their latent capacity to take control of development. There is a constant focus on the organic solutions that are generated in practice. International networking of organizations that represent the urban poor extends this process outward, beyond national boundaries. Like multinationals and speculative capital before them, the urban poor have recognized that national boundaries are merely constraints to information flow, opportunities and growth.

Chapter 9

Grassroots-driven Development: The Alliance of SPARC, the National Slum Dwellers Federation and *Mahila Milan*

Sheela Patel and Diana Mitlin

Introduction

This chapter describes the work of an Indian non-governmental organization (NGO), the Society for the Promotion of Area Resource Centres (SPARC), women's co-operatives (*Mahila Milan*) formed by pavement and 'slum' dwellers and the National Slum Dwellers Federation (a federation of slum dwellers' organizations and local federations). It explores how their work has resulted in local innovation and mass mobilization, securing both policy change and a better use of existing community and municipal resources. In doing so, it has made a tangible difference for hundreds of thousands of the urban poor. Over the last 18 years, this partnership developed the capacity to work on large-scale interventions with city governments and to influence local, state and national policy; by 2002, around 750,000 households were members and it was working in 52 cities in 8 states and 1 union territory. The three organizations who form this partnership have also supported organizations and federations of the urban poor in many other nations, as well as the development of Slum/Shack Dwellers International, which represents these federations in international fora and negotiations.[1]

SPARC's work cannot be understood without considering this alliance with grassroots organizations (*Mahila Milan* and the National Slum Dwellers Federation), referred to in the rest of this chapter as the alliance (see Figure 9.1). This alliance has been effective at many levels. Firstly, the approaches to urban

---

1 See www.sdinet.org for more details of Shack/Slum Dwellers International; see also www.achr.net and www.dialogue.org.za. Chapter 8 on the South African Homeless People's Federation also describes the importance of its links with SPARC, NSDF and *Mahila Milan*.

Figure 9.1 *The alliance and some of its local relationships*

development that the alliance evolved have been shown to work in many different sectors, such as housing construction, sanitation, resettlement and savings and credit (for emergencies, employment and housing), all of which have helped to expand access to basic amenities and services. Secondly, the scale and scope of the alliance's activities have grown in terms of the numbers of people reached, the nature of the support provided and the geographical coverage. Thirdly, the exchange programmes between India and several African and Asian countries through which slum and pavement dwellers visited each other and shared their experiences in organization, savings management and housing or upgrading projects have generated considerable interest among governments and international agencies regarding their capacity to promote and secure empowerment and shared learning.

This chapter concentrates on describing the first two aspects. It outlines SPARC's history from its early work to its present status as one of India's leading urban NGOs. Then, the relationships between the NGO and the people's organizations and their relative roles are described, with a discussion of how this has both supported communities' knowledge base and innovation capacity and enabled mass mobilization and, therefore, large-scale implementation. It goes on to describe the key approaches and perspectives that have become incorporated within the work of the alliance and considers the reasons for their success. This includes a discussion of how the creation of options changes the nature of participation from a passive to an active process, and how new options become part of a process to change policy through precedent-setting. The chapter then examines the effectiveness with which development assistance funds have been invested in this process and how – through blending external resources with communities' own resources – the urban poor can create viable financial systems to support their own development.

From the pavements of Mumbai

1984–1986: SPARC – 'learning on our own'

Pavement dwellers are among the poorest of India's urban poor and undeniably among the most vulnerable. When SPARC started its activities in 1984, its staff were clear that the pavement dwellers should be the central focus of their work. The first grant that SPARC received allowed it to start talking with women pavement dwellers, providing a better understanding of their experiences and perspectives. The pavement dwellers with whom SPARC worked were living in an area of Mumbai called Byculla, and they were in constant risk of having their homes demolished by the municipal corporation. SPARC did not have a solution to their problems; but it provided a space (an area resource centre) in which women could meet together and discuss their problems (hence, SPARC's full name: the Society for the Promotion of Area Resource Centres).

For the first three years, SPARC worked directly with women pavement dwellers of Byculla. Together, they developed an organizational form that invested knowledge in women's collectives rather than in male leaders. New teaching and learning strategies were developed, along with new ways of undertaking research. Most importantly, SPARC helped to set up an organization of women's collectives known as *Mahila Milan* ('Women Together') – decentralized groups of women pavement and slum dwellers who come together to set up and manage savings and credit schemes.

SPARC did everything possible to help the women explore how to break their isolation from the rest of the city. New strategies and tools were developed that are still in use today. These include community-based enumerations, the sharing of stories, dialogue to resolve community divisions or disagreements, community-managed savings, and credit and house construction. The women pavement dwellers worked out these strategies for themselves, and the logic of these processes is very much the logic of the informal city dweller. From a joint investigation on pavement dwellers in Mumbai, SPARC and pavement dwellers from Byculla developed a methodology for gathering socio-economic statistics and life histories. This led to the creation of an information base on the pavement dwellers, published as *We the Invisible* (SPARC, 1985).

One of the women's immediate needs was a capacity to help cope with the crises that were commonplace in their lives. These crises included coping with the constant threat of demolition for their pavement dwelling, coping with police harassment, and obtaining water, access to toilets and a ration card (which provides access to subsidized food and fuel). In each case, the community collectives of women and SPARC staff explored what women wanted and what they were entitled to, and then proceeded to find ways through which women could get these entitlements for themselves and could share what they had learned with other groups. For example, the women living on the pavement learned who was entitled to ration cards and how they could obtain them. One group of women used this information to obtain ration cards and then showed others how they, too, could obtain these cards.

The exploration of women's wants and needs soon addressed the issue of why pavement dwellers had no hope of a secure home. Gradually, housing strategies began to emerge and the women's collectives decided that they would start to save. All of the women living on the pavements were encouraged to contribute to a collective fund, which was then used to finance loans for emergencies and income generation (see Patel and d'Cruz, 1993).

Although the work in which SPARC is engaged has developed much since this time, and the work of the alliance now involves many other urban poor groups, the pavement dwellers remain at the centre of all activities. The pavements form the context within which all strategies for change are designed and tested. The leaders of the pavement settlements have become the main trainers for new *Mahila Milan* groups in Mumbai and elsewhere and for the National Slum Dwellers Federation.

1986–1988: An emerging partnership with the National Slum Dwellers Federation (NSDF)

After the initial work with pavement dwellers, SPARC sought to expand its outreach to the poor in the city. Recognizing that it was not likely to achieve the goal of getting land for pavement dwellers very easily, it sought wider support from the urban poor living in 'slums' to ensure that pavement dwellers were included in the official listing of the urban poor, along with slum dwellers.[2] To do that, SPARC sought a partnership with the National Slum Dwellers Federation (NSDF), an organization ten years older than SPARC. Both organizations could see that an alliance might be mutually useful. NSDF already had an existing network of federated slum communities. SPARC and women pavement dwellers had demonstrable skills that could be used to train these federations.

The NSDF was formed during the early 1970s by a group of community leaders. These leaders, primarily male, were all activists involved in fighting

---

2 In cities in India, the term slum is often used differently. Although originally used as a pejorative term (as in most other circumstances), and one used to classify settlements that the government sought to clear – with the recognition that 'slum clearance' does not diminish slum populations and often impoverishes those who move – there were advantages for the inhabitant of 'slums' in becoming officially recognized as 'slums'. Those living in informal communities may lobby hard to be officially designated as a 'slum' because this can bring particular advantages with regard to their relationship with the local authorities and the possibilities of obtaining basic infrastructure and services. They may also oppose being 'de-notified' (no longer being classified as a slum) because this makes them liable to pay service charges and property taxes.

demolition in their own settlements. The federation soon spread to over 30 cities in India and became a loose coalition of local federations. Many of these leaders had experience of working with NGOs; but they found the relationships with NGOs to be very unequal. Community members were not allowed to choose the issues on which to work, or the ways in which resources were used and allocated. As a consequence, the federation sought more autonomy. Some local organizations within the federation had registered their own trusts and societies in order to obtain direct funding from international NGOs. However, in practice, this strategy proved to be problematic. Talented and skilled community leaders were unable to fulfil the requirements of international agencies for reports and audits.

Many of SPARC's staff already knew the NSDF leaders, especially their president, Jockin. The struggle for Janata Colony, which had drawn Jockin into community organizing activities, was well known to many urban development professionals.[3] SPARC's activities in Byculla drew in Jockin and some NSDF members and, for almost a year, they offered advice and shared their experiences with *Mahila Milan* and SPARC. As the relationship between SPARC and NSDF grew stronger, NSDF's male leaders agreed that *Mahila Milan* should be gradually formalized to ensure that women had a separate and defined space within the local federations. Within *Mahila Milan*, women were able to develop the skills and experience to participate effectively in mainstream NSDF structures and activities.

Together, the alliance re-established NSDF activities in several cities and began to develop a wide range of activities to build local federations. SPARC decided not to open branches in other cities, but, instead, to work through these federations. During these years, the nascent alliance began to formulate an educational and organizational strategy that gathered knowledge on low-income settlements and allowed it to be articulated by their residents. Strategies to assist local communities to own this knowledge were refined so that local federations were able to reproduce, adapt and develop this process themselves. Thus, from the beginning, the process of knowledge creation, sharing of learning and expanding the learning circle itself became a skill located within the communities themselves.

1988–1990: Regional and international networking

The United Nations (UN) designed 1987 as the International Year of Shelter for the Homeless. SPARC increasingly took part in regional and international activities related to habitat, human settlements and urban development, with a range of development agencies, particularly NGOs and some UN organizations.

3 Janata Colony was initially a resettlement colony of households shifted from the island city of what was then Bombay (now Mumbai) during the 1950s. They were evicted and initially relocated in Chembur. Later, when the Bhabha Atomic Research Centre wanted that land for its recreational areas, residents of the settlement fought the eviction. Through a struggle that drew many community activists into the area of urban work, they obtained alternative land of their choice and secured a victory that still has many lessons relevant to today.

SPARC used these meetings to develop its networks and the contacts to address local needs.

A clear difference between SPARC and other groups emerged during these visits and exchanges. SPARC used opportunities to increase community leaders' exposure to global processes. It also encouraged community-to-community exchanges in which NGOs' roles were one of facilitation. These strategies brought out some differences between NGOs' objectives and operational styles, especially over the relationship between community members and professionals. Other NGOs struggled to adapt their role to one in which the poor, themselves, were at the centre of activities. For example, the savings and credit strategy within the alliance was developed by allowing *Mahila Milan* to work out its own rules and take time to develop its training capacity; there is minimal involvement of professionals and minimal supervision or control.

Between 1988 and 1990, exchanges between communities became a mainstream activity for the alliance. Community members, beginning with the pavement dwellers, travelled first to other settlements in their own city and later to other cities in India to visit other communities. They shared their knowledge and found many other people interested in acquiring their skills and understanding.

1990–1994: Participation in larger programmes

By 1990, the alliance was ready to start building houses, borrowing money and undertaking a series of larger-scale programmes in collaboration with other agencies. By now, community members of the alliance were training extensively in India and, primarily through the Asian Coalition for Housing Rights (ACHR), were obtaining international recognition.

The alliance developed the confidence to begin making unequivocal statements about the need for the poor to have the central role in developing workable and lasting solutions for urban development. The alliance also challenged Northern NGO donors to change the way in which they funded shelter-related activities. It established an exploratory dialogue with international (bilateral and multilateral) agencies on how a people's process might be structured into development assistance programmes from the outset. Perhaps most importantly, it challenged government agencies, arguing that no urban programmes can work in the long run until institutions are owned and controlled by the communities, and programmes are designed and executed by those who are meant to benefit from them.

A new partner for the alliance emerged during this period: the street children's federation, *Sadaak Chap* (Patel, 1990). The alliance recognized that existing NGOs were performing useful activities in providing street children with services that they needed. But they were not reaching a wider number of children in a way that could be easily maintained. Using the methodology developed with the pavement dwellers, the alliance assisted this process in two ways. Regular *mela* (parties) were organized, which enables 3000 to 5000 children to meet each other and the alliance. These parties provide an opportunity for the alliance to support a federating process among the children. The second kind of support is a residential care facility for 300 of the younger street boys to form a group. This group has allowed the children to participate fully in the process of change and transformation. The street children (at present, generally young boys who have run away from home) are now junior partners within the alliance. Many young people have begun to work actively with the federation. This relationship, in which everyone collectively takes care of the younger boys who live in the night shelter, has led to children learning skills from the federation leaders about negotiating and participating in dialogue with city officials.

1995 Onwards: going to scale

Between 1995 and 2000, the alliance continued to spread and share a development programme to communities of the urban poor. This programme includes a number of core activities that were first developed with the women living on the pavements of Mumbai.

Savings and credit

The alliance assists communities in establishing savings groups, which form the basis of community participation and ensure that women participate centrally in the process of change. Women are particularly attracted to savings groups and soon find that it transforms their relationships with each other, their family and community. Women who are interested in taking part are drawn into the training process and are shown how savings and crisis credit funds work in other communities. Within three months, most settlements are able to understand, agree and manage the rules and regulations to make the crisis credit fund operational (Patel and d'Cruz, 1993).

Surveys

Household, settlement and city surveys are an important tool in educating communities to look at themselves and in creating a capacity for communities to articulate their knowledge of themselves to those with whom they interact. The alliance helps communities to undertake surveys at various levels, including listing of all settlements (for instance, 'slum' surveys in cities), household enumeration and intra-household surveys. Questionnaires and other survey methodologies are discussed with communities and modified as necessary. As will be described in more detail later, these proved particularly important in allowing community organizations to manage a large resettlement programme for those who lived beside the railway tracks, which, in turn, developed precedents for use in other resettlement programmes.

Mapping

The alliance works with communities to build their skills in developing detailed maps of houses, infrastructure, services, resources and problems so that they can get a visual representation of how their physical situation relates to them. These maps are also particularly useful in developing plans for improvements with external agencies.

Pilot projects

Pilot projects are universally accepted as experimental learning tools that can be used to test possible solutions, strategies and management systems. The 'pilot projects' that the alliance sets up are activities that a particular community wants to undertake to address one of its problems. Once a task is accomplished, both the community and others, such as the state or the municipality, calculate what it would cost to scale up the pilot. Pilot projects also help to set precedents that are used to promote changes in policies, practices or standards (as discussed later).

Housing training

As communities secure land, they are eager to build. The federation members need to learn or improve many related skills, such as house construction, materials costing and how to manage the architects and planners who seek to influence their hopes and ambitions. There are also additional options, such as the production of building materials and the installation of infrastructure. Designs, life-size models and costings are developed and explored by community members – with many people and groups coming to visit the models and discussing possible changes in design.

There is not enough space here to include a description of the many different activities that the alliance is now undertaking; but these include house upgrading; new house construction (low rise and high rise); community-managed resettlement; and hundreds of community-designed, constructed and managed toilet blocks. The projects stretch from multilateral and bilateral agencies' development interventions to local government initiatives. The details differ in each case; but the process can be understood from the example given in Box 9.1 about the work of the alliance in addressing low-income households' sanitation needs in Mumbai.

The alliance has set up a new non-profit company, Nirman, to undertake projects, in part because of the greater scale and scope of the alliance's involvement in development projects, including the new Community-led Infrastructure Financing Facility (CLIFF), which is receiving support from the UK Department for International Development (DFID) and the Swedish International Development Cooperation Agency (Sida), as described in Box 9.2.

Description of roles and relationships

When SPARC began, the founding members sought to design an institution that enabled professionals to work in new ways with low-income communities. The challenge was to innovate, explore and evolve strategies that strengthened the capacity of the poor to participate at all levels of social change. Such a process inevitably involved enabling the poor to participate in many different aspects, such as creating their own institutional arrangements; designing educational and mobilization systems; identifying strategies for changing their circumstances; and dialogue and negotiation to enable them to be involved in executing, monitoring and managing the necessary changes in other institutions.

BOX 9.1 BOMBAY MUNICIPAL CORPORATION SLUM SANITATION PROGRAMME

In 1994, the Bombay Municipal Corporation Slum Sanitation Programme introduced a new programme to provide community toilets to 1 million people living in the 'slums'. This project was actually only a small part of a larger sewer and sewage treatment project for which the municipal corporation had been negotiating with the World Bank, and which concentrated on marine outfalls for sewers and sewage treatment. Some provision for sanitation in slums was included when the planners realized that half of the city's population did not have adequate toilets. In this first phase of the project, only settlements on municipal land were included. The project sought to provide 20,000 toilet seats to a population of 1 million people. The corporation considered a ratio of 50 persons to one toilet to be adequate.

What was unique and special about this project was that the municipal corporation's leadership sought to create new mechanisms to provide these toilets. The existing practice was for the city to organize the construction of public toilets, paying contractors to build them and ensuring that their conservancy department would maintain them. But most public toilets were poorly designed, badly constructed and not maintained. So the corporation planned to create new institutional learning, involving communities in the process of toilet design, construction, management and maintenance. If well-designed, well-constructed toilets were put into low-income settlements, residents should be willing to manage and maintain them. The challenge was to create a process that enabled this to happen.

The alliance has an interest in toilets because it believes that these can play a significant role in community development. Toilets unite communities, and community-developed toilets give them the confidence to undertake something which they need and which they can actually do. A further advantage is that the skills needed for toilet construction are not very specialized and women can participate in the process. The community toilet-block programme allows the local authority, usually at odds with the residents of slum settlements, to contribute to something that is good for the city and good for low-income settlements. Furthermore, when communities begin to undertake sanitation improvements, they look at their other amenities and often initiate the process of upgrading their homes and settlements. This partnership did not start easily. After an initially proactive partnership, the alliance considered that the way in which the World Bank team wanted to organize the design and funding of the community toilet programme, including getting communities to compete for tenders and separating the promotion, construction and maintenance of toilets, was inappropriate. As a result, the alliance walked away from the negotiations. The World Bank later agreed to change the funding and tendering arrangements, as well as the procurement procedures, to allow for more community management and NGO involvement. So, in October 2000, when the municipal corporation opened the bids for the ten wards where 20 toilet blocks each were to be constructed, the alliance filled out tenders for all ten projects. The alliance already had experience with developing community-managed toilet blocks in various cities, including a large-scale programme in Pune, where – with support from the municipal commissioner – they had constructed toilets with a total of 2000 seats. When the World Bank asked the Society for the Promotion of Area Resource Centres (SPARC) to participate in the bidding process and agreed to change this process, SPARC agreed because of the desperate need for toilets in Mumbai; because the funding allocated for sanitation was lying unutilized and would lapse shortly; and because it realized that the only way to change this whole process was to participate and change it from within.

SPARC placed a 24,938,500-rupee bid (about US$554,189) per ward (US$27,709 per toilet block). It sought to take on ten wards in this bidding round and a further four in the earlier round. It won the contracts as its bids were almost 10 million rupees less than any other group's tenders.

The inhabitants were involved in the design and construction of these toilets. Some women community leaders took on contracts to build toilet blocks themselves and managed the whole construction process, supported by engineers and architects from SPARC. The design of the toilet blocks introduced several innovations. Unlike the previous government models, they were bright and well ventilated (on all four sides), with better-quality construction (which also made cleaning and maintenance easier). They had large water storage tanks to ensure that there was enough water for users to wash after defecation and to bathe and to keep the toilets clean. Each toilet block had separate entrances and facilities for men and women, which gave women more privacy and which made queuing easier and quicker (and prevented men from pushing women out of the queue). A block of children's toilets were included, in part because children always lose out to adults when there are queues for a toilet (so they often defecate outside because they cannot wait), and in part because many young children are frightened to use conventional latrines (these are, generally, dark and smelly and often have large pits into which the children are frightened of falling). The children's toilets were specially designed for children's use – including smaller squat plates, handles (to prevent overbalancing when squatting) and no large pit openings. In many toilet blocks, there were also toilets designed for easier use by the elderly and the disabled.

Toilet blocks also included a room where the caretaker and his or her family could live – which meant that lower wages could be paid for maintenance, thus reducing the running costs. In some toilet blocks, a community hall was incorporated within the building; small fees charged for its use could also help to cover maintenance costs and having a community hall right on top of the toilets also places pressure on the caretaker to keep the complex clean. Despite these innovations, the cost of the toilet blocks was 5 per cent less than the municipal corporation's costing. As of July 2003, 180 community toilet blocks had been completed in Mumbai and another 110 were underway.

Source: Burra, Patel and Kerr (2003)

A further objective was to ensure women's central participation in all of these processes.

SPARC's initial goals changed and moved forward as its partnership with NSDF developed and *Mahila Milan* began to emerge. When SPARC and NSDF began to work together, they agreed on some general principles; over time, these have become the 'building blocks' of the relationships:

- Resources belong to local community organizations and should, ultimately, be managed by the women's collectives (loosely based around savings schemes).
- The federation and *Mahila Milan* should keep expanding their membership, building credibility and skills to represent the poor in dialogue with the state and other resource-providing institutions.
- SPARC should have a retreating and abdicating role, always seeking to ensure that current activities become embedded within the federation and finding new roles to support local federations. It should experiment with institutional

Box 9.2 THE COMMUNITY-LED INFRASTRUCTURE FINANCING FACILITY IN INDIA

The Community-led Infrastructure Financing Facility (CLIFF) is a financing facility to help the alliance of SPARC, *Mahila Milan* and the National Slum Dwellers Federation (NSDF) carry out and scale up community-driven infrastructure, housing and urban services initiatives at city level, in conjunction with municipal authorities and the private sector (including banks and landowners). This financing facility is also seen as a pilot project from which to draw lessons for setting up comparable facilities in other nations. It is unusual in that it provides funding for projects that are developed locally, on a larger scale than is usually available to NGOs and people's organizations, and in a form that helps leverage funds from other groups and, where possible, to recoup the capital for reinvestment.

The financing facility provides loans, guarantees and technical assistance to support a range of projects, including community-led high-rise developments in crowded areas (so that housing can be improved without displacing anyone), a variety of new housing projects and community-managed resettlement programmes. UK£6.1 million (approximately US$9.8 million) are available for bridging loans to kick-start large infrastructure, upgrading and resettlement projects, with the funding recovered as government subsidies are paid. Most government subsidies only become available when a project has reached a certain stage, and this often leads to such subsidies not being used, as few NGOs can afford to start major construction projects before funds become available. CLIFF also provides hard currency guarantees to secure local bank financing of projects, technical assistance grants (to develop projects to the point where they are ready for financing) and knowledge grants (to ensure that learning from the initiatives supported by CLIFF is widely shared by communities, municipal officials, technical staff and policy-makers).

A large part of the funding for the projects that CLIFF supports comes from the resources contributed by low-income households and their community organizations within the SPARC–*Mahila Milan*–NSDF alliance. In effect, CLIFF is only possible because of the strength and capacity of the long-established federations and savings and loan schemes. The Swedish International Development Cooperation Agency (Sida) and the UK Department for International Development (DFID) have contributed external funding to CLIFF, which is channelled through Cities Alliance and the UK charity Homeless International (which helped develop the concept of CLIFF with the alliance).

forms for the activities, all of which will, ultimately, be managed by the federations.

- SPARC's role includes fund-raising and financial management, research and liaising with state and international agencies. NSDF and *Mahila Milan* mobilize communities – particularly women – to participate in their own development.
- *Mahila Milan* groups should exist in every settlement where NSDF works. Their job is to help women in the collective to develop the skills that they need to be centrally involved in decision-making and, with the NSDF, to assist communities in accepting the role and contribution of women (and not to see women as being in competition with men).

Starting from these principles, the alliance has deepened and amended its working relationships. Initially, *Mahila Milan* members were unable to participate equally because the process was very new to the women. However, they soon became confident enough to deal directly with the NSDF; over time, women came to make up almost half of the federation's membership. The federation and *Mahila Milan* have created the space for local women to take on leadership roles. While the federation and *Mahila Milan* remain separate, much of their membership is shared.

When the federation offered to work with SPARC, there were mutual expectations. The federation sought the professional and support structure that SPARC offered, but kept its right to make decisions. The federation continues to see itself as a lobbying and advocacy organization, with day-to-day activities being based around the education and organization of small community groups who deal with essential needs. It seeks to retain its autonomy and vibrancy by not being registered as a legal entity.

The federation provided SPARC with a large social movement within which the pavement dwellers could fight for their cause and obtain the organizational support that they needed. Initially, SPARC was a great 'doer'. This role was due to the learning needs of its leadership and the absence of the relationship with NSDF between 1984 and 1987. For some time, most settlement organizing was done jointly; but, gradually, the local federations took over these tasks, with back-up and support from SPARC. Now, the back-up and support role is provided by the core leadership of NSDF and *Mahila Milan*, with SPARC taking on 'trouble-shooting' roles as required.

SPARC's current role is, in part, to act as a bridging institution, which:

- Obtains external resources for loan funds and grants.
- Highlights the difficulties that the urban poor face and the people's own proposals to address these problems.
- Makes the urban poor aware of government schemes and plans, and helps the federation to understand and critically review them.
- Attends conferences and other meetings to advocate for the central importance of people's organizations in development.

The NSDF leadership feels that a people's organization will always need support from an NGO because of NGOs' ability to deal with government and funding agencies, and their skills in writing project proposals, preparing documentation and representing to the external world the dialectics and outcomes of community processes.

There is no written memorandum of understanding between SPARC and the NSDF; but there is an understanding that the NSDF cannot be expected to participate in any activity or programme that it believes is not good for its constituency. SPARC does not try to promote or follow any particular line of action merely because funds are available or because of government invitation. There is dialogue and debate – although not always unanimity – before significant decisions are taken by members of the alliance. Differences are accommodated by recognizing that one party's passionate belief in something creates the basis for a conditional acceptance of further exploration of that perspective or plan. The proposal that develops out of this is later reviewed and accepted or rejected, based on the experience of trying it out. The president of the NSDF is always invited to SPARC board meetings, and this provides an opportunity for discussion on policy and direction. SPARC joins in federation meetings by invitation.

SPARC has few staff as its role is as back-up and facilitator. More and more activities need to be undertaken by the federation, and SPARC is involved in those aspects of the process that are complementary to the federation and *Mahila Milan*. The character of the process has to be decentralized and not determined by professional support, but, rather, by the urban poor themselves.

Core values

This section looks at how these organizational relationships are transformed into effective activities.

The learning cycle

Much of the alliance's work evolved from the initial learning strategy developed by SPARC. This learning strategy is so central to the alliance and its other strategies and activities that it is worth explaining in detail. The learning cycle includes several stages:

- Communities identify their priority concerns. A debate then takes place within the alliance, generally leading to the formulation of a strategy for seeking a solution.
- One or more communities come forward to design solutions to the problems. The alliance assists these groups financially and organizationally because they offer a living 'laboratory' of how change can occur and they will help the federation in achieving a sustainable solution through the learning process. Many failures occur during this initial phase.
- Once a crude solution has been developed in a settlement, groups take part in exchange visits to and from that settlement to see what has been achieved. This leads to the next generation of volunteers wishing to try out similar actions. Refinements to the solution emerge as a series of important additional factors are considered when other communities go through the process. Progress is always made, although frequent delays take place when external factors prevent communities from achieving change.
- Once a refined solution has been established, it is explored with city officials. Through inter-city exchanges, it is shared with other community organizations and federations and other city officials. Within a year, the federations in several other cities are exploring this possibility. The federation then creates a core team, made up of some of the members from the first settlement who experimented with the solution.
- This core team then visits other cities to demonstrate the solution that has

been developed. This process may have a long gestation period because large numbers of people need to participate to create an internal dynamic, which enables the local people's movement to believe that it can transform the situation of the poor. More and more communities are exposed to the innovation, and they put pressure on their local officials and politicians for change. Depending upon the external situation, there may be many possibilities for scaling up through participation in major state projects.

Over the last ten years, this strategy has been used on many occasions. Box 9.3 gives an example of what the cycle looks like in practice, through the alliance's work on savings and credit.

The alliance's training process involves several critical principles:

- There are never resident trainers, just visiting ones.
- Major training events are conducted by community leaders.
- Training encourages women to participate in the processes.
- Training teaches by doing rather than by telling.
- The trainers learn through training, acknowledge this and never consider themselves experts.
- The process helps people to develop a working relationship with professionals and other stakeholders, and helps to ensure that they are not treated as 'beneficiaries'.

This process helps more and more communities align with the federation, learn new skills and begin to reconsider their interaction with the external world.

Community exchanges

Exchanges between communities have been continually developed because they serve many ends. They:

- Are a means of drawing large numbers of people into a process of change.
- Support local reflection and analysis, enabling the urban poor themselves to own the process of knowledge creation and change.
- Enable the poor to reach out and federate, in this way developing a collective vision.
- Help to create strong, personal bonds between communities who share common problems, presenting them with a wide range of options to choose from and negotiate for, and assuring them that they are not alone in their struggles.

The exchange process is a vehicle that allows communication about all the strategies that people develop, refine and replicate. Although most exchanges are local (intra-city) or within nations, the exchange process has also broken national barriers, and evidence from the early exchanges with South Africa clearly showed that this process is validated across national boundaries (see Chapter 8). The international exchange programme has grown to encompass many countries,

Box 9.3 Savings and credit

Stages I, II and III

Women pavement dwellers started working with savings and credit in 1986. Gradually, they developed ways of recording savings payments and loan repayments. Most members are illiterate. However, this is more than compensated for by oral and memory processes and the use of symbols. *Mahila Milan* provides each woman with a plastic bag. This bag contains coloured squares of paper – for instance, pink represents 1 rupee, yellow 2 rupees and green 5 rupees. So, when she saves 10 rupees, her bag will contain two bits of green paper. All the bags from each cluster are stored in a larger black bag. Representatives from each area collect money every day from various people and bring it to the Byculla office where others, also nominated by the group, keep the money and put the bits of paper in the bags. With the Society for the Promotion of Area Resource Centres' (SPARC's) representatives' help, a register is maintained. Gradually, a literate person from *Mahila Milan* has begun to maintain this system.

Some of *Mahila Milan*'s leaders, who belong to the original, oldest collective, explain the origin of the scheme:

> *Everyone who meets the Byculla* Mahila Milan *has to hear about the* Mahila Milan *bank. We call it our bank; but it is actually a crisis credit scheme that has 600 households as its members. It was started in 1987. The residents of six pavement dweller clusters had just completed a process of exploration – designing shelter alternatives for themselves – and they discovered that their aim was not just a physical structure in which to live in but a new way of life. The crisis loans and savings scheme began when everyone felt that, if we all saved a little together – say, 1 to 2 rupees [equivalent to US$0.02–$0.04] – then, when any of us had a problem, we could use the money and repay the fund later.*

Stage IV

By 1988, *Mahila Milan* was training groups around the country to save; in 1989, the network was strong enough to support the transfer of loan funds between different savings groups. The credit and savings network has spread vigorously. At present, the alliance has over 25,000 households who save and about 5000 borrowers.

Stage V

In 1993, *Mahila Milan* began to borrow from external sources and to on-lend to its members. In the process, it developed a unique style of management and decentralized functioning.

The gradual increase in the savings and credit practices of *Mahila Milan* prepared the ground for the alliance to explore credit lines for communities. These processes focus as much on providing women with credit for their needs as they do on developing decentralized mechanisms for large federations to manage finance. Until now, savings and credit have been used primarily to build and strengthen women's collectives, to strengthen micro-community organizations and to build women's managerial capacity to manage and control resources. The Rashtriya Mahila Kosh (RMK), a government of India undertaking, provided the alliance with its first credit line of 3.2 million rupees. This fund was channelled through SPARC to various women's collectives in Mumbai, Bangalore, Chennai (formerly Madras) and Kanpur. Additional small-scale credit, in areas chosen by the communities but which the RMK does not provide for, is funded by community savings fund and a modest revolving fund from the Ford Foundation.

Another community need is housing finance. For many years, the alliance has been struggling to obtain housing loans for its membership. In 1991, it was able to access state housing funds, secured by a guarantee from SELAVIP, an international NGO. Since that date, it has been successful in obtaining loan finance for several more housing projects. Several federation co-operatives have now built their own houses, taking state loans and repaying them over 20 years.

especially in Asia and sub-Saharan Africa, and it continues to demonstrate its potential to develop people's confidence and capacities (Asian Coalition for Housing Rights, 2000).

The exchange process builds upon the logic of 'doing is knowing'. Exchanges lead to a good sharing of experience and, therefore, a new set of people can learn new skills. In the exchange process, communities and their leadership all over the country have the potential to learn and share teaching. The alliance's need to grow and multiply, combined with SPARC's own reluctance to expand, has led to this strategy, which is now the alliance's greatest achievement. The exchanges maintain a rapid learning and teaching curve, within which the alliance's core team supports new learning and helps more people to teach and to learn from each other. Since the first community exchanges between the pavement dwellers on the streets of Mumbai, there has developed an international alliance (the Shack/Slum Dwellers International) that links the urban poor organizations in different countries and draws together almost 1 million people in 11 countries (Patel, Bolnick and Mitlin, 2001)

Gender

The roles of women, both within the federation and within communities and families who are involved with the federation, have been evolving at a pace and in a way that has been selected by the women in the low-income settlements. The results that are emerging are very positive, demonstrating that the alliance is better able to address gender issues in this way rather than by directly demanding change.

The early contact between *Mahila Milan* and the NSDF led to *Mahila Milan* (at the time, solely the women of Byculla) attending local federation meetings. They were the only women present; but they remained confident because they had explored so many possibilities, trained so many people and were excited about their own learning. They inspired the men to invite them to work with women in their community. What *Mahila Milan* demonstrated was that women focus more than men on issues that require collective long-term investment. The federation leaders realized that they had 'used' women's presence for demonstrations and other activities, but had not enabled women to become leaders. Women in *Mahila Milan* did not compete with men. Choices about roles and activities should allow both groups the space that they require and meet the needs of both.

Over time, a new pattern has emerged. When federation groups within a settlement wish to undertake new activities, or the alliance wishes to assist communities to strengthen themselves, there is a general meeting where these issues are discussed. If, for instance, the community feels that the settlement's concern is with their relationship with the local police station, then the inputs would be those that help all of the people understand the roles and functions of the police, and the manner in which the community can use their collective strength to manage this relationship. In nine cases out of ten, it is women who are central to the resolution of a problem – for example, using the police to resolve a difficulty. The strategies suggested do not dissuade men from participating, but proactively support the participation of women. This allows women to work together to overcome their individual lack of confidence.

The example of housing training demonstrates how women are involved and why the federations undertake this training better than SPARC. Women can 'dream' about houses better than men, in part because they use the structure that they live in more than men. Men, therefore, concede that women can design the new structure better. Once that is achieved, men often concede that women who are trained to manage construction are the most effective supervisors of the process.

The starting point of the strategy means that women are the major innovators in the federations. Most solutions, therefore, require women trainers to assist communities, and women are involved in supporting the options as they develop. This opens up possibilities for participation and creates further opportunities for women. At every moment, women are central to this process.

Politics

The federation finds that as long as it can stay out of party political processes, it is able to grow and increase its membership. Within NGO movements, there is often debate about whether or not people's organizations should join mainstream politics in order to obtain more resources for their constituencies. The alliance leadership is convinced, based on its own experiences and the evidence of the last 40 years, that political parties rarely develop effective agendas for the poor, although their manifestos always 'hoist the flag of the poor'. Most elected politicians find themselves dragged into corruption and unable to address the needs of their constituency. The NSDF encourages all of its members who feel that they want to join parties to do so and to use what they have learned within the federation to influence party manifestos. So far, this has been possible because the political parties are not actively seeking federation support and none of the current leaders are committed to a specific party political direction. The partnership will be seriously affected if this happens.

Participation and the process of policy change

Participation and precedent-setting

The alliance has always been conscious of the need to work at a scale beyond conventional NGO projects and, therefore, to work with government. The tradition of policy advocacy among many local NGOs has been to consult communities and write up an alternative policy, which they campaign to have accepted. Often, the policies are good and much needed; but most communities lack the training, exposure or capacity to take advantage of such processes. As a result, many pro-poor reforms remain unused. The experience of urban professionals is that there are many ideal policies and programmes; but few make any positive impact on the poor and even fewer reach a significant scale.

SPARC and its partners decided to follow another route – that of setting a precedent and using this as the basis to negotiate for changes in policies and practices. Precedent-setting begins by recognizing that the strategies that the poor use already are probably the most effective starting point, although they may need to be improved. Hence, the alliance supports the refinement of these strategies and their demonstration to city officials. Because they emerge from the existing practices of the poor, they make sense to other grassroots organizations, become widely supported and can easily be scaled up. One of the first precedents to be established was the right of pavement dwellers to ration cards, which, once agreed by the government department, set a precedent that all pavement dwellers could use. The use of a mezzanine floor in the design of the houses developed by the federation is another example of precedent-setting, demonstrating what could be done (and how well it worked) before negotiating its approval. This mezzanine floor provides households with more room and more flexibility in their homes, but costs much less than a two-storey unit. The community-directed house modelling exercises described already have also produced precedents, showing how particular designs better serve low-income households' needs; so, too, have the community-designed and managed toilets.

All three partners in the alliance believe that there can be no social change that will benefit low-income communities if the poor do not participate in designing, managing and realizing this process of change. Community involvement in conceptualizing participation is as important as the participation itself. In SPARC's experience, before most conventional projects have even gone beyond the negotiating stage, the participation component is reduced and/or narrowly conceptualized. As a consequence, communities tend to be involved only peripherally or in a limited range of activities. SPARC's experience shows that active and multilevel participation by grassroots organizations can help to transform the relationships between the actors involved in any given project. Most social movements are designed to deliver high levels of participation; most development interventions are not.

There are many different kinds of participation and it has long been recognized that there are qualitative differences between these. Box 9.4 summarizes the types of participation with which federation members are familiar.

BOX 9.4 COMMUNITY PERSPECTIVES ON PARTICIPATION

Because you happened to be there. Just happening to be in a certain geographical location is probably the most passive version of participation, so passive that it might not look much like participation at all. But to people and communities suspicious of formal development programmes and afraid of getting burned, simply being there can be a start, and can begin to lay the foundation for more involvement. When a development intervention begins in your neighbourhood, even if it has nothing to do with what you want, the circumstances of location have created conditions for you to participate (for example, if you happen to live in one of the settlements on the banks of the Pata Nala, in Lucknow, your settlement finds itself part of a pilot project).

Because you didn't say no. The overall acceptance of a development intervention in your neighbourhood can create conditions that imply that you have been considered as having 'participated'. If the drain in your neighbourhood is being cleaned, for example, and you do not protest, that is a form of acceptance and acceptance is another form of participation, however slight. You may accept only because you do not see the project as hurting you in any way or compromising your interests; but, here again, acceptance may lead to enthusiasm and enthusiasm to greater involvement.

Because someone else persuaded you to jump in. Someone in your neighbourhood stirs things up and starts initiatives, which you can imagine yourself benefiting from. You may not have much commitment to the initiative yourself; but, because you see it as being potentially useful, you agree to go along. Or, you may participate because you follow someone else's leadership and because they've told you what to do. You may wait to see what happens, you may not resist this influence and, later, when things continue to improve, you may become more involved. Most communities naturally break down into only a few bold leaders, who may show this kind of initiative, and a lot of followers and 'hangers around'. The initiative of a few can kindle the participation of many more.

Because you feel it's worth it. And, finally, you participate because you have an urge to make a choice, to stick your neck out so that you or your community can move ahead. You are in the middle of things, a catalyst, and the leadership mantle falls on your shoulders. You may be an individual or a group. Once your behaviour becomes routine, and once benefits that you are working for are seen by all as being useful, more people will copy that behaviour and more will participate. You become a leader who has the potential to participate more and more actively in making choices for yourself and for the community.

The alliance believes that effective participation requires that an individual, group or community makes a choice to become involved in a given process or activity, can understand the options that the particular process opens up, and can appreciate the impact that the process will have upon their lives, their households, their community and their environment.

Creating options

In Indian cities, poor people who live in informal settlements or pavements survive by doing things in ways that nobody would ever choose, if they had any choice. However, for the most, part choices are non-existent or very restricted.

When a visitor to some of the women and men from *Mahila Milan* and the federation in Mumbai asked them how they described poverty, one woman replied: 'Poverty is never having any choices.' The routines that poor families follow reflect a tenuous balance between managing their own survival and managing the (almost feudal) relationships of dependency and patronage that enable that survival. Low-income families (many of whom are migrants) create their survival systems from extremely limited choices. People are constantly seeking potential opportunities, taking advantage of anything that comes along, are careful not to offend leaders and summon tremendous resources and innovation to stay alive. If being a passive participant helps one to survive, then they become adept at swallowing their own ideas before these ideas are verbalized. They learn to say only as much as their benefactors want to hear; they become experts at making themselves invisible. No strategy is perfect. Most of them involve exploitation, oppression and unimaginable hardship. But, for most, this is all that is possible.

The alliance believes that effective community development supports communities to undertake projects, and creates an environment that allows for experimentation and mistakes. The alliance does not try to create new standards; instead, it attempts to alter and influence circumstances in order to allow communities to develop options of their own. The difference between the alliance strategy for policy change and the more traditional NGO route of lobbying and advocacy now emerges. Through community exchanges, numerous communities are exposed to the innovation. These exchanges, which take place through the federation, have created a number of grassroots organizations that are ready to take up the new possibilities, should there be a change in government policy. In these circumstances, a change in policy is followed by immediate pressure for the changes to be implemented. If there is no change in policy after the precedent, when communities return to their locality, those who want this innovation start to push locally for the policy change; sooner or later, someone breaks through. This process is illustrated by the development of a community-rooted process to manage resettlement and to avoid the usual consequences of government-managed resettlement programmes, which impoverish those who are resettled. Box 9.5 describes what resettling meant to those individuals who live beside the railway tracks in Mumbai. The alliance also works with people who have settled on land owned by the airport authority and the port to improve conditions and develop new housing options.

Investing in development

SPARC's fundraising strategies have had to protect the community processes that are at the centre of the alliance's work. Donors often think that they know best, and that they can impose their perspectives and move funding away from community control. The alliance required funds from abroad, primarily to support learning and exchanges, in order to develop communities' capacity, confidence, knowledge, skills and negotiating abilities to initiate and manage their own development process. Some Northern NGOs recognized the need for

BOX 9.5 PEOPLE-MANAGED RESETTLEMENT PROGRAMMES IN MUMBAI

Mumbai relies primarily upon its extensive suburban railway system to get its work force in and out of the central city; on average, over 7 million passenger trips are made each day on its five main railway corridors. But the capacity of the railway system is kept down by the illegal railway settlements that crowd each side of the tracks. By 1999, more than 20,000 households lived in shacks within 25 metres of the tracks, including many living within less than 1 metre of passing trains. The households living there did so because they had no better option that they could afford as they needed the central location to get to and from work. Yet, they had to face not only the constant risk of injury or death from the trains, but also high noise levels, insecurity, overcrowding, poor-quality shelters and no provision for water and sanitation. Indian Railways, which owned the land, would not allow the municipal corporation to provide basic amenities for fear that this would legitimate the land occupation and encourage the inhabitants to consolidate their dwellings. So, the inhabitants had to spend long hours fetching and carrying water – a task that generally fell to women. Most people had no toilet facility and had to defecate in the open. Discussions within the Railway Slum Dwellers Federation (to which the majority of households belonged) made clear that most wanted to move if they could get a home with secure tenure in an appropriate location.

A relocation programme was developed as part of the larger scheme to improve the quality, speed and frequency of the trains. This was unusual on three counts. Firstly, it did not impoverish those who moved (as is generally the case when poor groups are moved to make way for infrastructure development). Secondly, the actual move involving some 60,000 people was voluntary and needed neither police, nor municipal force to enforce it. And, thirdly, the resettled people were involved in designing, planning and implementing the resettlement programme and in managing the settlements to which they moved. The process was not entirely problem free – for instance, Indian Railways started demolishing huts along one railway line and demolished over 2000 huts before the National Slum Dwellers Federation (NSDF) and the Society for the Promotion of Area Resource Centres (SPARC) managed to get the state government to decree that the demolitions must stop. Land sites were identified to accommodate the evicted households and the federation was given the responsibility for managing the resettlement programme. A pilot scheme involving 900 families was carried out to help develop the larger scheme

Perhaps the most important feature of this resettlement programme was the extent to which those who were to be resettled were organized and involved before the move. First, all huts along the railway tracks and their inhabitants were counted by teams of federation leaders, community residents and NGO staff. This was done in such a way that the inhabitants' questions about what was being done and how the move would be organized could be answered. Then, maps were prepared with the help of residents in which each hut was identified with a number. Draft registers of all inhabitants were prepared, with the results returned to communities for checking. Households were then grouped into units of 50; these house groupings were used to recheck that all details about their members were correct, and to provide the basis for allowing households to move to the new site together and to live next to each other when they were resettled. Households could choose to move from one group to another. Identity cards were prepared for all those who would move and visits were made to the resettlement sites. Then, the move took place, with a proportion of households moving to apartments in completed units and a proportion moving to transit camps as better-quality accommodation was being prepared.

A series of interviews with the relocatees in January and February 2002 highlighted the support that the inhabitants gave to the resettlement and their pleasure in having secure, safe housing with basic amenities. No process involving so many people moving so quickly is problem free – for instance, the schools in the area to which they moved (many railway stations from where they previously had lived) could not expand enough to cope with the number of children; many households had difficulties getting ration cards (which allow them access to cheap food staples and kerosene); and the electricity company overcharged them because they were on communal meters. The resettlement would have been better if there had been more lead time, with sites identified by those to be relocated and prepared before the resettlement. But this programme worked much better than other large resettlement programmes and has set precedents with regard to fully involving those relocated in the whole process. It is hoped that other public agencies in India will follow.

Source: Patel, d'Cruz and Burra (2002)

this. As community-based solutions develop, more resources are needed; but, at this point, these can often be negotiated from Indian government sources, although international support is a valuable source of bridging funds as government resources are often delayed or are only available when a project is underway or close to completion.

Many donors find it difficult to support community-directed processes because their procedures require outputs to be defined at the outset and achievements to be monitored during implementation. They are unwilling or unable to support processes whose objective is to transform the interaction between the state and the poor. They cannot see how support for local processes can strengthen poor communities' capacity to secure their own and external resources. But the process supported by the alliance has brought larger, more secure and more sustainable improvements to the lives of far more urban poor groups than any donor project. Hundreds of thousands of urban poor have access to emergency loans. Over 3500 houses have been built with permanent collective land tenure and community management, and, by 2002, 16,416 poor households had secured tenure. Savings for housing now exceed 25 million rupees a year. Table 9.1 gives details of the scale of community savings. More than 8 million rupees have been loaned to support income generation, with much of this money revolving. All of this is controlled and managed by communities, thus increasing financial management skills and capacities. Over 2 million rupees of community savings are now in high interest accounts, as the alliance's collective weight allowed it to negotiate a group scheme. Several hundred community-designed and managed toilet blocks serving hundreds of thousands of people have been built in Pune, Mumbai and Bangalore – with a total value equivalent to over US$10 million. The scale of the federation movement (built on the organic spread of small savings schemes) has enabled SPARC and the federation to be included in city negotiations in Mumbai. Recent legislation has combined the right to stay in low-income, high-density settlements, such as Dharavi, with the right to develop housing at higher densities than elsewhere in the city. Many new housing projects are being developed. Several hundred *Mahila*

Table 9.1 *Growth in community savings (rupees), 1991–1999*

	1991/92	1992/93	1993/94	1994/95	1995/96	1996/97	1997/98	1998/99
Local savings	125,000	125,000	134,375	322,500	765,625	1,750,000	4,375,000	10,500,000
Housing savings	684,833	345,333	6,983,109	9,411,640	9,274,786	18,344,057	24,451,150	3,853,053
Other savings*						300,000	3,765,400	
Other loan capital**			400,000	965,700	1,784,300	1,891,700	1,700,000	1,408,300

Note: * Housing and Urban Development Corporation (HUDCO) deposits and unit trust savings
** The federation's savings record has enabled it to access loan capital from special government schemes to capitalize revolving loan funds for income-generation lending.

Milan women have been trained in construction and have increased their earnings.

Many of the benefits to members of the federation (and other low-income households) cannot easily be given a quantifiable value. Such benefits include improved health, once housing is safe, secure and of an adequate standard, with less spent on medical bills and less work lost to illness or injury. There are also the resources obtained as a result of the increased ability of community organizations to negotiate with both NGOs and local authorities – which then results in improved access to basic amenities such as water, sanitation, electricity and solid-waste management. There are also those benefits that will always be difficult to measure, such as a reduction in social exclusion and an expansion of life choices for tens of thousands of people. This includes the increase in self-respect through involvement in federation activities and the reduction in vulnerability as a result of higher levels of cooperation between local residents. The objective of the community development process is the empowerment of individuals (and, therefore, communities) who decide to participate. Such an empowerment process enables life choices to be expanded and new options to be taken up. As described already, the dynamics within community organizations change as women are empowered to articulate and pursue their needs. Confident and articulate community leaders are able to build constructive relationships with city officials and politicians. The material results of these changed relationships may take years to show; but the investments in social networks are being developed and consolidated continuously.

Conclusions

Although the processes supported by the alliance of SPARC, the National Slum Dwellers Federation and *Mahila Milan* have faced many difficult issues, the core activities of learning and knowledge, organization and mobilization have proved their worth. The national movement has secured additional international and national loan funds, changed government programmes to favour the poor and begun to address basic needs for thousands of their members.

The rise of new options and development alternatives emerges from a process of community learning and knowledge creation. Unlike most conceptualizations of development plans and programmes, this knowledge is based upon the realities of the lives of the poor themselves. It emerges from the stories and experiences exchanged between communities as they visit each other and share each other's lives.

Needs are identified and priorities are refined. Solutions are tried and tested and then modified through replication. Gradually, a set of practices emerges that meets the needs of many communities. These practices are ritualized through constant sharing so that they become accepted ways of doing things. Communities have some new challenges to explore; but not everything is new. In some areas they follow the accepted practices of other communities. Problems are addressed through mutual support networks, communities gain in confidence and, in so doing, they gain in capacity. New innovations are put forward; other needs are addressed.

The better use of existing resources is key to many of the innovations that have developed. This, in turn, supports the long-term viability of many of the activities, particularly the re-creation of local organizations.

In general, community organizations do little to support the housing needs of low-income households, especially the poorest members. But the alliance has found that savings schemes based on accountability and trust do much to change the nature of the options that are open to those living in low-income settlements, including the poorest members. Individual members are less vulnerable; they can find the support they need in difficult situations. Collective activities become possible and neighbours work together to address mutual needs.

Drawing savings schemes into federations brings multiple benefits. The urban poor are no longer isolated. Communities can support each other in a range of areas, from addressing financial malpractice to avoiding eviction. Learning and knowledge can be accumulated and used for the benefit of all.

Mobilized through the federation, the women in the savings schemes become part of a movement of the urban poor. Together, they put pressure on government to secure changes that they need in order to advance their livelihoods and establish their place in the city. Through international networks, they learn more about the policies and programmes of international agencies and how these, too, can be influenced to further their cause. Through these networks, they can better use their resources to address their needs and those of other groups of the urban poor. This movement is rooted in the savings schemes and their practical activities to address members' poverty. As such, it cannot be easily co-opted or destabilized by government promises or led astray by a powerful self-interested leadership.

With regard to changing the approach of government, the federation leaders' increasing capacity to interact with senior government staff and politicians is related to the changes that have taken place, both in government and in the voluntary sector. Especially in housing, there is now – in principle, at least – official acceptance of the government's role as an 'enabler', and acceptance of the increased legitimacy of NGOs and community-based organizations. There is also an acknowledgement that increased responsibilities should be devolved to them. On the other hand, voluntary organizations have begun to shed their confrontational attitudes towards the state.

Engagement with government has been critical to the scaling-up of the alliance's work and impact. The alliance developed a new route to influencing policy. This involves working with community organizations to undertake demonstrable alternatives that communities want (such as toilets constructed and managed by communities), and then engaging local and national officials in a dialogue with communities about these pilot projects. Inevitably, the rules and regulations that restrict communities are breached by new practice. This in itself is more significant than a new policy because most administrations operate on precedent. Community access to this process expands, and direct possibilities for engaging the state emerge that are in favour of communities who, at the time, are ready to play their role. Furthermore, because communities have already developed the solution, their empowerment develops through subsequent negotiations and the scaling-up of the initiative.

This process focuses attention on what the poor can do for themselves. As a result, state agencies do not view them as beneficiaries. Instead, the poor increasingly operate as a constituency, lobbying to negotiate with the state and the agencies who have the resources to resolve the city's problems and to improve the quality of people's lives, as well. This is distinctly unusual and different. It is even more powerful when it appears at the same time that governments and international development agencies seek people's participation to make development interventions more effective.

This strategy has many implications, both for community organizations and NGOs, and for governments and international agencies. For all concerned, there is a clear message: organizational investments in communities have to be long term, developing capabilities in the communities to ensure that they become, and remain, central to mainstream city development. This is very different from organizational development and capacity-building, which is project-based, where communities are involved only to 'agree' to development interventions that are designed elsewhere. These can never result in a lasting institutional arrangement that works for the poor. Such interventions may even increase the alienation between the poor and the rest of the population, and further increase the problems that they face.

The alliance between NSDF and SPARC also has particular importance. If SPARC had undertaken its research and advocacy role without the support of a people's organization, its impact would have been limited – its perspective would not have been invigorated by the freshness of insights that the NSDF offers on poor people's problems. Had NSDF operated on its own, it would undoubtedly have affected the lives of large sections of the urban poor; but its impact upon policy would probably have been limited. In the absence of legal reform, receiving external funding would also have been problematic.

The demands that arise from this process are very different from those that have come before. The federation believes that the solution will not merely emerge from an acknowledgement by the state that the poor have needs. It believes that the present status quo must change, with a re-negotiation of the relationship between the city and its residents, between the state and civil society, and between the poor and other stakeholders. For dialogue to occur, there must be equality between the participants in any negotiation. Communities cannot compete with the city or the private sector on financial or technological terms. Moreover, their history of isolation makes even basic dialogue difficult. As a result, the strategy adopted by the alliance is one to strengthen their own capacities by designing a solution that works for the poor, and which also gives something of value to the city. With such solutions, the alliance can negotiate a more equal relationship with other urban groups and begin to create a more favourable urban future for the lowest-income city dwellers.

For more details on the work of the alliance of the Society for the Promotion of Area Resource Centres (SPARC), *Mahila Milan* and the National Slum Dwellers Federation (NSDF), see www.sparcindia.org.

References

Asian Coalition for Housing Rights (2000) *Face to Face: Notes from the Network on Community Exchange*, ACHR, Bangkok

Burra, S, S Patel and T Kerr (2003) 'Community-designed, built and managed toilet blocks in Indian cities', *Environment and Urbanization*, vol 15, no 2, pp11–32

Patel, S (1990) 'Street children, hotel boys and children of pavement dwellers and construction workers in Bombay: how they meet their daily needs', *Environment and Urbanization*, vol 2, no 2, October, pp9–26

Patel, S, J Bolnick and D Mitlin (2001) 'Squatting on the global highway', in M Edwards and J Gaventa (eds) *Global Citizen Action*, Earthscan, London, and Westview, US

Patel, S and C d'Cruz (1993) 'The Mahila Milan crisis credit scheme; from a seed to a tree', *Environment and Urbanization*, vol 5, no 1, pp9–17

Patel, S, C d'Cruz and S Burra (2002) 'Beyond evictions in a global city; people-managed resettlement in Mumbai', *Environment and Urbanization*, vol 14, no 1, pp159–172

SPARC (1985) *We the Invisible: A Census of Pavement Dwellers*, SPARC, Bombay

Part IV

Drawing Some Conclusions

Chapter 10

Addressing Deprivations in Urban Areas

Diana Mitlin and David Satterthwaite [1]

Local deprivation and local action

This chapter reflects on what the eight case studies in Chapters 2 to 9 tell us about addressing urban deprivation, while Chapter 11 considers how local and extra-local organizations can be more effective in supporting this – from local non-governmental organizations (NGOs) and local government to national organizations and international agencies. Each case study is about local organizations and actions or about national organizations that support local organizations and actions that address urban poverty. The focus on local organizations and processes is because, for the urban poor, the deprivations that they face are manifest and experienced 'locally'.

Chapter 1 noted the many different deprivations faced by large sections of the urban population in low- and middle-income nations. Perhaps it is stating the obvious that these multiple deprivations are experienced locally – inadequate food intakes and, often, reliance on poor-quality food; the health burden that arises from the health risks faced daily in their very poor-quality homes; the struggle to get water; the inadequacies in provision for sanitation; the difficulties they face in finding more secure and higher income sources; the inadequacies in the public transport system; the difficulties in getting healthcare and affording medicines; the difficulties (and often high costs) of keeping their children at school; the long hours worked and the often dangerous conditions in which they work; frequently, the constant risk of violence; and, for many, the constant threat of eviction or having to cope with the consequences of eviction. Many are particularly vulnerable to extreme weather – to flooding because they live on floodplains or beside rivers; the danger of landslides for those living on slopes; and the injuries, premature deaths and losses of property from accidental fires and floods. Of course, the scale and relative importance of these vary from person to person and

---

1 This chapter draws on two previously published papers, Mitlin (2003) and Satterthwaite (2002).

place to place; but large sections of the urban population in virtually all low- and middle-income nations face a mix of these deprivations.[2]

Many deprivations are caused or exacerbated by unequal power relations with external people or organizations – landlords or landowners, employers, government offices and government services that discriminate against the urban poor or exclude them (health services, police, schools, emergency services, law courts and other aspects of legal protection). The book *Squatter Citizen* (Hardoy and Satterthwaite, 1989) described the daily struggle that much of the urban population in low- and middle-income nations face in accessing necessities – the struggle to get water because of the distance of the water source and/or the queue; the struggle to get access to a toilet; to get seen by a doctor or nurse when sick or injured; to get a seat in a bus; or to get a land site upon which to live. All of these reflect failures or inadequacies of local organizations.

Low incomes and local governments' incapacity to ensure provision of infrastructure and services may be the result, or much influenced by, national or international factors; but they are experienced locally. These deprivations will not be addressed without local changes. Successful 'pro-poor change' has to have demonstrable local impacts. This has very significant implications for national governments and international agencies – in effect, they need to demonstrate how the measures that they are designing and implementing 'to reduce poverty' will bring positive benefits to (low-income) individuals and households in their daily lives, in what they can consume and save, in the quality and security of their homes and neighbourhoods, in the services to which they have access, and in their relationships with those who influence their incomes and lives (employers, local government or private infrastructure and service providers, the rule of law and, often, landlords).

This brings in the role of local organizations in poverty reduction. Virtually all of the deprivations that make up poverty in any particular urban setting can be (somewhat) reduced or increased by local organizations. Many of the deprivations noted above are caused by, or exacerbated by, the failures or limitations of local organizations. And as the eight case studies in this book show, there is considerable scope for local organizations to reduce or remove

---

2 The research programme in which we both work has long sought to document the scale and nature of these deprivations, both through our own writings and through our publication of the work of other people. See, for instance, the special issues of *Environment and Urbanization* on poverty (vol 7, no 1 and vol 7, no 2, 1995); on inequality (vol 8, no 2, 1996); on aspects of poverty relating to housing (vol 9, no 1 and vol 9, no 2, 1997); on poverty reduction and urban governance (vol 12, no 1, 2000); on the role of donors in reducing urban poverty (vol 13, no 1, 2000); and the role of civil society in reducing poverty (vol 13, no 2, 2001). The April 2005 issue of *Environment and Urbanization* will focus on meeting the millennium development goals, while an issue in 2006 will focus on chronic poverty. Many other issues of the journal have also had poverty reduction as part of their focus – see, for instance, vol 14, no 2 on the needs and priorities of children and youth and vol 15, no 1 on rural–urban transformations. With regard to our own work, see Hardoy and Satterthwaite (1989) on housing conditions; Hardoy, Cairncross and Satterthwaite (1990) on health burdens; Hardoy, Mitlin and Satterthwaite (1992; 2001) and McGranahan et al (2001) on environmental health risks; and Bartlett et al (1999) on children's needs and priorities; see also publications that the programme prepared for other agencies, including UNCHS (1996), focusing on housing conditions, and UN Habitat (2003), on the inadequacies in provision for water and sanitation.

most of the deprivations suffered by lower-income groups. This is not to claim that the underlying causes of poverty are local – as many are obviously linked to national and international factors, such as trade regimes, national government debt burdens, conflicts over scarce resources, unequal landowning structures, and civil strife and insecurity. What we argue here is that many of the deprivations can be reduced through solutions that are developed and implemented locally.

What underlies the gap between what people need and what they can get?

Comparing case studies

Each of the case studies in Chapters 2 to 9 are about local processes that sought to reduce the deprivations suffered by those with low incomes. Four are about national organizations who sought to support such local processes. The Urban Community Development Office/the Community Organizations Development Institute (UCDO/CODI, Thailand), the Mexican National Popular Housing Fund (FONHAPO) and the Community Mortgage Programme (the Philippines), in their very different ways, are about loan-based financing systems that support local actions and local control – for community organizations (and their members), local government organizations or partnerships between the two. The Local Development Programme (PRODEL, Nicaragua) is a national programme that supports local authorities in a range of cities with grants for infrastructure and service improvement and loans for low-income households in these cities for housing improvement or enterprise development. Two of the case studies are about community-based organizations and federations that sought regional (state/provincial) and national changes, as well as supported local processes (the alliance of the Homeless People's Federation and People's Dialogue on Land and Shelter in South Africa and the alliance of the National Slum Dwellers Federation, *Mahila Milan* and SPARC in India). The remaining two are more localized examples: *Cearah Periferia* in Brazil, operating in a few urban centres; Anjuman Samaji Behbood in Pakistan, operating within one city.

The eight case studies are not easily compared. Indeed, the authors of each case study have sought to relate the description of what was done or attempted locally to the local and national (and, where relevant, international) social, economic and political context within which they developed and operated. Strategies to reduce poverty vary according to opportunity. The work of the federations of the urban poor in India and in South Africa cannot be understood without understanding the political changes taking place in these nations. Priscilla Connolly's chapter on FONHAPO in Mexico makes clear the very specific economic and political circumstances that allowed this fund to emerge, the fund's political and organizational antecedents and the way that the political changes in Mexico shaped what the fund could and could not do. Successive political regimes in the Philippines changed conditions in ways that affected the functioning of the Community Mortgage Programme.

Comparisons of 'case studies' also run the risk of explicitly or implicitly assuming that what worked well (or, to some extent) in one location can be implemented elsewhere. Among many international agencies, there is almost a cult of the 'success story' and the search for 'best practice.' Ironically, many of the more successful experiences, including those described in Chapters 2 to 9, were very much locally determined (not based on some other 'success') and did not draw on international funding – or, if they did, this was only after they had developed an effective locally driven process. This chapter and Chapter 11 are not so much about comparing 'practice' in the eight case studies as about considering the 'good principles' that they had in common and how these often involved the use of comparable tools (see Turner, 1996).

The characteristics that urban centres share

Despite the differences in the measures that are developed to address urban poverty, there are certain characteristics that all urban centres share by being 'urban centres', which can cause or shape poverty. There are also certain factors that are present in most urban areas regardless of local social, economic and political circumstances that influence poverty, and it is worth being clear about what these are, as this allows a consideration of how these different organizations worked.

At its core, the contemporary urban centre is a concentration of profit-seeking enterprises that choose to locate there because of advantages to the owners and the resulting concentration of a work force who obtains or seeks employment opportunities from this concentration of enterprises. The demand for goods and services from these enterprises and from their work force creates a further concentration of enterprises and employment opportunities. Most urban centres are also concentrations of government organizations (who require a work force and create demand for goods and services) and government-provided or funded infrastructure and services.

This concentration in space of private enterprises (large and small, 'formal' and 'informal') and public agencies and organizations inevitably produces competition for land. Although the way in which this competition operates on the ground is influenced by many local factors, those individuals and organizations with the greatest monetary resources or political power get most of the best sites. For urban inhabitants, the unequal distribution of income that is part of contemporary urban development produces large differences in the capacity of different individuals and households to afford land and housing, and to afford to pay for infrastructure and services – even though all individuals and households in urban areas need accommodation and access to infrastructure and services, while most would wish their accommodation to provide good access to employment.

Each urban centre has these 'urban' characteristics that are independent of local specifics – although each is also located within its own unique and very particular local context with regard to the scale and nature of the economy and the enterprises that form it; site characteristics; transport and communications links to other places; and accumulated investments in the urban structure, including the stock of buildings, infrastructure and services. The role of history should also be recognized for its influence not only on this stock, but also on the ways in which urban poverty is manifest. All of these factors have been influenced by patterns of land ownership or control (and by the laws, regulations and traditions that influence this), and the influence of local political and bureaucratic systems (and their norms, codes and regulations, and the ways in which these have or have not been applied). Of course, regional and national contexts also influence each urban centre – in particular, the scale and nature of private investments there and of investments in infrastructure and services, as well as the form of local government permitted or supported by higher levels of government. Urban centres' economies and future possibilities are also influenced by national government's macro-economic policies and sectoral priorities – and, increasingly for many in a globalizing world, by international influences.

Within this mix of characteristics that are inherent in most or all urban centres, as well as characteristics rooted in very particular local, regional and national contexts, all urban residents have certain obvious, comparable needs that include some form of accommodation with access to infrastructure and services. One key characteristic of urban centres is that access to housing, infrastructure and services (and most other necessities) is commodified; you only get access to it if you pay money for it.[3] The more unequal the income distribution in any city, the more unequal this capacity to pay.[4] So, in every urban centre, there is the tension between the need of all residents for accommodation and the fact that access to housing and land markets is heavily influenced by the capacity to pay for it. This tension is increased by two factors: the scale of the inequality in income distribution and the extent of the competition for land. In general, the larger and wealthier the city, the greater the tension because of both these factors – unless resolved by government intervention. This intervention can take the form either of reducing the cost of reasonable quality accommodation or of increasing lower-income groups' capacity to afford or otherwise obtain (or build) better accommodation. In effect, all of the measures taken by the organizations or processes described in the eight case studies seek to do this, although the ways of doing so are very diverse.

---

3 There may be some possibility of getting access without paying (for instance, invading land and illegally tapping piped water supplies); but even illegal access to land, housing, infrastructure and services are often monetized – for example, the land agents who sell or rent illegal subdivisions, the landlords who operate in informal or illegal settlements and the profit-making operations that sell water and access to toilets. There are instances in societies where traditional landowning structures remain strong and where access to land is not monetized – although in cities where traditional landowning structures still predominate, these have generally become more monetized. See Yapi-Diahou (1995) and Kironde (1995). There are also accommodation arrangements within families or kin structures that allow individuals or households cheap or free accommodation (see, for instance, Beijaard, 1995), although these are generally part of complex reciprocal arrangements.
4 It is also important to remember how much the priorities of individuals or households vary with regard to housing in terms of what accommodation they want and how much they want to spend. Young, single people, such as temporary migrants who seek to minimize their expenditure on housing, obviously have very different needs and priorities from families who see their stay in the urban centre as permanent and have young children (see Hardoy and Satterthwaite, 1989, and vol 1, no 2, 1989 of *Environment and Urbanization* for a discussion of this diversity and how this links to the different housing sub-markets, through which those with limited income find accommodation).

Urban centres also bring another related tension – the need of all urban residents for infrastructure and services, but with many having a very limited capacity to pay for these. In high-income nations, this has been resolved by the recognition that government should ensure that all homes have basic infrastructure (water piped to the home, usually a connection to a sewer system, storm and surface drainage, paved roads and footpaths) and services (waste collection, accessible healthcare and schools, police, emergency services, postal services and telephones). The means to achieve this – and the balance given between guaranteeing people the income needed to afford these or subsidizing the infrastructure and services and the extent to which costs are recovered from users – may vary considerably from nation to nation, as does the quality of provision for low-income groups. But virtually all urban citizens in high-income nations have access to such infrastructure and services.

In most low- and middle-income nations, the gap between the cost of reasonable quality housing with the infrastructure and services that housing and residential neighbourhoods need, and the limited amounts that large sections of the population can afford, has been 'resolved' by high levels of overcrowding within existing housing (which reduces the cost per person) and large sections of the urban population going without the infrastructure and services that they require. In part, this is due to the accommodation that they rent or the housing that they develop themselves existing outside of the formal system of legally subdivided and developed land for housing and official provision for infrastructure and services. Despite the differences between nations and their cities within Africa, Asia and Latin America, in virtually all cities there is this twin manifestation of housing with extreme overcrowding and/or large sections of the population living in housing that was developed outside of conventional, legal systems of land acquisition and development, building construction and infrastructure, and service provision. The proportion of the population living in informal or illegal homes and neighbourhoods varies; but it is common for 30 to 60 per cent of cities' populations to live in these and for most or all of this proportion to have very inadequate provision for the familiar list of necessities: water, sanitation, drainage, waste collection, schools, healthcare and the rule of law. The forms that these kinds of housing take and their relative importance also vary considerably between urban centres – shaped by local circumstances and local and national political structures. But at their root is the gap between the cost of 'reasonable quality, secure accommodation with infrastructure and services' (and, for most people, a location that allows access to employment) and what a significant section of the population can afford to pay for this.

Closing the gap between what is needed and what can be afforded

All of the case studies are about organizations or processes that sought to reduce this gap between what all households need and what those with limited incomes can afford. All have focused primarily on reducing the gap on the 'housing, infrastructure and services' side – making it possible for those with limited incomes to get better-quality (and, often, more secure) housing with infrastructure and services – rather than the income side (increasing lower-income groups' real incomes). If urban poverty is viewed as being caused by inadequate income levels (and the inadequate consumption that results from this, including inadequate nutritional intake), with all other deprivations being directly or indirectly caused by inadequate income, then the success of these eight case studies is limited, even if several included significant initiatives to increase incomes among lower-income groups, to support local economic development and to help low-income groups cope with sudden falls in income or the sudden need for expenditure.

All eight case studies are examples of organizations who seek to make it possible for those with limited incomes to get better-quality (and, often, more secure) housing with infrastructure and services. Four routes to doing so are evident:

1   Reducing the cost of better-quality housing and/or infrastructure and/or services. Despite the diversity between them, all organizations recognized that, in part, this is achieved by keep down unit costs. Several also sought to reduce the cost of meeting 'official' standards by changing these standards or getting official acceptance for work that they had done, which did not meet official standards.

2   Using credit as a means to allow low-income households to afford better-quality and/or more secure accommodation by being able to spread the capital cost of a new house, core house, serviced site or housing improvement over a number of months or years. This was often accompanied by the use of credit to allow households to cope with fluctuating incomes and still manage to make regular payments.

3   Recovering costs from users (where possible), with the recovered funding returned to finance other improvements.

4   Strengthening community organizations to increase their capacity to improve conditions themselves and to negotiate with external agencies or organizations in order to secure additional resources and/or to contest measures that would impoverish them.

Most of the case studies focused on two or three of these; some, such as UCDO/CODI (Thailand) and the South African and Indian federations, sought to support all four. These strategies are further discussed below.

Many definitions of poverty do not consider the political power of low-income groups and their organizations. We recognize the significance of political power and would argue that a part of the reduced poverty in many of the case studies was driven by the greater political power and clout achieved by organized urban poor groups and federations (and, thus, also by the political circumstances that did not repress these).

The eight case studies

Table 10.1 uses the same eight aspects of deprivation listed in Chapter 1 to consider which aspects each of the case studies sought to address. Some of the case studies are on organizations whose work addresses many aspects of poverty. For instance, PRODEL (Nicaragua) provided small grants to support infrastructure and community works projects undertaken by municipal authorities and community organizations, credit programmes (with technical advice) to support house improvement; and credit to support the formation or expansion of micro-enterprises. In three of the case studies (UCDO/CODI in Thailand, the South African Homeless People's Federation and the alliance of SPARC, *Mahila Milan* and the NSDF in India) the work includes components in all eight aspects. The work undertaken by these organizations or alliances is difficult to categorize in terms of the sectors into which it falls, since the approach used combines concrete actions to address particular deprivations (especially inadequate and insecure housing and basic services), with changes in the relationships within and between urban poor groups and all other actors, including local political systems, local government agencies and international donors. This helps to emphasize the point made earlier with regard to the complex interrelations between the different aspects of poverty, especially the extent to which greater protection from the law and greater 'voice' helps to support improvements in other aspects. In these instances, the role of the local non-governmental organizations (NGOs) in India and South Africa and of UCDO/CODI in Thailand is to support urban poor groups in creating their own organizational structures and their own strategies for changing their circumstances.

Some case studies are of initiatives that focused on particular aspects. For instance, the work of the Anjuman Samaji Behbood in Faisalabad is specifically about a community-driven model for improving water, sanitation and drainage in the informally developed settlements in which most of Faisalabad's low-income population lives. It is also a smaller-scale initiative than the others. Its importance lies in the fact that it demonstrates a way in which low-income communities can address the multiple deficiencies that they face in the provision of water, sanitation and drainage, based on their own resources and in ways that are integrated within the larger organizational and infrastructural framework of Faisalabad (with all its constraints and deficiencies). Its relevance is not so much its scale but the potential of the (locally developed and financed) model that it has demonstrated to be implemented on a much larger scale.

The following sections discuss how the different case studies sought to increase incomes, reduce the gap between good-quality housing, infrastructure and services, and what those with limited incomes could afford.

Increasing incomes

All of the case studies include a focus on making it possible for those with limited incomes to get better-quality (and, often, more secure) housing with

Table 10.1 *Aspects of poverty that the case studies sought to address*

Case studies	Inadequate income	Inadequate, unstable or risky asset base	Inadequate shelter	Inadequate provision of public infrastructure	Inadequate provision of basic services	Limited or no safety net	Inadequate protection of poorer groups' rights through the operation of the law	Poorer groups' voicelessness and powerlessness
Government initiatives								
UCDO/CODI	**	**	**	**	***	**	*	***
Community Mortgage Programme		*	***	**	**		*	*
FONHAPO		*	***	**	**			*
PRODEL	**	*	**	**	**			*
Civil society initiatives								
Anjuman Samaji Behbood	*			***				
Cearah Periferia		*	**					*
South African Homeless People's Federation	*	**	***	**	**	**	*	***
SPARC–Mahila Milan–NSDF	*	**	**	**	**	**	**	***

Note: This table highlights how the eight case studies included different components. The more asterisks, the stronger the focus on that particular component. But it does not pretend to be a precise analysis of the relative priority given to each of these aspects of poverty reduction. It is also difficult to distinguish with any precision between these different aspects, since successful actions in one can spill over into others.

infrastructure and services; for some, it is their primary focus. It could be argued that increasing these people's incomes would be a more effective way of reducing their poverty since virtually all poverty is rooted in inadequate incomes, and increased incomes would allow individuals or households to choose which aspects of their deprivation they give priority in addressing.

But urban organizations, including city and municipal authorities and NGOs, have limited possibilities to change economic circumstances in ways that produce real income increases for significant sections of the urban poor – especially for those groups with the least assets or lowest educational attainments, or those who face discrimination in labour markets. This is especially so where the national or regional economy is stagnating or in crisis. In many nations, there are also the impacts of macro-economic policies that are (or were) intended to make the national economy more competitive, but that have contributed to increased unemployment and falling real incomes for large sections of the urban population. All of the case studies show the limitations for any organization (government, NGO, civil society) in contemporary economic settings of generating employment for lower-income groups or other means to increase the real incomes for those sections of the population with the lowest and/or least stable incomes. The measures taken in most high-income nations – a 'subsistence income' and/or provision of cheap or free accommodation for all those without work or income and assets – is either too expensive or politically unfeasible in these nations.[5]

Indeed, the main influence of local governments on poorer groups' incomes may be their potential to reduce or destroy them – as they limit, constrain or destroy livelihood and housing opportunities for low income groups (Amis, 1999). While local organizations may have a limited capacity to increase real incomes among poorer groups, there are two areas that have importance for incomes: the savings and credit groups, which support housing and which also support emergency or crisis credit needs; and the ways of integrating within upgrading programmes or new housing programmes opportunities for employment creation or local economic development. Three case studies (UCDO/CODI in Thailand and the alliances in South Africa and India) have as their foundation community-organized and managed savings groups who can provide their members with credit to cope with sudden falls in income or sudden increases in prices, and who can support members in enhancing their income-earning opportunities. UCDO/CODI has gone further in having trade-based networks in which much of the solidarity activity is to strengthen livelihood opportunities. The organization was also able to help community savings groups survive the 1997 economic crisis by providing low-cost subsidized loans to

---

5 UCDO/CODI (Thailand) is a partial exception. The programme supports community-managed revolving funds that offer loans to members for emergencies and income generation. The savings schemes have been involved in allocating welfare grants since the economic crises in Thailand, and there are special funds to support the elderly. In some cases, the schemes decide that a loan is what is required to address the welfare need and use the revolving funds for such a purpose. In some other countries, there are also programmes that make small payments available to particular groups, such as to low-income households who keep their children at school or to the elderly.

community-managed revolving funds that community organizations could use to provide grants or subsidized loans, as well as unsubsidized loans, to members – including small grants to help the elderly, sick or those who had lost their income sources during the economic crisis.

Several of the case studies include successful employment-generating or income-generating components. For example:

- the micro-enterprise loans for 2400 enterprises in Nicaraguan cities where PRODEL operated (with most enterprises taking on more than one loan), for which good levels of cost recovery and low default rates were achieved;
- the expanding income-generation loan programmes now integrated within the savings and credit schemes of the SPARC–*Mahila Milan*–NSDF alliance in India, and, to a lesser extent, the South African Homeless People's Federation; and
- the income-generation and community-enterprise loans provided by UCDO/CODI (Thailand).

Evaluations of programmes that supported housing improvement or new house development also found that many supported improved incomes for a proportion of the households. For instance, an evaluation of the Brazil case study found that some households had developed new businesses as their homes were extended, while others found new income-earning opportunities from the skills that they had developed while improving their homes. The savings groups and the housing improvements were also judged to have had positive consequences on the local economy. Many participants of the Community Mortgage Programme schemes in the Philippines found new opportunities for additional income from renting rooms or developing retail stores. In addition, in all of the case studies, most of the local economic multipliers in schemes to build or improve housing are local and, thus, help to stimulate demand for local building materials and components, as well as for local specialists. For instance, PRODEL (Nicaragua) found that housing loans had stimulated demand for building materials and components, and some extra construction jobs.

However, in general, perhaps the most noteworthy aspect of the case studies is that they show how the deprivations associated with low income could be reduced by other means than increasing household incomes – through increasing physical assets (especially access to land or legal ownership of it and better-quality housing); or improving basic infrastructure and services; or through political changes or changes in attitude by government agencies, which allowed low-income groups to negotiate more support (or less harassment). Regarding voicelessness and powerlessness (or its obverse, the right to make demands and get a fair response), some of the case studies show how organizations or federations formed by the urban poor and supportive local NGOs were able to successfully negotiate resources and/or room for autonomous action from government organizations and/or a halt to harassment. Thus, it is important to recognize that reducing many aspects of poverty depends only in part, or not at all, upon increasing low-income groups' real incomes (see Table 10.2).

Table 10.2 *Links between the different aspects of poverty and real income levels*

Aspect of poverty	Relation to real individual/household income	How this aspect of poverty exacerbates other aspects	Notes
Inadequate food intake	*Obvious direct relationship to income:* income influences how much food can be bought and its quality.	Inadequate food intake reduces work capacity (and, thus, earnings) and capacity to learn, with serious long-term consequences for physical and mental development.	Need to consider intra-household allocations.
Inadequate, unstable or risky asset base	*Obvious direct relationship to income:* lack of income limits capacity to increase asset base and assets may be sold to cope with inadequate income. Households who take loans to increase their asset base may face falls in income because of repayments (although many low-income households increase asset bases through building or developing their house through self-help and negotiation with government for land, or land tenure and infrastructure and services).	Lack of assets that can be used as collateral make it difficult or impossible to take out loans that would allow new income-earning opportunities to be developed, housing improved or connections to infrastructure afforded.	Government management of land a major influence on price, availability and appropriate location of land for housing for low-income groups.
Inadequate and/or insecure shelter	*Obvious direct relationship to income* as housing quality and security of tenure are related to how much can be paid (although many low-income households will trade off housing quality for the possibility of owning their own home, which then forms their most valuable asset – for instance, occupying land illegally and developing their own home in the hope that their tenure will be legalized).	Poor-quality and insecure housing increases the risk of asset loss and can be expensive as houses may need frequent repair because of the use of temporary materials. Limited value of the house as an income-generating asset through renting out rooms or home enterprise.	
Inadequate provision of infrastructure to homes: piped water, sewers, drainage,	*Some relationship to income* (as public, private or community provision depends upon individuals' capacity to pay), but also strong influence of government willingness to provide these, and the efficiency of providers (which influences cost and quality of provision).	Higher costs and fewer income-earning opportunities. Greater health burdens increase expenditure on healthcare and medicines and result in more days lost from work.	Efficient providers are often able to reach lower-income groups with better provision and cost recovery.

paved roads and paths		In some instances, inadequate public provision means that low-income households have to pay for education.
Inadequate provision of services:		
• education • emergency services (including rapid treatment for acute illness and injury, as well as ambulance and fire-fighting services)	*These services should be available to everyone, independent of their income*; much more influenced by the capacity of government to provide than by household income (although government provision is inevitably influenced by its capacity to raise revenues, which, in turn, is linked to income levels within the nation).	Lack of education is likely to reduce future incomes. Lack of emergency services will increase premature mortality and increase the health (and economic) impact of acute illnesses and injuries.
• healthcare • solid-waste collection	*Some relationship to income* (as public, private or community provision generally depend upon individuals' capacity to pay), but also strong influence of government willingness to provide these, and the efficiency of providers (which influences cost and quality of provision).	Lack of provision or inadequate provision, with obvious consequences for health; good healthcare also limits the physical and economic impact of illness and injury.
• public transport	*Some relationship to income* (as provision depends upon individuals' capacity to pay), but also critical influence of efficiency of providers and quality of government management. Transport is a significance employer in some cities.	Transport costs are often a significant proportion of poor urban households' expenditures; where households live in, or are pushed out, to peripheral locations in major cities, income earners may need to rent a bed in the centre of town. Isolated or otherwise poorly located land sites are often the only land that low-income households can afford.

Table 10.2 *continued*

Aspect of poverty	Relation to real individual/household income	How this aspect of poverty exacerbates other aspects	Notes
Inadequate law enforcement to ensure rule of law in low-income areas No, or inadequate, safety net Inadequate protection of poorer groups' civil and political rights Voicelessness and powerlessness within political systems and bureaucratic structures	*These are aspects of poverty that are related to governance failures; the rule of law, provision of safety nets, protection of civil and political rights, and responsive, supportive and accountable political systems and bureaucratic structures should be available to citizens, independent of their income* (although government provision for these is inevitably influenced by its capacity to raise revenues, which, in turn, is linked to income levels within the nation for national agencies and income levels within the locality for local governments).		

Making limited funding go as far as possible

Most of the case studies sought to reduce the gap between the cost of secure, reasonable quality housing with infrastructure and services and what lower-income groups could afford by one or more of six measures:

1   Seek all possible measures to reduce unit costs (to reduce or eliminate the need for subsidies).
2   Use credit to allow some, most or all costs to be recovered.
3   Share costs: combine individual, community, municipal and external support.
4   Procure land at below-market prices.
5   Avoid having to move.
6   Use subsidies carefully and strategically.

More details on each of these measures is given below.

Reduce unit costs

In most case studies, perhaps the most common to reduce costs was by using people's direct labour wherever possible – for instance, unskilled labour in housing and infrastructure construction, local management of construction and financial administration, and using local skilled labour at locally negotiated rates. Other common responses were to reuse existing materials from people's previous homes when building new units and to construct components (inspection covers, bricks, etc) on site using local labour.

Many of the schemes for new housing used smaller plots than were the norm and, where land was expensive, encouraged building upwards as it was cheaper to provide low-income households with adequate internal space through two- or three-storey dwellings, than with larger plots and one-storey dwellings. Community-managed new housing developments in India, Thailand and South Africa developed housing designs by house-modelling exercises involving all those who were seeking homes, and this included developing full-size model houses where different sizes and internal space configurations and their cost implications could be tested.

The four civil society-driven programmes and UCDO/CODI (Thailand) also devolved many tasks to community management, which in a conventional programme would be undertaken by paid professionals.

The savings groups around which new housing developments were based in the case studies from Thailand, India and South Africa undertook many of the management tasks that would normally be undertaken by professionals, thereby avoiding the professional salary costs that would have to be paid within any conventional project. Two key characteristics of these community-managed new housing developments were the careful records kept on costs and a constant process of exchange between them. Therefore, as one group developed ways of reducing unit costs, so other groups could learn from their experiences. The net result in South Africa was that a community-designed and managed new housing programme could construct a good-quality four-room house for the same cost as a serviced site or (often poorly constructed) two-room core house built by contractors.[6] In South Africa, some communities negotiated amendments to standards to enable them to reduce costs and make officially sanctioned solutions more affordably.

In the case study in Brazil (see Chapter 7), there was a recognition that there were effective means of reducing costs – for instance, through the use of cheaper materials than were conventionally used; but this was constrained by by-laws and regulations.

Using credit to spread the costs over time and to achieve cost recovery

The use of credit often requires non-conventional credit systems since conventional credit organizations require collateral that low-income households cannot provide and commissions that they cannot afford. It may also require an element of cross-subsidy within the community since not all members can afford to pay even reduced market costs.

Most of the case studies to support households in improving or extending existing homes or in building new ones relied partially or almost entirely on loans rather than on grants. This obviously allows far more to be done by those with limited capital. It also allows the capital cost of major improvements to be spread over a number of months or years, making such improvements affordable to lower-income groups. But considerable care is needed in any loan programme for low-income groups since such groups' capacity to repay is obviously limited. So, too, is their capacity to cope with sudden stresses (such as higher interest rates) or shocks (such as maintaining repayments when their income falls). *'Good practice' among loan programmes for low-income groups should support them in avoiding loans or taking the smallest loans that they need with rapid repayment periods (to minimize interest charges), rather than maximizing the size and number of loans (which would be the conventional measure of 'success' for most loan programmes).* Such loan programmes should also ensure that they have measures to help those who find it difficult to repay. And, obviously, loan programmes work best for low-income groups where the cost of what is to be funded by a loan is kept to a minimum.

Perhaps the most sophisticated loan programme for upgrading and for new housing among the case studies (and among other experiences) is the programme managed by UCDO/CODI (Thailand), as it offers a range of loans to any community, provided that they show they have the capacity to manage savings and loans. Although some of the loans have a subsidized interest rate, for the whole range of loans provided, the returns are sufficient to maintain the original capital base offered by the Thai government and to cover the management costs.

---

6 See also the experience of the homeless people's federation in the Philippines, which can build houses and construct infrastructure and services far more cheaply and efficiently than government agencies or developers (VMSDFI, 2001). See also the experience in Windhoek, where the city government supported low-income community organizations to develop infrastructure and services incrementally, which brought dramatic reductions in the cost of each plot (to the equivalent of roughly US$120 per plot; UN Habitat, 2003).

PRODEL (Nicaragua) also had unsubsidized loan programmes to support micro-enterprises and household improvements and both achieved good levels of cost recovery and low default rates, serving low-income households despite the economic difficulties within the nation. The Community Mortgage Programme in the Philippines uses loans to support over 100,000 low-income households to purchase the land upon which they are living or to acquire new land sites, and it also has the highest collection rate of any government housing loan programme in the Philippines (including a higher rate than many loan programmes to middle-income households). It also has a lower average loan than other programmes – although keeping down the loan amounts (so that they can be afforded by low-income households) has also meant that most loans only cover the cost of land acquisition, making it difficult for the households to afford site development and housing improvement. Casa Melhor/Better Home and Programme of Support for Self-building (PAAC, Brazil) introduced the practice of savings and loans for housing improvement to low-income housing programmes, and also had very good levels of cost recovery for the portion of the housing improvements that were funded by loans.

The Anjuman Samaji Behbood case study from Faisalabad is unusual in that it sought from the outset to develop a community-driven model for improving water, sanitation and drainage in informally developed settlements, with full cost recovery from the users. Offers of grant funding from international agencies were refused because of the organization's desire to demonstrate to the city authorities that substantial improvements could be made in providing water and sanitation in the kinds of informal settlements in which most of Faisalabad's low-income population lives, without the need for external funding. Obviously, if the costs of improvements can be funded through cost recovery from users, there are no funding constraints on the scale of programmes (except for the need for capital up front to allow the initial investment).

Some loan programmes had subsidies built in from the outset – so loans were used not to get full cost recovery but to make existing capital sources go further. FONHAPO (Mexico) had as a goal the recovery of half of the funding. In effect, available funding would go twice as far as it would if supported by grants. Although it did not achieve this goal – the best it achieved was 30 to 35 per cent recovery – it certainly reached a large number of those with relatively low incomes, providing improved housing or new housing, with a lower unit subsidy than other government programmes. Overall, between 1983 and 1994, it provided 180,000 home improvement loans and over 300,000 loans for serviced sites or core houses.

Sharing costs

In some of the case studies, a combination of individual, community, municipal and external support allowed more to be done without proving too expensive for any one of the groups. PRODEL (Nicaragua) did not seek to recover the costs from its support for community upgrading; but it made limited funding go as far as possible by sharing costs. It used two strategies to do so – requiring counterpart contributions from municipal authorities and using community participation. It made grants of up to US$50,000 available to municipal authorities for local investment. The funds could be used for a wide range of improvements, including piped water supplies; sewers and drains; treatment plants; roads and footpaths; electrification and street lighting; health centres and day-care centres; playgrounds; sporting facilities; and sites for the collection, disposal and treatment of wastes. External funding went twice as far by being matched by the combination of municipal and community contributions. The average cost per household was around US$100, with only half of this coming from external funding. Although the scale and range of improvements was not as comprehensive as those supported by some upgrading schemes – with costs that are equivalent to several thousand US dollars per household – this kind of model has far more possibilities of being afforded on a large scale.

In the case study from Brazil, the costs of housing improvement were met through a combination of household savings, grants and loans, with resources drawn from local government and external funding agencies, as well as from households.

The self-build model used in South Africa in which the household secures access to the state subsidy favours cost-sharing with the local residents. Many federation members who obtained the housing subsidy completed houses that are worth three to five times the value of the materials and skilled labour that the subsidy paid for. They added value because:

* Federation members provide unskilled labour free of charge (for construction and management).
* Skilled labour was provided at low cost as members negotiated with local artisans, or found skilled family members or friends to assist them.
* Materials were bought collectively, securing discounts from wholesale building suppliers.
* Materials used in their shacks were reused in the new houses.
* Federation self-builders paid more attention to quality than commercial contractors did. This is increasingly important as the value of the subsidy erodes under South Africa's moderate inflation rate (about 6 per cent annually) and rising material costs (Baumann and Mitlin, 2003).

Getting land cheap

The cost of land in cities is, perhaps, the most difficult gap to address between the cost of 'good-quality' accommodation with access to income-earning opportunities and what low-income households can afford. This is especially so in prosperous cities and/or in cities where governments have not taken measures to help increase the supply and reduce the cost of land. The Philippines case study pointed to the growing gap between land prices and urban real incomes between 1992 and 2000. In Metro Manila, the high price of land meant that it was not possible to purchase land with the largest loan that the Community Mortgage Programme could provide. The high price of land also meant that most of the loans provided by this programme only funded land acquisition, although their original intention was also to fund housing and site improvement.

In several cities, local governments sought to procure land at below-market prices, but faced strong opposition from landowners.

Governments who tolerate low-income groups invading or illegally occupying land are, in effect, allowing them to get land at non-market prices, although neither governments nor landowners and real-estate interests would permit low-income groups to occupy the better-quality and more valuable sites. Local governments are often reluctant to allocate the better-quality, more valuable land that they own or control to 'poor people' and to 'incremental' development as it looks messy and middle-class groups object. However, low-income groups may decide to invade a good-quality land site, not because they expect to be able to stay there but because this starts a negotiation. The Homeless People's Federation in South Africa supports community negotiation for land from local authorities, although there are examples of savings groups who invade land because they were getting nowhere in negotiations or they saw land that they thought they had been promised being allocated to other groups; having invaded, they then negotiated (People's Dialogue on Lands and Shelter, 1999).[7] Despite particular instances of federation successes, getting access to well-located land in South Africa remains very difficult.

Upgrading programmes that include provision for tenure are, in effect, cutting the costs of acquiring legal land tenure, unless – like the Community Mortgage Programme – they are supporting the illegal dwellers in purchasing the land from the landowner. In Thailand, UCDO/CODI supports community organizations in their negotiations with landowners to procure the land they already occupy – which may take the form of complete purchase, or agreement to divide the site (land-sharing) or the purchase of particular land plots to allow some dedensification and reblocking as infrastructure is introduced or improved.

For many of the new housing developments supported by FONHAPO (Mexico), land acquired by public agencies that was then provided at below-market value was important for many of the new housing schemes that it supported.

There are examples in India and South Africa of community organizations looking for land for their housing schemes and purchasing this. Obviously, there are more possibilities of this occurring in smaller and/or less prosperous cities. Smaller urban centres enable communities to locate on the periphery and manage either without motorized transport, or with a low expenditure on transport, whereas this is far more difficult or impossible in larger cities.

Avoiding having to move

All of the case studies have as a central component to their work improving the homes and neighbourhoods in which low-income households already live, at least for a proportion of the urban poor groups with whom they work. Obviously, this does not work for large section of the poor who want a new home. Many of the pavement dwellers in Mumbai may have more security and even some

---

7 There are various case studies from other nations showing this tactic of invading land as a way of opening negotiations with local authorities; see Peattie (1990) and Arévalo (1997).

infrastructure for their pavement dwellings; but they don't want to live on the pavements if they can get their own homes. As the Indian case study also describes, the squatters who were living beside the railway track also wanted to move, when offered reasonable alternatives within a resettlement programme that they could manage. Many low-income groups are tenants or boarders and, therefore, have no possibility of developing the house in which they are currently living. But many low-income households would prefer to stay where they are – with tenure, infrastructure and services improved. There are also costs to moving, especially if the move is to cheaper land that is not well located with regard to employment opportunities. Moving can also disrupt social networks.[8]

The experience in Thailand is interesting as it shows how low-income households' attitudes to moving changed – and this also highlights the importance of investing in community learning. The first communities threatened with eviction were eager to purchase land and to resettle. But networks saw the problems with this strategy: the households who moved were far from existing sources of livelihood and they struggled to stay on the new site and to repay their loans. Now, networks actively discourage households from relocating; instead, they help them to fight eviction threats and secure the right to upgrade their existing homes. The costs are lower and the location is better in terms of income-earning opportunities.

Use of subsidies

This focus on making limited funding go as far as possible, or even seeking completely self-financing systems paid for by low-income households, could be considered exploitative. And, as noted above, there are dangers in relying on credit since this can create impossible debt burdens for low-income households. A large part of the 'cost saving' achieved in the lower-cost upgrading or new house construction schemes is from transferring most of the building and management tasks to staff of community organizations, for which they are not paid (or are paid far less than professionals). But the case studies that sought to keep down unit costs and use credit are examples of 'what was possible' in particular circumstances. The use of credits has the advantage not only of significantly increasing what low-income households can afford to do, but also of reinforcing people's sense of capacity and responsibility.

There are examples of upgrading schemes and new housing schemes with very large subsidies per household; but these (and the political circumstances that permit them) are rare. Furthermore, if large unit subsidies are being used to reach only a proportion of low-income households, cheaper models are needed to allow the funding allocated to subsidies to go further. In addition, high-subsidy programmes tend to be more 'top-down' because they do not need community contributions and, therefore, often forget to work with low-income groups and their organizations in ensuring that the externally funded interventions make best use of available resources. And 'high-subsidy' solutions may also result in

---

8 It need not do so; see the case study of community-managed resettlement described in Patel, d'Cruz and Burra (2002) and summarized in Chapter 9.

their capture by relatively wealthy households – as is so often the case with public housing programmes and subsidized mortgage schemes.

Several case studies made strategic use of subsidies by directing them to necessary expenditures that people might not be willing to pay for (such as technical assistance), or by seeking to focus on those most in need (as in the housing subsidy available to low-income households in South Africa). PRODEL (Nicaragua) funds upgrading programmes with grants, but avoids subsidies for loans for improving housing and for community enterprises – showing that it is possible to reach low-income groups with conventional loans. Anjuman Samaji Behbood (ASB, Pakistan) did not provide any direct subsidies, although the technical assistance for installing the pipes was provided free of charge. UCDO/CODI (Thailand), in addition to its loan programmes, used small grants strategically – for example, small infrastructure grants helped to support a community organization who was managing savings and loans, and helped develop relationships between community organizations and local governments. The Community Mortgage Programme (the Philippines) provided an interest rate subsidy to reduce the repayment burden of loans – although, even with this, the poorest groups had difficulty in affording loans or making loan repayments.

Both the Brazilian and the Mexican case studies provided a mix of grants and loans, seeking to recognize state responsibilities to support the poor and to secure the benefits of a loan-based housing improvement programme.

The NGO–community organization alliances in India and South Africa provide grants for community learning through exchanges, networking and federating and for communities who want to experiment with a new innovation. Both use loan-based systems that charge less than market-based systems, but which charge a significant rate of interest.

Addressing urban poverty through building the assets of low-income groups

The range of assets

All of the case studies can be reviewed for their contribution to building the asset bases of lower-income groups. Each case study sought to strengthen the capacity of community-based organizations, although in very different forms. Four components are worth highlighting (and most case studies use more than one, with some using all four):

1 Support community organizations' capacity to save and use their existing financial assets.
2 Support the development of collective knowledge – for instance, how to manage finance, develop homes, establish and enhance enterprises, and strengthen social organizations and participation. This influences residents' capacity to plan their lives and realize their goals. Most case studies also sought to develop collective knowledge and learning with new solutions to traditional urban development programmes.

3   Encourage households to invest in their own physical assets in terms of household assets (their homes and enterprises) and community assets (water supply networks and community centres).
4   Build stronger, more representative, local organizations for what they can do collectively and the new relationships that this permits with external agencies, especially local authorities.

Many of the case studies do not address a single type of asset but seek to support a set of social change processes that are mutually reinforcing. For example, group savings and credit can provide financial capital, strengthen social organization, teach skills, and provide capital for investment in buildings and income-generation. In several of the case studies, the creation, consolidation and enhancement of assets emerges as part of a conscious strategy to achieve social change, and this is underpinned by three underlying change processes:

1   the transformation of relationships within the community to become open and accountable, with leaders and members involved in working together to improve their local settlement;
2   the transformation of relationships between the community and the state, with a move away from confrontation and opposition to collaboration and partnership; and
3   new ways of 'doing' development, with a reconsideration of the technical details for housing and infrastructure installation and, underlying such a reconsideration, a changed relationship between civil society and the state.

The following sections discuss these three processes.

Relationships within community organizations

With regard to strengthening grassroots organizations, the case studies do not seek to replace existing organizations, but develop or augment a number of capacities:[9]

•   Manage practical self-help development activities, in addition to activities such as lobbying the state for more resources.
•   Competent community financial management through community contributions for self-help activities: financial management skills help to ensure that local communities can manage external funding, once secured.
•   Greater transparency and accountability within the organization: financial contributions are just one strategy to increase the stake that local residents have in their organization.

9 In South Africa and India, new organizations were set up or strengthened, such as the women's savings groups; but these were not established in ways that challenged existing leaders and community organizations. The case study from Brazil describes some tensions between community organizations set up for the programme and existing community organizations (see Chapter 7). See also Díaz et al (1999) for a case study of upgrading from Guatemala City, where the external funders set up 'new' community organizations to help ensure that their projects were implemented. This had significant drawbacks as the projects threatened and weakened existing community organizations.

- Achieve greater and more active participation from members, especially those with the lowest incomes, as well as more scope for the participation of women.

To different extents, the case studies seek to reconstruct grassroots organizations and the ways in which they operate within settlements or neighbourhoods. Grassroots organizations exist in some shape and form throughout low-income urban settlements; but many do not appear to be effective in increasing the development options for individuals and families and in realizing the best of these options. In particular, existing community organizations may simply offer legitimacy to the more wealthy and powerful groups in the settlement, who dominate negotiations with external agencies to advance their own interests.

Within several of the case studies, practical local activities help to consolidate a leadership who is concerned with securing immediate and continuing local benefits. These neighbourhood-based activities help to increase knowledge and confidence between residents and to build solidarity. Financial commitments from external groups change the relationships even further. Leaders and members learn the skills needed for financial accountability. In the case studies from South Africa and India, the support NGOs sought to support grassroots organizations who developed democratic internal organizational capacities; in doing so, both also ensured high levels of women's participation. In the Community Mortgage Programme (the Philippines), beneficiaries attest that, by becoming homeowners and lot owners, they have greatly increased their status and changed their relationship with retail stores and other businesses in the area. They feel that businesses trust them now because they are not squatters or renters anymore, who may move anytime they want. As owners of their home/home lot, they are more bankable and appear trustworthy/reliable, including being potential business partners.

An important element in reconstructing grassroots organizations in the case studies from India, South Africa and Thailand has been the encouragement of federating and networking activities between groups. Federating strengthens the solidarity between groups, breaking down the isolation faced by individual grassroots organizations and their leaders and enabling the federation to negotiate credibly on city-wide issues. In India, the National Slum Dwellers Federation (NSDF) has linked local communities to achieve a mass movement; they have secured housing and services with the strengthening of neighbourhood groups and a new sense of confidence among leaders. In Thailand, UCDO/CODI has increasingly supported networks of community organizations formed by those organizations within a city, within a region or with a common interest and it is the networks that manage much of the funding. Strong grassroots organizations and federations can also help to keep good programmes going in the face of political change. The fact that effective social programmes are often withdrawn as governments change is, perhaps, in part a reflection of the lack of grassroots strength to prevent this from happening.

Changing relationships with the state

A second similarity in the strategy of most case studies is the systematic attempt to change the nature of the relationships between grassroots organizations and local authorities and, in some cases, other organizations (state and private). Many of the case studies place emphasis on reforming relationships between the state and urban poor. They seek such reforms in order to secure a more equitable division of government resources, more effective development expenditures and a better dialogue between communities and the state (including specific state agencies responsible for specific forms of infrastructure and services). This can change the way in which the state undertakes its formal development programmes, as well as prevent individualistic bargaining by leaders and local politicians. As shown by the case studies, the willingness to restructure relationships may come from either party. In the case of PRODEL (Nicaragua), UCDO/CODI (Thailand), FONHAPO (Mexico) and the Community Mortgage Programme (the Philippines), the lead was taken by government (although drawing on civil society initiatives and, often, staff from civil society), while SPARC (India), the People's Dialogue (South Africa), *Cearah Periferia* (Brazil) and ASB (Faisalabad) work with grassroots organizations as the key group to initiate change.

Reforming these relationships is never easily achieved, especially since they threaten existing political interests and may be contrary to what external agencies need. The case study on PRODEL mentions a community in a Nicaraguan town who did not want to take part in PRODEL activities, believing that it could find a state agency that would offer them money without requiring 'anything in exchange or effort'. In Faisalabad, the ASB had to face sceptical local authorities who showed little interest in their work; local factions within the settlements in which they worked who opposed what they were doing; a local politician who sought to undermine their activities by promising households free connections if they stopped participating in the ASB programme; and external funders keen to pump money into their work (which could threaten their whole strategy to demonstrate that it was possible to greatly improve provision for water, sanitation and drainage without large external funding).

Through working together on practical activities that involve high levels of local participation, new perspectives are gained by the poor, state officials and politicians. On the one hand, joint activities help the local authority to see that grassroots organizations and their members have their own resources to contribute; these also help to erode the unfair and inaccurate stereotyping of 'the poor' by local authority staff as illegal citizens or foolish migrants or criminals who should be pushed away from the city.[10] They start to consider organizations of the urban poor as potential partners in the development process. With the active collaboration of local grassroots organizations and new ideas for addressing poverty, government officials may recognize that their responsibilities are not so difficult to achieve. At the same time, local residents

---

10 These may sound like extreme views, but it is remarkable how often these views of 'the poor' come out in discussions with local authorities.

begin to view their relationship with the local authority (and, sometimes, other state agencies) differently. They see that not all officials and politicians are there to secure personal or political profit. They may realize that state funds can provide a useful additional contribution to their own scarce funds in improving their local neighbourhood. Residents may also be more willing to pay the service charges that are required.

In Nicaragua, at the heart of many of PRODEL's strategies lies the need to restructure the relationship between citizens and the state. Once a public works project has been approved, PRODEL signs a contract with the municipal government and places its share of the project costs in a special account. The contract makes the obligations on both sides transparent and helps to improve accountability. The community and municipality then have to contribute their own shares before PRODEL's own funds are released. Funding is only forthcoming if the project addresses local need. Before signing the contract, there is a participatory planning process with the local communities and local authority staff. Politicians often take part. This helps to ensure that activities are relevant and affordable. Over time, members of the municipal staff have begun to use the participatory methodologies that PRODEL developed with communities in other spheres. Through their experience with PRODEL, they realize that local residents often have many good ideas about what needs to be done and how the activities should be completed. Instead of believing that they know best, they have acquired new skills in listening and consultation. At the same time, as the case study describes, citizens' attitudes to working with local authorities and contributing payments to their work also began to change.

Through building closer and more open relationships between politicians, officials and grassroots leaders, programmes seek to alter the way in which development activities take place in order to make outcomes more favourable for the poor. Several case studies use precedent-setting as a way of showing what can be achieved and of changing relationships with official agencies. Both SPARC (India) and the People's Dialogue (South Africa) explicitly use precedent-setting to move their negotiations with the state forward. ASB's experience in Faisalabad is similar in approach. Precedents are created by a community who wishes to invest in a process of change, either to improve its housing or to provide essential services. That community explores the options that might address its needs, identifies what appears to be the best option and begins to invest in it. The difficulties such communities face can be significant. There may be disputes among members who are suspicious of change and prefer a more established practice, even if it has proved inadequate. In an ideal situation, there is already an agreement with the local authority to support this exploration; but sometimes this does not occur until a second stage. Without local authority support, precedent-setting is likely to involve breaking municipal rules and regulations. Once the solution has been developed – for example, a mezzanine floor in the design of the houses developed by the NSDF in India – then other communities, state officials and politicians are invited to an event. Whatever stage the municipality becomes involved in, the process has a necessary phase of development. Together, around a tangible option, officials and communities work out what needs to change to make it work. Both communities and officials become engaged around the practical issues at stake.

Redeveloping urban solutions

Turning to the physical process of urban development, it has long been recognized that there has been a dichotomy between conventional professionally led urban development strategies and the realities of urban development as experienced by the poor (Choguill, 1996). However, although John FC Turner highlighted these problems several decades ago (see, for instance, Turner, 1968; 1976), there has been limited action to address this situation. Many agencies turned to supporting self-help, but not to the increased community participation and control that was meant to go with it. The case studies can be seen as joining (to different degrees) a relatively underused tradition that has sought to bring the resources of the state behind the development strategies that are being employed by urban poor groups.

While these programmes seek to support the urban development strategies as they emerge from people's own activities, none of them accepts current solutions in their entirety. Instead, they attempt to improve self-help solutions to better meet the needs of the urban poor. As SPARC makes clear, as an NGO they support circumstances in which the poor, themselves, can develop a range of improved options.

Are there valid generalizations about how the case studies redeveloped urban solutions? These solutions, for the most part, address very basic needs. They are concerned with sanitation, housing, water supplies and other basic services and infrastructure. In a few cases, they are also concerned with economic development and livelihood opportunities. The solutions may involve new technological options and/or new financing options. But perhaps their most outstanding characteristic is the way in which they sought to involve a new division of responsibility between the citizen and the state, with a more substantive role for collectives of the urban poor. This is unusual in that many urban development strategies, including upgrading schemes and new serviced sites or core houses, are still managed by professionals within a model in which the state provides and local residents pay for the services (and, sometimes, contribute to the capital costs). It presupposes a state with a capacity to collect taxes, invest and maintain these services. It also presupposes a populace who is, for the most part, able to pay the state for infrastructure and services. There is often meant to be a cross-subsidy from richer to poorer families. As argued by Choguill (1996), none of these preconditions hold in many cities, and new models of financing and management are needed to reach low-income households with better-quality housing, infrastructure and services. Hence, the focus in most of the case studies is keeping down costs and recovering costs, where possible.

There are evident synergies between stronger grassroots organizations, better relationships with officials and politicians and developing more effective urban solutions. Stronger grassroots organizations are able to create new relationships and more actively manage urban services. Better relationships help to minimize the risks of more traditional clientelist influences from politicians and state officials, and to build grassroots organizations who address the needs of their members. Strong grassroots organizations and new relationships with municipalities enable both parties to contribute to new solutions in urban development. New ways of undertaking urban development can strengthen grassroots organizations as the people become involved in managing collective resources.

Conclusions

This chapter has sought to pull out some key points from the eight case studies – particularly with regard to increasing incomes, making available funding go as far as possible and increasing asset bases.

With regard to increasing incomes, the case studies demonstrate both the potential and the limitations of local actions. On the one hand, they show the concrete improvements that were possible with modest or no external funding in addressing deprivations other than inadequate incomes. All show tangible improvements in living conditions and access to infrastructure and services for low-income groups, with many also bringing other important benefits, such as secure (or, at least, more secure) tenure. In many instances, the quality of the living conditions of urban poor households was transformed and their asset base much enhanced. The case studies show how much can be done to address many of the most serious deprivations faced by low-income households, often with modest resources. But they also show the difficulties in addressing the most immediate cause of poverty – inadequate and often unstable incomes – even if several case studies had successful income-generation components.

Most of the initiatives are likely to have directly or indirectly increased real incomes for many low-income households by lowering the costs of basic services (for instance, piped water costing less than their previous reliance on vendors) or by reducing other costs (especially the income lost to ill health, injury and premature death, and expenditure on treatment and medicines). Although this book emphasizes the many aspects of poverty other than inadequate incomes that can be addressed by local actions, poverty reduction will always be limited if the poorest groups do not get higher and more secure incomes. The key point for those who consider that poverty is only reduced by increasing the incomes of those with below poverty-line incomes is that many aspects of poverty can be reduced by other means (and many of these do, directly or indirectly, increase incomes). The key point for those who focus on 'improving living conditions' is to stress the limitations of such an approach, especially in cities or nations with stagnant or declining economic bases, and the need to incorporate, wherever possible, measures that increase incomes, protect incomes, make incomes more stable and provide safety nets for those who lose their incomes. Table 10.2 and the case studies are reminders of the complex interrelationships between the different aspects of poverty, their causes and their consequences.

With regard to improving housing conditions, perhaps the four most important lessons are:

1   Local governments must be involved, and even those governments with limited monetary resources can still do much – for instance, in improving access to land, improving tenure and permitting non-conventional approaches, such as the many described in the case studies.
2   There needs to be a switch from one-off projects to constant local processes supported by local authorities in partnership with residents and their organizations.
3   These local processes are more successful when they act on various fronts (infrastructure and services, land tenure, housing improvement, housing extension and credit, supporting better income-earning opportunities, where possible).
4   Higher-level government agencies are often needed to support such local processes.

With regard to the use of funds, the case studies emphasize the importance of making available funding go as far as possible. This was generally achieved through a combination of using loans and seeking all possible measures to reduce unit costs (to reduce or eliminate the need for subsidies). The more that unit costs are reduced, the more useful credit becomes and the more it can be afforded by low-income households, without imposing difficult or impossible debt-repayment burdens. For households, the use of credit increases what they can afford to do; for the larger programmes, it provides new funding streams when repayments begin.

Other measures highlighted by the case studies that helped to make available funding go as far as possible included:

•   Devolve tasks to community management (including financial management and construction management), which in a conventional programme would be undertaken by paid professionals.
•   Combine individual, community, municipal and external support so that costs are shared (and not prohibitive for any one of these groups).
•   Procure land at below-market prices – especially important in larger and more prosperous cities; this usually requires action by local authorities.
•   Avoid solutions that require low-income communities to move.
•   Careful and strategic use of subsidies to cover those aspects that are not easily afforded, that help to ensure the poorest groups are included and that help to develop innovations which have potential for much larger application.

In terms of building assets, four points need stressing:

1   Support the capacity of community organizations to save and to use their existing financial assets.
2   Support the development of collective knowledge within community organizations on how to organize and do things.

3   Encourage households to invest in their own physical assets, in terms of household assets (their homes, their enterprises) and community assets (water supply networks and community centres).
4   Build stronger, more representative, local organizations for what they can do collectively and the new relationships that these permit with external agencies, especially local authorities.

Most of the case studies strengthened community organizations, improving such organizations' accountability, encouraging leaders to represent their members' interests and developing new relationships between community organizations and local authorities. The case studies from India, South Africa and Thailand have gone one step further as they work with, and build, networks or federations of community organizations. In many of the cases, the relationship between community organizations and the state was transformed with a move away from confrontation, opposition or clientelist practices to real collaboration and partnership. This changed relationship also meant that local authorities permitted community organizations to develop new ways of doing things that were outside conventional land-use planning, building and infrastructure norms and codes; this often brought significant cost savings and greater effectiveness.

All poverty reduction programmes need to be assessed for the extent to which they involved and met the needs of women and of the lowest-income groups. The two final sections consider these issues.

Meeting women's needs

All poverty reduction programmes need to be assessed for the extent to which they meet women's practical and strategic needs (Moser, 1993). As the primary focus of all the case studies was more secure, better-quality housing and/or better-quality infrastructure and services, this responded to women's practical needs in terms of managing the home and having primary responsibility for child care. But in many of the case studies, the changes also addressed strategic needs (reducing discrimination against women) as they opened new opportunities for women to own housing, enhance their income-earning opportunities, develop new skills and increase their involvement (and leadership) in community organization.

The initiatives in India and South Africa had at their foundation women's savings groups who also helped to increase women's roles and status within low-income settlements. In India, *Mahila Milan* groups were set up to help women in the collective develop the skills they need to be centrally involved in decision-making within the alliance and, with the National Slum Dwellers Federation, to assist communities to accept the role and contribution of women. The case study from South Africa describes how the federation drew from the experience of *Mahila Milan* and set up savings schemes as places in which women can begin to address their needs. It found that many residents in low-income areas were not involved in existing grassroots organizations, especially women and the poorest groups. Through the Homeless People's Federation, women's savings collectives were able to gain recognition in their settlements and to take on key leadership roles, managing community processes with the traditional male leadership. In both India and South Africa, most of the leaders have been women, first within the savings schemes and then within the larger federations.

One important part of the success of many of the case studies was the possibility that women had to become involved – or, as in India, the Philippines, South Africa and Nicaragua – that they had to take on many of the leadership tasks and management roles. In South Africa, among the 100,000 members of the Homeless People's Federation, 85 per cent are women. In the Community Mortgage Programme in the Philippines, 70 to 90 per cent of the community-based organization officers and board members were women. In the case study from Brazil, more women than men were involved. In PRODEL (Nicaragua), three-quarters of all team leaders and half of those in management and supervision were women. In part, this high involvement of women can be explained by the fact that the programmes addressed women's practical needs for better-quality and more secure homes with basic services. But, in many programmes, the new possibilities opened for women went beyond this – supporting women in taking on stronger public roles (as leaders and organizers), helping them to become property owners, providing credit to help them develop new income-earning possibilities and supporting them in developing skills. For instance, in the Philippines, women's involvement in the Community Mortgage Programme gave them the experience and the confidence to assume public roles, such as becoming a member of *barangays* (district councils) or community legislative councils. This greater involvement by women in community-based organizations, or in setting up their own community-based organizations, also brought a greater focus on addressing other practical needs, such as day-care and health services, both through actions by the community organizations and through negotiations with external agencies.

Chapter 5 on PRODEL (Nicaragua) includes a section discussing how the measures that PRODEL supported helped to promote the involvement of women in all phases of the infrastructure projects and encouraged their participation in the two loan programmes. The chapter includes a comment from a mayor and a municipal official who acknowledged how the role taken by women in other programmes has changed since PRODEL gave them equality in participating in the various stages of the project; this was something that had never been done before.

Most of the case studies described how the programmes allowed women to become property owners. For instance, for the case study in Brazil, in interviews with households who were participants in the programme, 61 per cent had the title registered with the woman. However, the Philippines case study noted that there were instances of common-law arrangements and consensual unions, where the male manages to keep membership of the Community Mortgage Programme when he leaves his former partner and she loses out. The Philippines case study also noted that women had to adjust their working hours and activities to accommodate their new public responsibilities; but there was no evidence that their male partners increased their share of domestic work. One suspects that this was also likely to occur in most other case studies.

Reaching the poorer and/or more vulnerable groups

Not all of these programmes reached the groups with the lowest incomes. For instance, FONHAPO (Mexico) certainly reached low-income households, but not the lowest-income households. FONHAPO provided subsidies to lower-income population with substantially lower subsidies than those channelled to (generally) higher-income groups by housing finance agencies and banks. The same is true for the Community Mortgage Programme (the Philippines), which had a small proportion of beneficiaries with very low incomes but was not reaching the poorest of the poor. Casa Melhor/PAAC (Brazil) reached much further down the income scale than other government programmes, but did not reach the families living in the worst conditions. The case study gives details of the difficulties that a (small) proportion of those who took loans faced in repaying them.

In part, this is because of the difficulties of reaching the poorest groups with programmes that seek to improve housing and housing tenure. Many of the poorest groups have to focus on survival and therefore have priorities other than better-quality or more secure housing. Those programmes or programme components based on credit will also tend to exclude the poorest groups since they cannot afford the repayments or lack the minimum qualifications to allow entry. However, the case studies of programmes developed by the federations of the urban poor in India and South Africa (and of similar federations in other nations, too[11]) are notable because they do seek to develop models that are affordable for the lowest-income groups. So, too, does UCDO/CODI in Thailand. Their commitment to doing so provides a constant pressure to keep down unit costs and to ensure that credit repayments are flexible. However, there are both internal pressures (higher-income community leaders, a desire to replicate conventional housing, the desire to take larger loans) and external pressures (local authority expectations, market-based subsidy systems that work for those able to adapt to the formal world) that favour those who are less poor.

References

Amis, P (1999) *Urban Economic Growth and Poverty Reduction*, Urban Governance, Partnerships and Poverty Research Working Paper 2, International Development Department, University of Birmingham, Birmingham

Arévalo, T P (1997) 'May hope be realized: Huaycan self-managing urban community in Lima', *Environment and Urbanization*, vol 9, no 1, April, pp59–79

Asian Coalition for Housing Rights (2001) 'Building an urban poor people's movement in Phnom Penh, Cambodia', *Environment and Urbanization*, vol 13, no 2, pp61–72

Bartlett, S, R Hart, D Satterthwaite, X de la Barra and A Missair (1999) *Cities for Children: Children's Rights, Poverty and Urban Management*, Earthscan, London

Baumann, T and D Mitlin (2003) 'The South African Homeless People's Federation – investing in the poor', *Small Enterprise Development*, vol 14, no 1, March, pp32–41

---

11 See Asian Coalition for Housing Rights (2001) and Urban Poor Development Fund (2003) for Cambodia; Chitekwe and Mitlin (2001) for Zimbabwe; VMSDFI (2001) for the Philippines; and Gold, Muller and Mitlin (2001) for Namibia.

Beijaard, F (1995) 'Rental and rent-free housing as coping mechanisms in La Paz, Bolivia', *Environment and Urbanization*, vol 7, no 2, October, pp167–182

Chitekwe, B and D Mitlin (2001) 'The urban poor under threat and in struggle: options for urban development in Zimbabwe, 1995–2000', *Environment and Urbanization*, vol 13, no 2, pp85–101

Choguill, C (1996) 'Ten steps to sustainable infrastructure', *Habitat International*, vol 20, no 3, pp389–404

Díaz, A C, E Grant, P I del Cid Vargas and V Sajbin Velásquez (2000) *El Mezquital - A Community's Struggle for Development*, IIED Working Paper 1 on Poverty Reduction in Urban Areas, IIED, London

Gold, J, A Muller and D Mitlin (2001) *The Principles of Local Agenda 21 in Windhoek: Collective Action and the Urban Poor*, Urban Environmental Action Plans and Local Agenda 21 Series Working Paper 9, IIED, London

Hardoy, J E, S Cairncross and D Satterthwaite (eds) (1990) *The Poor Die Young: Housing and Health in Third World Cities*, Earthscan, London

Hardoy, J E, D Mitlin and D Satterthwaite (1992) *Environmental Problems in Third World Cities*, Earthscan, London

Hardoy, J E, D Mitlin and D Satterthwaite (2001) *Environmental Problems in an Urbanizing World: Finding Solutions for Cities in Africa, Asia and Latin America*, Earthscan, London

Hardoy, J E and D Satterthwaite (1989) *Squatter Citizen: Life in the Urban Third World*, Earthscan, London

Kironde, J M L (1995) 'Access to land by the urban poor in Tanzania: some findings from Dar es Salaam', *Environment and Urbanization*, vol 7, no 1, April, pp77–95

McGranahan, G, P Jacobi, J Songsore, C Surjadi and M Kjellén (2001) *The Citizens at Risk: From Urban Sanitation to Sustainable Cities*, Earthscan, London

Mitlin, D (2003) 'Addressing urban poverty through strengthening assets', *Habitat International*, vol 27, pp393–406

Moser, C O N (1993) *Gender Planning and Development; Theory, Practice and Training*, Routledge, London and New York

Patel, S, C d'Cruz and S Burra (2002) 'Beyond evictions in a global city; people-managed resettlement in Mumbai', *Environment and Urbanization*, vol 14, no 1, pp159–172

Peattie, L (1990), 'Participation: a case study of how invaders organize, negotiate and interact with government in Lima, Peru', *Environment and Urbanization*, vol 2, no 1, April, pp19–30

People's Dialogue on Lands and Shelter (1999) 'Negotiating for land: the construction and demolition of Ruo Emoh's show house in Cape Town in August 1999', *Environment and Urbanization*, vol 11, no 2, pp31–40

Satterthwaite, D (2002) *Reducing Urban Poverty: Some Lessons From Experience*, Poverty Reduction in Urban Areas Series Working Paper 11, IIED, London

Turner, J F C (1968) 'Housing priorities, settlement patterns and urban development in modernizing countries', *Journal of the American Institute of Planners*, vol 34, pp354–363

Turner, J F C (1976) *Housing By People – Towards Autonomy in Building Environments*, Ideas in Progress, Marion Boyars, London

Turner, J F C (1996) 'Seeing tools and principles within "best practices"', *Environment and Urbanization*, vol 8, no 2, pp198–199

UN Habitat (2003) *Water and Sanitation in the World's Cities; Local Action for Global Goals*, Earthscan, London

UNCHS (1996) *An Urbanizing World: Global Report on Human Settlements, 1996*, Oxford University Press, Oxford and New York

Urban Poor Development Fund (2003) *Fifth Anniversary of UPDF; Celebrating Five years of Active Partnership with the City Government and with the People*, UPDF, Cambodia, May

VMSDFI (Vincentian Missionaries Social Development Foundation Incorporated) (2001) 'Meet the Philippines Homeless People's Federation', *Environment and Urbanization*, vol 13, no 2, pp73–84

Yapi-Diahou, A (1995) 'The informal housing sector of the metropolis of Abidjan, Ivory Coast', *Environment and Urbanization*, vol 7, no 2, October, pp11–29

Chapter 11

The Role of Local and Extra-local Organizations

Diana Mitlin and David Satterthwaite

Having considered the different routes through which deprivations were addressed by local processes in the eight case studies in Chapter 10, this chapter considers the role of different kinds of organization – from non-governmental organizations (NGOs) and city and municipal government to national agencies and international donors. The chapter ends with a discussion of the links between urban poverty reduction, local institutional capacity and the Millennium Development Goals (MDGs).

Changing roles for city and municipal governments

Figure 11.1 lists the different aspects of poverty described in Chapter 1 and highlights the immediate external causes or influences on them.[1] Most of these immediate external causes are linked to the failure or limited capacity of local government agencies or departments to meet their responsibilities. Even if some are the responsibility of state or national governments (for instance, if responsibility for schools and healthcare falls under state or national governments), it is still the quality and capacity of local branches of such agencies that are the main influence on the quality and extent of provision on the ground. As noted already, the inadequacies in provision for many forms of infrastructure and services are often more the result of the limited capacity or disinterest of government organizations than of individuals or households with incomes too low to allow payments to be made. This is evident in many of the case studies as improved provision for infrastructure and services, or loans to micro-enterprises or to support housing improvements have recovered their

1 Obviously, not all of these external causes are present in all places – and for those that are present, their relative importance varies considerably from place to place.

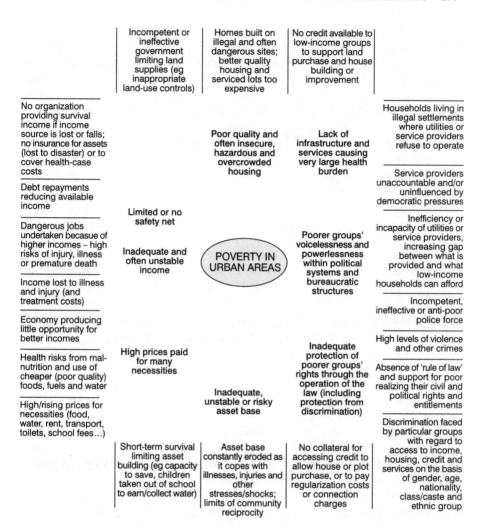

Figure 11.1 *Deprivations associated with urban poverty and their immediate external causes*

costs. If costs are fully recovered from the users, this demonstrates that the key issue was not the inadequate incomes of the population (in terms of their incapacity to pay), but the inadequacies in local infrastructure, service or credit providers.[2]

---

2 Some caution is needed in assuming that what low-income households currently pay for informal provision of infrastructure or services is what they will pay for formal provision – for instance, the assumption that what they currently pay for water to water vendors would be available to pay for piped water. Inevitably low-income (and higher-income) households often act opportunistically to avoid making payments if they think that they can get away with doing so; the likelihood of this decreases where there are representative and trusted community institutions who are involved in the improved provision.

The reasons for government failure may stem from the government's:

- unwillingness to act appropriately (for political reasons or for the lack of profit; no democratic pressures; no accountability to populations; no developmental state; national or state/provincial governments allocating city and municipal governments' responsibilities without the necessary powers and resources);
- inability to act (weak; lacking funding and professional competence; hampered by inappropriate legal, regulatory and financial frameworks);
- inefficiency (infrastructure and service provision costing more than they should, with the potential for cost recovery untapped; the capacity of government agencies to greatly expand the proportion of people who benefit from infrastructure and services is always influenced by the extent to which agencies can meet people's needs at costs that they can afford and are willing to pay for);
- official standards that require levels of investment which are unrealistic with regard to what much of the population can afford and what investment capital local authorities have available – unaffordable standards create an impasse; it often requires both technical support (to legitimize an alternative lower-cost approach) and significant mass action (to persuade politicians or civil servants that they should support a change in standards).

Of course, government failure is also frequently linked to the fact that this serves the interests of politicians and government officials. Political interests can use the promise of infrastructure and service improvements to get votes, while government employees and politicians may be able to extract bribes for this (as was described in several of the case studies).

This emphasis on the extent of government failure is not meant to imply that government agencies provide, or should provide, all forms of infrastructure and services. But the government is meant to establish the framework of incentives and regulations that ensure provision. The inadequacies in provision may also relate to:

- the costs being too high (for instance, low-income groups may have settled in areas where the costs of providing infrastructure and services are particularly high);
- unfortunate synergies between deprivations (for example, very dangerous living environments and no healthcare, which reduces the inhabitants' available incomes and, thus, their capacity to contribute towards the costs).

The different case studies show how much the extent of local government incapacity varies. In the case studies of national programmes, this variation is also evident between cities within the same nation or between local government units within large cities. Where the lack of provision for land management, infrastructure and services is underpinned by the incapacity or unwillingness of local governments to meet their responsibilities, the possibilities of poverty reduction are connected to the capacity of low-income groups and their community organizations to develop their own plans and projects, as well as to make demands and negotiate – although, clearly, there are many places where government structures are too repressive to permit this. These possibilities have been shown by the many examples of organizations and federations of the urban poor demonstrating more effective approaches (such as building or upgrading their own homes, developing new settlements, and installing infrastructure and services) and negotiating with local authorities – and, in some instances, changing national policies. This was particularly evident in the case studies from India, South Africa and Thailand. But it is not only in these nations that active federations of the urban poor exist, which are led by elected leaders embedded within representative structures and accountable to strong community-based savings groups – these federations are also evident in many other countries (such as Cambodia, the Philippines, Sri Lanka, Zimbabwe and Namibia) and are developing in many more (for example, Kenya, Uganda, Zambia and Nepal).[3]

What this suggests is that democracy will not deliver for the urban poor unless they are organized and have the capacity to identify improved urban development processes; make demands; and develop their own autonomous actions, as well as work with formal agencies (including local government, higher levels of government and international agencies). Even a well-functioning democracy only provides equality of 'voice' and vote, and not of market power (where power is measured by the money available to each individual or household).[4]

The role of NGOs

Relations with grassroots organizations

Local NGOs had significant roles in all of the case studies. In India and South Africa, the federations of the urban poor worked in alliance with local NGOs – for example, the Society for the Promotion of Area Resource Centres (SPARC) in India and the People's Dialogue for Land and Shelter in South Africa. Staff from the Pakistan NGO Orangi Pilot Project Research and Training Institute helped to advise and train staff in the Faisalabad case study. In Fortaleza and three other local authorities, Cearah Periferia supported the development of the programme by raising funds from international donors and providing professional expertise to the grassroots organization. The role of NGOs in the Mexican National Popular Housing Fund (FONHAPO) was slightly different in that, as Priscilla Connolly describes in Chapter 4, the form of this national government organization was much influenced by the earlier experience of Mexican NGOs working with urban poor groups. Many of FONHAPO's staff

---

3 See *Environment and Urbanization* (2001), vol 13, no 2, October, for descriptions of the work of many of these organizations and federations. This can be accessed on the web at www.ingentaselect.com/09562478/v13n2/; see also www.sdinet.org/ and http://www.achr.net.
4 If it is accepted that an important part of poverty reduction in urban areas is supporting the capacity of the organization of the urban poor to make demands and develop their own solutions, this presents a considerable challenge for official external-funding agencies in that they were not set up to provide support for urban poor organizations. Their institutional structure is also ill suited to doing so. This is a point to which this chapter returns in its final sections.

had previously worked for these NGOs. Similarly, the Community Mortgage Programme (the Philippines) also drew on NGO experiences to support secure tenure, and its design gave an explicit role to NGOs as one possible technical support agency for communities applying for loans. In Chapter 2, Somsook Boonyabancha also describes how the Urban Community Development Office/ Community Organizations Development Institute (UCDO/CODI, Thailand) drew on NGO experiences and worked with NGOs to facilitate improvements in relations between communities and the local authority. The Local Development Programme (PRODEL) in Nicaragua relied on NGOs for some of its programme components, and its forms and mode of operation also draw on NGO experiences.

Certainly in the cases in India, South Africa, Brazil and Pakistan, local NGOs recognized that their work must strengthen the bargaining power of low-income or otherwise disadvantaged groups and their capacity for organization and action. This includes developing within the urban poor a greater capacity to negotiate for resources and to gain appropriate responses from local agencies (for housing, land for housing, water, sanitation, drainage, waste collection, emergency services, schools, electricity and police services). It also includes building a greater capacity to successfully oppose, for example, anti-poor measures in order to ensure that urban poor groups have their civil and political rights, their rights to 'public goods and services' and their rights to unpolluted environments respected. This point is particularly evident in the case studies from India and South Africa, where the local NGOs recognized from the outset that poverty reduction requires more than an official recognition of the poor's needs. *It has to include strengthening an accountable people's movement that is able to renegotiate the relationship between the urban poor and the state (and its political and bureaucratic apparatus at district, city and higher levels), and also between the urban poor and other stakeholders.* Such a renegotiation requires not only an effective dialogue, but also more equality within the dialogue; the way in which state structures exclude the urban poor from dialogue or limit its scope makes this difficult. This is why the local NGOs in South Africa and India have always supported solutions that are developed by the poor, that work for them and that give them a more equal relationship with other groups. Without organizations of their own, the poor will always be isolated and easily weakened.

NGOs may find it difficult to work with low-income/disadvantaged groups when these groups are, themselves, developing alternatives to professionally driven solutions. Many NGOs find it difficult to accept that they do not have the answers to the problems faced by these groups. Many participatory processes are shaped by professional interventions. The experience in the civil society-driven case studies (and also in the case study from Thailand) suggests that professionally designed responses to the problems faced by these groups are often inappropriate, and a much more equal relationship with these groups needs to be created to allow more appropriate responses to be developed. The federations and networks of urban poor groups described in the Indian and South African case studies help to address the balance in favour of these groups.[5]

5 Studies such as Benjamin and Bhuvaneshari (2001) point to some of the difficulties that NGOs face if they are unable to relinquish control. See also Gazzoli (1996) for a Latin America example.

The role of the NGO is shifted to one of support and facilitation; it does not take on what individuals or community organizations can do on their own. As the role of the local NGO becomes more to create a positive 'space' for low-income groups or communities in their dealings with state officials, each agency can adopt a more constructive role.

NGOs also need to consider how they can become accountable and transparent to the urban poor groups with whom they work. One aspect that can be particularly challenging for NGOs is transparency concerning their costs, including the salaries paid to their staff. This may cause difficulties when NGO staff are questioned by the community groups with whom they work about the use of externally provided resources, including the size of their incomes, even when their income levels may be low in light of their professional competence or in comparison to what they would earn if working in government or in the private sector.[6] If poverty reduction programmes require large amounts of staff time from professionals – for instance, in negotiating with local agencies or developing consensus among diverse groups regarding what is to be done – the cost of such staff time can appear to be excessive in overall project budgets. This is especially problematic for projects with international funding, since many international funders (or their supervisory bodies) see high staff costs, or high proportions of project budgets allocated to staff costs, as 'inefficient'. Yet, this 'inefficiency' may be because more appropriate models of intervention and action are being developed that work with grassroots organizations and that maximize the use of local resources, get support from local government agencies and minimize dependence on external funding.

However, high costs for professional staff may occur because of the assumption that professionals need to be involved in many tasks that low-income groups or their community organizations can do for themselves. With a confident community, professional costs can often be significantly reduced. Two added advantages of community organizations taking on tasks normally assigned to NGO professionals are that the community has a chance to add to its skills and confidence, and that the process is able to spread without the constraint of professional time. The NGOs profiled in the case studies in South Africa and India have encouraged urban poor groups to take on many of the tasks that are usually reserved for professional NGO staff.

Scaling up with civil society-driven strategies

In Chapter 1, we suggested that the orientation of NGOs or other agencies who work with the urban poor can be summarized in four categories to highlight the different ways in which they interact with urban poor groups: market orientation; welfare provision; claim-making on the state; and self-determined solutions. Here, we return to consider these in the light of the case studies.[7]

---

6 For two discussions of these in relation to particular NGOs, see Jellinek (2003) and Magedi (2004).
7 This section draws on Mitlin (1999).

Market orientation

This consists of initiatives to increase low-income groups' incomes or assets, or to pay for improved housing, infrastructure and services that seek full-cost recovery or that achieve this by being implemented through local entrepreneurs. Most of the case studies had elements of such an orientation because of the possibilities this provides for reaching more households without external funding (or external funding only to start the process). Furthermore, among the multiple problems faced by residents in low-income settlements, there are those that can be addressed through improving the functioning of markets. For example, the Anjuman Samaji Behbood's initiative in Faisalabad to improve provision for water and sanitation and provide loans for micro-enterprises sought to be completely financed by market demand. This is also the case for the credit programmes for micro-enterprises and for household improvements in PRODEL (Nicaragua). A market orientation was chosen because it could increase the number of houses upgraded and micro-enterprises supported, and could be sustained after the programme finished, as good repayment records allowed returned funding to be used to provide further loans. The savings and loans programmes of SPARC–*Mahila Milan*–National Slum Dwellers Federation (NSDF) in India and of the South African Homeless People's Federation also seek to sustain themselves by ensuring good repayment rates on loans – although there is considerable caution about whether or not the market really can deliver to the poor. One of the most important aspects of the hundreds of savings and credit schemes set up by urban poor groups in India for emergencies is their capacity to be effective without the need to negotiate external funding. UCDO/CODI's range of loans in Thailand seek full-cost recovery across the whole spectrum, although some of the activities had loans available at below-market rates. They were also encouraged to adopt a market approach to interest rates by some of their board members who were anxious to ensure that financial loan markets were not disturbed by low-interest lenders.

Welfare provision

Here, local agencies (governmental or NGOs) offer services or particular forms of assistance or improvements (for instance, upgrading programmes) to those in need. Where an NGO undertakes this, this is often to fulfil a role that government agencies provide in high-income nations. Although this is a very conventional role for NGOs, this is not the main orientation of any of the case studies. Nevertheless, as discussed in Chapter 10, many programmes do draw on grants and have elements of subsidy and are seen, at least in part, as social development and poverty reduction programmes.

Claim-making on the state

In this case, the NGO is active in the advocacy of citizen rights and in putting pressure on local authorities or other state agencies to provide infrastructure or services to the poor, or to provide tenure to squatters. There has been a considerable growth in the number of NGOs working in this area as more attention has been given to the 'rights-based approach' to development.

Although not widely acknowledged within development agencies who have adopted the rights-based approach, it can be argued that among NGOs working on housing issues, the rise of the rights-based approach took place during the 1980s. During the 1970s, the focus of much of the literature was on what might be termed the 'needs-based approach', which stressed the advantages for governments in improving the housing conditions of lower-income groups (more political support, healthier work force, etc) and explained how the costs were not prohibitive, especially when using upgrading and serviced sites. The rights-based approach became prominent when the arguments based on 'needs' showed little success in most nations. It was also strengthened by the recognition, among NGOs, of the scale of evictions and the devastations that forced evictions brought to those who were evicted and by the success of anti-eviction struggles in some countries.[8] The willingness of the United Nations (UN) Social and Economic Commission on Human Rights to consider issues related to land and housing further strengthened the rights discourse within anti-eviction struggles. There was also an older influence on this shift – associated with social movements such as those pioneered and supported by Alinsky in the US during the 1950s and 1960s. Here, the suggestion was that access to basic services could be a first step to new forms of pro-poor government, 'complementary to the representative institutions of liberal democracy' (Castells, 1983, p61). Within such mobilization, claiming rights is the way in which social movements are strengthened and empowered. Moving on to the following decade, the shift to the rights-based approach among local NGOs also owes something to the shift in many nations to elected governments and away from repressive, unrepresentative governments.[9]

In the case studies, it can be seen that through more equal relationships with local authorities and other state agencies, there is a strong element of recognizing and securing the right of the urban poor to be involved in those aspects of development that are within the remit of these organizations, as well as the need for more competent and accountable local government organizations. But, at the same time, all of the programmes go beyond a passive (albeit assertive) campaign for rights to an active, creative engagement of the poor and the state in new relationships. The programmes go beyond asserting the urban poor's rights to public goods and services to an active involvement in demonstrating what should be done and, in many instances, in providing it themselves. *Strong 'pro-poor' advocacy has limited value if there are no practical models of pro-poor development that can be implemented.*

---

8 See, for instance, the development of the Asian Coalition for Housing Rights and its work with groups in South Korea to halt evictions (ACHR, 1989), the growing volume of work on the right to housing (for instance, Leckie, 1992) and the October 1994 issue of *Environment and Urbanization*, vol 6, no 2, on evictions. This shift was also discussed in Hardoy and Satterthwaite (1989).

9 There were many NGOs who worked with urban poor groups within nations governed by dictatorships. In Latin America, many of the best-known NGOs with strong urban agendas were formed during the 1960s and 1970s when dictatorships were in power, set up by urban specialists who were excluded from government and often expelled from universities. But the possibilities of 'claim-making' on the state are obviously limited under repressive regimes.

Self-determined solution

From the case studies, this is the orientation with the greatest potential to 'scale up' – to reach large numbers of the urban poor. It is self-determined in the sense that it is driven by what organized urban poor groups design and implement themselves; but this is not done (or intended) as actions that are independent of the state. Indeed, the designs and their implementation demonstrate what urban poor groups can do for themselves and help to assess what is needed from government agencies. The development of self-determined 'precedents' becomes a strategy to draw in government agencies for discussions and, then, agreements about their possible contributions.

The models developed involve a combination of community and state support to provide housing, infrastructure and services in non-traditional ways.[10] As noted in Chapter 1, this approach is of particular interest to NGOs because it combines direct action – working with low-income groups to improve conditions – and a strong emphasis in improving local governance. NGOs working in this area recognize that they must strengthen the bargaining power of low-income groups and their organizations, along with their capacity for organization and action.

So, while each of the programmes in the case studies is concerned with rights – and, therefore, their programmes might be considered to be compatible with, or, indeed, a central part of, the rights-based approach – there are important differences. Firstly, while self-determined approaches share with rights-based approaches the belief that state finance should support a more equal access to basic services, there is no assumption that the state should provide services. On the contrary, the underlying assumption is that the state often does not have workable models that can address the scale of need. Thus, low-income groups need to be supported in order to develop new models that the state can then replicate. There is no belief that the state should provide services to citizens 'by right' because of doubts that the state can do so effectively at scale.

The second important difference, although linked to the first, is that to do this successfully, a non-confrontational approach to the local authority is required. Community organizations need to ensure that their new proposals are accepted and listened to. As shown in the case study of Anjuman Samaji Behbood (ASB) in Faisalabad, the organizations work with the courts and the local council as required in order to ensure acceptability. By contrast, rights-based campaigns may rapidly become confrontational and governments are forced onto the defensive. In addition, local authority officials and politicians may be frustrated that people do not accept responsibilities, while claiming their rights. The people are frustrated that they are not provided with services of a sufficient standard; and while many are ready to help themselves, a strong emphasis on state provision means that they

---

10 Some self-determined solutions are market-based because if they can be initiated, continue and expand using only market mechanisms, it allows them to be self-determined and independent of external agencies. See, for instance, the example of Orangi Pilot Project in Karachi (Hasan, 1997). However, they are very different from traditionally accepted market-based solutions for urban development, and may have implications for state investments in bulk infrastructure and/or in regulations and by-laws.

do not have a role in provision. In the experience of FONHAPO (Mexico), as noted in the case study in Chapter 4:

> *Protesta con propuesta* (protest with proposal) became the dominant theme, a position whose logical conclusion was the realization of housing and urban development projects, controlled by the community organizations themselves.

Prior to FONHAPO, community organizations had lobbied intensively, but had not achieved the improvements that their members required. The approaches embedded within FONHAPO helped to change the existing antagonistic relations between the groups (residents, leaders, NGO professionals and the state) – essential to the development process – to a more constructive engagement in which each could see new roles and identify the benefits.

The third important difference is in relation to political structures. Political parties may offer to secure rights and encourage NGOs and community-based organizations (CBOs) to support them. The NGOs who work with 'self-determined' solutions seek to have a more instrumental approach to politics, offering to engage with any political party who is interested in learning more about the solutions being developed by the poor. At the same time, experience has made them cautious about being too closely associated with any political grouping. Although there are obvious overlaps and complementarities between NGOs working on rights-based approaches and NGOs supporting urban poor groups to develop self-determined solutions, tensions between these approaches can arise. NGOs working on rights-based approaches can find the self-determined approach's commitment to work with whoever is in power unacceptable. Meanwhile, the NGOs who work on self-determined approaches may criticize the rights-based NGOs for inadequate attention to working with, listening to and developing accountability to low-income groups and their community organizations.

Most self-determined initiatives to scale up civil society-driven strategies are relatively small; but three of the case studies, in India, South Africa and Thailand, show how these can expand because of their capacity to negotiate (mostly local) resources and support a rapid growth in the number of local initiatives (often underpinned by community savings and credit groups), combined with a supportive institutional environment and new partnerships with state agencies.[11]

The methodology developed by the Indian NGO SPARC has particular relevance, and is one that has been followed (with local adaptations) by the South African Homeless People's Federation and by many NGOs. This involves two components:

1   support for low-income groups and their community organizations in developing pilot projects to show alternative ways of doing things (building or improving homes; setting up emergency credit schemes; developing

---

11 See also one interesting large-scale civil society-driven programme for new housing in Goias, Brazil, described in Barbosa, Cabannes and Moraes (1997).

emergency credit schemes into savings and credit schemes for housing; setting up and running community/public toilets; organizing community-determined and managed resettlement); and

2   engaging local and national officials (and staff from international agencies) in a dialogue with communities about these pilot projects, and about how they can be scaled up (or the number of such initiatives multiplied) without removing community management.

With working models already implemented, negotiations with government agencies can be undertaken, referring constantly to what has already been achieved. An important part of this involves taking government officials and politicians to visit the pilot projects and talking to those who implemented them. This approach inevitably includes 'claim-making'; but, by also being able to demonstrate solutions, engagement with the state occurs in order to request support for non-conventional approaches, rather than for state provision. At the same time, the case studies from Thailand and Mexico demonstrate the effectiveness of the state, when they are able to use strategies that catalyse, rather than replace, local community self-help energies and activities.

The community-developed pilot projects also serve as learning experiences. They begin when communities identify their own needs and priorities and, through discussions within the SPARC–*Mahila Milan*–NSDF alliance, develop strategies to address them. One or more communities agree to try out this strategy and, in this way, become a living laboratory of how change can occur, from which the alliance can learn. Once a solution is developed, many community exchange visits stimulate the next generation of volunteers to try out and refine strategies to suit their local circumstances. The refined solution is explored within the city on a larger scale and is shared through community exchanges. The alliance builds a core team consisting of those who implemented the strategy, who visit other cities to demonstrate how it worked and who expose more communities to the innovations. They also put pressure on local officials and politicians for change to support more community action.

The case studies from India and South Africa describe the importance of these community exchanges; they have become the means through which learning is spread and shared. The constant interchange between those involved in different community initiatives stimulates other urban poor groups into initiating comparable actions. This can lead to work on changing local institutional constraints on community initiatives – for instance, as in the work of SPARC, changing building regulations to enable housing developments to better suit the needs of low-income groups; participating in the design and realization of a new state policy for legalizing and improving housing for the poor in Mumbai; developing community designs for toilet provision and then implementing them on a large scale; and proposing and implementing schemes for the resettlement of urban communities in which the resettled people play a key role in determining the location, timing and form of their relocation. Community exchanges also serve to stimulate and support initiatives in other cities and even in other nations (see Asian Coalition for Housing Rights, 1999; Patel, Bolnick and Mitlin, 2001).

Most of the case studies emphasize the importance of participation and local involvement, and thus have elements of a self-determined approach. However, the South African and Indian examples are the ones that best illustrate such an approach, as they centre on building local capacity to improve conditions and install services (both for civil society and for government organizations). To make a self-determined approach effective requires a basic capacity at community level in building and financial management, infrastructure maintenance, conflict resolution (to deal with disputes within the community) and negotiation (with a range of government departments involved). It also requires recognizing the heterogeneity within low-income settlements. The community organizations and NGOs within the case studies in India and South Africa make provision for ensuring that the needs and priorities of the poorer, less organized and less articulate individuals within 'low-income groups' are addressed. In addition, as is noted in Chapter 10, women have a central role, from the lowest level (for instance, in the organization and management of savings and credit schemes), to being elected settlement representatives, to being on the staff of the federations and support NGOs.

The role of local organizations in poverty reduction

The eight case studies suggest that one of the critical determinants of the success of poverty reduction is the quality of the relationship between 'the poor' and the organizations or agencies who have the resources or powers that can help to address one or more aspects of the deprivations that they suffer. This holds true whether these organizations are local or national NGOs, local government agencies, agencies from higher levels of government or international agencies. Obviously, the extent of success also depends upon the extent to which such organizations have resources or decision-making powers that can support urban poor groups, and on the space given by such organizations to urban poor groups in defining priorities and developing responses – or, more fundamentally, as the SPARC–*Mahila Milan*–NSDF case study points out, in actually conceptualizing participation. The quality of this relationship is influenced by the transparency and accountability of these organizations to the urban poor. What the case studies emphasize is how much urban poor groups and their community organizations can achieve with relatively limited resources if they have good relationships with local (and other) organizations and appropriate support for their actions. Some case studies also suggest that the capacity of low-income groups to form their own representative organizations and to work together is enhanced by supportive, accountable local (governmental or non-governmental) organizations.

The case studies also suggest that the form of the local organizations who 'deliver' to poorer groups, in terms of resources and a satisfactory relationship, varies considerably. They can be community organizations or federations of community organizations (as in South Africa and India); community organizations and local NGOs (as in Pakistan); or national organizations who are characterized as part NGO and part government, set up by an international agency working with community organizations and municipal authorities (as in PRODEL Nicaragua). In the case studies from Mexico, Thailand and the Philippines, a national agency supported local organizations, including local government and community organizations. What these organizations actually deliver, the form in which it is delivered (and paid for) and the role of low-income groups in the planning and delivery also varies greatly with local context; but it always includes a more detailed and context-specific understanding of the needs and priorities of different low-income groups. Most of the organizations whose work is documented in the case studies are also more accountable to low-income groups than is the norm. UCDO/CODI (Thailand) and the Community Mortgage Programme (the Philippines) are unusual in this respect since both have representation of urban poor communities on their boards, even though they are national government agencies.

The case studies show how the scale and scope of poverty reduction interventions need to be related to local circumstances and local capacities. In effect, they have to be guided by what is possible on the ground. Obviously, all poor households want higher and more stable incomes. However, in many locations, local organizations may have little scope for boosting these households' incomes, whereas there may be considerable local capacity to work with urban poor groups to extend basic infrastructure and services, support improvements to housing and, for those in illegal settlements, to provide more secure tenure. The problem of what to prioritize is reduced if local authorities and other agencies involve urban poor groups in discussions and if urban poor groups understand the limitations that local government agencies face. Most of the case studies document measures taken to ensure that urban poor groups themselves have more influence on what is done and how it is performed.

Many local public agencies and private organizations (including NGOs) have some influence on one or more of the eight aspects of deprivation listed in Chapter 1, and thus have some capacity to contribute to poverty reduction. Table 11.1 illustrates the range of actions that can address different aspects of poverty. The interventions that are listed draw from the case studies and from other experiences. Table 11.1 is included not as an attempt at a comprehensive list, but to highlight the many ways in which one or more aspects of poverty can be reduced by local actions.

Many of the case studies suggest that there can be powerful complementarities between actions to address the different aspects of poverty – for instance, better infrastructure and services improve health, reduce fatigue (for instance, water piped into the home replaces a long trek to fetch water from a standpipe) and increase income (for instance, reduced incidence of illness and injury means less time off from work and lower costs for healthcare and medicines). But there can also be trade-offs – see, for instance, the FONHAPO case study in Mexico showing how living conditions and service provision was often poorer in the 'new' homes that low-income households received (although, in the longer term, with tenure of their new homes, conditions would improve).

Table 11.1 *Different aspects of urban poverty and the range of local means to address them*

Aspect of poverty	Local means to address poverty
Inadequate income (and, thus, inadequate consumption of necessities, including food and, frequently, safe and sufficient water; often problems of indebtedness with debt repayments significantly reducing income available for necessities)	• *Better-paid job opportunities* (linked to educational attainment and contacts) *and more possibilities to work* (linked to good health, less discrimination against women in labour markets, tolerance of informal activities and, for households with children, access to day care/schools). Opportunities for self-employment. • *Greater possibilities of self-production* (linked to adequate space within home for informal activities and/or land/space for urban agriculture, access to credit, wholesale suppliers and markets). • *Access to a safety net or emergency credit or to a public works programme that seeks to provide a minimum income for those without work.* • *Government land-use and business regulations and practices* that do not unnecessarily inhibit poorer groups' income-earning opportunities. • *Cheaper housing and basic services* (so that existing incomes go further). • *Availability of relevant training/skills' development.*
Inadequate, unstable or risky asset base (non-material and material, including housing) for individuals, households or communities	• *Income level* that allows some savings in inflation-proof assets. • *Access to emergency and asset-building credit*, including community-based savings and credit schemes that make savings possible or more feasible. • *Social relations* that provide access to resources, services or capital (including those provided through rural–urban links). • *Access to education/training* (to enhance income-earning capacity). • Ability to invest in housing as an asset. • *Asset 'safety nets'*, such as insurance for property or health.
Inadequate shelter (typically poor quality, overcrowded and insecure)	• *Income level or credit* that allows more to be spent on buying, building or improving housing. • *Access to suitable land sites* on which housing can be built through invasion, purchase or negotiation with local agencies. • *Measures to cheapen the costs of building* (cheaper materials, sites, fixtures and fittings; better control of external contractors). • *Shacks being made legal.*

Table 11.1 *continued*

Aspect of poverty	Local means to address poverty
Inadequate provision of 'public' infrastructure (piped water, sanitation, drainage, roads, footpaths), which increases health and work burden	• *Adequate income*, providing more capacity to pay for infrastructure. • *Access to credit* (to help pay connection charges or for investments in these). • *Access to land* (or tenure), which ensures public provision of infrastructure through political or bureaucratic structures and processes. • *Increased capacity of local government or other (private, NGO, CBO) organizations* to provide these more cheaply and efficiently.
Inadequate provision for basic services (such as day care/schools/vocational training, healthcare, emergency services, public transport, communications, law enforcement)	• *Adequate income* (to allow more to be spent on services, especially for private provision). • *Greater public provision* (linked to local political structures, attitudes and capacities of local government agencies) or *greater capacity of other organizations or enterprises* to provide affordable services efficiently. • *Access to land* (or tenure), which ensures public provision of services through political or bureaucratic structures and processes.
No safety net to ensure basic consumption can be maintained when income falls, as well as access to shelter and healthcare when these can no longer be paid for	• *More competent, adequately resourced local organization(s)* capable of providing safety net and with funding (including public works programme, which also seeks to provide a minimum income for those without work). • *Food/nutrition and other programmes* targeted at poorest and/or more vulnerable groups (for example, pregnant mothers, infants and children). • *Role of safety nets, such as pensions or regular 'subsistence income' payments to retired people.*

Underlying causes of inadequate government responses

Inadequate protection of poorer groups' rights through the operation of the law, including laws and regulations regarding civil and political rights, occupational health and safety, pollution control, environmental health, protection from violence and other crimes, protection from discrimination and exploitation	• *Legal/judicial system* to which poorer groups have access and which functions to protect/promote their rights and entitlements (including protection from forced eviction from homes). • *Effective measures and public agencies* for ensuring/promoting occupational health and safety and pollution control. • *Effective policing* in low-income areas, with emphasis on crime prevention, uncorrupted police and good liaison between police and the inhabitants. • *Strengthened capacity of disadvantaged groups to demand legal protection* (for instance, support for women's groups and immigrant groups). • *New codes of practice for local government agencies to allow more scope for informal enterprises.*

Poorer groups' voicelessness and powerlessness within political systems and bureaucratic structures, leading to little or no possibility of receiving entitlements, organizing, making demands and getting a fair response; no means of ensuring accountability from public/ private/NGO agencies	• *Accountable political structures* with transparent decision-making and publicly audited collection, allocation and use of revenues/resources. • *Representatives of citizen groups* in public agencies and supervisory bodies of private utilities. • *Decentralization of decisions to accountable sub-municipal groups.* • *Measures to support community-driven processes and organizations of urban poor groups* to gain adequate responses to their demands and to support them in identifying problems and developing solutions. • *Public funds, over whose use poorer groups have a more direct say* (including participatory budgeting and locally based funds for community initiatives).
Limited power and resources available to local government agencies to address the above as control of resources is concentrated at state/ provincial or national level	• *Decentralization and democratization* (which has eased this constraint in some countries). • *Regional and national federations of urban poor groups* with the capacity to negotiate with supra-local agencies.

Addressing the broader constraints that inhibit local action

One common criticism of poverty reduction initiatives that focus on local projects or actions is that they only act 'within their project' and do not address broader city-wide or national constraints. They also 'simply build a roof over our poverty,' as one memorable comment made by an inhabitant of a squatter settlement in Guatemala City states, in response to what had been a relatively successful upgrading programme, but where the inhabitants felt that they had been abandoned, once this had been implemented (Díaz et al, 2001). For Casa Melhor/Better Home and Programme of Support for Self-building (PAAC) in Brazil, there was a recognition that although it improved quality of life and increased the asset base of low-income households, it did not 'remove poverty'.

One partial solution to this is seeing poverty reduction initiatives as not only building a stronger relationship between 'the poor' and government, but also initiating or supporting continuous processes. Among the government initiatives, UCDO/CODI (Thailand) supports such processes; its whole structure is designed to support continuous action, not just one-off projects. For the PRODEL programme in Nicaragua, from the outset, its intention was to develop and institutionalize a participatory model for providing infrastructure and services and for supporting housing improvement and micro-enterprise development that can be sustained in all urban areas of Nicaragua. Both these national programmes put great stress on supporting stronger ties between urban poor groups and local governments. FONHAPO (Mexico) was intended as a continuous national-scale financial support programme. All four government programmes described in Chapters 2 to 5 are examples of changed national policies, partially created by bottom-up pressure and community organization, and partially by new attitudes developed by NGO staff who had worked with the urban poor.

Among the civil society initiatives, those in India and in South Africa have long had clear strategic goals, which include the intention to remove legal, institutional or political constraints that inhibit community-driven development – from the local (for instance, negotiating permission to change house designs that go against local codes or practices), to the national (in India, getting the federal government to support community-managed public toilet blocks), and to the international (for instance, in India, changing the procurement regulations used by the World Bank because existing regulations made it impossible for community organizations and Indian NGOs to create major programmes). In South Africa, the Homeless People's Federation sought to change the way in which the national government's main housing programme for low-income groups operated, so that the housing subsidy programme could provide subsidies direct to low-income households – in this way supporting self-determined housing development, rather than giving funds to contractors to build units 'for the poor'. The federation claims some success in initiating changes to national policy. For the Anjuman Samaji Behbood's initiative in Faisalabad, the intention was to demonstrate a way of improving provision for water, sanitation and drainage that could be widely implemented within Faisalabad, without external support. For Casa Melhor/PAAC in Brazil, one key aim was to show the potential and importance of community-managed savings in a nation where development associations and savings groups were not allowed to receive money from individuals or to hold savings.

Some implications for international donors

Setting new models for donor support

All of the case studies received some international funding – although UCDO/CODI was initially funded by the Thai government (which is still its primary source of funding), and the Faisalabad case study saw the funds it received from WaterAid as a start-up fund that would become self-perpetuating. FONHAPO (Mexico) received support from the World Bank, although the second loan it received had to be repaid as a commercial loan. The case studies from India and from South Africa have received substantial funding from international donors; but this represents a relatively small part of the total value of investments made that draw heavily on people's own savings, their capacity to implement initiatives, and resources negotiated from local and national governments.

Perhaps the two key lessons that these case studies can offer international donors are:

1   A growing scale of impact was largely the result of local organizations having the capacity to support a constant programme (or process) through which the success of one initiative or project supported and stimulated other initiatives or projects.
2   Part of the reason for the growing scale of impact was the capacity of the local initiatives to change the ways in which local government agencies operated and interacted with urban poor groups.

This has enormous implications for donors because it suggests a need to engage with, and support, local processes (contrary to the shift that many donors are making away from this), but with a different model of external support from that of conventional project cycles, which feature exit strategies. It implies a need not so much for specific projects (for example, upgrading projects and installing water supply systems), but for continuous support for local initiatives that allow low-income communities and support agencies to innovate, develop workable models and implement them, and then build on their successes and tackle other issues. This may initially cost far less than supporting conventional donor-funded projects, especially if every effort is made to keep down unit costs in order to ensure that funding goes further and to prevent a dependence upon large amounts of external funding. As scale increases, more substantial support may be needed. Again, one returns to the point that low-income communities need local organizations from whom they can obtain advice and support for their own initiatives. Given the multiple deprivations suffered by most low-income groups, 'moving out of poverty' is a slow process, and this has to build not only the capacities and asset bases of low-income groups but also of local organizations.

The case studies emphasize the importance for poverty reduction of local initiatives and (government and non-government) organizations that:

• Respond to the urban poor's own needs and priorities and are flexible to emerging opportunities (ie, that are not time constrained).
• Support the organizations formed by the urban poor themselves, and have funds for them to experiment and to network.
• Include support for multiple sectoral initiatives in an integrated programme.
• Develop greater accountability to urban poor groups as well as to external funders.
• Have a continuous programme of support so that success can build on, and learn from, previous achievements.

This is very different from the main characteristics of most international donor-funded activities. It is also very different from the evident shift in many agencies' attitudes towards 'budgetary support', which implies no engagement with, or support to, local processes.

Official development assistance is dominated by the donor agency–national government relationship and this makes it difficult for international agencies to engage in what are, perhaps, the two most important long-term processes for reducing urban poverty – namely:

- supporting (directly or indirectly) the development of accountable, effective city and municipal local governments (and their agencies) who are able to undertake or support the many different local interventions that can reduce different aspects of poverty; and
- supporting the organizations formed by lower-income groups, both in their capacity to act (to set precedents and to demonstrate how much they can do with their own resources) and in their capacity to influence the resource allocations, policies and practices of government agencies and the political systems that oversee them.

New funding channels

New funding channels need to be found to:

- Engage with, and support, local government, where government agencies have the potential to become more effective.
- Amplify funding channels that go outside government to ensure that funding reaches low-income groups and their organizations. More support is also needed for the work of local NGOs who have the capacity to engage with the urban poor in ways that strengthen the urban poor and are accountable to them. This implies a more careful evaluation of the relationship between local NGOs and urban poor groups before providing support through NGOs.

Most international agencies already channel some funding to each of these; but this represents a very small proportion of total funding flows. However, there is an increasing recognition among many international donors of the need for funding channels that support local processes – for instance, to set up local funds in cities in low- and middle-income nations, or to provide funding to local organizations to allow them to support local initiatives. The support of the Swedish International Development Cooperation Agency (Sida) for PRODEL in Nicaragua and for other comparable initiatives (as well as national organizations who support local processes) in Central America was based on this recognition. This shifts the decision-making process about what is to be funded, and most of the administrative burden and transaction costs, to the place where the local proposals originate. From there, it is much easier, quicker and cheaper to check on proposals and monitor their implementation, using a network of people with local knowledge. In the case of PRODEL, each of the 260 projects designed to support municipal authorities did not have to go to Sida's central offices in Stockholm for approval. Pushing the decision-making process regarding who should receive funding down to local organizations can also minimize the need for ex-patriate staff. All international agencies who have expanded their offices in low- or middle-income nations face difficulties regarding high staff costs. This also, generally, means a constant turnover in staff, inhibiting in-depth knowledge of local circumstances. But it is a big step for any international donor to entrust the funding that it manages (and for which it has to be accountable) to local organizations or local funds.

UCDO/CODI is unusual in that this is an official national Thai government agency, yet it strengthens and supports local processes involving community organizations (and their networks) and local governments. Also, unusually for any national government agency involved in poverty reduction, it provides support for local processes by having a clear range of credit lines and support services that seek, wherever possible, to recover costs. And many of the decisions about what is funded are made at the level of the community organization, with many of decisions about loans made by networks of community organizations. Having a national agency such as this presents international agencies with far more scope to channel their funds to support local processes. FONHAPO (Mexico) also provided international agencies with a national agency through which to channel support to local processes during the 1980s and early 1990s. The case studies in South Africa and India are of federations of the urban poor that operate in many cities and regions and also are 'national' in their explicit attempt to change national policies. Usually, such civil society-driven initiatives can only draw international funding from international NGOs as the 'official' bilateral and multilateral agencies are meant to only work with, and through, governments. Certain international NGOs – CORDAID, MISEREOR and Homeless International – have helped to support these federations; but both these federations are unusual as they have also sought (and received) support from official bilateral and multilateral agencies. For instance, SPARC-*Mahila Milan*-National Slum Dwellers Federation in India have received support from Sida, the World Bank and the UK government's Department for International Development (DFID). The South Africans have had support from Sida, the Swiss Agency for Development and Cooperation (SDC), the US Agency for International Development (USAID) and the British High Commission.

There has long been a recognition of the limitations that official bilateral and multilateral agencies face in poverty reduction if their funding can only go through national government agencies (and be subject to such agencies' control). The initial response to this was to channel a proportion of 'official donor assistance' to international NGOs, who could then channel it to grassroots organizations and initiatives. More recently, a few official donors have sought ways of supporting these directly, as in DFID's funding of City Community Challenge (C3) funds to support municipal and community initiatives in two cities in Zambia and two cities in Uganda[12] and DFID and Sida's support for the

---

12 For more details, see Kiyaga-Nsubuga et al (2001); see also 'Local Funds – And Their Potential To Allow Donor Agencies to Support Community Development and Poverty Reduction in Urban Areas', Report of an international workshop on Reducing Urban Poverty through Innovative Local Funds; Sharing Donor Experiences, *Environment and Urbanization*, vol 14, no 1, 2002. This workshop in 2002 attracted staff from 23 international donors. This highlighted the range of experiences with local funds to date – including many that are funded by local governments and some by national governments (the Thai government's Community Organizations Development Institute being the largest and best documented). See also the special issue of *Housing by People in Asia* published by the Asian Coalition for Housing Rights on Community Funds (ACHR) – available from ACHR, 73 Soi Sonthiwattana 4, Ladprao 110, Bangkok 10310, Thailand; email: achr@loxinfo.co.th; website: www.achr.net.

Community-led Infrastructure Finance Facility (CLIFF) being developed in India to support SPARC-*Mahila Milan*-National Slum Dwellers Federation in India and intended for application in other nations. These recognize the need to make funding available to support local initiatives and processes through organizations located in each city who can respond rapidly, who can fund community organizations directly, and who can finance a large and diverse range of initiatives, including those requiring very small grants or loans. Most of these local funds have sought to strengthen community–local government partnerships. Obviously, these have more possibility of success in cities where there are representative organizations of the urban poor and municipal authorities who are prepared to work with them and are able to do so.[13]

Resolving conflicts between supporting local processes and donors' own institutional structures[14]

It is always difficult for international donors, who have most of their senior staff in head offices in Europe, Japan, Australia or North America, to make sense of the complex and often rapidly changing local context within which each of their projects operates. They also need to spend their money (or, for multilateral development banks, lend large sums), and they are judged positively by the people and institutions who supervise them if they can spend the funds allocated to projects rapidly. Within conventional donor logic, they also want to avoid a permanent engagement in each locality and to have a clear exit strategy; many also wish to avoid supporting more than one project in one location.

This conflicts with the point brought out by the case studies, and the discussion in this chapter and Chapter 10, that – in most urban areas – what is needed is more long-term support, less 'big, expensive projects' and less pressure for rapid implementation, at least in the initial stages. The case studies suggest that the best development course is often to minimize the amount of external funding needed. If, in Faisalabad, a local organization can support community-managed provision for water, sanitation and drainage that integrates within the official water mains and trunk sewer system, and where costs are covered by user payments, this has far more potential to reduce the huge city deficit that such projects bring than any expensive, donor-funded programme. But the response of most international donors to this model is to fund it. ASB refused this support – no doubt causing much puzzlement among some donors. But ASB recognized that all of its hard-won, hard-developed goals of demonstrating what was

---

13 When our research programme first suggested the idea of international agencies supporting local funds for community initiatives located in the cities where the support was to be provided in 1989, this included the suggestion that these should be set up first in cities with strong and accountable community-based organizations. This was so that a good working experience could be developed before the initiatives were applied in cities without such community organizations. When these local funds were first suggested and discussed in DFID, the hope was that the first City Community Challenge Funds would be piloted in cities in India and South Africa, where there were such community organizations. However, it was not possible to get DFID to support them in these nations.

14 This is discussed in more detail in Satterthwaite (2001).

possible, based on local resources and local capacity to pay, would be lost if it shifted to a reliance upon donor-funded development. *Thus, there is a need for all international agencies to avoid external funding that damages or competes with local development processes, which require no external funding.* Again, there is the potential conflict between donor agencies who must spend their budgets and the need to avoid subsidizing those projects or programmes that should be generated, funded and managed with local resources. Donors who seek to spend their budgets can fund local initiatives in ways that create unsustainable programmes that depend upon external funding, and which destroy local processes that do not.[15]

Complex and changing local contexts in each city also mean that effective donor agencies either require an intimate knowledge of local context and local possibilities, or they must support local organizations who can provide them with this. This is a point recognized by the Swedish International Development Cooperation Agency (Sida) in its urban programmes in Central America; in each programme, its funding has been channelled through a non-profit organization that it helped to set up, with staff drawn from the region. In Costa Rica, this was through FUPROVI (La Fundación Promotora de Vivienda – Fund for Housing Promotion) (Sida, 1997); in Nicaragua, it was through PRODEL. This point was also recognized by the multilateral and bilateral agencies who were prepared to allow their funding to go through UCDO/CODI in Thailand and the local processes that had been developed.

Each of the case studies in this book describes the efforts of local organizations who have a constant local presence or a national organization to support local processes. This also means a greater capacity to adapt to changing local circumstances – for instance, to change or adapt an existing programme to respond to a particular crisis (such as a flood or a sudden rise in food prices). See, for instance, FONHAPO's response to the earthquake in Mexico City, PRODEL's response to the damage caused by Hurricane Mitch in Nicaragua or the response of UCDO/CODI (Thailand) to the Asian crisis in 1997. International donors need to be able to respond to particular opportunities, too, such as a local election, which brings a new mayor into office who is more committed to addressing urban poverty. But without local organizations as partners, they are usually unable to do so. The case studies have also highlighted how the form of the local organizations who have demonstrated a capacity to meet the needs of the urban poor varies considerably with context.

One other reason why relatively little official development assistance goes towards supporting the work of the kinds of organizations described in the case studies, and the low-income groups with whom they work, is because many international agencies (and most national governments) still identify and measure poverty through income-based poverty lines, and fail to recognize the need for

---

15 This does not imply that external funding is not needed. In most cities, there are large backlogs in the 'big infrastructure' necessary for water, sanitation and drainage (especially the trunk infrastructure, water treatment plants and waste-water treatment) that external funding can help to address. But even here, it is important to develop models for financing and implementation that make best use of local resources and reduce dependence upon external funding.

poverty reduction programmes to address other aspects of deprivation. As a result, they fail to see the great potential role of local organizations to address the many non-income aspects of deprivation. They also fail to recognize that addressing these other aspects of deprivation can often contribute to increased real income, as discussed earlier in this chapter and Chapter 10.

It is also common to find cities where different international agencies (both official agencies and international NGOs) are busy funding 'their' projects, with little or no coordination between them and little attempt to work together in order to help strengthen the capacity of local organizations. For the official bilateral agencies, development banks and international NGOs, it may be that this is not so much by choice, but related to the lack of local staff who know how and when to support local processes. There are various efforts underway to change this – for instance, through international support for cities to develop their own development strategies and through international agencies working more closely together in their urban programmes (for example, through their collaboration with each other within the Cities Alliance).[16]

Channelling official funds outside of governments

There is also the obvious political difficulty faced by any official multilateral or bilateral agency in being able to channel funds directly to organizations formed by the urban poor and the local NGOs who work with them. Most recipient governments seek to limit the extent of such funding; no national government in Africa, Asia or Latin America is going to sanction an increase in funding to organizations over which they have little control, or approve of external agencies steering funding to citizen groups or NGOs who do not support them, or might even oppose them.

International NGOs usually have fewer constraints than official bilateral or multilateral agencies on their capacity to channel support directly to local NGOs or, through them, to urban poor groups. This is one reason why certain international NGOs have long been particularly important in urban poverty reduction despite funding programmes that are far smaller than belonging to the large official donor agencies. International NGOs such as SELAVIP in Belgium, MISEREOR in Germany, Cordaid in the Netherlands and Homeless International and WaterAid in the UK provided funding for some of the case studies reviewed here. This does not imply that support from official multilateral and bilateral agencies is not needed; but such agencies are generally less able to identify and support new community-based initiatives that draw most support from local resources or local demand. Perhaps there are two key roles for official donors: firstly, to fund intermediary organizations who can support new community-based initiatives (for example, through the local funds for community initiatives mentioned earlier), and, secondly, to support the scaling-

---

16 The Cities Alliance is a global alliance of cities and their development partners (which includes many of the main bilateral and multilateral development assistance agencies) who are committed to improving the living conditions of the urban poor through city development strategies and city-wide and nation-wide slum upgrading. For more details, see www.citiesalliance.org.

up or multiplication of these initiatives as the possibility for greatly increasing their scale and scope becomes evident. Civil society-driven programmes, such as those described in the case studies in India and South Africa, require more external funding when they develop to the point where they have engaged the interest and support of local governments (and higher levels of government), while greatly expanding the scale and scope of their work.

One example of an alternative approach by an international funding agency is the support provided by the Sigrid Rausing Trust to community organizations formed by the urban poor in order to procure land. An initial grant of UK£200,000 was made available to members of Shack Dwellers International, the umbrella organization formed by federations of the urban poor.[17] This could be drawn on to support local initiatives by low-income urban dwellers to negotiate for land for housing or to negotiate for legal tenure of the land that they already occupied. The trust did not specify the means that these groups must use to obtain the land. It allowed for quick disbursement with a minimum of bureaucratic procedures; in effect, it relied upon the (already demonstrated) capacity of local NGOs through which the funds were channelled to make sure that the funds were used well. Our own institute (IIED) managed this process. The initial UK£200,000 grant in 2001 supported the acquisition of secure land and the construction of housing in 13 different communities in Cambodia, Colombia, India, South Africa and Zimbabwe. Over 40,000 people benefited and many more should gain from the processes that this funding supports, in part because cost recovery is sought wherever possible so that any recovered funding can be used to support new initiatives. In many instances, the funding allowed local financial sources to be tapped. Many governments have grant funding available to low-income groups or particular 'disadvantaged' groups to support their housing schemes; but the funding is only available when the housing is finished. The trust's funds can pre-finance housing projects with the funds recovered when government financing becomes available (when the project is completed). The trust provided a further UK£220,000 to support this programme in 2003 (see Mitlin, 2003, for more details).

One final point regarding income generation. Although these final two chapters have stressed the importance of paying far more attention to addressing aspects of poverty other than inadequate incomes (and the positive influences that these can have on real incomes), there is a need for international donors to support more creative thought and experimentation on how to support more adequate incomes for low-income groups, especially for those people with the least possibility of finding adequately remunerated work and for those unable to go to work. One way to do this would be to support urban poor groups and the NGOs that work with them and that have been successful in addressing other aspects of poverty in expanding employment-creating or income-enhancing initiatives within their work programmes. As in their work in other aspects of poverty, success will often depend upon changing local contexts, removing local

---

17 See www.sdinet.org for more details of Shack/Slum Dwellers International; see also www.achr.net/ and http://www.dialogue.org.za.

constraints and developing the effectiveness of local organizations. For example, too many income generation programmes that work within national economies growing at 3 per cent or more a year have been transposed into economies with negative, zero or very low growth. There is also the need to develop local safety nets that are effective in helping urban poor groups who lose their income sources or are unable to work. The UCDO/CODI programme in Thailand to support community-managed revolving funds, which can provide grants or soft loans in cases of particular hardship, is worth noting.

Final thoughts: urban poverty reduction, the Millennium Development Goals and local institutional capacity

Any discussion of the role of international agencies in reducing poverty has to consider the role of the Millennium Development Goals (MDGs) because most international agencies have publicly committed themselves to these, and many are making changes in their institutional structures in the hope that this will allow them to be more effective in getting these goals met.

Will these goals mean more effective international aid to reduce urban poverty? Certainly, many of the MDGs are compatible with this; according to these goals, development now has to:

- Achieve universal primary education by 2015.
- Greatly reduce infant and child mortality (reducing under-five mortality by two-thirds between 1990 and 2015).
- Greatly reduce maternal mortality (reducing it by three-quarters between 1990 and 2015).
- Halve the number of people without safe drinking water, adequate incomes and food intakes by 2015 compared to 1990.
- Significantly improve the lives of at least 100 million slum dwellers by 2020 (which includes increasing the proportion of people with 'improved' sanitation and access to secure tenure).
- Halt and begin to reverse the spread of AIDSs/HIV, malaria and other major diseases.[18]

This obviously has very large implications for urban development for the reasons outlined in Chapter 1:

- A significant proportion of the people whose needs have to be met live in urban areas. Close to half of the world's population live in urban areas, including hundreds of millions who lack safe drinking water, adequate food intakes, good-quality sanitation and access to secure tenure, and who live in settlements with very high child and maternal mortality rates and high incidence of AIDS and other major diseases.

---

18 For the full text on the Millennium Development Goals, see www.undp.org.

- In most nations, most of their increase in population between now and 2015 or 2020 will be in urban areas.
- The potential advantages that urban areas have for meeting the MDGs, because of the economies of proximity, scale and agglomeration (cheapening the unit costs of most forms of infrastructure and services).

But it is the choice of international donors with regard to how they seek to achieve the MDGs that will determine their effectiveness in reducing urban poverty. There are two contrasting ways of addressing urban poverty. One is directed by national governments and international agencies, designed by 'experts' drawing upon (usually woefully inadequate) official data and crude definitions of 'who is poor' and 'who is in need' to identify 'target groups' and design policies to meet their 'basic needs'. Needs are conceived in clear and limited physical terms – for example, adequate nutrition and access to 'safe' water. Here, much attention is given to identifying 'indicators' to monitor progress. For most international agencies, the 'experts' involved are drawn primarily from high-income nations. The other way to address urban poverty is to make resources available to respond to, and support, local democratic processes in which the rights of all citizens to basic services, the rule of law and accountable organizations are stressed. The case studies in this volume have shown what this kind of approach can deliver, drawing heavily upon local resources and capacities.

One of the difficulties with expert-led 'solutions' is the lack of knowledge that experts have about the specifics of each city or urban neighbourhood, and their lack of engagement with the local population. Foreign experts often cannot speak the language of the inhabitants of settlements, where recommendations will be implemented. Their recommendations are also biased by their experience in other nations or by their reading of other 'success stories'. Thus, will donor support for achieving the MDGs be based upon strengthening and supporting local organizations and local democratic processes, or will it be through top-down, 'targeted' approaches? Will they support representative organizations of the urban poor to renegotiate better deals with local authorities? Will they recognize the importance of more effective local processes over particular, measurable outcomes, related specifically to their funding? For instance, will donor-funded initiatives to 'significantly improve the lives of at least 100 million slum dwellers' be rooted in supporting local processes that are more citizen directed and more accountable to slum dwellers? Or will they be feature (often expensive) one-off, externally directed 'upgrading' projects, over which 'slum' dwellers have little influence and which may be 'putting a shelter over poverty'?

It is worth considering the example of UCDO/CODI (Thailand) in this context. Should it be judged by the number of houses that its loans have helped to finance or improve – or by the impacts of what has been achieved by the community organizations, networks of community organizations and local government–community organizations partnerships that it has helped to build, nurture and support (which is very difficult to measure but far more important for poverty reduction)? UCDO/CODI recognize that part of their success should be in helping community organizations to avoid having to use its loans.

But for any external funder, the number of loans and the total amount of loans made by a national or local organization that it supported would be viewed as a key indicator of a programme's success. This contradiction is particularly relevant for international financial institutions, such as the World Bank and the regional development banks, whose very institutional basis depends upon lending large sums. In development terms, these banks should be supporting local and national organizations that can mobilize local and national resources and cut costs to the extent that they no longer need to borrow money – but this hardly accords with these banks' own organizational priorities.

With regard to unit costs and cost recovery, there is nothing inherently wrong with upgrading programmes that help to 'significantly improve the lives of slum dwellers' being designed, implemented and managed by professionals if all measures are conducted in full consultation with the inhabitants. A new generation of upgrading programmes in Brazil may seem expensive at a cost of US$4000 or more per household, and with no cost recovery. But this is, generally, much cheaper than providing new housing – and in many middle-income nations, probably less than the subsidy provided to lower-middle and middle-income groups through subsidized mortgages or public housing or tax benefits. Such upgrading schemes can also be seen as a form of redistribution that is less visible and politically controversial when funded by an international loan that the government (and, ultimately, the tax-payers) have to repay. But the difficulty with such expensive solutions is, primarily, that all available funding 'significantly improves the lives' of only a small proportion of slum dwellers. And large, expensive programmes generally have the greatest difficulties in truly involving the 'slum dwellers' and their organizations in their design and implementation. In terms of matching the funding available to the scale of needs, spending US$4000 or more per household hardly develops models that can be greatly expanded. If we can estimate that there are at least 150 million households in urban areas in Africa, Asia and Latin America in need of upgrading programmes,[19] and if upgrading costs US$4000 per household, the total cost of reaching these households would be US$600 billion. This is far beyond any possibilities of available international funding. However, reduce the costs of upgrading per household to US$50 to $200 per household, with the costs shared by households, municipal authorities and external agencies, and reaching 150 million households seems far more feasible. Similarly, reduce the cost of good-quality, well-located 'new housing' to between US$800 and $2000 – as has been demonstrated by the Indian and South African case studies – and, again, with the costs shared between households, local government and national and international agencies, the gap between costs and needs does not seem insurmountable.

But the extent to which the MDGs support realistic and effective poverty reduction in urban areas also depends upon whether international agencies recognize the scale of deprivation in urban areas. Many international agencies have little or no involvement in urban poverty, either because their staff or the

19 See UN Habitat (2003) for estimates of the number of households that need improvements in water and sanitation.

politicians or civil servants who supervise them think that virtually all poverty lies in rural areas. We hope that this volume will help to encourage more international agencies to reconsider this, and that the case studies help to highlight how much can be done to reduce urban poverty by supporting more effective local organizations who can work with low-income groups and their community organizations, be guided by their needs and priorities and be more accountable to them. This does not require huge sums. It does not imply taking funds away from addressing rural poverty. But it does depend upon more international agencies supporting the kinds of local processes and organizations described in this volume.

References

ACHR (Asian Coalition for Housing Rights) (1989) 'Evictions in Seoul, South Korea', *Environment and Urbanization*, vol 1, no 1, April, pp89–94

ACHR (Asian Coalition for Housing Rights) (1999) *Face to Face*, Newsletter of the Asian Coalition for Housing Rights, Bangkok

Barbosa, R, Y Cabannes and L Moraes (1997) 'Tenant today, posseiro tomorrow', *Environment and Urbanization*, vol 9, no 2, October, pp17–41

Benjamin, S and R Bhuvaneshari (2001) 'Democracy, Inclusive Governance and Poverty in Bangalore,' *Urban Governance, Partnerships and Poverty Research Working Paper*, no 26, Stage 2 Case Study, University of Birmingham, Birmingham

Castells, M (1983) *The City and the Grassroots*, Edward Arnold, London, 450

Díaz, A C, E Grant, P I del Cid Vargas and V Sajbin Velásquez (2001) 'The role of external agencies in the development of El Mezquital in Guatemala City', *Environment and Urbanization*, vol 13, no 1, pp91–100

Gazzoli, R (1996) 'The political and institutional context of popular organizations in urban Argentina', *Environment and Urbanization*, vol 8, no 1, April, pp159–166

Hardoy, J E and D Satterthwaite (1989) *Squatter Citizen: Life in the Urban Third World*, Earthscan, London

Hasan, A (1997) *Working with Government: The Story of the Orangi Pilot Project's Collaboration with State Agencies for Replicating its Low Cost Sanitation Programme*, City Press, Karachi

Jellinek, L (2003), 'Collapsing under the weight of success: An NGO in Jakarta', *Environment and Urbanization*, vol 15, no 1, pp171–180

Kiyaga-Nsubuga, J, R Magyezi, S O'Brien and M Sheldrake (2001) 'Hope for the urban poor: DFID City Community Challenge (C3) fund pilot in Kampala and Jinja, Uganda', *Environment and Urbanization*, vol 13, no 1, pp115–124

Leckie, S (1992) *From Housing Needs to Housing Rights: an Analysis of the Right to Adequate Housing Under International Human Rights Law*, Human Settlements Programme, IIED, London

Magedi, E (2003) 'Housing mobilisation in Calcutta – Empowerment for the masses or awareness for the few?', *Environment and Urbanization*, vol 15, no 2

Mitlin, D (1999) *Civil Society and Urban Poverty*, Urban Governance, Partnership and Poverty Working Paper 5, International Development Department, University of Birmingham, Birmingham

Mitlin, D (2003) 'A fund to secure land for shelter: supporting the strategies of the organized poor', *Environment and Urbanization*, vol 15, no 1, pp181–192

Patel, S, J Bolnick and D Mitlin (2001) 'Squatting on the global highway', in M Edwards and J Gaventa (eds) *Global Citizen Action*, Earthscan, London, and Westview, US

Satterthwaite, D (2001) 'Reducing urban poverty: constraints on the effectiveness of aid agencies and development banks and some suggestions for change', *Environment and Urbanization*, vol 13, no 1, pp137–157

Sida (Swedish International Development Cooperation Agency) (1997) 'Seeking more effective and sustainable support to improving housing and living conditions for low-income households in urban areas: Sida's initiatives in Costa Rica, Chile and Nicaragua', *Environment and Urbanization*, vol 9, no 2, pp213–231

UN Habitat (2003) *Water and Sanitation in the World's Cities; Local Action for Global Goals*, Earthscan, London

Index

Page numbers in *italic* refer to Tables, Figures and Boxes. Page numbers followed by 'n' denote footnotes.